Spring Bulbs

Daffodils, Tulips and Hyacinths

Geoff Stebbings

B T BATSFORD

Acknowledgements

First published 2005

© Geoff Stebbings 2005

The right of Geoff Stebbings to be identified as Author of this work has been asserted by him in accordance with the Copyright, Designs and Patents Act 1988.

Volume © B T Batsford

ISBN 0 7134 8924 3

A CIP catalogue record for this book is available from the British Library.

Printed in Singapore by Kyodo
for the publishers
B T Batsford
Chysalis Books Group
The Chrysalis Building
Bramley Road
London W10 6SP

www.batsford.com

A member of Chrysalis Books plc

I would like to thank the following people for their assistance in the production of this book:

Alan Shipp, Holder of the National Plant Collection of Hyacinths, for his help and for allowing me to pick flowers for photography. Ron Scamp for sharing his enthusiasm and time, and allowing me to pick daffodils for photography. Marie Blom of Bloms Bulbs, and Johnny Walkers, for allowing me to photograph their flowers. The staff of the Keukenhof and Hortus Bulborum, in particular, Joop Zonneveld who allowed me to pick flowers for photography and tolerated my enthusiasm for anything that was not commercial. Also Floratuin Julianadorp and the International Flower Bulb Centre, and George Hogervorst, who took me to all the right places in the Netherlands.

All photographs © Geoff Stebbings

To Steve

Contents

Preface   4

Chapter 1
Bulbs in the wild and in cultivation   5

Chapter 2
Daffodils   12

Chapter 3
Species and cultivars of daffodil   32

Chapter 4
Tulips   95

Chapter 5
Species and cultivars of tulip   112

Chapter 6
Hyacinths   181

Chapter 7
Species and cultivars of hyacinth   192

Glossary   202

Contacts   203

Bibliography   204

Index   204

Preface

My intention, when I had the idea to write this book, was to produce something that would be of use to the average gardener; someone who was not content with the vague information on the standard tulip pack. Many millions of words have been written about tulips and daffodils, but much of it is specialized and not easily accessible.

Bulbs are victims of their own success. You buy them, you plant them and they flower. What more do you need to know? Even articles in magazines do not help much. They are either just captions for luscious photographs, or give such cursory information that the reader is left wanting more. Most articles only mention the most common cultivars, while specialist articles confine themselves to plants that most mortals can only dream of possessing. So this book was written to address what I perceived as a need for a book that dealt with the kinds of plants that are available from garden centres and other commercial sources.

Daffodils, hyacinths and tulips are the most important bulbs in our gardens and I wanted to provide an insight into how we have ended up with such fabulous plants, the effort that was needed to produce them, and the great diversity that may not be obvious from the mainstream press. I wanted to concentrate on garden plants but, in describing the breeding of cultivars, it was necessary to stray into the territory of wild species too, an area that is the preserve of experts and botanists – an intimidating place to be.

I have been interested in bulbs for most of my gardening life from the time when my family moved into a rather rundown Victorian vicarage, two-thirds of which was uninhabitable, but a wonderful place to be as a child. In the grounds were remnants of an ancient garden, and in spring there were double daffodils and rows of pheasant's eyes in grass and in the woods. I can still smell those flowers if I close my eyes.

All three of these wonderful flowers have progressed from delicate wild things to a level of perfection that was probably not even imagined by the gardeners who first brought them into a domestic setting. I hope that I will be able to stir a passion in you and a need to explore each genus. In the case of each plant, there is beauty in every stage of its development, from the finest show daffodil to the oldest, scruffy double, and from a wild tulip to the best the English Florists can produce.

These three plants, although all spring flowers, are treated in very different ways by gardeners at the start of the 21st century. Daffodils are important commercial crops, but vast numbers of new cultivars are produced by amateur growers and small, specialist nurseries. To list all the new cultivars would be impossible. Tulips are treated in a casual way by most gardeners and most bulbs are bought, flowered and discarded. This probably suits the Dutch growers, who dominate the industry, perfectly well. And the poor hyacinth is not taken seriously at all. It gets hardly a look-in, even though we all love the perfume and colour of hyacinths in spring.

I realize that the dedicated daffodil exhibitor, the grower of cut tulips, the casual gardener who just wants some colour in March, and the serious flower historian, will all find this book wanting. It is a compromise, but I hope it will be useful.

Chapter 1
Bulbs in the Wild and in Cultivation

Bulbs have always fascinated me, and I know I am not alone. Bulbs include some of the most commercially important ornamental plants in the temperate world, with daffodils, tulips and hyacinths dominating. From a commercial viewpoint, few plants are easier to sell. After all, you can dig up your tulips, clean and grade them, put them in storage ready for shipment, or put them in packs with a big colourful picture on the front and hang them in a garden centre for months until they sell. No other plant material can be treated in this way except seeds, but seeds do not offer the guarantee of flowers in the same way as bulbs, often proving difficult to germinate and needing experience to get them to maturity. Given even basic care, however, your bulbs will flower. Being free from soil, which may harbour pests and disease, bulbs can also be shipped all over the world without the restrictions imposed on other live plant material. So people in Europe can enjoy daffodils bred all over the world, and

people in North America can import tulips from the Netherlands, still the world's greatest producer of these popular flowers.

This ease of growth is a major reason why gardeners or even casual plant buyers love bulbs. In today's busy world, it is convenient to be able to go to a garden centre and fill a basket with bulbs knowing that, if you have to leave them for a week or two before you have time to plant them, they will still be alive and ready to grow when you do so.

For me, the love of bulbs stems from a fascination with monocotyledons, that huge division of the plant kingdom made up of plants that have just one seed leaf (cotyledon) when the seed germinates. This differentiates them from the dicotyledons, with two, but there are other differences. Most monocotyledons have narrow, grass-like leaves (grasses are probably the most successful and most widespread monocotyledons) and the veins are parallel, unlike dicotyledons,

Alan Shipp, commercial hyacinth grower, rogueing bulbs in the field.

which have branching veins. The roots are also different: monocotyledons do not form taproots, and their formation of fresh roots, often in rings, is from the base of the stem. There are internal differences too, which make woody monocotyledons rare (palms and cordylines are notable exceptions) and mean that they cannot be grafted – their vascular tissue is not packed around the outside of the stem in a way that would allow the joining of two parts (the feature that makes the uniting of rootstock and scion possible in dicotyledons such as apples).

The Power of Three

From the ornamental point of view, however, it is the flowers that make monocotyledons so special. Dicotyledons have flower parts in multiples of four and five – think of a single rose with five petals – but monocotyledons have flower parts, usually, in threes. Three is a very satisfying number, not only visually but also structurally, being strong and economical – just look at the structure of a pylon, made of strong triangles.

The trinity of flower parts is common to the three important families of temperate bulbs: *Iridaceae* (including irises, freesias and gladioli), *Liliaceae* and *Amaryllidaceae*. All have three outer petals – which protect the flower when in bud in a similar way to the calyx in a rose – and three inner petals. *Iridaceae* have only three stamens, but they need not concern us further here because they are not relevant to the three genera in this book.

Both *Amaryllidaceae* and *Liliaceae* have six stamens, but members of the two are easily distinguished because the ovary, which contains the seeds, is below the flower in *Amaryllidaceae* so it can be seen even when the flower is immature or closed, as is easily shown in snowdrops (*Galanthus*), houseplant amaryllis (*Hippeastrum*) and daffodils (*Narcissus*). In *Liliaceae*, the ovary is inside the flower and cannot be seen except when the flower is open. In recent years botanists reviewing the classification of the vast *Liliaceae* have split it into a number of smaller families so that, although *Tulipa* is still a subfamily of *Liliaceae*, Hyacinthus has its own family, *Hyacinthaceae*, which includes the genera *Muscari*, *Bellevalia*, *Scilla* and others. For the

purposes of the following description, I shall ignore this recent change because tulips and hyacinths have the same basic structure.

Both have three outer petals and three inner ones. In the case of tulips, the outer petals are often smaller and may be a different shade, usually with greenish flushing, while in hyacinths the outer petals may be narrower. In most flowering plants the term 'petals' would refer only to the inner three, the outer three being known as sepals, which are usually green and leafy. However, although the sepals and petals of tulips and hyacinths do show small differences in size, shape and often colour, this is not as marked as in other flowers, and a new term has been coined denoting sepals and petals that are essentially indistinguishable: tepals. I have used it throughout the book.

So hyacinths and tulips have flowers with six tepals and an ovary inside the flower, while daffodils (*Narcissus*) have flowers with six tepals and an ovary behind the flower. *Narcissus* also differs in that the outer tepals are wrapped around the flower and have less protective value, but the buds are kept in a spathe – a thin sheath – until ready to open. Hyacinths and tulips have flowers with even less protection. The observant will also notice that *Narcissus* flowers have something extra, a trumpet (corona) in the centre of the flowers. This seems to go against all I have written previously, but in fact this remarkable organ is an extension that grows from the base of the stamens, and is not truly a petal at all.

Why Bulbs?

It is interesting that so many of the monocotyledons have developed bulbs. Bulbs are not seen in dicotyledonous families, although there are tubers and other storage organs. It is common to refer to anything that is a dormant storage organ as a bulb, but there is a distinct difference between tubers, corms and bulbs, and I have lost many an argument with a marketing manager who wanted to glue free gladioli 'bulbs' (properly corms) on a magazine cover.

Corms are annual structures and are replaced every year. They have no leafy structure and, when dormant, consist of a lump of storage tissue with a tiny bud on the top. As the plant grows, it consumes this store of starch and sugar and produces a new corm on top. If lifting crocosmia or gladioli, you discard the old, spent corms and keep the upper, new ones.

Bulbs, on the other hand, consist of a compressed stem at the base (basal plate) and a series of concentric leaves around the growing point. Like any other plant, there are potential buds at the base of each leaf and, in *Narcissus*, as these grow, they develop into new bulbs. The main bulb grows from the centre and the outer leaves die and become scales. Any side shoots that develop into bulbs gradually make their way to the outside and are eventually released as the outer leaves decay. This is the basic bulb structure (as can be seen in an onion, if you do not want to cut precious *Narcissus*), but there are subtle differences between this and the bulbs of tulips and hyacinths.

So why do plants form bulbs in the first place? The answer, as in so many things in nature, is survival. In temperate lands, and in subtropical climates, growing conditions are not consistent all year round and plants have had to develop ways to survive adverse conditions such as cold or drought. Annuals have become the sprinters among plants, germinating, growing, flowering and producing seed in the few months when conditions are good. They survive hard times as seed. Herbaceous plants take several years to reach flowering size but survive by hiding underground, able to tolerate cold but not always drought. Trees and shrubs usually drop their leaves and batten down the hatches, protecting their buds in scales.

Bulbs take a similar approach to herbaceous plants, retreating under the soil, but they are fully dormant, for a while at least, and protected from drying out. The amount of drought they can survive depends on where they naturally grow. Lilies, most of which evolved in moist soils, have fleshy bulbs without protective coats, and are prone to desiccation.

Narcissus can cope with some drought, their outer scales being thin and papery. This is logical because many come from Northern Europe where conditions are not completely dry in summer. Tulips, on the other hand, largely evolved in areas with baking summers, and so have a thick, tough coat to protect them from drying. This is especially evident in those that

have small bulbs, which are particularly susceptible to drying out – just compare the bulbs of the small *Tulipa linifolia* Batalinii Group with any large hybrid.

Bulbous plants usually take several years to reach flowering size, so they invest for the future. The leaves manufacture sugars that are stored in the bulbs as starch, and these give the plants the ability to make a remarkable spurt of growth as soon as conditions are suitable. They can grow and flower and set seed quickly before growth becomes impossible. In the case of autumn-flowering daffodils such as *Narcissus serotinus*, this allows the plants to flower before the leaves or flower stem have made any food, the flowers being sustained by the stored starch of the previous year. This quick growth is even more important for woodland bulbs that need to make food in late winter and early spring before new leaves on the trees plunge the woodland floor, and the bulbous plants, into darkness.

This all emphasizes the need for bulbs to keep their foliage attached and photosynthesizing for as long as possible so that every particle of food possible can be re-absorbed by the bulb. And I hope it will make all but the most heartless of gardeners stop tying their daffodil foliage into knots as soon as the flowers have faded.

In summer, or in the dormant period, nothing seems to be happening to the bulbs, as far as we can see on the surface. But this is an important

Hyacinths beds.

time for the bulb, for it is then that it will be forming its flower buds. Some bulbs do not flower or may even not grow if they have not had a baking summer the previous year, but this rarely applies to the bulbs in this book.

Development of the Bulb

Many thousands of words have been written about how to plant bulbs, and I will add to this later in the book, but just how a bulb gets under the ground when its seeds, in nature, fall on the surface may puzzle the quizzical gardener. Of course, some seeds will fall into crevices in the soil or get lodged under stones. Tulip seeds are flat while those of hyacinths and daffodils are round. All produce a small, grass-like leaf when they germinate, and they quickly start to form a bulb. Over several years this increases in size but every year the bulb will form a few special 'contractile' roots. These thick roots grow down and anchor themselves at the base. Then, as the season progresses, they contract and actually pull the bulb deeper in the soil. Tulips also produce bulbs called 'droppers' on shoots that grow deep into the soil.

However, although I will write more on planting later, a good guide is to plant the bulbs so that the depth of soil above the top is about twice the height of the bulb, so a bulb 7 cm (2.75 in) high will need a hole 21 cm (8.25 in) deep, to allow for the bulb height plus 14 cm (5.5 in) of earth above. If you are only planting for bedding and intend to discard the bulbs after flowering (shame on you!), the planting depth is not critical, as long as they are deep enough not to overbalance when they grow. However, reasonable planting will help the bulbs flower for several years, not least by helping them avoid being pierced by later cultivation.

Basic Requirements

Most of the bulbs in this book are easy to grow and are hardy. The exceptions are some of the species of daffodil and tulip. The species are necessarily varied, often having evolved to a specific niche in nature and it is too much to expect them all to adapt well to sometimes very different garden conditions. As mentioned earlier, tulips are largely from the Middle East and need drier conditions than daffodils, some of which are native to Northern Europe. But there are always exceptions, such as the North African narcissus, which requires warmth in summer and protection from the worst of winter weather in Northern Europe. The smaller species are also best suited to growth in a cold greenhouse (such as an alpine house) or with other protection because of their size, which makes their flowers a tasty snack for a slug.

Outside, all three genera in this book require a sunny spot, though daffodils will tolerate some shade. However, you should note that all three, grown as a commercial crop, are grown in full sun and though you may plant some daffodils partly in shade – either because they look nice there or because you wish to protect the red coloration of the coronas from burning in the sun – they will not increase as fast as in full sun.

These plants also require a soil that is well-drained. Read a gardening book about almost any plant and it will say that you need a 'moist, well-drained soil'. It sounds something of a contradiction, but it really means a soil through which water is moving (downwards), rather than collecting, and in fact it covers most soils except those in which the water table is high and the roots will sit in ground water for long periods. So areas that are prone to flooding in winter, especially if the soil is heavy clay where water does not drain quickly, may cause problems. The answer may be to create raised beds of free-draining soil above the natural earth level, or to grow bulbs in pots, which allow easy drainage and to which they are admirably suited.

Dryness in summer is not a problem. Many years ago, when I embarked on the restoration of Myddelton House Garden in Enfield on the northern outskirts of London, the former home of E A Bowles (whose name will crop up many times in this book), I spent the first year discovering what had survived 30 years of minimal care on a soil that is poor and gravelly. In summer, the few herbaceous plants were cooked to a crisp and even weeds struggled to survive, but come spring, the soil was covered in a carpet of bulbs, including ancient *Narcissus* cultivars, crocus, snowdrops and clumps of *Tulipa sprengeri*.

So summer drought in the garden is not likely to be a problem, the only obvious exception being some late double daffodils that will not tolerate dry soil in late spring and will abort their buds. And, of course, plants in pots need watering because dry soil when the plants are growing will not suit any bulb.

These flowers are very tolerant and bulb roots will put up with wet soil. Proof of this is the way that hyacinths and 'Paper White' daffodils can be grown in nothing more than pebbles and water. But it is important that the water level does not come higher than the base of the bulb, known as the basal plate. If it rises above this the roots and bulb will rot.

A note on the terminology used in this book. Because this is a gardeners' book and not a botanical treatise, I will refer to *Narcissus* hybrids, from now on, as daffodils and hybrid tulips as tulips, and the species as *Narcissus* and *Tulipa*. Because there is only one *Hyacinthus* species in common cultivation today, I will refer to them all as hyacinths unless I mean the wild plant. I will use the term cultivar when I mean a 'cultivated variety' to differentiate between these and wild varieties. It may be an ugly word but it maintains some accuracy.

Use in the Garden

Of all the spring bulbs, daffodils, tulips and hyacinths reign supreme in popularity. Between them they provide many months of colour and fragrance. If you are planting solely for effect, you can use them almost anywhere, from borders to window boxes and pots for the home. It is no accident that millions are produced and bought by gardeners every year. With thousands of cultivars from which to choose, if you are lucky, you can find just the right bulb for your circumstances, whether you need a dwarf daffodil for the rock garden or a tall tulip to come up through wallflowers.

Although I will deal with the development of the three plants in their own chapters, and suggest ways to use them, it is appropriate to mention here what I see as their differences as far as garden use is concerned.

The big changes in the development of daffodils have been more recent than in tulips and hyacinths, the latter having changed little in the last hundred years. Although this book will deal with some super-fine flowers that are of more interest to show growers rather than those who simply want to enjoy them in the garden, most of

Daffodil bulbs

Top row:
'Minnow',
'Spellbinder' cut,
'Earlicheer'.
Lower row:
'Baby Moon',
'Spellbinder' cut,
mother bulb,
'Sugar Bush'.

the daffodils you can buy in shops are for putting in your borders. Here they retain some of the informality of their wild cousins and I still think that, beautiful though the show flowers may be, you cannot beat the sight of daffodils in grass. I gaze in admiration at the perfection of a show flower in a green vase, but my heart lifts when I see golden daffodils set free under apple trees in an orchard, or in a meadow.

Daffodils are less suited to formal bedding because, unlike tulips and hyacinths, they can turn their back on you. Wherever you plant them, remember that, as the buds escape the confines of the spathe, they will turn to wherever they can detect warmth or light. So if you put them in a window box, they are unlikely to peer in to see what you are doing; if planted against a hedge they will face the centre of the garden; under a tree they will peer out, and in any bed they will all smile to the south (in the northern hemisphere, and vice versa). More than tulips and hyacinths, gardeners see daffodils as permanent residents, and they are planted in borders among herbaceous plants and shrubs where they can stay for many years. There is no need to lift them every year.

Hyacinths, on the other hand, are ideal for formal bedding, their stiff stems closely set with flowers. They look good from all sides and their short height, few exceeding 25 cm (10 in) high when in flower, makes them ideal for the front of borders and all containers. They are used predominantly for bedding but there is no reason why they cannot be used in borders too, and their wide range of colours allows many unusual combinations with coloured foliage. After several years the bulbs may get crowded and the flower spikes get thinner with fewer florets, but do not let their resemblance to bluebells fool you into thinking these are woodland plants – in shade they pine for the sun's rays. As the most expensive of the three bulbs, they are a luxury in the open garden, but there is no need to buy the biggest bulbs for the garden, or for containers. They are so reliable and colourful that I am always glad I bought as many as I have when they flower in spring. I always think that hyacinths look best when viewed from the side so you can see the flowers at their best, and they are my favourite spring bulbs for containers and raised beds. They are also the easiest of the three to grow in pots for the home; I like to have a succession of potted hyacinths to bring into the house so I can have flowers from Christmas until the end of March.

Tulips are probably the most varied of the three, at least in terms of the range available in garden centres, but most people use them in bedding schemes. This is quite a new idea, in gardening terms, becoming popular only at the beginning of the last century. The classic combination of wallflowers and tulips is one of the most glorious partnerships of the whole year, whether you plant a mixture of colours or a carefully chosen pair. Tulip flowers face upwards and look the same from every side but change personality as they mature, from slender or oval buds to great saucers or stars when the sun coaxes them open. With heights from 10–80 cm (4–32 in), there are tulips for every part of the garden.

In containers or borders, you can combine daffodils, tulips and hyacinths, and you can often buy packs that include all three, with a suggested planting layout. Though these can work well, read the pack to make sure you are getting enough of the most expensive part (hyacinths) to make a good show, and bear in mind that, lovely though the flowers may be, the leaves of bulbs are rarely ornamental. Plant the earliest-flowering bulbs in the centre of the pot and later-flowering, taller plants around the edge. That way the later flowers will disguise the leaves of the earlier ones.

Hyacinth bulbs
Blue and pink hyacinths have red-skinned bulbs, while white bulbs signify white or yellow flowers.

The Commerce of Bulbs

Tulips, daffodils and hyacinths are important garden plants but, perhaps because they are so easily grown and give their beauty so freely, they are not always given the serious treatment they deserve. All three have had their times in the horticultural limelight, and have captured the imagination of breeders and gardeners.

Of the three, it is hyacinths that have suffered the most neglect, and most gardeners now grow them only for spring colour and then throw them away. Most hyacinth cultivars we grow today are a century old. Tulips are taken more seriously and even today the type of flowers that led to the Dutch tulipomania of the 1630s are grown by a few dedicated gardeners. But the cultivation and breeding of tulips is now largely a matter for commercial companies, particularly in the Netherlands. Most gardeners grow their tulips for one year, something that I am sure suits the bulb producers.

The daffodil is rather different and is being actively developed by amateur breeders and small commercial concerns. These dedicated individuals are pushing the boundaries of the flower in ways that would have seemed entirely fanciful 50 years ago. As a result, there are thousands of daffodil cultivars, some of which are available only from the raiser. They command high prices, and only a tiny fraction can hope to attract the attention of commercial growers and, through them, reach the general gardening public.

Despite the vast amount you might think you spend on your garden, the amateur gardening market is small compared to the municipal, corporate and cut-flower markets, and commercial breeders do not always create plants with us in mind. When you buy the latest bedding plant, remember that it was chosen for production in massive numbers because it will flower in a smaller pot, a week earlier, in a greenhouse one degree cooler than other competing varieties, or because its seed is easier for a machine to sow – not because it is better in the garden. In the same way, the latest commercial daffodil is more likely to make it on the garden centre shelves because it increases readily, because it has big bulbs that attract the attention of gardeners when buying, or because it is a good cut flower. So, with daffodils, more than with tulips and hyacinths, we can directly support the people who are actually producing the latest developments, and make sure that gardeners in the future can look forward to the next generations of flowers.

Tulip bulbs
Top row:
T. turkestanica,
hybrid from garden
showing growth of bulbs
after one year – one
large replacement bulb
and one small one,
T. praestans.
Bottom row:
T. batallinii,
'Uncle Tom',
'Corsage'.

Chapter 2
Daffodils

I am sure that daffodils are the most popular garden flowers. Almost every garden has a clump and, apart from those who profess to hate yellow flowers, they are welcomed by everyone. Discarded bulbs and those deliberately planted can be seen in often unlikely places, regularly marking the gardens of long-demolished houses or orchards that succumbed to honey fungus in decades past. The general public and gardeners alike often make a distinction between daffodils

Drifts of daffodils planted in grass bring cheer to urban parks.

and narcissi, and I too fell into this trap as a child. In my early years a narcissus was a flower with white petals and a short trumpet and a daffodil was yellow with a big trumpet. This was fine at the time, but strictly speaking incorrect. Today the distinction is even more erroneous; what do you call something that has yellow tepals and a pink trumpet or a flower that has a trumpet split into six, flat segments?

It is simpler to stick to daffodil as a common name and use *Narcissus* as the botanical name for the whole genus. The confusion is long-established, as shown by the fact that, in 1629, the herbalist John Parkinson in his famous *Paradisi in Sole Paradisus Terrestris* wrote 'Many idle and ignorant Gardeners … doe call some of these Daffodils Narcisses, when, as all that know any Latine, that narcissus is the Latine name and Daffodill the English of one and the same thing'.

But where do the two names originate? It is usually supposed that Narcissus is named after the beautiful youth in Greek mythology, a handsome mortal. Women longed to be with him but he rejected them all in the hope of finding someone as handsome as he. His fate was sealed when he died while vainly trying to embrace his reflection in a stream. Some versions have it that the thwarted nymph Echo, who was such a chatterer that Hera condemned her never to start a conversation, only to end them, persuaded Cupid to make Narcissus fall in love with his reflection. As a result he gazed at his reflected beauty for the rest of his life, till he died on the spot. He did not find love, but his beauty was retained as he was transformed into a flower that bent its head to face the water rather than the sun. This explantation of the name seems to fit the look of the plant, since the flowers of daffodils do, usually, hang down. Oddly, the Victorians, who saw a moral in everything, associated daffodils with chivalry, perhaps because of the bright, golden colour and cheerful nature of the flowers, ignoring the Greek myths.

Although the name of the psychological condition of narcissism stems from the myth, that of the flower does not. Instead it is derived from the Greek *narkao*, to be numb, because of the supposed narcotic properties of the plant. Pliny the Elder (AD 23–79), in his *Natural History* (AD 77) describes it as *Narce narcissum dictum, non a fabuloso puero* – 'named narcissus from *narce*, not from the fabulous boy'. It seems surprising that such a common plant could be considered such a powerful medicine but Socrates (470–399 BC) called it the 'Chaplet of the Infernal Gods' because of its effects, and it is generally emetic if eaten.

The name 'daffodil' is from 'asphodel' (originally from the Greek *asphodelos*), the name of a group of some fifty mostly Mediterranean liliaceous species. In 15th-century England, it was called 'affadille' or 'affodylle', and in 1538 the word 'daffydilly' is first recorded. It is not known for certain where the initial 'd' comes from, but it makes the word easier to say and it may simply have been added for convenience. A possibility is that it is from the Dutch article *de* (the) in *de affodil* (the asphodel), the Netherlands being a likely source for bulbs brought into England.

John Gerard, the Elizabethan physician, in his *Herbal* of 1597, suggested that it was useful for wounds and burns, and 'draweth forth thorns and stubs out of any part of the body'. Not always known for his accuracy, he concludes his description of the plants: 'But it is not greatly to our purpose, particularly to seeke out their places of growing wilde, seeing we have them all & everie one of them in our London gardens, in great abundance. The common wilde daffodil groweth wilde in fields and sides of woods in the West parts of England.' So we know that daffodils have been popular for a long time.

Today we do not consider daffodils a dangerous plant, though there are inevitably odd stories of poisoning when the bulbs are mistaken for onions or, in a bizarre case in Toulouse in 1923, for leeks. A more serious problem can be the crystals of calcium oxalate in the tissues, which dissuade browsing animals from eating the foliage but which can also make the skins of dried bulbs an irritant to the skin. It is often stated that the narcotic effect of the plant is not related to any medicinal properties but to the strong perfume of some species. This is possible since many southern European species such as *N. jonquilla* and *N. tazetta* have a heady perfume. We accept tales told today about people being stupefied if they

'Berlin' has become popular because of its frilly, bright corona.

fall asleep under a brugmansia in bloom, and it is possible that if you were of a delicate constitution you might be overcome if you fell asleep in a field of *N. papyraceus* or *N. poeticus* – I must give it a try one day!

Breeding

Daffodil breeding began in earnest in the 1950s. Daffodils have suffered from the attentions of many who have tried to classify the burgeoning hoards of hybrids that were produced in the latter part of the 19th century. What we would now call Division 1, the trumpet daffodils, were the Magnicoronati, with eight groups. Division 2 of the system that was in place until 1908 were the

Mediicoronati, including the *Incomparabilis*, *Barrii* and *Leedsii* groups. The Parvicoronati comprised plants with small coronas. This system was published in J G Baker's *Handbook of Amaryllidaceae* in 1888.

Trumpets

The big yellow daffodils of Division 1 (the Magnicoronati) derive from *N. hispanicus* and *N. obvallaris* and not, as might be expected, from the familiar *N. pseudonarcissus*, a plant that produced offspring with drooping heads. The other two parents of today's daffodils are *N. moschatus* and *N. bicolor*. *N. hispanicus* was also known as *N. maximus*, *N. maximus var. superbus*, or just 'Maximus', and had rich yellow flowers on 75 cm (30 in) stems. Ironically it is now called *N. pseudonarcissus subsp. obvallaris var. maximus* so, according to modern nomenclature, it could be said that all the daffodils are derived from *N. pseudonarcissus* after all. Keeping the older names, *N. hispanicus* contributed size, golden colour and blue stems and foliage, *N. obvallaris* has good flower shape, a reason why it is so popular today, *N. moschatus* brought white to the colour mix, and *N. bicolor* brought vigour and the combination of yellow corona and paler perianth, though not in a precise pattern. In the early days, there was no red or orange in the flower, and this was added to the genetic mix from *N. poeticus*. It was not long before further species were added to the pot.

White Trumpets

It is remarkable to look at the beautiful *N. moschatus* and then at a recent white Division 1 flower, and see the difference. Among the earliest white trumpets of the 1880s were 'William Goldring', snow-white and dog-eared; 'Colleen Bawn', with a twisted, propeller-like perianth and long, cylinder-like trumpet; and 'Leda', perfumed like old oak. E A Bowles mentioned these in 1934 (in *The Narcissus*) but even then they were no longer available, and he comments that they were generally poor plants. But everything changed with the introduction of 'Madame de Graaff' (1W-W, de Graaff Bros, 1887 – see the introduction to the listing of daffodil varieties on page 32 for an explanation of notations such as

'1W-W'). This was a cross between the Backhouse's bicolour 'Empress' and the white *N. albescens* and it had, according to Bowles, an 'opaque whiteness and well-balanced trumpet, with its fascinatingly rolled-back rim'. It was not just beautiful, it was vigorous, and it was soon immensely popular. When self-fertilized ('selfed'), it produced 'White Knight' (1W-W, de Graaff Bros, 1907), which was better still, and when crossed with 'King Alfred', 'Madame de Graaff' gave 'Mrs Ernst H Krelage' (1W-W, E H Krelage & Son, pre-1912).

It is interesting that these big breakthroughs are largely Dutch, but work was happening in the UK and Revd G H Engleheart of Hampshire took 'White Knight' and produced 'Beersheba'. A new standard had been achieved and the short stems and rather demure posture of the whites was gradually being shed. Bowles said of Beersheba that it 'attracts the notice of all by its great size and glittering whiteness. It has achieved 5 inches in diameter on a stalk of 20 inches … Its outline is unusual and very striking; the perianth segments have long points and clean-cut edges forming a six-rayed star, or two triangles. The trumpet is curiously narrow at the base, and widens gradually to the open mouth in a curve that recalls the outline of a Convolvulus flower'.

The Scottish aristocrat Ian Brodie, the 24th Brodie of Brodie, was busy too, producing 'Trappist' (1W-W 1912) and then 'Askelon' (1W-W 1919), which set the standard with its broad perianth and led to 'Courage' (2W-W 1923). This was used by Guy Wilson to create 'Kanchenjunga' (1W-W 1934), which led to his 'Empress of Ireland' and the perfect flowers we expect today.

Yellow Trumpets

It would seem to be easier to create a yellow trumpet daffodil, not having to rely on such a small gene pool, but the perfection of form we expect today was not easy to create. *Narcissus hispanicus* may have golden flowers, but also the notched trumpets and twisted tepals that give its familiar propeller form. The first big breakthrough was 'King Alfred' (J Kendall, pre-1899). It is astounding that this ancient variety is still the one that people ask for. Its exact parentage is not known.

Revd Engleheart produced 'Magnificence' (1Y-Y pre-1914), with flowers 115 mm (4.5 in)

across, and P D Williams produced 'Crocus' (2Y-Y). Brodie used 'King Alfred' to create 'King of the North'.

Other Colours

The 20th century saw remarkable advances. We now have a Division 1 with reddish trumpets, such as Michael Jefferson-Brown's 'Hero' (1Y-O), bred from 'Brer Fox' (W O Backhouse 1959, 1Y-O) and 'Corbiere' (1Y-YOO). There are bicolours of excellent form, such as 'Newcastle' (W J Dunlop 1957), and the white and yellow flowers have been joined by new combinations such as white and pink 'Chinese Coral'.

One of the most beautiful developments has been the reverse bicolour, a pattern that is now found in many other divisions. The father of these was Guy Wilson who, having had success with 'Binkie' (2Y-W), crossed 'King of the North' (1Y-Y, Brodie of Brodie, 1909) with 'Content' (1W-WWY, P D Williams, pre-1927) to produce flowers unlike any that had been seen before. One in particular combined the colour of the two parents to perfection, having yellow tepals and a yellow corona, but this faded with time and the colour bleached from the corona to leave the inside, in particular, white, with a rim of yellow around the mouth. This was named 'Spellbinder' (1 Y-WWY) and it is still popular today.

The cross that produced 'Spellbinder' in the UK was repeated by Grant Mitsch in the US, and he sowed 10,000 seeds. Throughout history it has proved worth repeating a cross because the results vary; the second time you may be blessed with something completely different yet still of great merit. Mitsch crossed these with 'Binkie' and his introductions include 'Honeybird' (1Y-W) and 'Moonlight Sonata' (1Y-W 1960).

Cups

We now have a simple system to divide the large from the small cups (Division 2 and Division 3). But it was not always like this. Before the present system these were called the *Incomparabilis*; before that they were known as 'The Great Peerlesse Daffodil' or 'The Incomparable' by the 17th-century English botanist John Parkinson. They were even given their own genus at one time – *Queltia*, after Nicholas le Quelt who collected them in the wild – and they then had the common name of 'mock-narcissus'.

Large Cups

The large cups are the biggest group, and it is easy to see why. If you are breeding for a Division 1 and the corona is just a bit short, it will slip into Division 2. If the hunt for a Division 3 results in a good plant that has a cup that is just too large, it too can move into Division 2. But there is more to it than this. Most hybridizers are breeding for flower colour and shape but also vigour, and this strong growth seems to be associated with Division 2, again perhaps because it is such a mixing pot.

The first great achievements in yellow flowers were made by Engleheart, who raised 'Helios' (2Y-O), which Bowles compared with 'Fortune', though it was probably far less orange in the cup. 'Fortune' (1923) was an extraordinary development that still dominates its class in the

'Spellbinder' was the first of the commercially popular reverse bicolours.

garden centre even though it was swiftly followed by wonderful plants such as 'Carbineer' (1927) and its offspring 'Ceylon' (1945). The *Incomparabilis* sported to produce doubles, and the ancient 'Butter and Eggs' and others, as well as the 'Phoenix' group, arose as sports.

Small Cups

Now called Division 3, the small cups were classified as *Barrii* and *Burbidgei* at the beginning of their development. These short cups were created by crossing the trumpets with *N. poeticus*, and this last species brought red and then orange into the mix. The red rim of *N. poeticus* has a nasty habit of burning and dissolving in the sun; this was a common problem with early orange cups and can still be seen in some common plants today, but breeders have worked hard to make their flowers more sunproof. The first *Barrii* daffodils were raised by W Backhouse of Durham and 'Conspicuus' (also known as 'Barri Conspiucuus', 3Y-YYO) was one of his greatest achievements, still loved today. 'Bath's Flame' (3Y-YYO) was also significant but once again the name of Engleheart appears because of his great 'Beacon' (3W-R pre-1897).

Doubles and Splits

Double flowers always attract attention. Some people love double flowers, some hate them, and others judge them individually. I hope I fall into this last category. Double flowers are of no use in nature. While the daffodil may have developed its corona and nodding stance to protect the pollen and stigma from wet weather, it would never want the flowers to be double because this usually involves the sexual parts being converted to petal tissue. Consequently, most truly double flowers are sterile – you only have to look at the ovary of a double flower, and even at an early stage in development it will be rather thin. But these mutants have arisen many times and gardeners have selected them and ensured their survival. Perhaps the best known of the old doubles is 'Van Sion' (also known as 'Telamonius Plenus', 4 Y-Y). Mutations, or sports, have been the source of many doubles, such as 'Golden Ducat' from 'King Alfred', and 'Sulphur Phoenix' from one of the *Incomparabilis*, but since World War II the

potential for producing doubles has increased dramatically. This is because in 1934 a flower of 'Mary Copeland' (4W-O), a hybrid of the old 'Orange Phoenix', set a seedpod. This was unusual and it is fortunate that it happened in the garden of Lionel Richardson. It seems a miracle that such a rare event occurred by chance in the garden of a daffodil expert. In a similar tale to that of the chance happenings that led to 'Tête-à-Tête', just two seeds were produced. One produced a weakly plant but the other had a white and orange flower, which was named 'Falaise'. It was only semi-double, so was fertile, and it provided a way to get double genes into seedlings at last. You may not have heard of 'Falaise', but most modern doubles can trace their ancestry back to this breakthrough plant.

The structure of doubles also varies. In most, there are many rows of tepals with segments of corona between, a hint at how the split coronas could have appeared. But in others, the corona is intact and stuffed with pieces of tepal. For example, 'Falaise' was such a good plant that it helped to strengthen the stems of its children, improving their garden performance, but some doubles still have a tendency to abort their flower buds while still in the spathe if they are allowed to dry out when growing.

Perhaps the most extraordinary recent development in breeding has been the split-corona daffodils. Coronas may have split before, but it was Jaap Gerritsen who spotted such a plant in 1929 among a batch of seedlings. With great dedication and conviction – many fanciers considered his creations ugly – he used this flower to create a race that is now more or less accepted.

Ron Scamp is among those who have developed these flowers. He first saw them in Dan du Plessis's field and thought they looked like 'a "King Alfred" someone had sat on'. Ron obtained more bulbs from Rodney Ward on the Scilly Isles and got seeds from Gerritsen. At first he crossed splits with splits but the results were not great, so he moved on to use Division 1 flowers instead, producing big, ugly splits. He therefore changed to Division 2 varieties as parents, and got better results. Ron's plants now set the standard in this division.

Ron Scamp is also a great breeder of doubles, and started with the best he could obtain. He bred for vigour and for good foliage. He likes plants with upright foliage. This is not just cosmetic: it is also easier to pick flowers from rows with upright foliage, making any cultivar a better prospect to be grown commercially as a cut flower (often the making of a new daffodil). Good stems are also vital, and Ron likes 'a flower that smiles at you when you smile at it'. He also breeds for strong stems and for flowers that open fully and easily in any weather. One of his greatest achievements is 'Madam Speaker'.

The Plant and Flower

The Bulb

The daffodil is a true bulb, with its stem reduced to a basal plate and the leaves growing directly from this, swollen to form a food store for the plant. The bulb grows from a central growing point, the leafy scales being pushed to the outer edge of the bulb as it grows, and eventually becoming dry and being sloughed off as skins. The scales in a bulb that you buy will not grow into new leaves – they simply sustain the new leaves and the flower that grows from the centre of the bulb. These scale leaves not only provide food for the developing plant, but also protect the delicate growing point in the centre. You may know from experience that even if you severely damage a bulb, chopping through its scales, it will still grow. Sideshoots that form in the axil of a leaf will develop into new bulbs, which will be released as they eventually reach the edge of the mother bulb.

Hyacinth and tulip bulbs are graded according to size, and they vary only a little between the main cultivars (the bulbs of tulip species are the exception and are often small). Daffodil bulbs, on the other hand, vary greatly in size because of the many divisions, some of which are closely allied to wild species.

Bulbs are graded according to their relative size, with double-nosed (DN) bulbs the most common commercial grade, ranging in size from the largest (DNI) to the smallest (DNIII). These, and single-nosed bulbs, should all flower. The other popular choice are mother bulbs, which have a central bulb with many offsets attached. These offsets may not flower (see the section on Cultivation on page 20).

Leaves and Stem

The leaves that grow from the bulbs can be green or greyish, flat or rounded, and tall and upright or floppy, but a seed always produces just one leaf and it will be round in cross-section.

Although I use the word 'stem' throughout the book, it strictly refers only to the base plate, and the green 'stick' that holds the flower should properly be called a scape. This is leafless and cannot branch. It may be smooth or furrowed, often markedly so in some tazettas, or it may be rather flattened with ribs down opposite sides. At the top of this scape is the pedicel, or neck. As soon as the flower escapes the confines of the protective spathe the pedicel bends to allow the flower to assume its nodding stance.

Structure of the Flower

The pedicel joins the ovary, which is usually brighter green and distinct because of its swollen shape, although in double daffodils this may not be so obvious. The ovary contains three compartments (locules) and each can produce up

'Tête-à-Tête'
is widely available and is exceptional in the garden for borders and pots.

17

and look ghastly, so this is a big consideration when breeders select seedlings. Fortunately, nature tries to prevent such a monstrosity because most wild daffodils have their (male) anthers and the stigma – the receptive female part – in the centre of the flower, protected from the elements by the corona.

The corona is a special bonus in the *Narcissus* flower: it is an extra row of tissue that springs from the base of the tepals or filaments. You can see a similar structure in *Pamianthe*, *Pancratium* and *Hymenocallis*, all relatives in the *Amaryllidaceae*. It is impossible to say why it developed or what its use may be, but it seems likely that it had the evolutionary advantage of protecting the sexual organs from rain. The autumn-flowering species, which are mostly native to drier climates than the northern range of long-cupped species such as *N. pseudonarcissus*, tend to have small or rudimentary coronas, suggesting either that they did not need to develop such structures because of the climate, or that they are primitive species, and the origin of the genus that developed its own 'umbrella' as it headed north for wetter climes. The corona must have an advantage in this way because once a daffodil has opened its flower it does not close it again, come rain or shine – unlike the tulip, which watches the skies continually, clamping its flower shut as the sun disappears.

Finally, there is the bulk of the flower, the perianth, composed of three outer tepals and three inner ones. These may be very similar, or the inner may be smaller.

The Show Flower

Everyone can appreciate the beauty of a daffodil, and even the most ragged and primitive hybrid has its charms. As breeders have developed the plant, we have enjoyed bigger flowers, more colours, brighter shades, new colour combinations, greater vigour, a longer season of blooms, completely new flower shapes and forms and more perfect blooms. I do not wish to delve deeply into the world of showing but I have, in the accompanying list of species, suggested some as being good for showing.

When showing any flower, there are a few basic rules. The exhibit should be as specified in the

to 30 seeds, in two rows. Gardeners usually remove the seed pods to prevent the formation of seeds. Between the ovary and the flower, as we usually see it, is the tube. The stamens are usually attached to this, deep in the heart of the flower. Its size is a way of identifying some plants, but it is usually of little importance except where its green or yellow colour is clearly seen, in which case it affects the eye of flowers with short or split coronas.

The stamens are attached to the tube, and they consist of the filament on which is attached the anther, which bears the pollen. The stamens may be held in a single ring of six, or in two rows of three. In trumpet daffodils, the filaments are long and the anthers are held near the mouth of the flower. If stamens of this length were produced in a short cup or *poeticus* flower they would extend beyond the end of the trumpet schedule. The flower should be in good condition, free from disease and pest, of the right type, and a good example of that type – of good size, form and colour. If you are exhibiting more than one flower, they should be of consistent size. This is often the most difficult part – we can all find one good daffodil in our garden, but can we find three, five or more of the same age, size and condition? Your fridge can help here and you can keep flowers in good condition for a few days, at least, in a domestic fridge.

Where you do your showing will influence what daffodils you grow. It is fair to say that breeders have improved the perfection of our plants. The wild *N. pseudonarcissus* and its relatives have tepals that twist and are thin in width and texture, and flowers that hang down. Most breeders have aimed to improve the texture of the flowers, to make the tepals broad and stand back at 90 degrees to the axis of the corona, and to make the flowers with a strong pedicel so that they face, at least at the horizontal, though this has often been the most difficult thing to achieve.

There are many fine flowers that have to be lifted slightly to see the perfection of their form. But today we have blooms with broad tepals creating a round perianth, often overlapping by a third or half of their length. Though broad, they can still vary in shape; some are rounded while others are triangular, so there is a great variation among these 'perfect flowers'. The tepals should be as flat as possible, with no creasing, waving and in-rolling, making them as far from the imperfections of the original wild plant as possible. An interesting feature is the mucro, a white hook, that is seen in many flowers. In nature these overlap to hook the tepals together until they are ready to open. In the show flower it may add to a starry outline of the flowers, and as long as they are even, it is not usually regarded as a fault. I actually like prominent mucros on lots of flowers – it gives them a bit of extra sparkle. Some cultivars have flowers where the tepals overlap in the bud in an awkward way so that the open flower shows nicks or tears as the tepals open, usually in the upper half. These are not good show flowers.

What you grow for showing will depend on who you are competing against. A stock of good commercial daffodils is fine for the local village show, but if you are taking part in national,

specialist competitions you will need to get some modern daffodils of good form to stand a chance. Bear in mind that the requirements of a good show daffodil and a good garden daffodil are not always the same. Some that are useless in the garden because the intense orange or red coloration burns in the sun are nevertheless fine for a show, where the flowers will have been picked just as they open and kept in shade.

Before I leave showing I should mention a few other points for those who are interested. I have already mentioned that it is essential to read the schedule. I make no apology for repeating that even if you stage a wonderful exhibit, with the best flowers ever seen, but you enter the wrong class, you will not win. A kind steward may notice and advise you of your error but, just as you were always told when starting an exam in school: read the question!

Staging is the next hurdle. Even a mediocre flower can look classy when it is staged well in a clean vase. Grooming is also crucial. You should always leave yourself plenty of time to 'dress' your flowers. All the daffodils in the photos reproduced here have been picked and photographed *au naturel*. Many are top-notch show winners, but they are like models without make-up. Catalogues will show you flowers as they look on the showbench – the show flower's equivalent of the catwalk – whereas I show them here in the buff. Any daffodil flower can be transformed by a little manipulation, straightening tepals to create a flat perianth; covering lobes at the edge of the corona. But be careful and use a large, soft brush to avoid damaging the flowers.

If you are keen to try showing, the points for different aspects of your flower, according to the criteria used by the Royal Horticultural Society, are as follows:

Colour: 5 points
Form: 5 points
Condition: 4 points
Size (for cultivar): 3 points
Texture: 3 points
Poise: 3 points
Stem: 2 points
– making 25 points in total.

For a vase of three or more blooms the points are:

Colour: 4 points
Form: 4 points
Condition: 4 points
Size (for cultivar): 3 points
Texture: 3 points
Uniformity: 2 points
Poise: 3 points
Stems: 2 points
– again making 25 points in total.

Commercial Production

Daffodils are important commercial crops in many temperate areas of the world including the UK, the Netherlands, the US, New Zealand, Australia and Canada. In the UK, the main daffodil growing areas are in Cornwall and Lincolnshire, where in spring you will not only see hectares of flowers in bloom but gangs of pickers harvesting the flowers for market. You may also see people tending rows 'rogueing' the bulbs – painting a leaf with glyphosate weedkiller to destroy a bulb that would otherwise produce a rogue flower in the stock.

Most commercial daffodil cultivars, which are grown in tonnes rather than dozens, were originally bred by amateurs or specialist growers and then taken up for large-scale production. They were evaluated for their novelty, beauty and ease of growth but, more importantly, for their earliness (making them a good cut flower), and their ability to make a big, healthy bulb without falling prey to disease.

In the garden we are happy for bulbs to increase naturally, but for commercial growers the need is always to speed up the process. To make one bulb produce many more, you need to carefully and deliberately damage it in a similar way to that used for hyacinths. But while the hyacinth bulb is left in one piece, with daffodils you cut them into eight pieces. The aim is to produce a piece of base plate with some sections of scale attached. Only healthy bulbs should be used for propagation. It will take three to four years to produce flowering bulbs by this method, and it is vital that the original bulb is free from viruses to start with. The process starts in June or July (in the northern hemisphere). Round, single-nosed bulbs are best, and they are prepared by slicing off any narrow neck to leave the lower two thirds of the bulb's height. Then the bulb is sliced through, into two identical halves, from top to bottom. The halves are cut again and these portions cut once more so there are eight sections (fewer for a smaller bulb: cutting the bulb into many sections may give you more bulbs in total, but small pieces are also more liable to die). Ideally the sections are then soaked in a solution of fungicide before they are put in moist perlite or vermiculite, labelled, and kept in a temperature of about 20° C (68° F). You must watch the segments carefully and if any show signs of rot they must be removed. After two months there should be signs of growth, with small roots and bulbs forming around the base of the scales. At this stage they can be carefully planted out, about 5 cm (2 in) deep, either in pots, the open garden or in frames, and the following spring there will be grassy foliage. The small bulbs can be lifted the following June and July and replanted the following autumn. These should flower after another two or three years. This method will produce 15 to 40 bulbils from a single average original bulb, but commercial growers can take the process a stage further and, having cut the bulb into eight or more segments, they cut these into pieces of basal plate with two scales. As many as 100 bulbs can thus be produced from a single bulb, but there is a greater chance of the scales rotting, the bulbils that are produced are smaller, and they may take one more year to reach flowering size.

Cultivation

Daffodils are easy to grow. Buy a bulb and it already has a flower formed inside. It just needs minimal care and it will flower and provide you with colour and fragrance the following spring. But this is just the advertisement. In practice, you should treat your daffodils with a little respect. You can use daffodils to be a splash of colour in the border but, with their variety and beauty, they can be much more.

If you buy from a specialist, you are spared the worry of picking out good bulbs yourself – you will not get soft or infected bulbs. If you do get bad bulbs by mail order, inform the supplier immediately. A healthy bulb is heavy for its size and solid. The skins should not be mouldy, but if any mould present is only on the surface, it is only the result of recent moisture so may not be serious. Bulbs should be stored in cool, airy conditions and not in plastic bags unless they have ventilation holes.

Daffodils do not like to be out of the ground for too long, and they should be planted in September and October (in the northern hemisphere). Miniatures and poets (Division 9) are particularly prone to drying out. If you dig up some bulbs in your garden in August you will find that they have already started to form roots, giving you an idea of what they really want to do instead of being strung up in a shop waiting for you to put them back in the ground. If bulbs have been stored in damp conditions they may start to form roots in the pack. This is not a good situation, but if you can plant them without damaging these short roots they should be alright. Try to select bulbs without long shoots (except in the case of 'Paper White', where this is almost inevitable).

If you are a frequent shopper at garden centres you may see that, in October, the bulbs start to get squeezed out by tinsel and baubles. By November the bulbs are in the way of holly wreaths and the prices of daffodils may be reduced. Are they a good buy? I would hesitate to recommend them without reservation for a couple of reasons. Regarding the condition of the bulbs themselves, if they have been stored in a cool, airy place they may still be alright, but if they have been stored in a heated shop, they may be dead before the end of November. Second, when bulbs are planted late they do not have a chance to develop good roots before flowering. Late planting therefore increases the risk of stunted growth and aborted flowers. I have planted daffodils on Christmas Eve before now and they have grown, but with late flowers and on stunted stems. They recovered, but I cannot recommend it as good practice, and I was ashamed to be stuffing 'Ice Follies' into the ground when I should have been stuffing a turkey.

I have already mentioned planting depth, which should be approximately twice the height of the bulb. If you do not get it right, do not panic: like hyacinths and tulips, daffodils have contractile roots and will pull themselves down to the correct depth. Deep planting does not seem to bother most bulbs provided you are sensible and do not plant them deeper than 25 cm (12 in) – the average depth of topsoil in most gardens.

Growing in the Border

Most people grow daffodils in borders. Their bright flowers are so cheerful in spring. But as soon as the flowers have faded the situation is different. Daffodils will grow in a wide variety of soils, from light and sandy to heavy clay. They do not like soils that are waterlogged in winter, but a damp slope that is wet in spring is fine. E A Bowles's meadow at Myddelton House Garden, home to wonderful old daffodils that have survived to this day, was damp throughout the

'Ice Follies' is possibly the most popular daffodil today.

year and kept a huge gunnera happy as well as his *Incomparabilis*. Many cultivars, because they have such a mixed pedigree, will tolerate most soil types and degrees of acidity or alkalinity (pH) though most species are more fussy. If you want to grow daffodils well, it is good practice to dig the soil over and add some organic matter such as well-rotted manure, garden compost or mushroom compost. You can add some slow-release organic fertilizer too, but it is easier to add a general fertilizer when the shoots appear through the ground.

It seems an obsession with many people to buy mother bulbs, or bulbs with numerous offshoots. These will produce one flower, or perhaps two, and a mass of foliage as the offsets develop. Though you have got lots of extra bulbs developing, these will be crowded around the main bulb, will not have a chance to develop, and will need lifting and replanting after a few years. If you do buy mother bulbs, remove the outer bulblets at the side and plant them separately.

Daffodils are informal and I always think they look better if planted in drifts and informal clumps in the border, rather than in rows. But, if you are planting for showing and cutting, rows may be best. The spacing of the bulbs in your border will depend on the cultivar. Large cultivars should be planted about 15 cm (6 in) apart, closer for miniatures. The depth should be about 10–15 cm (4–6 in). What tool you use to plant with is up to you, but I usually prefer a spade, digging a hole at least 15 cm (6 in) deep and putting three in each so they are about 15 cm (6 in) apart. A trowel is useful if you have forked over the soil beforehand but trowels are hard work in heavy soils and, if you have more than a few dozen to plant, you will probably end up with blisters.

You may be tempted to try a bulb planter. These are usually of two types. The cheapest take out a cylinder of soil that should fall out when the handle is compressed. I am not keen on planters and have never used one for more than two minutes with any satisfaction. The other type, which is large and more expensive, is designed so you can take out the hole without bending, though how you get the bulb in the hole or replace the core, I can only guess. I'd prefer to spend the money on good quality bulbs instead. You can mulch the border after planting, but be

careful how you tread on the soil afterwards so as not to damage the emerging shoots. When they appear you can give the soil a scattering of rose fertilizer to provide a good, balanced feed with plenty of potash.

When flowering has finished, you should remove the dead flowers, complete with the developing seed pod. This need not take too long and it will prevent the bulb wasting energy making seeds that no one wants.

There is then just the problem of the leaves. The leaves are there to continue to manufacture food, replenishing the bulb after it has given you a lovely flower, and to make sure you get another flower next year. It is best to leave the foliage to die down naturally, though trials at the Royal Horticultural Society gardens in England showed that no harmful effects result if you cut the leaves six weeks after flowering. If you leave them longer, the bulb will continue to be replenished, but six weeks should be regarded as the minimum time.

Those who tie their daffodil leaves in knots as soon as the flowers have faded, or who strip them off the surface with a hoe, are failing to understand how bulbs function: they need their leaves to photosynthesize food for next year's growth. Please leave the foliage to feed the bulbs for another year and do not tie it in knots, however neat it looks or how bright the string.

That being said, daffodil foliage is ugly in the border, turning brown just as other plants are looking their best. A little careful planning can disguise daffodil leaves, and I always think that peonies are the perfect companions. The red shoots of peonies always look good with the daffodil flowers, and the peony flowers return the compliment by covering the daffodil foliage later in spring. It is not impossible to plant other, larger herbaceous plants among the daffodils, and if you wait six weeks and then hoe off the leaves you should not have too much of an ugly foliage display to look at.

Daffodils make good companions for roses too, but only if the roses are cut down quite hard. If their stems are at the same height as the daffodil flowers the blooms tend to get ripped to shreds by the thorns – this is a common problem, especially if the weather is windy. Another alternative is to plant miniatures under the roses.

If all goes well, your bulbs should thrive, and they may need to be divided after two or three years. The best time to divide bulbs is in the summer when they are dormant, but this is not always possible and it is easy to forget because there are so many other things to do. An ideal time is when the foliage is starting to die down, from six weeks after flowering finishes. You can lift the clumps, divide them, pull off the foliage and replant them, and the bulbs will be all the better for it. You can also divide daffodils when they are in full growth. It is not ideal because daffodil roots do not branch and will not grow afresh if they are broken off, but if someone offers you a daffodil you want when it is in flower and it's the only chance you are going to get, take it. Make sure the plant is kept cool and is not allowed to dry off; you should also expect it to have a rest from flowering the following spring.

Growing in Grass

Daffodils look their best in grass. If you have an orchard, you should plant it with masses of daffodils. But you do not need to plant on a grand scale to enjoy daffodils in grass, and in my present garden a corner of the small lawn is planted with pale yellow-and-white miniature 'Segovia' with 'Valerie Finnis' *Muscari* and white celandines. If there are two gardeners in the household, remember that the grass in which daffodils are planted cannot be cut for at least six weeks after the bulbs have flowered. For this reason it is best to choose early daffodils such as 'February Gold'. Make sure you both agree that the daffodils can be included in the lawn before you plant.

Never buy cheap bulbs to plant in grass. You should go for the same quality as you would buy for any other part of the garden. It is usually recommended that you avoid mixtures sold for naturalizing, and stick to one or two cultivars instead, and I have to agree with this advice. 'Naturalizing Mixtures' are often the commercial growers' 'floor sweepings', and may be small bulbs. They could also be a mix of cultivars that were simply not available in sufficient quantity to be listed separately. Such a mixture might include lovely flowers, but not all daffodils look perfect in grass. I tend to prefer smaller, simpler and older

daffodils for naturalizing. The old, scruffy doubles are alright, but modern super-smooth flowers look too much like a fashion model slumming it in the jungle, and that would not be of interest to anyone! One of the worst uses of double daffodils I have ever seen was a steep bank below a castle in Scotland, which was studded with rocks, overlooked the ocean, and was dotted at regular intervals with 'Petit Four' (4W-PPY) – pink, double and totally out of context.

There is no need to stick to wild daffodils, but be selective and restrained, if only because it will not be easy to remove and replace the bulbs after planting. While the planting should be irregular, it should be artfully so, not randomly. I have never got on very well with the idea of throwing the bulbs over your shoulder and planting them where they land. Rather, the traditional, overlapping drifts of similar varieties work best. Stand back to look at the area and, if possible, direct someone who has a bucket of sand to create the outlines of the drifts on the ground, which you can then follow when planting. A word of caution if the ground is irregular: you may have problems with bulbs in the hollows rolling together.

There are various ways to plant, and it will depend on the soil you have and the size of the area. The counsel of perfection is to lift the turf, fork over the soil and put the bulbs in before replacing the turf on top. But I usually just push

'Paper White' daffodils are ideal for indoor display or for cutting.

23

a spade into the soil, wiggle it back and forth, remove it and push a bulb or two into the slit. The effect is fine, the bulbs are deeper, which is important, and it is quicker than lifting turf. How you go about it will also depend on how much you value the grass surface you are planting under: you'll want to employ a lighter touch on a carefully manicured lawn than on the rough grass in an orchard. If you do have a lot of mother bulbs, pull off the offsets and plant them at the same spacing as the other bulbs so they have room to grow to flowering size.

Growing in Containers Outside

It is easy to grow daffodils in containers, and you can buy daffodils in bud at garden centres in

'Quail'
in a hanging basket
with euonymus, violas
and scilla.

spring, ready to place into your borders or patio pots. However, with a bit of planning, you can easily grow your own at a fraction of the cost. Just remember that your bulbs will be better the following year if you use a good, John Innes compost (see Glossary on page 202), and that your pots will need to be watered throughout the winter because winter rains will not usually be sufficient to keep the compost moist. You can really pack in the bulbs to make a colourful display, and you can plant them in two layers. Put drainage material, such as gravel, broken clay pots or broken chunks of expanded polystyrene, in the base of the container, and then compost. When there is a gap of about 20 cm (8 in) from the compost to the top of the container, put in a layer of bulbs. Then add enough compost to almost cover the bulbs and put in another layer of bulbs so they sit between the noses of the lower layer. This way you will get a really good, densely packed display, but you will need to make sure you water and feed the bulbs well. You can either use a single variety for this or two different daffodils, but if mixing them, try to arrange for them to flower at the same time or for the earliest to be shorter so the later covers the foliage of the earlier. Of course, you can also use this method to mix daffodils with bulbs of other flowers.

I always like to use single-nosed or double-nosed bulbs when planting in containers, rather than bulbs with lots of offsets. This is because the former produce large flowers and less foliage than mother bulbs, or bulbs with lots of offsets that are not of flowering size.

Daffodils are hardy but, if you have the strength, you could put your patio pots in an unheated greenhouse in winter so that they come into flower slightly earlier than usual. You can move the pots out of the way when the flowers have finished, but do not neglect to water them because they have been put out of sight. When the foliage has died down you can then lift the bulbs from the pots and plant them in the border.

Growing in Pots for Indoor Display

Daffodils can be grown for indoor display or to brighten the greenhouse. Any can be grown in this way but the easiest are the Tazetta or Division 8 daffodils, especially the tender cultivars such as

'Paper White' and 'Sol d'Or', which do not need a period in the cool and dark. They can be planted in pots or in gravel and water, and placed on the windowsill to grow. Details of cultivation are given in the section on Division 8 (p. 82). The hardy kinds can be grown for indoor use but they will not tolerate high temperatures, especially in the early stages of growth, and should be treated in the same way as hyacinths. Choose firm single- or double-nosed bulbs and put these in pots so the noses of the bulbs are just above the rim of the pot. Cover with compost and then either place them outside in a cold-frame under 10 cm (4 in) of bark or put them in a dark, cool place indoors. Keep them moist and when the shoots are 5–10 cm (2–4 in) tall, bring them into the light. Keep them watered and fed after flowering.

Miniature daffodils are especially lovely when grown in this way, which allows you to best appreciate their beauty and fragrance. If you get hooked on miniatures you will inevitably progress to the species to which these small plants are so closely related. The species are not always easy to find or grow in the open garden, but these challenges are just what gardeners who eschew large hybrids seek. Though these are at their best in a cold greenhouse – an alpine house is ideal – they can be grown in a cool greenhouse too, and I have a few that fit quite happily into the routine I use for my collection of winter-growing South African bulbs, which need frost protection.

Problems

Daffodils are generally easy to grow and suffer from few pests and diseases.

The most common problem is 'blindness' – the failure of bulbs to flower. This has several possible causes, and if the clump has been growing untouched for many years it could simply be that the bulbs are too crowded and not able to grow to flowering size. Dig up the clump as the foliage is starting to die down and divide the bulbs. Fork over the soil, add some organic matter and replant the bulbs, in clusters of two or three, 15 cm (6 in) apart. They will not flower the following spring but, if they are given a good feed as they start to grow, they should have achieved enough size to flower in the year after that. Blindness can also be caused by shade. Daffodils grow beside trees but they do not flourish in dense shade, especially under evergreens where there is no light in spring while they are in leaf. This can be a problem in gardens where shrubs have grown and spread over areas where bulbs have been planted.

A more serious cause of blindness is narcissus fly (two species, the large and the small narcissus flies). Both lay their eggs on the bulbs under the soil, getting there by crawling down the tunnel left as the leaves wither. The eggs hatch and the larvae tunnel into the bulbs, destroying the centre. The outer leaves are usually left, however, and the bulb responds by sending up a clump of narrow foliage in a type of natural twin-scaling. You can stop the female fly in her tracks by hoeing off the foliage just as it starts to turn yellow – by disturbing the soil surface you prevent her getting to the bulbs. When daffodils are grown in grass, narcissus fly is less of a problem because the mass of foliage makes it less easy for the flies to find their way down to the bulbs. The large narcissus fly (*Lampetia equestris*) lays one egg per bulb and this becomes a large (1 cm/0.5 in) long dirty-grey maggot. The small narcissus fly (*Eumerus tuberulatus*) lays several eggs on each bulb, but is less of a problem. You should never get a bulb with narcissus fly from a specialist grower, but if you are scooping up handfuls from a garden centre, reject any lightweight or soft bulbs, or those that look black under the skin – they might be infected.

The other serious pest of daffodils is eelworm. These minute creatures live within the bulbs and may be in there when you buy the bulbs. But good, specialist growers will regularly treat their stocks so you will get clean bulbs. Symptoms of infection are generally a decline in vigour, with stunted stems and distorted flowers, not just patchy colouring as you see with virus infection. If you cut a bulb in half you may see brown colouring in the scales. Commercial growers kill the eelworm by heating the bulbs in hot water at 44–46° C (111–115° F) for three hours. Higher temperatures kill the bulbs, so this is not something to try at home. In the year following heat treatment the flowers are often abnormal on the bulbs, showing how close the bulbs come to dying in the process of getting rid of the eelworm.

The only other common problem is viral diseases. You will spot these because the foliage will be stunted, streaked with yellow or white, and the flowers will have pale patches where there should be none. Once a plant is infected you cannot get rid of the virus and, unfortunately, you will find that some commercial bulb stocks are infected. If you have a collection of good daffodils you will not want virus to infect your collection so you should destroy any infected bulbs. But in the open garden you may decide to put up with the problem because it rarely affects the plants enough to reduce the garden value of the flowers. Aphids spread viral diseases, so control these pests in spring.

Classification

The classification of daffodils is complicated and this is not the place to offer anything but a brief outline of the way they are grouped. Gardeners and botanists take two different approaches. For the gardener there is a classification of cultivars to simplify things, with all the hybrids slotted into 12 divisions. Into the 13th division are lumped all the individual species found in the wild (plus their hybrids), which is a convenient way of dealing with them. Botanists, who are usually more interested in wild plants than cultivars, have instead divided the genus into sections to try to make sense of this complicated genus. The problems are compounded by the fact that the genus is actively evolving – hardly surprising given its intensive cultivation – and species such as *N. bulbocodium* show a wide range of variation. Some botanists may treat plants throughout the range as species, while others prefer to give them only varietal rank. These problems started early in the history of daffodil growing because many species in the section *Narcissus* were originally described from garden plants that did not breed true and were obviously not true species.

Sections

At present, botanists recognize ten sections in the genus *Narcissus*. This shows the diversity of *Narcissus* in the wild, but few of the sections are of importance to gardeners. The section names are not used often but they do group species together with certain characteristics, so if you are keen to grow the species, the sections give you an idea of the relationships between them and the kind of conditions the plants may need.

The sections of the genus *Narcissus* are *Apodanthi*, *Aurelia*, *Bulbocodium*, *Ganymedes*, *Jonquillae*, *Narcissus* (confusingly), *Pseudonarcissus*, *Serotini*, *Tapeinanthus* and *Tazettae*.

Apodanthi: These are plants from Spain, Portugal and Morocco and are similar to the jonquils but differ because the foliage is usually glaucous (bluish) rather than green, and the seeds are round and shiny rather than angular and matt in colour, among other things. The *Apodanthi* usually show their foliage in spring while the *Jonquillae* appear in autumn. Most importantly, hybrids of two species within each section are fertile, but hybrids of two species from different sections are sterile. The flowers in *Apodanthi* can be solitary or in small clusters and include yellow *N. rupicola*, white *N. atlanticus*, and multi-flowered, yellow *N. scaberulus* and *N. calcicola*. Division 7 includes hybrids of these species. This section was separated from the *Jonquillae* in 1966.

Aurelia: This includes just one, autumn-flowering species from Morocco, and it is the most southern of all daffodils apart from *N. canariensis*. *N. broussonetii* is unusual because it has no corona, but otherwise looks a bit like *N. papyraceus*, with white tepals and good fragrance. It will not tolerate frost.

Bulbocodium: These cannot be confused with any other type of daffodil because of the large, inflated corona and tiny tepals. The species are widespread throughout Spain and Portugal and into northwest Africa. Those that flower in spring are generally suitable for the garden but the African species, which usually flower in the depths of winter, are best grown in an alpine house. This is a complicated group for the botanist, though gardeners will easily recognize them, and includes *N. bulbocodium*, *N. cantabricus*, *N. hedraeanthus* and *N. romieuxii*. Its hybrids are included in Division 10 (p. 84).

Ganymedes: This is a simple section with just one species, *N. triandrus*, but this is itself divided into subspecies and varieties based on flower colour and size. *N. triandrus* has round stems and several, drooping flowers with reflexed tepals and a cup-shaped corona that is rarely flared at the mouth. The anthers are carried on filaments of two different lengths – three anthers are held inside the corona and three are held at the mouth of the corona or beyond the rim. It has given rise to its own division of hybrids (Division 5, p. 68).

Jonquillae: These species are mostly native to southern Spain and its islands in the Mediterranean, with some from Morocco, Portugal and southwest France. The flower stems carry from one to five (rarely more) flowers on round stems. The flowers are yellow, never white, with a cup-shaped corona that is wider than it is long, and they are fragrant. Species include *N. jonquilla* (the tallest), *N. fernandesii*, *N. cordubensis*, *N. assoanus*, and the strange *N. viridiflorus* – the only species of the section to flower in autumn and the only species in the genus to have green flowers. The hybrids of *Jonquillae* are in Division 7 (p. 74).

Narcissus: Despite its name, which coincides confusingly with that of the genus, this section does not include flowers of the familiar golden daffodil shape but rather the 'poets', *N. poeticus*. With a wide natural distribution across Europe from northern Spain to the Black Sea between the latitudes 42 and 45 degrees North, as well as down into Greece, these are widespread plants and often found in large quantities. The species and variants are spring flowering, with one (occasionally more) flower per stem. The small corona is edged with red. The stems are compressed and the leaves are flat and not channelled. The hybrids of this section are found in Division 9 (p. 85).

Pseudonarcissus: This is a large section, with many species that have been grown in gardens for centuries. They flower in spring and there is usually one flower per stem. The stems are usually compressed and the flowers are white, yellow or both, with a cylindrical corona. There is never any orange or red colouring in the flowers. Among the many species are *N. cyclamineus*, which is unusual because of the reflexed tepals, and *N. longispathus* and *N. nevadensis*, which are exceptional because they have two to four flowers per stem. More typical are *N. asturiensis*, *N.*

pumilus, *N. hispanicus*, *N. obvallaris*, *N. pseudonarcissus* and *N. moschatus*.

Serotini: This is an odd section, with just one species, *N. serotinus*. But it is widespread, growing in coastal areas around much of the Mediterranean. *N. serotinus* has small, white, fragrant flowers in autumn.

Tapeinanthus: Another section with just one species, *N. cavanillesii*. It has only recently been classified as a daffodil at all. It is found in Gibraltar and down the west coast of Morocco, and flowers in autumn with one yellow flower per stem. There is no corona as such, but there may be six small protrusions from the base of the tepals – as though the flower is thinking about making a corona.

Tazettae: The 12 or so species in this section come from around the Mediterranean and the south and east coasts of the Black Sea. They have compressed stems with three to 20 flowers and white, yellow or bicoloured flowers, which are usually fragrant. They differ most obviously from the *Jonquillae* because the leaves are glaucous (blue). Apart from *N. papyraceus* and *N. canaliculatus*, the species are rarely seen in gardens, but others include the all-white *N. dubius*, *N. canariensis* and *N. polyanthus*, and the

N. cantabricus and other species in the section Bulbocodium are difficult to classify but a delight for gardeners.

yellow *N. italicus*, *N. aureus* and *N. bertolonii*. For more information on common species see the listing on page 91.

Divisions of Cultivars

Daffodil cultivars are grouped according to the flower shape or obvious alliance to a few common species. The listing (p. 32) is organized by this system. The divisions are as follows:

Division 1: Trumpet daffodils – the corona as long as or longer than the tepals (p. 32).

In mild climates, *N. canaliculatus* flowers freely outside.

Division 2: Large-cupped daffodils – the corona more than one third but less than the length of the tepals (p. 40).

Division 3: Small-cupped daffodils – corona less than one third the length of tepals (p. 54).

Division 4: Double daffodils – doubling of the perianth and/or corona (p. 60).

Division 5: Triandrus daffodils – plants obviously descended from *N. triandrus* (p. 68).

Division 6: Cyclamineus daffodils – plants obviously descended from *N. cyclamineus* (p. 70).

Division 7: Jonquilla daffodils – many flowers per stem with fine fragrance (p. 74).

Division 8: Tazetta daffodils – up to 20 fragrant, little flowers per stem; not always hardy (p. 79).

Division 9: Poeticus daffodils – fragrant white flowers; tiny, often red-rimmed, corona (p. 83).

Division 10: Bulbocodium daffodils – flowers clearly descended from *N. bulbocodium* (p. 84).

Division 11: Split corona daffodils – flowers with coronas split at least half their length (p. 85).

Division 12: Other daffodils – those that do not belong in the other sections (p. 90).

Division 13: Individual daffodil species and their hybrids (p. 91).

Daffodil Breeders

This chapter has mentioned several famous daffodil breeders. Here are some biographical notes, in approximate chronological order.

Engleheart, Revd George Herbert
(1851–1936) Hampshire, UK
He began to breed daffodils in 1882. George Engleheart's name is famous among daffodil fanciers and lovers of old plants, and he really set the progress of breeding in motion. His flowers are not comparable to modern daffodils, but they are still collected by enthusiasts, and he dabbled in many divisions. He raised 'Beacon' (3W-R) and the famous 'Mitylene' (2W-Y), which was used as a parent for decades. He bred 'White

Lady' (3W-Y), and one of his most lasting achievements was 'Beersheba' (1W-W).

Backhouse, Mrs R O
(1857–1921) Herefordshire, UK

She started raising daffodils in 1888. Mrs Backhouse and her husband raised many fine daffodils, but few are important today except the double 'Texas' (4Y-O). However, the name of Backhouse is best known for the daffodil that bears her name, a flower that launched many more pinks. It is not of great form compared to today's flowers but still deserves a place in the garden.

Williams, Percival Dacres
(1865–1935) Cornwall, UK

Williams began raising daffodils in 1895. Cornwall, as well as Ireland, has long been a hotbed of daffodil breeding, and is still an important area for breeding and production today. Although Williams's achievements are rarely mentioned, his daffodils form some of the most important commercial cultivars. Where would bulk sales be today without 'Cragford' (8W-O), 'Peeping Tom' (6Y-Y), 'Tresamble' (5W-W) or 'Carlton' (2Y-Y)?

Brodie, Ian, the 24th Brodie of Brodie
(1868–1943) Grampian, UK

He started raising daffodils in 1898. Brodie was a dedicated breeder and was accomplished in the production of lemon and pink shades. 'Seraglio' (3Y-YOO) was one of his greatest achievements, and fathered 'Green Island' in the hands of the Richardsons.

Wilson, Guy Livingstone
(1885–1962) N. Ireland, UK

Wilson began breeding daffodils in 1906. One of the most important hybridisers of the 20th century, Guy Wilson began creating new plants in his youth and by 1930 he had started to name and introduce them. One of his great, early achievements was 'Chinese White', a big flower of good form and a cool, greyish-white colour. It was widely used as a parent, and with the beautiful 'Green Island' (2W-GWY) it led to many better things such as 'Pontresina' (2W-Y), bred by J L Richardson. Wilson also produced the fabulous 'Empress of Ireland' (1W-W) which can draw crowds today, 50 years after its

introduction. Wilson also started the race of lemon reverse bicolours, and 'Spellbinder' (1 Y-WWY) is his creation.

Richardson, Lionel J
(1890–1961) Waterford, Ireland

He started raising daffodils in 1911. Lionel Richardson began hybridizing at an early age and his impact on the world of daffodils was continued by his wife (Helen K Richardson) after his death. A list of their achievements includes some of the most famous and important daffodils of the 20th century. Perhaps their greatest achievement was to create 'Falaise' (4W-O), a rather poor plant that was raised from a seed on the usually sterile 'Mary Copeland'. 'Falaise' was not fully double, but it was fertile, and it led to marvellous plants such as 'Acropolis' (4W-O), 'Double Event' (4W-Y), 'Gay Time' (4W-R) and 'Unique' (4W-Y). Their other speciality was orange cups, but they will also be remembered for 'Kingscourt' (1Y-Y), 'Salome' (2W-PPY) and 'Romance' (2W-P).

Gerritsen, Jaap (Jack)
(1909–1992) Voorschooten, Netherlands

He began raising daffodils in 1920. Introducing his daffodils under the name of his company, J Gerritsen & Son, he was the source of some fine, small daffodils including 'Topolino' (1W-Y) and 'Baby Moon' (7Y-Y). But his greatest contribution to the development of daffodils must be the introduction of split coronas (Division 11).

Gray, Alec
(1895–1986) Cornwall, UK

Gray started raising daffodils in 1927. Alec Gray concentrated his attention on miniature daffodils and had huge success. Though most of his plants are maintained by specialists and are not commercially grown, a few are, and 'Tête-a-Tête' may be the most widely grown of all daffodils. He and his wife were also responsible for superb plants such as 'Segovia' (3W-Y) and the similar 'Xit' (3W-W), as well as the successful 'Minnow'. Our gardens would be poorer without his pioneering work.

Blanchard, Douglas
(1887–1968) and **John** (1930–) Dorset, UK

'Payday', a large, Division 1 daffodil with 'ace of spades' tepals.

'Honeybird', 'Daydream' and 'Payday'. He did not concentrate on just one division, and his work includes the lovely pink-and-white Division 7 'Cotinga', and the superb pair 'Itzim' and 'Jetfire'. He formed Grant Mitsch Novelty Daffodils and his fine, world-famous work is being continued by Elise and Richard Haven, his daughter and son-in-law.

Dunlop, William J

(died 1990) N. Ireland, UK

Dunlop started raising daffodils in 1937. He will be remembered for introducing fine flowers such as 'Craigywarren' (2Y-R). He also raised many fine red and white daffodils such as 'Kildrum' (3W-R), but he will be best remembered for his superb 'Newcastle' (1 W-Y), which has been a favourite since 1957.

Jefferson-Brown, Michael

(1930–2003) Essex, UK

He began raising daffodils in 1943. Michael Jefferson-Brown was one of the greatest promoters of daffodils and of other bulbous plants. He raised many fine varieties and introduced the work of other breeders through his company. Among his achievements are 'Hero' (1Y-O), 'Lemon Cloud' (1Y-Y), 'Bandleader' (2Y-O) and 'Soldier Brave' (2Y-R).

Lea, John

(1911–1984) Worcestershire, UK

He started to raise daffodils in 1948. John Lea began his long list of introductions with white daffodils, and then yellow and orange flowers such as 'Achduart' (3Y-R), but his most memorable commercial daffodil was the double 'Delnashaugh' (4W-P).

Board, Frederick

(died 1966) Derbyshire, UK

Board began raising daffodils in 1948. Among the fine daffodils bred by Frederick Board are the yellow trumpets 'Exemplar' (1Y-Y) and 'Golden Vale' (1Y-Y), while 'Broomhill' (2W-W) is prolific and a super flower for the garden or for showing.

Evans, Murray W

(1912–1988) Oregon, USA

He started raising daffodils in 1953. Murray and Estella Evans introduced in excess of 200

Blanchard Sr began to raise daffodils in 1927, and his son in 1954. This father-and-son team introduced fine miniature and standard daffodils. Among the fine Douglas Blanchard daffodils are 'Arish Mell' (5W-W), 'Icicle' (5W-W) and 'Tiffany' (10Y-Y). John Blanchard has given us 'Bryanston' (2Y-Y), which received the Royal Horticultural Society's Award of Garden Merit (AGM) in 1998, 'Hambledon' (2YYW-Y), and 'Badbury Rings' (3Y-YYR) AGM (also 1998).

Fowlds, Matthew

(1880–1972) Oregon, USA

Among the many fine miniatures raised by this American breeder are 'Chit Chat' (7Y-Y), the triandrus 'Little Lass' (5W-W) and 'Tiny Tot'(1Y-Y), introduced after his death.

Mitsch, Grant E

(1907–1989) Oregon, USA

Grant Mitsch, who started his gardening growing gladioli, began raising daffodils in 1934. His name is associated with an enormous number of great daffodils, especially those with subtle colouring and his reverse bicolours such as cultivars before the mid-1970s, when their work was continued by Richard and Elise Haven (see Mitsch, Grant above) and others. Among their achievements were good pinks such as 'Artful' (2W-P), and the fine doubles 'Ensemble' (4Y-Y) and 'Peach Prince' (4W-O).

Reade, Kate

(1923–) N. Ireland, UK

Kate Reade began to breed daffodils in 1957 and founded Carncairn Daffodils. She produced some astoundingly good flowers. 'Foundling' (6W-P), with its 'cyclamineus' form and pink corona made a real impact when introduced, and 'Gin and Lime' is still sought after, receiving an AGM in 1998.

Roesé, Bill

(1927–2000) California, USA

Roesé began to raise daffodils in 1958. Though his daffodils are not well known in the UK, Bill Roesé, who held the post of President of the American Daffodil Society, raised many fine flowers. One of the last to be registered was 'Super Seven' (7Y-Y), a fragrant flower for show.

Duncan, Brian

(1934–) N. Ireland, UK

He started raising daffodils in 1964. Brian Duncan's name is synonymous with quality, and his catalogues of new cultivars are eagerly awaited. He is a gifted hybridizer and has produced a stream of excellent plants such as 'Sportsman' (2Y-R) and 'Bossa Nova' (3O-R), as well as the superb 'Pink Paradise' (4W-P). He ran the companies Rathowen Daffodils (1973–1988) and Brian Duncan Daffodils (1989–).

Scamp, Ron

(1943–) Cornwall, UK

Scamp started raising daffodils in 1969. Part of the renowned daffodil-farming family du Plessis, Ron Scamp has made a name for himself by producing new daffodils that combine show form with great vigour and garden value. He has catholic tastes, and his introductions include fine doubles and split coronas.

Pannill, William G

Virginia, USA

Bill Pannill has made important developments in developing flowers with yellow perianths and pink coronas. His white and pink Division 2 'Chromacolour' has an AGM, and he has registered 187 cultivars. He introduced 'Virginia Walker' in 1992 and considers it his best white Division 1. His 'Indian Maid' and 'Kinglet' are popular jonquils and his 'Toto' is one of the select band of Division 12 flowers.

Abel-Smith, Barbara

(1914–1995) Hertfordshire, UK

Barbara Abel-Smith concentrated on good pinks such as 'Pink Clover' (2W-P), but among her other fine introductions were 'Brackenhurst' (2Y-O) and 'Park Springs' (3W-WWY).

Hamilton, Max

Waikato Region, New Zealand

Max Hamilton started raising daffodils in 1956. With Peter Ramsay, he founded Koanga Daffodils, which has become the home of some great plants. These include 'Baldock' (4 Y-P) and 'Kiwi Magic' (4W-Y).

Millett, Paul

Cornwall, UK

Paul Millett worked at Rosewarne Experimental Horticultural Station in Cornwall until 1989, and is especially interested in old daffodils. With the help of Ron Scamp he has saved many old cultivars for the future by making them available again. His exhibit of ancient flower varieties in Falmouth opened my eyes to what was still available.

Fry, Barbara

(died 1997) Cornwall, UK

Barbara Fry was Senior Recorder at Rosewarne Experimental Horticultural Station in Cornwall, and worked on breeding programmes to produce daffodils as commercial cut flowers in Cornwall. Some of these are still being assessed but some of her achievements are already available to enjoy, including 'Radical' (6Y-Y) and 'Alliance' (6Y-Y).

Throckmorton, Dr Tom D

Iowa, USA

He is best known for developing and introducing the daffodil colour-coding system in 1975, but he was also interested in breeding flowers that changed colour as they matured.

Chapter 3
Species and Cultivars of Daffodil

This list of daffodils is split into the main, official divisions used by gardeners, listed alphabetically within each division. If you are looking for a cultivar and do not know to which division it belongs you should be able to cross-refer in the index. By grouping them in divisions it makes the list more manageable and will also be more use to those looking for cultivars with particular characteristics, such as a split corona or a small cup.

This list cannot hope to be complete, but I have tried to include all common cultivars, a good selection of novelties and some older rarities and important antiques, to try to give an overview of the genus. Only a few individual species are included because most are not common garden plants. Heights are not given because they do not vary enormously between cultivars, and most daffodils can be expected to grow to about 45 cm (18 in) high when in bloom. Only when a plant is exceptionally small or tall is reference made to its height.

After the name is the horticultural classification. The number defines the division but this is followed by two sets of letters, divided by a hyphen. The first letter refers to the perianth and the second to the corona. Where there is more than one letter, it is because that part of the flower has different colours in its various zones. When describing the perianth the letters start at the outer edge, then the middle region, then the centre. The second set describe the corona from the base, the centre and the rim. So 'Ballygarvey' 1WWY-Y is a Division 1 variety, with tepals that are white at the edge and centre but yellow near the base, and a corona that is pure yellow. 'Corbiere' 1Y-YOO has yellow tepals and the corona is yellow at the base but predominantly orange. If the colours are non-concentric – something that is most common in split corona daffodils – the two colours are separated by a slash, such as in 'Sorbet' 11b W-Y/OW, which has white tepals and a corona that is yellow and orange with a white edge.

The abbreviations for colours are as follows:

W = white or whitish
G = green
Y = yellow
P = pink
O = orange
R = red

After this, I have provided an approximate guide to flowering time. Most daffodils flower in early April, which is mid-season, the earliest usually flower in March or even February and the latest are at their best in mid-April onwards. Much depends on the geographic location, the position in the garden and the particular season. A warm spring will shorten the season and you may not notice much difference in most flowering times, while a cool spring will extend the flowering period and early cultivars may be over before the late cultivars have started to open.

After the entry I have given the name of the raiser, and then that of the introducer, or person or company who registered the plant, if different, and the date(s), where known, of its registration, introduction or first recorded flowering. I have also noted if the variety has received the Award of Gardening Merit (AGM) of the Royal Horticultural Society (RHS), and the year.

The official registrar for daffodils in the UK, as well as the International Daffodil Registrar, is: Mrs Sally Kington, Royal Horticultural Society, Vincent Square, London SW1P 2PE UK

DIVISION 1
Trumpet Daffodils

These, the traditional daffodils, are more varied than most gardeners think. They are dominated by golden yellow and white flowers, but the colour range is increasing every year. This is probably the most difficult Division in which to make an impact as a breeder, because most potential parents that could add variation by bringing pink or red to the coronas have short cups, and to be in Division 1 the corona must be as long as, or longer than, the perianth segments (tepals). The overall size of the plant or the flower is not important, however, so this Division includes some miniatures such as 'W P Milner', as well as giants including 'Unsurpassable', but common to all of them is that there is only one flower per stem.

'American Shores' 1Y-P mid

Pink trumpets with yellow perianths are not common, and this is one of the best. Its tepals are lemon yellow with a vague ivory stripe and a flared, bright pink trumpet that is smooth and sun-proof. Good for showing and 9 cm (3.5 in) across. It is similar to 'American Heritage' – it comes from the same stable (1983, 1992) and parents ('Memento' x 'Lorikeet') – but the latter has larger flowers (11 cm/4.5 in) with a narrower, brighter trumpet. (R & E Havens 1992)

'Arctic Gold' 1 Y-Y early

This is vigorous and has wonderful, traditional, golden yellow flowers 9.5 cm (3.75 in) across. It flowers freely and is a good garden plant. (J L Richardson, pre-1951; AGM-RHS 1993)

'Arkle' 1Y-Y

A fine, golden daffodil in deep yellow of great flower size (12.5 cm/5 in) and vigour. The corona is cylindrical with a slightly expanded mouth, and the tepals are broad and have a slight twist. (J L Richardson, Mrs H K Richardson 1968; AGM-RHS 2001)

'Ballygarvey' 1WWY-Y mid (p. 35)

Large flowers (10.5 cm/4 in) with white tepals, shaded yellow at the base. They are slightly wavy and ribbed, but overlap deeply. The contrasting yellow corona is cylindrical and widely expanded at the rim. (W J Dunlop pre-1947)

'Barnum' 1Y-Y mid

This is a fine flower, of similar shape and size to 'Empress of Ireland', with big, broad tepals of 'ace-of-spades' form and a big trumpet with flaring mouth. It is a deep, golden yellow and has good substance. Bred from 'Midas Touch' (1977)

and resembling it, but bigger. (Brian S Duncan, Rathowen Daffodils 1986; AGM-RHS 1998)

'Bawnboy' 1Y-Y

This is a strong, deep yellow trumpet daffodil with bright yellow flowers 10 cm (4 in) across and a slightly darker, ribbed corona. (G L Wilson 1960; AGM-RHS 1993)

'Bell Rock' 1W-Y mid (p. 33)

Mid-sized flowers (9 cm/3.5 in) with broad, white tepals overlapping in the lower half. The broad, dumpy trumpet is beautiful, bright yellow, with a widely expanded, rolled and frilled rim. (R A Scamp 1997)

'Biscayne' 1Y-Y mid

Bred from the great 'Spellbinder', this is a reliable

Division 1 daffodils
Top row:
'Newcastle' 1 W-Y,
'Bravoure' 1W-Y.
Second row:
'Corbiere' 1Y-YOO,
'Lorikeet' 1Y-P.
Bottom row:
'Bell Rock' 1W-Y,
'Gin and Lime' 1W-WWY.

golden yellow daffodil, with blooms 12.5 cm (5 in) across. The tepals are greenish yellow, white at the base and apex and slightly twisted. The ribbed corona is flared and frilled at the mouth and vivid greenish yellow, creamy white inside except at the mouth. The blooms have good poise and it is a wonderful garden plant.(P de Jager & Sons 1966; AGM-RHS 1993)

'Brabazon' 1 Y-Y early
This is a bright, golden-yellow daffodil with flowers 9.5 cm (3.75 in) across with a slightly expanded mouth to a corona that is a touch deeper in colour than the slightly reflexing perianth. It has strong stems and is good for the garden. (G H Johnstone pre-1950; AGM-RHS 1993)

'Bram Warnaar' 1Y-Y early
This child of 'Arctic Gold' and 'Golden Harvest' is vigorous with golden flowers and a bold corona that lasts well in the garden. (W J M Blom 1973, W Blom & Son 1984; AGM-RHS 1993)

'Bravoure' 1W-Y mid (p. 33)
This extraordinary, huge flower is 12 cm (4.75 in) across and has bright white tepals that are yellow at the base. They are broad and overlap, though the inner three are narrower than the outer. The corona is yellow, smooth and barely expanded at the rim, with few notches, though it is sometimes edged with white. Great for use in the garden and for local shows. (J W A van der Wereld 1974; AGM-RHS 1993)

'By Jove' 1Y-Y mid
A good, all-round flower for the garden and showing. Deep yellow with wide tepals and slender trumpet. (M J Jefferson-Brown 1968)

'Chinese Coral' 1W-P mid
This is a short plant with flowers 8.5 cm (3.3 in) across. The perianth is greenish white and the beautiful corona is orange-pink and heavily ruffled around the mouth. It hangs its head a little but it is a real charmer. (J Gerritsen & Son, Van Eeden Goohof 1995)

'Chivalry' 1W-W mid
Though showing its age, this fine white is still popular and has the superb 'Broughshane' as a parent. (J L Richardson, F E Board 1955)

'Corbiere' 1Y-YOO mid (p. 33)
This cheery flower has broad, smooth, rounded tepals of bright gold. They reflex slightly and have a white mucro. The corona is funnel-shaped and narrow, and the rim is slightly dentate, deep yellow at first but becoming flushed with orange. The 10 cm (4 in) flowers on tall stems have a touch of the 'cyclamineus' about them. (J S B Lea, Clive Postles Daffodils 1988).

'Cristobal' 1 W-Y mid
A pretty flower with broad, white tepals and a yellow trumpet that is funnel-shaped and attractively rolled at the rim. Good poise and fine form, and rather like 'Newcastle'. (J L Richardson, Mrs H K Richardson, 1968)

'Crock of Gold' 1 Y-Y mid
A large (11.5 cm/4.5 in) flower of bright yellow with a slightly deeper trumpet that is notched and flared. (G L Wilson pre-1948)

'Dispatch Box' 1Y-Y early–mid
This outstanding yellow daffodil has large flowers of deep gold, and a cylindrical corona with an expanded mouth. It is vigorous and free-flowering, ideal for the garden because it holds its flower well clear of the foliage. (Brian S Duncan, Rathowen Daffodils 1988; AGM-RHS 1999)

'Donore' 1Y-Y late (p. 35)
This rich gold trumpet daffodil flowers later than most and has rather creased tepals and a broad corona that is deeply scalloped at the mouth. (G L Wilson 1956)

'Drumlin' 1W-Y mid
This is a large (11 cm/4.25 in) flower with a broad perianth that opens cream and ages to white, making a strong contrast to a deep yellow corona that is beautifully flared and rolled at the mouth. The flowers are freely produced and last well, making it a fine garden plant. (Ballydorn Bulb Farm 1981, 1993; AGM-RHS 2002)

'Dutch Master' 1Y-Y early
Any garden centre will offer this traditional daffodil with large (11 cm/4.25 in), bright yellow flowers on short stems. Among such illustrious and modern kin it is easy to dismiss this flower because of its slightly creased tepals. It is not of

show standard but it is fine for the garden with its beautifully expanded and rolled corona. It is vigorous and ideal for naturalizing in grass, being inexpensive and increasing well. (pre-1938; AGM-RHS 1995)

'Empress of Ireland' 1W-W mid

This stately and imposing flower has smooth, overlapping tepals forming a perianth up to 12 cm (4.75 in) across and a cylindrical trumpet, of slightly deeper tone, with a rolled frilly mouth. Superb for the garden with a long history of show wins. One of the finest of all white trumpets. (G L Wilson pre-1952; AGM-RHS 1993)

'Entrancement' 1Y-W early

A greenish yellow flower with broad, overlapping tepals that are sometimes wavy. The trumpet opens the same colour but ages to almost white, with a notched frilled mouth. (G E Mitsch 1958)

'Envoy' 1W-W mid (p. 59)

This large flower is pure white with a broad perianth and a beautiful corona that is funnel-shaped and flared and rather split at the mouth. (G L Wilson – unregistered)

'Exception' 1Y-Y early

This hybrid of the popular 'Dutch Master' does not have perfect form, the tepals being rather twisted, but the golden yellow blooms are large (10 cm/4 in) and freely produced. It has a glorious funnel-shaped corona, deeply notched around the flaring mouth, and it flowers early in the garden. (D van Buggenum 1971; AGM-RHS 2001)

'Exemplar' 1Y-Y mid

A classic, golden flower with broad tepals that overlap in the lower half. The corona is narrow with a widely expanded mouth to create an attractive bloom. Suitable for the garden or exhibition, though the inner tepals are narrower than the outer, and more pointed. May be better for showing than 'Saint Keverne', but is not super smooth. (F E Board 1965)

'Fort Knox' 1Y-Y mid

A fine flower with ace-of-spades tepals that overlap well. The trumpet is slightly deeper yellow than the perianth. Fine for showing, and floriferous. (M J Jefferson-Brown 1975)

'Gin and Lime' 1W-WWY early–mid (p. 33)

A large (11.5 cm/4.5 in) flower with sulphur-yellow tepals that are rather narrow and may be creased or wavy. The corona is cylindrical with a broad mouth and notched rim. It opens yellow but fades to white with a ring of yellow around the rim. It may not be of perfect form but it is a charming, early flower that deserves special place in the garden. (Carncairn Daffodils 1973; AGM-RHS 1998)

'Glenfarclas' 1Y-O mid

Orange trumpets are not common (see 'Corbiere' and 'Uncle Duncan') but this is one of the best. The flowers are 10 cm (4 in) wide with good golden tepals that inroll slightly and a smooth, lightly frilled corona of deep, bright orange. As might be expected of a colour combination that is new to the division, the corona length is not always long enough to fulfil the dimensions required of Division 1. (J S B Lea 1976; AGM-RHS 1998)

Yellow and white daffodils

Top row:
'Golden Aura' 2Y-Y,
'Donore' 1Y-Y.
Second row:
'Camelot' 2Y-Y,
'Ballygarvey' 1WWY-Y.
Bottom row:
'Lapwing' 5W-Y,
'High Note' 7Y-W.

'Golden Rapture' 1Y-Y mid

This has many fine attributes as a garden plant, not least the massive size of the flowers, 12.5 cm (5 in) across, and its fragrance. The perianth is bright yellow and the corona is slightly deeper in colour with a flared, frilly mouth. (J L Richardson pre-1952; AGM-RHS 1993)

'Golden Riot' 1Y-Y mid–late

This is a useful garden plant because it blooms late and the bright yellow flowers have neat perianths and coronas that are slightly toothed. (G L Wilson pre-1948)

'Golden Vale' 1Y-Y mid

This hybrid of 'Golden Rapture' has big blooms, 12 cm (4.75 in) across, with smooth, vivid yellow tepals and a wonderfully flaring corona that is narrow at the base and frilled at the edge. (F E Board, W A Norton 1976; AGM-RHS 1995)

'Goldfinger' 1Y-Y mid

This seedling of 'Golden Jewel' is one of the finest of its class and is a proven show-winner as well as a good, if at present expensive, garden plant that flowers freely and has long-lasting flowers. Their staying power is down to the fine substance; they are also of great form with smooth, flat tepals forming a double-triangle perianth. The cylindrical corona is slightly expanded at the mouth and serrated, and the flower has good poise. (Brian S Duncan, Rathowen Daffodils 1983; AGM-RHS 2001)

'Gold Medal' 1 Y-Y mid

A good, rather old, yellow daffodil, ideal for garden display because the large flowers are held on short (30 cm/12 in) stems. (G Lubbe & Son, pre-1938)

'Grasmere' 1Y-Y very early

This fine, tall, golden daffodil has a large flower (10 cm/4 in across) with a neatly frilled, funnel-shaped corona. (J S B Lea 1984, Clive Postles Daffodils 1994; AGM-RHS 1998)

'Honeybird' 1Y-W mid

This has the same parentage as 'Entrancement' but was released later, probably because its merits took time to show. It is similar in all respects, with flowers of lemon yellow and a trumpet that ages to white. But it is generally considered of better substance and is a better grower than its sister, and is among the most popular of all reverse bicolours. Recommended despite its lack of AGM. (G E Mitsch 1950, 1965)

'Hero' 1Y-O mid

This is a beautiful flower with a neat golden perianth of overlapping tepals and an orange trumpet that is lobed and elegantly flared. (M J Jefferson-Brown 1984)

'King Alfred' 1 Y-Y mid

This ancient daffodil is probably the most famous of all, though most bulbs sold under the name – because people recognize and want it – are not true. It attracted huge prices at first (£10 a bulb at the turn of the 20th century, equivalent in purchasing power to more than £620 today) because it was such a breakthrough in the development of big, golden daffodils, but it was not always a good grower, splitting into small bulbs that did not flower. The flowers are large (10 cm/4 in) and the rather twisted, bright yellow tepals overlap at the base. The corona is deeper yellow, and the flared mouth is deeply notched. It is really now only of historical importance because it is not a strong grower, true examples are rarely available, and there really are better yellow trumpets on the market now, such as 'Arctic Gold', 'Goldfinger' and 'King's Ransom'. It sported to produce the double 'Golden Ducat'. (J Kendall, pre-1899)

'Kingscourt' 1Y-Y mid

Not all the best yellow garden daffodils are modern, as this fine flower with excellent form and substance shows. The blooms are 11 cm (4.25 in) across and the tepals are broad and overlap, though are slightly twisted. The corona is ribbed and funnel-shaped with a deeply notched mouth. (J L Richardson pre-1938; AGM-RHS 1993)

'King's Grove' 1Y-O mid

This beautiful show-winning, yellow and orange daffodil is tall, with good poise and a flawless perianth. The corona is cylindrical and attractively lobed at the mouth, and opens deep yellow, developing its orange colour as the bloom matures. (Brian S Duncan, Rathowen Daffodils 1987; AGM-RHS 2001)

'King's Ransom' 1 Y-Y mid
This fine flower, produced by crossing 'Kingscourt' and 'Goldcourt' (pre-1937), has large, golden flowers with broad, slightly wavy tepals and a smooth corona, notched and flared at the mouth. (J L Richardson pre-1950)

'Lemon Cloud' 1Y-Y early–mid
Vigour makes this huge (15 cm/6 in), pale-yellow flower so special. The blooms have long, narrow trumpets and rather pointed and twisted tepals, and inherit their colouring from 'Spellbinder' and 'Moonstruck'. (M J Jefferson-Brown 1969)

'Lemon Glow' 1Y-Y early (p. 76)
This is almost a reverse bicolour, with primrose yellow tepals and a flared corona that gets paler as it ages but retains a darker rim. It is not of great form but is robust, early and good for the garden. (G Lubbe & Son 1958)

'Little Beauty' 1W-Y mid
This dwarf plant has pretty flowers with white tepals that open with a green tinge, and a yellow corona that shades to white at the base, is nicely flared, and almost rolled at the rim. It is superior to 'Bambi'. (J Gerritsen & Son pre-1953; AGM-RHS 2001)

'Little Gem' 1Y-Y early
Another dwarf, this time with bright yellow flowers 4 cm (1.5 in) wide, it is distinguished as a garden plant by its great vigour. The blooms have rather wavy tepals and the corona is slightly darker around the flared, notched mouth. (J Gerritsen & Son 1938; AGM-RHS 1997)

'Lorikeet' 1Y-P mid (p. 33)
An attractive flower (9.5 cm/3.75 in) with broad, smooth, pale yellow tepals. The flaring corona has a lobed rim in a soft, apricot pink colour. (G E Mitsch 1979)

'Millgreen' 1Y-Y early
Like many Rosewarne daffodils, this is a fine garden plant. The blooms are acid yellow with a distinct green tinge, especially on opening. (Rosewarne E H S 1964, Gee Tee Bulb Co. 1985)

'Mount Hood' 1W-W mid
This is the most popular white trumpet for the garden. The flowers are 10 cm (4 in) across and have beautifully rolled and notched trumpets. The perianth is rather narrow and creased and this is not a show flower, but it is short and superb for the garden. (P van Deursen pre-1938; AGM-RHS 1995)

'Mulatto' 1Y-WWY early
An old, vigorous and usually inexpensive cultivar with sulphur yellow perianths and slightly twisted tepals, the inner three being narrower than the outer. The trumpet is yellow and ages to white so that only the frilled, lobed, flaring mouth retains its colour. (C G van Tubergen pre-1931)

'Newcastle' 1 W-Y mid (p. 33)
A bold, large flower (12 cm/4.75 in) with white tepals, greenish yellow at the base, that overlap in the lower half. The gold corona is cylindrical with a wide mouth and wavy rim. (W J Dunlop 1957)

'Nosie Posie' 6Y-Y mid
This golden flower has a lot of *N. cyclamineus* in it. The corona is long and is flared at the mouth, and bulbs produce a second crop of flowers as the first fade, making it a possibility for landscape use.

'Panache' 1W-W mid
This super white flower has narrow trumpets that widen to a wide mouth set against an 11.5-cm (4.5-in) wide perianth that has spreading, well-formed tepals. (G L Wilson, F E Board 1962)

'Pay Day' 1YYW-W late (p. 30)
This is a large (10.5 cm/4 in) flower with lemon yellow tepals with a band of white at the base of the perianth, and a funnel-shaped corona. This opens lemon yellow and fades to white with the mouth frilled and flared. A nice flower and a vigorous plant. (Elise Havens, G E Mitsch 1976)

'Pink Dew' 1 W-P early–mid (p. 38)
This may not be the correct name for a plant I have grown but it is sold as such and is a large flower with white tepals and pale pink corona. The tepals are rather creased and twisted and of thin texture. It is fine for the garden but unexceptional. (Unregistered)

'Potential' 1W-P mid
A fine flower, 10 cm (4 in) across with a smooth,

'Rijnveld's Early Sensation' 1 Y-Y very early
The large flowers (9 cm/3.5 in) have yellow petals and a deeper, large corona that is funnel-shaped with a wavy, notched rim. As the name suggests, it is very early but also lasts well and is good for the garden. (F H Chapman,1943, F Rijnveld & Sons, 1956; AGM-RHS 1993)

'Silent Valley' 1W-GWW mid
Bred from 'Empress of Ireland', this is a great flower for garden and show, with cool colouring. The double-triangle perianth is smooth and of heavy texture, the inner tepals curling slightly, and the cylindrical corona is smooth with a slightly wavy edge. (T Bloomer 1964; AGM-RHS 1999)

'Spellbinder' 1 Y-WWY mid (p. 14)
This great favourite from Guy Wilson was the first reverse bicolour I grew and is a beautiful flower that has been used to create other fine flowers such as 'Gin and Lime'. The large flowers (11 cm/4.25 in across) has brilliant, greeny yellow, twisted tepals with obvious mucros. The coronas open yellow but quickly fade to white with a yellow zone around the frilled, widely expanded rim. Widely available and recommended for the garden. (G L Wilson, pre-1944) (*AGM-RHS 1993*)

'Standard Value' 1Y-Y mid (p. 41)
Standard is the word for this unremarkable but pleasant enough, yellow daffodil with no extraordinary features. Good for the garden because it is not too big, but it takes up room that would be better filled with something else – I gave mine away. (P Geerlings pre-1949)

'Tedstone' 1W-W mid
A good garden plant, the bulbs increase well and produce plenty of large, white flowers with good proportions. (M J Jefferson-Brown 1985)

'Topolino' 1W-Y early (p. 38)
This charming miniature daffodil has all the grace of species trumpet daffodils. It has nodding flowers with creamy white, narrow tepals and a yellow, frilled corona. Larger than 'Little Beauty' and commonly available. The name means 'little mouse' in Italian. (J Gerritsen & Son 1965; AGM-RHS 2001)

Daffodils in mid-March
Photographed with hellebores and celendines.
Top row:
'L'Innocence' 8 W-Y,
'Bridal Crown' 4 W-Y.
Second row:
'Martinette' 7Y-O,
'Jetfire' 6Y-O,
'Tete-à-Tete' 12Y-Y.
Third row:
'Variant' 2Y-O,
'Pink Dew' 1W-P unreg,
'Topolino' 1W-Y.
Bottom row:
'Obdam' 4W-W,
'Itzim' 6 Y-R young flower,
'Replete' 4W-P.

flat perianth of broad, white tepals and a cylindrical, bright pink, sun-proof corona. (R & E Havens 1982, 1993)

'Princeps' 1W-Y early (p. 39)
This old daffodil resembles *N. pseudonarcissus* but is about twice the size. The flowers are 9.5 cm (3.75 in) across with narrow, pale yellow tepals that are twisted and only overlap at the base. The corona is ribbed and yellow. It has a rather flimsy substance, especially in the perianth, but it is a fine plant for naturalizing and often self-seeds, but it does not breed true, as would be expected of a cultivar. (Italian? pre-1830)

'Prophet' 1 Y-YYP early
This early flower has delicate and ethereal colouring of lemon yellow in the tepals, and a narrow corona, but the rim of the trumpet becomes shaded with pink for a while. (H R Barr, M J Jefferson-Brown 1975)

'Trousseau' 1W-Y early

Not of the best form because the tepals are creased and the inner three are narrower than the outer, but it is still a pretty flower, with milky white perianth and a pale yellow, nicely flared trumpet. Tall and early. (P D Williams pre-1934)

'Tyrone Gold' 1Y-Y early–mid

This has everything you could want from a golden daffodil, whether for a special place in the garden or for showing. The flowers have perfect perianths and smooth, cylindrical coronas with a flared mouth, all in rich gold. The flowers face upwards, with perfect poise. It is also vigorous and healthy. (Brian S Duncan, Rathowen Daffodils 1986; AGM-RHS 1998)

'Ulster Prince' 1Y-Y early

This large (10 cm/4 in) flower has brilliant, greenish yellow, pointed tepals and a bright yellow, frilly, expanded corona. (G L Wilson pre-1950; AGM-RHS 1993)

'Uncle Duncan' 1Y-O early (p. 46)

One of the best of its colouring, this has a fine, smooth, golden yellow perianth and a perfect corona, frilled and rolled at the rim, in rich orange and with a bright green eye. It is sun-proof and has good stems, making it good both for showing and for the garden. (A J R Pearson 1991)

'Unsurpassable' 1Y-Y very early

It may have been surpassed in the 80 years since its introduction but this is still a good garden plant with large (11 cm/4.25 in) lemon yellow flowers with big coronas on tall stems. (G Lubbe & Son pre-1923)

'Valley Forge' 1YYW-Y

This is a great garden daffodil with bright colouring. Raised from 'Burnished Gold' and 'Daydream', it has a rounded perianth in bright yellow that is white around the base. Its broad, ribbed corona is lemon yellow, fading almost to white. A really striking flower. (W G Pannill 1985)

'Vigil' 1W-W mid

This is a giant (12.5 cm/5 in) flower, of good substance, with angular, rather twisted tepals and a slightly frilled and flanged trumpet, all in pure white. (G L Wilson pre-1947; AGM-RHS 1993)

'Viking' 1Y-Y mid

This resembles 'Kingscourt' but is larger, with bright yellow flowers 11.5 cm (4.5 in) across. (J L Richardson 1956; AGM-RHS 1995)

'Windjammer' 1Y-Y mid

This has large, sulphur yellow flowers with broad tepals. (W J Dunlop, M J Jefferson-Brown 1964)

'W P Milner' 1W-W early (p. 39)

This is a pretty little plant with dainty, 6 cm (2.3 in) flowers with pale, sulphur tepals and a slightly deeper, cylindrical corona that usually fades as it matures. It is more than a century old but its nodding stance and delicate colouring, reminiscent of *N. moschatus*, make it highly prized. (W Backhouse pre-1869)

Mixed old daffodils

Top row:
'Ruston Pasha' 2Y-O,
'Sir Watkin' 2Y-Y.
Second row:
'Elvira' 8 W-YYO,
'W P Milner' 1W-W
(two blooms).
Bottom row:
'Princeps' 1W-Y,
N. obvallaris.
Bottom left:
N. moschatus.

DIVISION 2
Large-cupped Daffodils

To fit into Division 2, a daffodil's corona must be more than one third of the length of the tepals but must not exceed their length: those that do are part of Division 1. Perhaps because it is the middle group of the three defined by coronal length, this is also one of the largest, with a mass of cultivars that have a variety of coronal colours and shapes. A failed flower, bred for Division 1 or Division 3, if it has other merits, can be caught in this group, provided it is consistent. There is only one flower per stem.

This is a good division for garden display because the corona is long enough to be showy and, if the flowers are bicoloured, there is enough substance in the corona to ensure that a good contrast is made, even if the flowers hang their heads a little. The greatest breakthrough in this division was 'Fortune' in 1923, a giant leap in the race to create big, bold, sun-proof yellow and orange flowers. It could be argued that these have now been improved as far as is possible, and attention is now focused on other colours, notably pinks with white or yellow perianths.

'Abalone' 2W-YYP mid (p. 59)
This delicately coloured flower is large (12.5 cm/5 in) with white tepals and a broad corona that opens pale yellow and develops pinkish shades around the rim. (G E Mitsch 1962)

'Aberfoyle' 2Y-YOO early
This has a bright yellow perianth with tepals forming a double triangle,. and has a deep orange-red corona that is yellow at the base. Growing strongly and flowering profusely, it is ideal for the garden. (J S B Lea 1983, Clive Postles Daffodils 1994; AGM-RHS 2001)

'Accent' 2W-P mid
This is a large (10 cm/4 in) sturdy flower with a white, starry perianth and a deep, salmon pink, filled corona. The foliage is grey. (G E Mitsch 1960; AGM-RHS 1995)

'Ambergate' 2O-O mid (p. 40)
This is the best known of the all-red cultivars, and it is difficult to believe that a colour that is so unfamiliar to the general public is so old. The tepals are soft orange and the broad, flat corona is brighter orange. It burns and fades in bright sun, so plant in light shade and use for cutting. (D B Milne pre-1950)

'Amberglow' 2Y-Y mid
A fine flower with bright lemon yellow tepals giving a starry background to the frilled crown that opens pale yellow and ages with a hint of buff. (G E Mitsch 1969)

'Arcady' 2 W-YWP mid (p. 59)
Considered an improved version of 'Rainbow', with broad tepals of crisp white and a bowl-shaped, frilly corona edged with dark pink. (M J Jefferson-Brown 1985)

'Armada' 2Y-O early
A good, strong, garden daffodil, the flowers are

Mixed daffodils
Top row:
'Buffawn' 7Y-Y,
'Ambergate' 2O-O.
Second row:
'Kissproof' 2Y-O,
'Bandleader' 2Y-O,
'Soldier Brave' 2Y-O.
Bottom row:
'Gouache' 2W-O – unreg,
'Amor' 3W-YYO.

11 cm (4.25 in) across with bright yellow tepals and a bright orange corona that is funnel-shaped, wavy and cut at the mouth. (G L Wilson pre-1938; AGM-RHS 1993)

'Ashmore' 2W-GWW mid
This beautiful, cool flower has a smooth, white perianth 9.5 cm (3.75 in) and a neat, toothed cup with a green heart. (J W Blanchard 1974)

'Avalon' 2Y-W mid
This is a beautiful flower with slightly reflexed tepals forming a broad, smooth perianth. The bloom is lemon yellow becoming white at the base of the tepals, and the corona fades to white with age. It is larger than 'Daydream' and smoother than 'Camelot', its two parents, but the flowers hang their heads a bit – at least they did when I saw them on an admittedly miserable day in the Netherlands. The stems are short, so may be good for exposed gardens. (Mrs H K Richardson 1977)

'Bandleader' 2Y-O mid (p. 40)
This is a smart flower with a gold perianth and smooth, deep orange, almost scarlet, cup-shaped corona. (M J Jefferson-Brown 1967)

'Barleythorpe' 1W-Y mid
This bright yellow and white daffodil sometimes has coronas that are too long for this division, but it is good for the garden. (F E Board, pre-1966)

'Bantam' 2Y-O late
A bright, perky flower 8.5 cm (3.3 in) across. The rounded tepals are a bright, acid yellow, and the neat, orange, six-lobed, smooth corona is often rimmed with red, adding to its crispness. (Barr & Sons pre-1950; AGM-RHS 1993)

'Bedruthan' 2W-YYR late (p. 53)
This large (10 cm/4 in) flower is suitable for showing, with broad, pure white tepals and a funnel-shaped corona that opens pale yellow and fades as the flowers mature, showing off the red rim to perfection. (R A Scamp 1996)

'Ben Hee' 2 W-GWW mid
This supremely beautiful flower is pure white with a green eye at the base of the corona. The tepals form a double triangle, with the inner three slightly narrower than the outer, and the

cylindrical corona is only slightly expanded and frilled at the mouth. A cool and tailored flower. (JSB Lea 1964; AGM-RHS 2001)

'Berlin' 2 Y-YYO mid (p. 13)
This recent cultivar has already made its mark as a popular and readily available daffodil because of its extraordinary corona. This is pale orange, shading almost to red around the highly frilled edge. It is set off against the yellow perianth composed of broad tepals. The 8.5-cm (3.3-in) perianth is rarely flat and is not of show form, but it is a beautiful flower. (W F Leenen 1980)

'Binkie' 2Y-W mid (p. 41, 70, 88)
This is a super-cool flower with rather ribbed tepals and corona – so not of perfect form by any means, but loved by gardeners for its colouring. The tepals are pale, greenish yellow and white at the base, and the corona is white with a lemon-

Mixed daffodils
Top row:
'Saint Keverne' 2Y-Y,
'Redhill' 2W-R,
'Pink Smiles' 2W-P.
Second row:
'Standard Value' 1Y-Y,
'Delibes' 2Y-YYO,
'Binkie' 2Y-W.
Third row:
'La Argentina' 2W-O/WY,
'Ring of Fire' 2W-WWR,
'Geranium' 8W-O.
Bottom row:
'Quail' 7Y-Y,
N. bulbocodium
'Golden Bells' 10Y-Y.

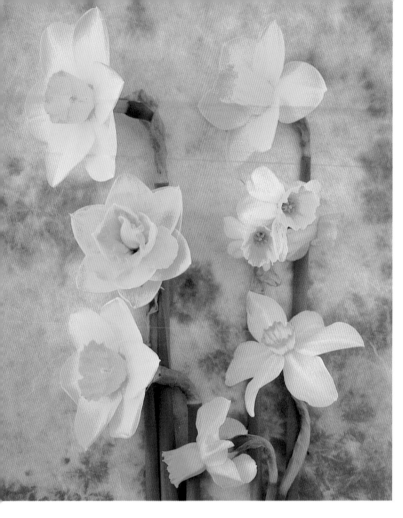

Mixed daffodils

Top row:
'Cape Cornwall' 2Y-R,
'Trebah' 2Y-Y.
Second row:
'Madam Speaker' 4Y-O,
'Cornish Chuckles' 12Y-Y.
Third row:
'Millennium Sunset' 2Y-O,
'Conspicuus' (syn 'Barri
Conspiucuus') 3Y-YYO.
Bottom:
'Coombe Creek' 6W-O.

lime rim. It is a good garden daffodil, strong enough for naturalizing and very popular, though I recently bought stocks that were badly virused. It is the sort of unusual colour that ends up being described as 'new', which it most certainly is not. (G L Wilson, W Wolfhagen pre-1938)

'Border Beauty' 2Y-R mid

This well-named, showy cultivar is vigorous, and the deep, orange-red corona is sun-proof. The flowers are large (11 cm/4.25 in), and the triangular, yellow tepals form a smooth perianth. (Brian S Duncan 1992; AGM-RHS 2001)

'Boulder Bay' 2Y-YYO mid

It is the wavy-mouthed, rolled corona with its orange rim that makes this modern daffodil stand out from the rest. This is set against a smooth, 9.5-cm/3.3-in), deep yellow perianth. (Brian S Duncan 1996; AGM-RHS 2001)

'Brackenhurst' 2Y-O mid

This is a fine, sun-proof garden flower with deep

yellow-coloured tepals forming a rather starry outline and a deep orange cup. Far better than older, reddish cups. Bred from 'Ceylon'. (Mrs J Abel-Smith 1977)

'Broomhill' 2W-W mid

Ideal for show and the garden, this sparkling white flower is 10 cm (4 in) wide with a greenish tinge. The corona is ribbed and frilled. (F E Board 1965; AGM-RHS 1995)

'Bryanston' 2Y-Y early

This is a deep yellow of good form, with upward-facing flowers, 10 cm (4 in) across and a straight-mouthed, funnel-shaped corona. (J W Blanchard 1977; AGM-RHS 1998)

'Camelot' 2Y-Y mid (p. 35)

This is a large, rounded, deep yellow flower of good form, but the inner three tepals are narrower than the outer, and not always flat. The slightly ribbed corona has a flared, frilled mouth. Good for the garden and much used in breeding. (J L Richardson, Mrs H K Richardson 1962; AGM-RHS 1995)

'Cape Cornwall' 2Y-R late (p. 42)

Good for showing, this has fine form with triangular tepals, the inner three narrower than the outer, forming a golden perianth 10.5 cm (4 in) across. The yellow corona has a slightly frilly, bright red mouth. (R A Scamp 1996)

'Carib Gipsy' 2Y-WWY late

This is strong and vigorous with a pale yellow perianth, paler at the tepal tips and bases, and with a white corona with a broad golden rim. (A J R Pearson 1987; AGM-RHS 1998)

'Carlton' 2Y-Y mid–late

This must be the most popular of all yellow daffodils and is grown in huge quantities, partly because it is such an important crop for cut flowers. It is one of a batch registered by P D Williams in 1927, of which 'Havelock' received the greatest accolades. But 'Carlton' grows like mad and has huge bulbs that are reassuringly heavy and appealing when filling bags in the garden centre. It has flowers 12 cm (4.75 in) across, with rather twisted and creased tepals, the inner ones particularly wavy. The corona is deeper yellow, and has a notched, frilled and expanded mouth. Useless on the show bench, it is still good for the garden and grows and flowers well. (P D Williams pre-1927; AGM-RHS 1995)

'Caro Nome' 2W-WPP mid
The pure white perianth is the perfect foil for the small, pink bowl-shaped corona, which is darker around the rim with an alleged hint of lavender. (G E Mitsch pre-1954)

'Ceylon' 2Y-O early
One of the best garden daffodils, with bright yellow perianths 10 cm (4 in) across and an orange corona that is often slightly split. The tepals are often creased and wavy, so it is not of show form, but the corona is sun resistant, the flowers last, and it grows well. (J L Richardson pre-1943; AGM-RHS 1995)

'Charter' 2Y-WWY early–mid
Bred from 'Binkie', this is a large flower with rather narrow tepals that recurve slightly and form a perianth 11 cm (4.25 in) across. The tepals are a bright lemon yellow, and white at the base. The corona opens lemon yellow but quickly fades to white with a rim of yellow to leave a luminous flower that lasts well and is freely produced. (G E Mitsch, M J Jefferson-Brown 1964; AGM-RHS 1993)

'Chromacolour' 2W-P mid
Bigger and with better colour than 'Accent', this has large (12 cm/4.75 in) flowers with pure white tepals and a bright pink, trumpet-shaped corona. (W G Pannill 1976; AGM-RHS 2001)

'C J Backhouse' 2Y-O mid (p. 58)
An historical plant with starry perianths and a frilled, orange corona that burns in the sun. (W Backhouse pre-1869)

'Coquille' 2W-P mid
The vigorous bulbs produce large (10 cm/4 in) flowers with ivory white tepals behind a pretty, ribbed and frilled corona of rich, orange pink. (J L Richardson, W Blom & Son 1966)

'Corbridge' 2W-Y mid
This seedling of the beautiful 'Green Island' has tall stems with a perfect 11.5-cm (4.5-in) white

perianth of excellent substance. The corona is pale yellow, slightly darker at the rim. (G Harrison 1968)

'Craigywarren' 2Y-R mid–late
A bright flower that increases well in the garden and produces lots of flowers with deep yellow tepals, the inner ones narrower and ribbed. The split corona is cup-shaped and reddish orange. (W J Dunlop pre-1949)

'Dawn Mist' 2W-WWP mid
Bred from, and resembling, 'Maiden's Blush', this has white perianths that never quite open flat, behind a short, funnel-shaped pink corona that has a flared, frilly rim where the colour is concentrated. (G Barr 1954)

'Daydream' 2Y-W mid
'Binkie' may not have super form but has passed on its vigour and colouring to many descendants, including this beautiful flower. It is only of moderate size, 8 cm (3 in) across, but has a rich lemon, flat perianth composed of broad tepals with white mucros on the outer three. The base is white, like the corona, except for a thin yellow ring around the frilly mouth. Of show form. (G E Mitsch 1960; AGM-RHS 1995)

'Delibes' 2Y-YYO early (p. 41)
This has large (9.5 cm/3.75 in) flowers with bright, greenish-yellow tepals and a bright yellow, bowl-shaped corona that is orange at the frilly mouth. (F Rijnveld & Sons pre-1950)

'Desdemona' 2W-W mid
This reliable, tall white flower has tepals that are slightly wavy and incurved, and a long corona with a flared and frilled mouth. A lovely garden flower with good stems. (G L Wilson 1964; AGM-RHS 2001)

'Duke of Windsor' 2W-OOY mid
This marvellous flower has large, white tepals that are rather creased and a broad, apricot-coloured corona that is ribbed and frilled. It was one of the first daffodils I ever knowingly grew, given to me by an expert gardener, Elizabeth Christie, who instilled in me the need to weed carefully – something that has stood me in good stead in my career. (G A Uit den Boogaard pre-1936)

Division 2 and 3 daffodils
Top row:
'Eastern Dawn' 2W-P,
'Precedent' 2 W-P.
Second row:
'Passionale' 2 W-P,
unnamed.
Third row:
'Redstart' 3W-GWO,
'Blarney' 3 W-OOY.
Bottom row:
'Kimmeridge' 3W-YYO,
'Kilworth' 2W-YOO.

'Eastern Dawn' 2W-P mid (p. 44)

This is a relatively small flower in this division, and seems to have distinct cyclamineus genes in it. The broad, white tepals reflex gently and the corona is broad and salmon pink. It flowers freely and is fragrant too. (G L Wilson 1964)

'Elysian Fields' (or 'Elysian') 2 W-P mid

This is a superb pink and white, with broad, white tepals of exceptional purity and a vibrant pink, broad corona. (M Jefferson-Brown 1985)

'Evendine' 2W-GWW mid–late

This crisp, cool, almost perfect flower is white with a touch of lemon. The 8-cm (3-in) perianth is formed by broad tepals that open pale yellow and have slightly rolled margins. The broad corona has a toothed, frilled edge that is tinted pale yellow but soon fades to pure white with a green eye. (M J Jefferson-Brown 1985)

'Favourite' 2W-Y late

This pretty flower has an attractive starry perianth of pure white, with a pale yellow, broad corona. (F E Board, M J Jefferson-Brown 1965)

'Feeling Lucky' 2Y-R mid–late

This daffodil increases well and has beautiful flowers with acid, lemon yellow, well-formed tepals and a broad, lobed and split corona of orange scarlet. (J L Richardson, M J Jefferson-Brown 1969; AGM-RHS 1993)

'Festivity' 2W-Y mid

The perianth of this garden or show flower is smooth and white, but the inner three tepals are narrower than the outer and may be incurved at the apex. The corona is lightly frilled, broad and deep yellow. (G E Mitsch pre-1954)

'Filly' 2W-YYP mid

This is not the pinkest of the pink and whites, but it is vigorous. The lightly ribbed, white tepals are often wavy, and the rather narrow corona opens pink but ages to yellow with a pink rim. The flowers are only 6 cm (2.3 in) wide but change as they mature. It is superb for cutting. (J W A van der Wereld, Tom Parker Farms 1984)

'Flower Record' 2W-YYO mid

Though not of show form, this popular plant is superb for the garden because of its short stems and large flowers, with white tepals tinged yellow at the base and a cup-shaped corona in yellow with a frilly, orange edge. A sweet perfume adds to its charms. (J W A Lefeber pre-1943)

'Flying Saucer' 2W-Y mid

The corona is broad, flat and pale yellow, set against an ivory white perianth. Will impress the neighbours. (G E Mitsch pre-1954)

'Fortune' 2Y-O early

Few daffodils can match the impact that 'Fortune' made on its introduction. Exhibited in

Birmingham in 1915, it was bigger and brighter than anything that preceded it. Its parentage is still not certain but may have involved 'King Alfred' and 'Sir Watkin'. It was greatly in demand and it is difficult to imagine, now that 'Fortune' is most often found in 'fill-a-bag' bins, that ten years after its introduction it commanded £25 a bulb, equivalent in purchasing power to more than £900 today! Its earliness was its downfall as far as being a parent was concerned, and it has trouble standing up to March weather but it is an important cut-flower crop. The flowers are 11 cm (4.25 in) wide with bright yellow tepals and a strong orange corona with overlapping lobes. There are far better plants for the garden, and orange cups that stand sunlight better, but because of its now bargain price and vigour, it will be with us in quantity for a while yet. (W T Ware pre-1917)

'Fragrant Breeze' 2W-O mid
This is a good garden daffodil with 11-cm (4.25-in) creamy white perianths and a broad, flaring corona in yellow. It is tall and very fragrant, good in the garden and worth planting in a pot for the house. (W F Leenen & sons 1976, O A Taylor & Sons 1993)

'Fragrant Rose' 2W-GPP mid–late
Extraordinarily beautiful flowers with extraordinary fragrance. The white, waxy tepals create a 9.5-cm (3.75-in) perianth against which the deep, rich pink, sun-proof corona with green eye is beautifully displayed. The fragrance is said to be of roses or raspberries. (Brian S Duncan, Rathowen Daffodils 1978)

'Freedom Rings' 2Y-P mid (p. 49)
A beautiful, softly coloured flower with neat flowers 8 cm (3 in) across, the tepals are slightly reflexed and lemon yellow. The sun-proof corona is apricot pink and flared. (R & E Havens 1994)

'Gaylord' 2Y-YOO early
A yellow and orange flower, 9 cm (3.5 in) across with bright yellow tepals, and a strong orange corona that is a strong yellow at the base. (D F Lee 1979)

'Gigantic Star' 2Y-Y mid
This offspring of 'Carlton' and 'Magnificence'

has, as you might expect, huge flowers (12.5 cm/5 in) with overlapping tepals and a trumpet-shaped, frilly and notched corona, all in golden yellow. A strong and colourful garden flower with strong stems. (G Helmus 1960)

'Gold Convention' 2Y-Y mid
The large (11 cm/4.25 in) flowers have smooth, vivid yellow perianths and a lightly frilled, deep yellow corona. It grows strongly and the flowers are held well on strong stems. (J S B Lea 1978; AGM-RHS 1995)

'Golden Aura' ('Gold Aura') 2Y-Y mid (p.35)
This is a beautiful flower for the garden, and it is also good enough for showing. The tepals are well rounded to give a deep gold perianth of excellent shape 9.5 cm (3.75 in) across, and the slightly deeper corona is neat and lightly frilled. This flower comes highly recommended. (J L Richardson, Mrs H K Richardson 1964; AGM-RHS 1995)

'Golden Jewel' 2Y-GYY mid
This has golden tepals, the inner three narrower and slightly wavy, and a funnel-shaped, frilled corona with a green base. It is strong and has good stems. (T Bloomer 1973; AGM-RHS 1995)

'Good Measure' 2W-W mid
Another excellent white from Jefferson-Brown with smooth white tepals and a cup-shaped corona that opens cream but passes to white. (M Jefferson-Brown 1975)

'Gouache' 2W-O mid (p. 40)
This beautiful flower has a perianth of round tepals with some creasing, and a large, flat, frilled, ruffled and cut corona of soft orange. (W F Leenen pre-1993, unregistered)

'Hambledon' 2YYW-Y mid
Bred from great parents, 'Golden Aura' and 'Daydream', this daffodil is a fine variety. Its bright, acid yellow flowers have ace-of-spades tepals and a tubular corona that is paler at the base and shows some buff colouring around the mouth. It is a strong grower and it is excellent for showing, resembling the daffodil 'Amber Castle' but of better form. (J W Blanchard 1985; AGM-RHS 2001)

famous Engleheart daffodils that still have their following among those who like floral antiques. The blooms are 10 cm (4 in) wide and have creased, twisted and wavy, soft yellow tepals, and a yellow corona that ages to coppery orange. (G H Engleheart pre-1912)

'High Society' 2W-GWP mid–late
This has a well-formed white perianth with a yellow corona edged with pink. Good for the garden and for showing. (Brian S Duncan, Rathowen Daffodils 1979; AGM-RHS 2001)

'Holiday Fashion' 2W-WPP mid
This has huge (12 cm/4.75 in) perianths with broad, slightly ribbed tepals of pure white and a ribbed, frilled, salmon pink cup that is brighter pink at the mouth. (G E Mitsch 1956, 1967)

'Hospodar' 2Y-O mid (p. 58)
Bred from 'King Alfred', this has yellow tepals, often notched, and a ribbed, funnel-shaped corona in deep orange with a slightly flared mouth. It is not of great form but it is sun-proof. (J C Williams pre-1914)

'Ice Follies' 2W-W early–mid (p. 21, 66)
This is rapidly becoming the most popular daffodil in the UK, being beautiful and easy to grow. It is not of perfect form because the tepals that form the 9.5-cm (3.75-in) perianth are not flat, but ribbed and have wavy margins. However, it is so free with its flowers that it is perfect for the garden and for naturalizing, where the subtle colouring is an advantage. The corona is large and spreading, ribbed and frilled, opening pale yellow and ageing to creamy white. This must be among the top ten daffodils for the garden. (Konynenburg & Mark, pre-1953; AGM-RHS 1993)

'Irish Minstrel' 2W-Y
Bred from 'Green Island' and 'Tudor Minstrel', this is a big (10 cm/4 in) flower with white tepals forming a smooth perianth and a deep yellow, loosely frilled corona. (J L Richardson 1958; AGM-RHS 1993)

'Jubilation' 2W-Y mid
This offspring of 'Green Island' is tall, with white perianth and a broad corona that is frilled and opens yellow, ageing to buff. (G E Mitsch 1959)

Gold and orange daffodils
Top row:
'Uncle Duncan' 1Y-O,
'Ensemble' 4Y-Y.
Second row:
'Helford Dawn' 2Y-W,
'Tamar Fire' 4Y-R.
Third row:
'Crackington' 4Y-O,
'Perimeter' 3Y-YYO.
Bottom row:
'Liverpool Festival' 2Y-O,
'Lundy Light' 2Y-R.

'Helford Dawn' 2Y-W mid (p. 46)
One for the show bench, this pristine flower, of great charm, has soft yellow tepals and a cylindrical corona that is slightly flared at the mouth, opening soft yellow and fading to white. It is a beautiful bloom. (R A Scamp 1996)

'Helford Sunset' 2Y-P mid (p. 49)
Combining the tepals of a reverse bicolour with a pink corona, this state-of-the-art flower is a sure bet for showing. The tepals are pale, primrose yellow that fades to white at the base, and the corona is long and slightly flared, in deep pink. (R A Scamp 2002)

'Helios' 2 Y-O mid
This was *the* yellow-and-orange flower to grow before 'Fortune' was introduced, and one of the

'Kilworth' 2W-YOO late (p. 44)
This important cultivar has a fine, 11-cm (4.25-in) white perianth tinged yellow at the base, and a bowl-shaped corona of deep orange tinted yellow and green at the base. It is lightly frilled. A superb flower and good for the garden. (J L Richardson pre-1938)

'Kissproof' 2Y-O mid (p. 40)
The name suggests that the kiss of the sun will not burn away the vibrant scarlet corona that sits like a pleated disc in the centre of the creamy white perianth. Indeed, it is quite sun-proof except in strong sun and the pale, sulphur-yellow perianth highlights the bright cup. (Warnaar & Co 1964)

'Klamath' 2W-Y mid
This lovely, fresh flower is large (11.5 cm/4.5 in) with white tepals and a pale yellow, flaring corona that ages to buff. It is similar to, but bigger than, its pollen parent, 'Penvose'. (G E Mitsch 1960)

'Krakatoa' 2Y-O mid
The great 'Fortune' provided the pollen for this good garden plant with massive flowers 12 cm (4.75 in) across with vivid yellow tepals and a funnel-shaped, sun-proof, orange corona. (J L Richardson pre-1937)

'La Argentina' 2W-O/WY mid (p. 41)
The deeply lobed corona, almost making this a split corona, may put many people off this flower, but it is a good garden plant and has been a welcome sight in my border for many years, though the stems are sometimes a little lacking, enforcing its addition to vases of flowers. Each lobe of the corona is spreading and golden orange, shading to yellow with a white margin, all set against a pure white perianth that is creased but good enough to be effective in the garden. (P van Deusen pre-1953)

'Lady Ann' 2W-GPP mid–late
This super flower is 10 cm (4 in) across, and the perianth is pure white. The corona is broad, deep pink and beautifully shaped. I saw this when it was cloudy and blowing a gale, but it still looked lovely. (Brian S Duncan 1992)

'Limbo' 2O-R mid
This superior orange and red cultivar has a 10-cm

(4-in) orange perianth with paler tips to the tepals, and a shallow corona that is bright orange-red. A vibrant flower and superior to older cultivars such as 'Ambergate'. (Brian S Duncan, Rathowen Daffodils 1984)

'Liverpool Festival' 2Y-O mid–late (p. 46)
Fine, smooth, golden tepals; a perky orange corona, attractively frilled, combined with good poise, makes this a fine flower. (J S B Lea 1974, Clive Postles Daffodils 1985)

'Lizard Light' 2Y-O early
A neat flower with evenly sized and placed golden tepals, often nicked, with a ribbed, notched corona of deep orange with overlapping lobes. (M P Williams pre-1947)

'Loch Hope' 2 Y-R early
A bright flower with greenish yellow, slightly incurled tepals, creating a smooth perianth 10 cm (4 in) wide, and a frilled, straight, bright orange corona. (J S B Lea 1970)

'Loch Owskeich' 2Y-O mid
This is a sturdy and short-stemmed plant with sun-resistant yellow and orange flowers 10 cm (4 in) across. (J S B Lea 1971; AGM-RHS 1993)

'Lucifer' 2W-YOO mid–late (p. 62)
Not as bright as we might expect of such a name in the 21st century, this pretty old plant has starry flowers that measure 10 cm (4 in) across, with twisted, recurved, white tepals flushed with yellow at the base, the inner three particularly narrow, and a golden, ribbed and frilled corona that is flushed with orange. (Mrs Lawrenson pre-1890)

'Lundy Light' 2Y-R late (p. 46)
Great for showing, this 11-cm (4.25-in) wide flower has a golden yellow, evenly shaped perianth and a cup-shaped, bright orange corona with light frilling. Long stems and great vigour add to its charms. (R A Scamp 1996)

'Manon Lescaut' 2W-YYO mid
This large (11.5 cm/4.5 in) flower, with 'Actaea' in its ancestry, has a smooth, white perianth and a pale yellow corona with a brilliant orange rim. (Konynenburg & Mark 1960)

'Marlborough' 2W-P early–mid (p. 53)
One of the earliest in its class, this is a good show flower with a fine, white perianth 11.5 cm (4.5 in) across, and a wavy-mouthed, funnel-shaped, pink corona. (R A Scamp 1991)

'Millennium Sunset' 2Y-O mid (p. 42)
A vigorous plant, producing many flowers of show form, it is smooth with a golden perianth and a soft orange corona. (R A Scamp 1999)

'Misty Glen' 2W-GWW mid
Bred from 'Easter Moon', this is a good white with a green eye and slightly creased tepals. (F E Board, W A Norton 1976; AGM-RHS 1995)

'Mitylene' 2W-Y mid–late (p. 62)
One of the most influential of all Engleheart's many fine hybrids, this has silky white tepals that were used to breed later whites. The large (10.5 cm/4 in) flowers have rather wavy tepals and a broad, primrose yellow corona. It cannot compare in substance and form with later cultivars, but is charming in the garden. (G H Engleheart pre-1923)

'Modern Art' 2Y-O mid–late
Everyone loves this showy flower. The 9-cm (3.5-in) perianth is composed of almost round, bright yellow tepals, but the corona is deeply split and frilled like parsley leaves, despite its deep orange colour. The plant is prolific and, even better, the blooms are sun-proof. (W F Leenen 1973)

'Mona Lisa' 2W-W mid
This vigorous seedling of the good 'Chinese White' is pure white with a wide, spreading cup. (F E Board, M J Jefferson-Brown 1965)

'Mongleath' 2W-P early–mid (p. 49)
This is a sister seedling to 'Marlborough' and has large (10.5 cm/4 in) flowers with broad, chalky white tepals and a rosy pink corona. It is not as vigorous as its sibling but is superior, when on form, for showing. (R A Scamp 1994)

'Mrs R O Backhouse' 2 W-P mid
One of the reasons why it pays to go to a specialist is that you will get the best bulbs, and also good information. It amazes me that 'Mrs R O Backhouse' is still listed by some general suppliers as 'new'! In fact it is probably the oldest of all pink daffodils, and was first shown in 1923. In 1934 E A Bowles wrote 'The fact is that no really rose-pink form has yet been seen by the general public' and added, of 'Mrs R O Backhouse': 'Though it had more pink in it than any previously known, there is also so much pale orange in the lower portion of the corona that the general effect is nearer to a pale apricot shade, with a salmon-pink rim when at its best.' He concludes by writing that 'most people are reluctant to accept it as a pink daffodil'. Today it is quite common, and is sold as a pink daffodil, and those gardeners who know only this exemplar probably still refuse to accept that daffodils *can* be pink. But, whatever the colour, it is still a pretty garden plant with rather twisted tepals forming a 9.5-cm (3.75-in) wide perianth and a frilly corona. Look for something more modern if you want a true pink, or just glory in growing the flower that started a wonderful trend. (Mrs R O Backhouse pre-1921)

'My My' 2W-P late
This is a majestic flower with broad, white tepals forming a flat perianth. The large corona is salmon-pink in colour. (J L Richardson, M J Jefferson-Brown 1967)

'Nansidwell' 2W-P mid (p. 49)
This is a large flower, 13 cm (5 in) across, with a pure white perianth and a bright pink corona, beautifully frilled at the mouth and pale at the base. It is strong and rather special for the garden. (R A Scamp 1993)

'New World' 2Y-YYP mid
This lovely pastel-coloured flower has pale yellow tepals and a broad, frilled corona that opens yellow but flushes with pink with age. (M J Jefferson-Brown)

'Notre Dame' 2W-GYP late
Bringing the daffodil season to a close, this distinctive flower is also good for showing. The 10.5-cm (4-in) perianth has broad, white, slightly reflexed tepals, and the corona, constricted at the mouth, is deep orange-pink, shading to yellow and then green at the base. It is free-flowering and sun-resistant. (Brian S Duncan 1992; AGM-RHS 1999)

'Nuage' 2W-W mid

A good garden variety in pure white with a fine, flat perianth. (G H Johnstone pre-1949)

'Orange Ice Follies' 2W-O (p. 66)

This was bought under this name and has flowers that resemble 'Ice Follies'. It also blooms at the same time, but the corona is a soft, amber orange. (unregistered?)

'Ormeau' 2Y-Y early–mid

This is a smooth, beautiful flower of good form in vivid, greenish yellow. (W J Dunlop 1949; AGM-RHS 1993)

'Osmington' 2W-R mid

A vibrant flower 9.5 cm (3.75 in) wide with a broad, smooth, white perianth and a slightly frilled, bright-red corona. (J W Blanchard 1974)

'Paricutin' 2Y-R mid–late

This wonderful flower has bright yellow tepals that make the perfect foil for the wide, almost flat corona in bright scarlet. This daffodil has a well-balanced shape and really zingy colouring. (G E Mitsch pre-1952)

'Passionale' 2 W-P (p. 44)

A refined flower, with great vigour. The smooth, flat perianth is 10 cm (4 in) wide and pure white, and the funnel-shaped corona is salmon pink with a frilled mouth. Readily available and recommended. (G L Wilson, F E Board 1956; AGM-RHS 1993)

'Pastorale' 2Y-WWY mid

These large flowers (11 cm/4.25 in) have wide tepals that reflex away from a corona that is slightly flaring and ruffled. The bloom is pale, greenish yellow, and the corona fades to white, with a zingy, yellow rim. A tall flower. (G E Mitsch pre-1954, 1965)

'Pengarth' 2YYW-WWY mid

This is a really exceptional flower, measuring 8.5 cm (3.3 in) across with round tepals of lemon yellow, with a white base and a stripe through the centre. The corona is yellow at first but ages to white with a yellow rim, and is gently frilled. Elegant and distinctive. (Brian S Duncan, Dan du Plessis 1996)

'Penkivel' 2W-P mid (p. 49)

Another show-winner from Ron Scamp, this precise flower has a 10.5-cm (4-in), smooth perianth of ace-of-spades, white tepals, and a smooth, intense pink corona. (R A Scamp 1992)

'Pimpernel' 2Y-O mid

This has large flowers with yellow tepals, and a small corona of sun-resistant orange. (J Gerritsen & Son 1984; AGM-RHS 2001)

'Pinafore' 2W-W mid

A big (10 cm/4 in) flower with a white perianth composed of broad tepals, and a broad corona with a rolled rim. (G E Mitsch 1955, 1966)

'Pipe Major' 2Y-O late

This bright flower has a neat perianth of golden yellow, the inner tepals being narrower than the others, and a vibrant, small, lightly frilled corona of scarlet. (F E Board 1965)

Division 2 daffodils with pink coronas

Top row:
'Nansidwell' 2W-P,
'Precocious' 2W-P.
Second row:
'Mongleath' 2W-P,
'Penkivel' 2W-P.
Bottom row:
'Freedom Rings' 2Y-P,
'Helford Sunset' 2Y-P.

'Pink Charm' 2W-WWP mid

Moderately sized (9 cm/3.5 in), pure white, flat perianths show off a pale corona that is rimmed with coral pink. (P de Jager & Sons, van Eeden Bros 1977)

'Pink Smiles' 2W-P mid (p. 41)

This good garden plant has bright flowers with rather incurved, white tepals and a brilliant, deep pink corona, nicely frilled at the mouth and shading to white at the base. (W J Dunlop pre-1953)

'Pink Tea' 2W-P mid

The pink corona of this pretty flower fades slightly as it ages. The stigma is longer than the length of the cup. (Murray W Evans 1979)

'Pinza' 2Y-YYO mid

This is a sun-resistant flower with a perianth 9.5 cm (3.75 in) wide in bright yellow, and an orange-yellow corona that is deeper in colour at the frilled mouth. Good in the garden with nicely held, bright flowers. (J L Richardson, Mrs H K Richardson 1962; AGM-RHS 1993)

'Precedent' 2 W-P mid (p. 44)

Introduced in the same year as 'Accent', this is one of the many fine pink-cupped flowers to come from Grant Mitsch that led to redder colouring. The blooms are 11 cm (4.25 in) wide with slightly reflexed, white tepals, and the corona is salmon pink, deeper around the rim. (G E Mitsch 1960)

'Precocious' 2W-P mid–late (p. 49)

This extraordinary flower is unlike most others, and one of the best if you like frilly, unusual flowers. The ivory white tepals form a lovely background to the broad, flat, heavily frilled corona that is deep pink at the edge, shading to yellow at the base. Its only fault is that the flowers hang their heads slightly. It was love at first sight when I saw this. (G E Mitsch 1966, 1976; AGM-RHS 2001)

'Professor Einstein' 2W-R mid

This standard red and white has a wonderful perianth of pure white with thick tepals and a flat corona that is a bright, deep orange and almost disc-like in shape. Unfortunately the corona burns badly in bright sun, so it needs a semi-shaded spot unless picked when just open. (J W A Lefeber pre-1946)

'Queensland' 2 W-P late

Now quite a common pink-cup, this has flowers 9 cm (3.5 in) wide with creamy white, rather creased tepals and a funnel-shaped, lobed and frilled corona in salmon pink, paler at the base. Does well in the garden, where it looks appropriate with its less than perfect form and moderate size. (G Barr 1954, E B Champernowne 1985)

'Rainbow' 2W-WWP late (p. 53)

This has white tepals and a notched, pink corona with a salmon-pink rim. A good choice for the garden. (J L Richardson 1961; AGM-RHS 2001)

'Red Devon' 2Y-O mid

This child of 'Fortune' has flowers 10.5 cm (4 in) across with wavy, acid yellow tepals and a short, funnel-shaped, orange corona. It is vigorous and scented. (E B Champernowne pre-1943; AGM-RHS 1993)

'Redhill' 2W-R mid (p. 41)

This is a good, vigorous plant that is good in the garden and has 9.5-cm (3.75-in) perianths of pure white and good substance, often curling in at the apex. The corona is bowl-shaped, ribbed and bright orange-red. (P de Jager & Sons 1958, G A Preyde 1978)

'Regal Bliss' 2W-GWW mid (p. 51)

This is a big flower, having a long, cylindrical corona with a slightly expanded mouth. The white perianth is 12 cm (4.75 in) across and flat. A fine garden daffodil. (Brian S Duncan, Rathowen Daffodils 1982)

'Ringleader' 2W-YYO mid

A free-flowering bulb with smooth white tepals and a flat, yellow corona edged with pinkish orange with a greenish eye. (Mrs H K Richardson 1972; the name is also used for a J N Hancock & Co cultivar with characteristics 2Y-YYO)

'Ring of Fire' 2W-WWR mid (p. 41)

A real find, this has huge flowers, more than 12 cm (4.75 in) across. Don't consider it for showing because the white, broad tepals are nicked and creased, but they do show off the frilly ribbed corona that shades from white to pink and red at the edge. Not of perfect form but lovely for the garden, for cutting, or to impress neighbours who might not appreciate the subtleties of finer things! (Dutch, pre-1995)

'Romance' 2W-P mid
It is the deeply lobed, deep-pink corona and fragrance that make this flower stand out. The 9-cm (3.5-in) perianth is made of pure white tepals of good substance. Recommended. (J L Richardson 1959; AGM-RHS 1995)

'Rustom Pasha' 2Y-O mid (p. 39)
This large (10 cm/4 in) flower has an old-fashioned charm with rather narrow tepals of bright yellow and a flaring, bright orange corona, nicely toothed, that deepens in colour as it ages. (A M Wilson/Miss G Evelyn pre-1930)

'Saint Keverne' 2Y-Y early (p. 41)
This is not only a fine garden daffodil with 10-cm (4-in) wide perianth and cylindrical corona in bright yellow, but it has proved a good parent. This is because it is resistant to basal rot which makes it, and its progeny, exceptional for garden planting. Even better, it is a tall, bright, handsome flower and deserves to be planted far more than other common daffodils. (M P Williams 1934; AGM-RHS 1993)

'Saint Patrick's Day' 2Y-Y early
This is a superb, vigorous garden daffodil of fresh colouring and good form. The perianth is 10 cm (4 in) across and pale yellow with some creasing. The corona is quite flat and broad, heavily ribbed and pale yellow with a deeper rim that is split and frilled. Genetics seems entirely predictable when you know that the parents of this great flower were 'Ice Follies' and 'Binkie'. (Konynenburg & Mark 1964)

'Salome' 2W-PPY mid
Patience is needed with this flower, as the narrow corona opens yellow and matures to pink with a yellow rim. The 9-cm (3.5-in) perianth is pure white. (J L Richardson 1958; AGM-RHS 2001)

'Sarah' 2W-P mid
The white perianth has sharply pointed, rather

creased tepals with curled edges, while the frilly corona is pale pink. Not of perfect form but good for the garden. (G Barr 1955)

'Satin Pink' 2W-P mid–late
A well-formed flower with an ivory white perianth and amber pink corona, ideal for the garden. (J L Richardson, Warnaar & Co 1958)

'Sealing Wax' 2Y-O mid
This sprightly flower has a crisp perianth of acid yellow and a petite ribbed, bright orange corona. The plant is tall and grows well. (Barr & Sons, Wallace and Barr 1957)

'Silvermere' 2W-W mid (p. 59)
This flower, with 'Empress of Ireland' as one parent and 'Easter Moon' as the other, has broad,

Pale mixed daffodils
Top row:
'Kenellis' 10W-Y,
'Erlicheer' 4W-Y.
Second row:
'Praecox' 9W-GYR
(*N. poeticus praecox*),
'Frostkist' 6W-W.
Third row:
'Regal Bliss' 2W-GWW,
'Sparnon' 11aW-GYY.
Bottom row:
'Skerry' 2Y-Y,
'Countdown' 3W-Y.

fine tepals that incurl at the edge to form a lovely setting for the precise, trumpet-shaped corona. Described as a better 'Ben Hee', it is a beautiful bloom of precise form. (Brian S Duncan, Rathowen Daffodils 1981)

'Sir Watkin' 2Y-Y mid (p. 39)

This is another ground-breaking development in the history of daffodils. Bowles in *The Narcissus* records that its origins are rather obscure, but that it was probably found in the garden of the house bought by W Pickstone in 1868. He also notes that as early as 1934 many considered that it was losing vigour. It is rarely seen today because of its old-fashioned form. The flowers are 11 cm (4.25 in) wide with rather wavy, incurved, greenish-yellow tepals, while the ribbed corona, of a slightly more golden shade, is lobed and frilled. It may be old, but few flowers would look nicer in an orchard. (W Pickstone pre-1868)

'Skerry' 2Y-Y mid (p. 51)

This flower, of moderate size (9 cm/3.5 in), has lovely, rounded flowers with pale, greenish-yellow tepals, which fade to white at the midrib. It has a lightly ribbed, frilled, attractive corona, slightly rolled, to form a really pretty bloom. (Carncairn Daffodils 1991)

'Snow Frills' 2YYW-W mid

This beautiful flower, 9 cm (3.5 in) across, does not have the greatest form, but stands out because of its cup, which is very heavily frilled and stands out against the yellow perianth. It is tall and strong. (G E Mitsch 1977)

'Soldier Brave' 2Y-R late (p. 40)

This fine plant, one of Jefferson-Brown's 'military' hybrids, has excellent poise and substance. The perianth is deep gold with broad tepals, and the corona is orange at first, becoming red as it ages. Being late it is exposed to stronger sun than most, but is sun-proof. Recommended. (M J Jefferson-Brown 1985)

'Special Envoy' 2Y-Y early

A superb show flower, this all-yellow bloom is 9.5 cm (3.75 in) across with super-smooth tepals and a flared corona. It grows well and presents the flowers perfectly. (J S B Lea, Clive Postles 1991; AGM-RHS 1998)

'Sportsman' 2Y-R mid (p. 56)

This 'Ceylon' hybrid is a super plant, producing masses of beautiful flowers of rich colouring, fine both for the garden and for showing. The blooms are 9.5 cm (3.75 in) across, the broad tepals creating a rounded profile. They are deep yellow with a hint of orange, and the corona is bowl-shaped, ribbed and lightly frilled, of deep, reddish orange. It is tall and holds its flowers well. (Brian S Duncan, Rathowen Daffodils 1979)

'Spring Dawn' 2W-Y early

Its genetic inheritance from 'Rijnveld's Early Sensation' has ensured that this is among the first to flower in the garden, and its white perianth and frilly lemon corona are especially welcome so early in the season. The creamy white tepals are rather narrow and twisted, so plant for the garden rather than the show bench. (Rosewarne E H S, O A Taylor & Sons 1986)

Tulips and daffodils
Photographed with polyanthus 'Guinevere' and *Muscari* 'Valerie Finnis'.
Top row:
Tulip 'Red Riding Hood',
Narcissus 'Stainless' 2W-W,
Tulip 'Za-za'.
Second row:
Tulip 'Scarlet Baby',
Tulip 'Peach Blush',
Tulip 'Upward'.
Bottom row:
Tulip 'Purissima',
Narcissus 'Segovia' 3W-Y,
Narcissus 'Bell Song' 7W-P.

'Stainless' 2W-W mid (p. 52, 70)

A fairly good flower that is readily available, this has flowers 9.5 cm (3.75 in) wide with white tepals, the inner three rather narrower and more wavy than the outer three, and with a shallow, ribbed corona, also in white, all with a greenish cast. A lovely, cool plant for the garden. (G L Wilson 1960)

'Strines' 2Y-Y mid

This is a beautiful flower of bright, acid yellow, 12.5 cm (5 in) across, with good form. The tepals overlap and the corona is funnel shaped with a frilled, slightly flared rim that gives the flower a neat, pretty shape. (F E Board 1965)

'Stromboli' 2W-O mid

The fiery orange, large corona is shown off by the white perianth. (J L Richardson 1959)

'Swaledale' 2Y-Y mid

This hybrid of 'Daydream' is similar but has more pointed tepals. (Jan Dalton 1989)

'Tamar Snow' 2W-GWW mid (p. 53)

The elegant, cool flower has rather pointed, smooth white tepals, and a cylindrical, gently ribbed, pure white corona, tinged green at the base. (Brian S Duncan, du Plessis Bros 1986)

'Testament' 2W-YPP mid

Like a superior 'Passionale', this has super form with a large, flat, smooth white perianth, and a wide pink corona with a yellow base. (M J Jefferson-Brown 1985)

'Tibet' 2W-W mid

This white flower opens very pale yellow and the perianth is 9.5 cm (3.75 in) across. The corona has a flaring mouth, notched and frilled, and the flower has a good scent. It grows strongly and is good for the garden. (G L Wilson pre-1942)

'Torrianne' 2W-W mid–late (p. 53)

Bred from 'Ben Hee' and 'Brierglass', this daffodil has moderately sized, pretty flowers of pure white, with a flat perianth and a lobed and frilled, gently flaring corona. (R A Scamp, S Holden 1997)

'Trebah' 2Y-Y R mid (p. 42)

Combining the merits of 'Saint Keverne' and 'Golden Aura', this excellent, strong-growing plant has good flowers of deep, golden yellow, with tepals that overlap by half, and a cylindrical corona. (R A Scamp 1993)

'Trewarvas' 2W-Y late (p. 53)

This clean-cut flower has smooth, white perianths 11.5 cm (4.5 in) across and a smooth, slightly ribbed, barely flared corona of rich, egg-yolk yellow. (R A Scamp 1991)

'Tudor Minstrel' 2W-Y

This famous and well-regarded flower, bred from the equally famous and ancient 'Mitylene', has enormous flowers. The white, smooth, sulphur-flushed tepals form a perianth 13 cm (5 in) across, and the broad, funnel-shaped corona is brilliant yellow. (J L Richardson pre-1948)

Division 2 daffodils with white tepals

Top row:
'Trewarvas' 2W-Y,
'Marlborough' 2W-P.
Second row:
'Bedruthan' 2W-YYR,
'Torrianne' 2W-W.
Bottom row:
'Rainbow' 2W-WWP,
'Tamar Snow' 2W-GWW.

'Variant' 2 Y-O mid (p. 38)
I am sure this flower, with a creased and notched perianth, and a corona that changes from yellow to orange, has some special feature that makes it a commercial proposition, but it is lost on me. In an age of exciting and beautiful flowers, this one cannot justify taking up space in the garden. (J L Richardson, G Zandbergen-Terwegen 1959)

'Vulcan' 2Y-O early
This tall plant, bred from 'Carbineer' and 'Ceylon', is as good as you would expect from such illustrious parents. The perianth is bright yellow and the small, cup-shaped corona is bright orange. It does not burn in the sun. (J L Richardson 1956; AGM-RHS 1993)

'Widgeon' 2Y-P mid
This seedling of 'Daydream' has flowers with soft yellow perianths (10 cm/4 in across) and a flared, bell-shaped corona of pink-flushed pale yellow. (G E Mitsch 1975)

'Willy Dunlop' 2W-Y mid–late
This has enormous flowers of good substance with pure white tepals, shading yellow at the base, and a deep yellow, cylindrical corona. (W J M Blom 1968, W Blom & Son 1984; AGM-RHS 1998)

'Winfrith' 2W-W mid
This white flower is similar to 'Snowshill' but with a more frilly corona, and it also has pure white tepals that form a double triangle. Its straight-sided corona has a green eye. (D & J W Blanchard 1966)

'Woodgreen' 2W-WYY early
This plant has large flowers with 11-cm (4.25-in) creamy white perianths, and a yellow corona with a pale base. (W J Dunlop 1956)

'Worcester' 2W-W mid
This large flower has spade-shaped tepals that sometimes reflex slightly. The corona opens pale cream and ages to white with a frilly edge. (M J Jefferson-Brown 1975)

'Yes Please' 2W-P mid
The big (10 cm/4 in) flowers have slightly laid-back white tepals, the inner three of which are

slightly incurved at the tip. The bright pink corona is lightly frilled. (F E Board, M J Jefferson-Brown 1965)

DIVISION 3
Small-cupped Daffodils

Division 3 includes some of the prettiest daffodils, with neat coronas not more than one third the length of the tepals, and with only one flower per stem. It is quite a difficult division to breed for because, in increasing vigour, the result is often that flowers produce longer coronas than this division specifies. Historically, many are closer to *Narcissus poeticus* than the previous divisions, and this has resulted in the cultivars being late in flower and rather prone to have cups that burn in sunlight. *Narcissus poeticus* bulbs are also thin and light in weight, and most gardeners tend to prefer bulky bulbs. Many of these problems have been resolved by breeders, and Division 3 is the place to look for more delicate flowers than you will find in the previous two.

'Achduart' 3Y-R mid
This bright flower, 10.5 cm (4 in) across, has an overlapping perianth of deep gold and a smooth red corona. Good for showing. (J S B Lea 1972)

'Aircastle' 3W-Y mid
A beautiful flower with illustrious parents ('Green Island' and 'Chinese White') with colours that vary according to the weather conditions. The perianth is white and develops some yellow colouring, and the tepals overlap well. The corona is flat, ribbed and pale yellow, touched with apricot and darker at the lightly frilled rim. It has been an important plant for breeding and has been involved in the development of cultivars in many divisions, including jonquils, where its genes have imparted a tendency to change colour as the flowers develop. (G E Mitsch 1958)

'Altruist' 3O-R mid
This good, bold flower of good form resembles 'Ambergate' but has a smaller corona. The 8-cm (3-in) perianth opens orange and fades with age, while the shallow corona is a dark, orangey-red, and also fades slightly – more so in sun. (F E Board 1965)

'Amor' 3W-YYO early–mid (p. 40)
This seedling of the standard 'Flower Record' is a good garden plant with huge (13 cm/5 in) flowers. It has an ivory white perianth and a shallow, pale yellow corona with an orange rim. (W F Leenen 1957, 1971)

'Audubon' 2W-WWP mid
This large (10 cm/4 in) flower has a pure white perianth. The inner tepals in particular are somewhat in-rolled, but have good substance. The corona is bowl-shaped and creamy white, with a pretty, coral pink rim. (G E Mitsch 1955, 1965)

'Badbury Rings' 3Y-YYR mid
This is popular on the show bench and is also a fine, fragrant garden plant. It has 10-cm (4-in) flowers with smooth yellow tepals, and a shallow corona of a deeper shade with a clearly defined orange-red rim around the slightly frilled mouth. (J W Blanchard 1985; AGM-RHS 1998)

'Bath's Flame' 3Y-YYO very early (p. 58)
This, the next stage in the development of Division 3 after 'Conspicuus', resembles it but has darker yellow tepals. The starry flowers are 10 cm (4 in) across, and the yellow corona is six-lobed and frilled around the orange-rimmed mouth. Bowles wrote that it was 'rather gaudy' – I wonder what he would make of modern cultivars! (G H Engleheart pre-1913)

'Beige Beauty' 3Y-Y mid (p. 59)
A large (10.5 cm/4 in), flat flower in pale lemon shades with a hint of buff, the perianth opens ivory and becomes pale beige-yellow. The flat, ribbed corona is a similar shade. A lovely, soft flower. (G E Mitsch 1995, 1996)

'Birma' 3Y-O mid
This is a popular garden cultivar with masses of vibrant flowers on tall stems. The perianth is bright yellow, and the corona is cup-shaped and bright orange, paler at the base. (J W A Lefeber 1938, 1960)

'Blarney' 3 W-OOY (p. 44)
Bred from the old 'Mitylene', this 10-cm (4-in) flower has white tepals and a flat corona of salmon orange with a paler base and a cream rim. It was used to produce 'Blarney's Daughter' (2W-

OOY), which has a larger corona. (J L Richardson, pre-1935)

'Bossa Nova' 3O-R mid–late (p. 56)
One of the best orange flowers, the blooms have slightly incurled tepals of rich gold – flushed with orange except at the tips and the midribs – and a neat, bright-red corona that is ribbed and frilled. The flower colour intensifies when cut. (Brian S Duncan, Rathowen Daffodils 1983)

'Bullseye' 3W-R mid–late
Well-named for its small, orange-red corona, which stands out against the ivory white perianth. (F E Board, M J Jefferson-Brown 1975)

'Capisco' 3W-GYR mid (p. 57)
A fine flower with snow-white tepals, the inner smaller, and a hexagonal, frilly, ribbed, short corona edged in red. (Ballydorn Bulb Farm 1969)

'Carrara' 3W-GWW mid
Though this 9-cm (3.5-in) wide flower opens with a pale yellow rim to the shallow corona, it soon fades to pure white with a green eye. (Mrs H K Richardson, Rathowen Daffodils 1979)

'Centrefold' 3W-YYR mid (p. 57)
Sometimes producing flowers that straddle Divisions 2 and 3, this is a large (10.5 cm/4 in), showy flower with broad, smooth, heavy-textured tepals. The corona is lobed and shallow with a heavy band of red at the rim. (G W E Brogden 1975, Brogden Bulbs 1991)

'Cheer Leader' 3YYO-R mid (p. 56)
This fine, bold flower has a smooth, golden perianth with slightly incurled tepals and a brilliant, bowl-shaped, ribbed corona. (Brian S Duncan, Rathowen Daffodils 1987)

'Chickerell' 3Y-YYR early (p. 57)
This is a fine, large (11 cm/4.25 in) flower with a primrose yellow perianth with broad tepals and a broad, slightly lobed and ribbed yellow corona, edged with orange. It is tall and early. (J W Blanchard 1985)

'Clockface' 3W-YYO late
This is a big flower (11.5 cm/4.5 in) with milky white tepals and a flat corona that is bright yellow

**Division 2 and 3
daffodils**
Top row:
'Tamar Lad' 3Y-O,
'Dimity' 3Y-OW.
Second row:
'Tiffany Jade' 3Y-YYR,
'Nonchalent' 3Y-GYY.
Third row:
'Ferndown' 3Y-Y,
'Bossa Nova' 3O-R.
Bottom row:
'Cheer Leader' 3YYO-R,
'Sportsman' 2Y-R.

with a bright scarlet rim. A tall and dazzling flower. (G L Wilson pre-1947)

'Conspicuus' (also known as 'Barri Conspiucuus') 3Y-YYO mid (p. 42)

This old flower is one of the first of the Division 3 daffodils, created by crossing Division 2 (an *Incomparabilis*) with Division 9. The group was even called *Barrii* at first, and 'Conspicuus' was popular because of its vigour and ability to grow anywhere. The starry flowers open with deep yellow tepals, but these fade. The short corona is strongly ribbed, and shaded orange at the frilly mouth. (W Backhouse pre-1869)

'Countdown' 3W-Y mid (p. 51)

This large, majestic flower does not have super show form, but the white tepals form a smooth perianth, and the distinctive corona is broad and spreading, ribbed and lobed, of deep yellow for its outer part and paler in the centre. (New Zealand, not registered)

'Dimity' ('Demure') 3Y-OW mid (p. 56)

A smooth, golden perianth backs the neat, bright orange cup. The style protrudes beyond the stamens almost to the length of the corona. (Jackson Sr, W Jackson Jr 1968)

'Doctor Hugh' 3W-GOO mid

This vibrant flower has pure-white tepals and a flat, split, bright-orange cup with a green eye. It is good for showing. (Brian S Duncan, Rathowen Daffodils 1975; AGM-RHS 2001)

'Dream Castle' 3W-W mid (p. 59)

This is similar to, but slightly smaller than 'Chinese White', one of its parents. It increases well and has white flowers with broad tepals forming a perianth nearly 11 cm (4.5 in) wide. The corona is broad and opens cream, aging to white. (G E Mitsch 1963)

'Edna Earl' 3W-OOR mid

A bright flower with white perianth and a small cup that is yellow with a bright red rim. (G A Uit den Boogaard, pre-1950)

'Eminent' 3W-GYY mid

This cool flower has greenish white perianths (9 cm/3.5 in wide) and a small, ribbed corona that is greenish yellow with a green base and deeper yellow rim. Bred from 'Bithynia', it has a smoother perianth. (G E Mitsch 1963)

'Ferndown' 3Y-Y mid (p. 56)

This is a must for show-growers, with 8.5-cm (3.3-in) wide flowers, a smooth perianth, and rounded, pale yellow tepals. The pretty corona is funnel-shaped and notched at the rim, of a slightly deeper yellow with a darker rim to complete the finely finished form. (J W Blanchard 1971, introduced 1990)

'Firebrand' 3WWY-R mid (p. 62)

An old cultivar with small, starry flowers, it has narrow white tepals, stained yellow near the base. The corona is ribbed, straight and brilliant orange. A delicate flower that deserves a place in grass or in shrubberies. (G H Engleheart, 1897)

'Gossamer' 3W-YYP mid
This delicate flower has white perianths (10 cm/4 in across) with slightly reflexed tepals, and a cup-shaped corona that is pale yellow with a narrow pink rim. (G E Mitsch 1962)

'Hammoon' 3W-Y mid
This is a large flower (nearly 11 cm/4.25 in) with broad white tepals that are slightly wavy and a shallow, bowl-shaped corona that is pale yellow with a darker colour around the frilly rim. (D & J W Blanchard 1952, 1968)

'Kazuko' 3W-R mid
A pretty flower with a white, 10-cm (4-in) perianth and a short, flared, red corona. Of smooth substance and a possibility for showing. (J A O'More 1963, P & G Phillips 1975)

'Kildrum' 3W-R mid
A good, bright flower with pure white tepals and a deep, crimson-red corona that is disc-shaped. (W J Dunlop pre-1950)

'Kimmeridge' 3W-YYO mid (p. 44)
A pretty flower, 9.5 cm (3.75 in) across with white tepals and an intricately coloured, ribbed corona that is pale yellow with an orange band around the rim. (D & J W Blanchard 1966)

'Last Word' 3W-GYY late
This hybrid of the *poeticus* 'Cantabile' has white tepals with green and yellow at the base, and a small, yellow corona with a green base. (M J Jefferson-Brown 1985)

'Lichfield' 3W-GYR mid (p. 59)
This cool and pastel flower has a broad, smooth perianth with tepals that have some curling, and a scalloped corona in pale primrose with a delicate band of red at the rim. (C R Wooten 1956)

'Little Jewel' 3W-P mid (p. 57)
A neat flower with rather starry, white perianth and a funnel-shaped corona that is pale yellow at the base and pink around the lobed, frilly edge. The style is prominent. (J A More 1971, intro R G Cull 1985)

'Merlin' 3W-YYR mid
This popular plant is good for showing and for the garden and has white perianths (7.5 cm/3 in wide) shaded yellow at the base and slightly incurled at the apex. The corona is quite flat, deeply lobed and frilled, and is yellow with a reddish rim. (J L Richardson 1956; AGM-RHS 1993)

'Mrs Langtry' ('Lily Langtree') 3W-W mid–late (p. 58)
Though rarely grown today, this was an influential variety in the breeding of later plants with its white colouring, which is only seen on mature flowers. The starry blooms are 8.5 cm (3.3 in) wide with twisted, narrow tepals, and the frilled, straight corona is yellow on opening and ages to white with yellow at the rim. (W Backhouse pre-1869)

Division 3 daffodils
Top row:
'Little Jewel' 3W-P,
'Ravenhill' 3W-GYO.
Second row:
'Park Springs' 3W-WWY,
'Chickerell' 3Y-YYR.
Third row:
'Centrefold' 3W-YYR,
unnamed flower.
Bottom:
'Capisco' 3W-GYR.

'Nonchalant' 3Y-GYY mid–late (p. 56)
Good for showing, this smooth, rounded daffodil has a 9.5-cm (3.75-in) wide perianth of bright, greenish yellow, with heavy-textured, slightly in-curled, tepals and a frilly, flared, slightly darker corona with a green eye. (Jackson's Daffodils 1989)

'Park Springs' 3W-WWY early (p. 57)
This is a fine, beautiful flower for the garden or for showing, with greenish-white tepals forming a perianth 9.5–10.5 cm (3.75–4 in) across. Against this is set a shallow, funnel-shaped corona that is cream-coloured with a rim of buffy yellow around the finely frilled mouth. The bloom is accented by a cold green eye. (Mrs J Abel Smith 1972)

'Perdredda' 3O-R mid
A bright flower with a 9-cm (3.5-in) orange perianth, and a red, bowl-shaped corona. It sometimes produces two flowers per stem. (Brian S Duncan, Dan du Plessis 1996)

'Perimeter' 3Y-YYO early (p. 46)
For many years the standard in its class, this is still a worthy garden plant, and useful for showing. The primrose yellow tepals back a bowl-shaped, deeper yellow corona that is slightly frilled, with a fine reddish rim. (J L Richardson 1956)

'Purbeck' 3W-YOO mid
This superb flower is a good show winner and has broad white tepals forming a perianth 9.5 cm (3.75 in) across, and a small, orange-pink banded, frilly corona that is yellow at the base. (J W Blanchard 1971; AGM-RHS 2001)

'Ravenhill' 3W-GYO mid (p. 57)
This bright flower has a brilliant white perianth, the inner tepals narrower than the outer, and stained yellow at the base. It has a neat, shallow, yellow corona that is lobed and minutely toothed with a bright red rim. (T Bloomer, introduced by Rathowen Daffodils 1984)

'Redstart' 3W-GWO mid (p. 44)
The bright white perianth backs a short, ivory white corona, green at the base and with a coral pink rim. (G E Mitsch 1959)

'Riding Mill' 3W-Y mid–late
A fine flower with a white, circular perianth 10.5 cm (4 in) across and a pale yellow, shallow corona that is deeper at the rim. (G Harrison 1968)

'Sabine Hay' 3O-R mid
This show-winning daffodil is also good for the garden, where its rich colouring will always turn heads. The 9.5-cm (3.75-in) orange perianth is made up of broad tepals that overlap by half their length or more, while the small, flattish corona is a bright, orange-red. Best in some shade to prevent fading. (D B Milne, B C James 1970)

'Seagull' 3 W-Y mid–late (p. 58)
This is a large flower, up to 12.5 cm (5 in) wide, with white tepals stained yellow at the base, and a ribbed, yellow corona that is rimmed with

orange at first but ages to pure yellow. It is similar to 'Albatross', although that retains its orange rim. (G H Engleheart pre-1893)

'Segovia' 3 W-Y mid–late (p. 52)

At last this pretty flower is becoming widely available, and it is a fine addition to the garden. Dwarf in habit, it has 5-cm (2-in) wide flowers with a slightly reflexed, white perianth, and a disc-shaped, greenish-yellow corona. (Mrs F M Gray 1962; AGM-RHS 1996)

'Sidley' 3W-GYY mid

This short, good garden plant has flowers 7 cm (2.75 in) across with white tepals, and a short corona that is yellow, green at the base, and darker at the rim. (T Bloomer, Rathowen Daffodils 1982)

'Sunrise' 3W-YYO mid (p. 58)

Obviously popular in the early 20th century, Bowles describes it as 'too well known as a popular market flower to need lengthy description'. It has rather irregular and flimsy flowers that face downwards and have white tepals, streaked through the midrib with gold, and a shallow, bright-orange split corona. Like many early orange flowers, it burns in the sun. Bowles should have the last word: 'It is unsuitable for garden decoration, burning quickly and possessing limp, yellowish green leaves, which always look unhealthy.' (Mrs R O Backhouse pre-1901)

'Tamar Lad' 3Y-O mid (p. 56)

This fine flower, with a smooth, broad perianth 9.5 cm (3.75 in) across, has golden tepals with an orange tint when young, and a shallow, bowl-shaped, lightly frilled corona in deep orange. (Brian S Duncan, introduced by Dan du Plessis 1996)

'Tiffany Jade' 3Y-YYR mid (p. 56)

The 9.5-cm (3.75-in) wide flowers have broad, pale yellow tepals, and a shallow, yellow corona with a band of red around the lightly frilled rim. (R A Scamp, introduced by S Holden 1996)

'Tranquil Morn' 3W-W mid (p. 59)

From the same breeding as 'Dreamcastle' ('Green Island' and 'Chinese White') this huge flower has a broad white perianth (12 cm/4.75 in) and a small, flat corona that is cream-coloured on

opening and changes to white with age. Similar to 'Chinese White', but larger and with better poise. (G E Mitsch 1962)

'Triple Crown' 3Y-GYR mid

This lovely flower has golden yellow tepals that are incurved at their edges, and a small, bowl-shaped corona with dark red rim. It is vigorous and quick to increase. (Brian S Duncan, Rathowen Daffodils 1987; AGM-RHS 1998)

'Tullybeg' 3W-GYR late

A beautiful flower with a pure white, smooth, 8.5-cm (3.3-in) perianth and a corona that is green at the base, merging to yellow and tipped with red. (Ballydorn Bulb Farm 1979)

Pale daffodils
Top row:
'Envoy' 1W-W, unregistered,
'Abalone' 2W-YYP.
Second row:
'Lichfield' 3W-GYR,
'Arcady' 2 W-YWP.
Third row:
'Silvermere' 2W-W,
'Tranquil Morn' 3W-W.
Bottom row:
'Beige Beauty' 3Y-Y,
'Dream Castle' 3W-W.

'Vernal Prince' 3W-GYY mid

This cool flower, 10 cm (4 in) across, has smooth white tepals, slightly reflexed, and a lemon yellow, bowl-shaped corona that is deeper at the edge and green in the eye. (T Bloomer, Rathowen Daffodils 1982; AGM-RHS 2001)

'Verona' 3W-W mid–late

Yet another offspring of 'Green Island' and 'Chinese White', this has long been a popular show flower because of its 10-cm (4-in) wide white flowers with smooth perianths. The corona is small and lies flat against the perianth; it opens cream-coloured but ages to pure white. (J L Richardson 1958; AGM-RHS 1993)

'Virginia Waters' 3W-GWY mid

This is a cool, pretty flower with broad tepals of pure white, well overlapped to produce a circular, 9-cm (3.5-in) perianth and a white, flat corona that is green at the base and yellow at the frilly rim. (R A Scamp 1995)

'Whitbourne' 3W-GYR late

This flower has pure white tepals and a frilly, small cup that is green at the base, shading to yellow, and rimmed with red. It resembles 'Merlin' but is even better. (M J Jefferson-Brown 1975)

'White Lady' 3W-Y mid (p. 58)

This pretty old flower, with *N. triandrus* subsp. *pallidulus* as the pollen parent, has a white perianth, 8.5 cm (3.3 in) wide with fairly broad tepals for its time, and a ribbed, lobed corona of bright yellow. Its delicate appearance and fragrance endear it to lovers of old things but Bowles (in *The Narcissus*) was rather mean when describing it: 'She can provide as good a drift of white as any *poeticus*, but for inside there is a cup so ragged that it would disgrace a recent seedling. It has been described as "daintily crimped", though to others it suggests the remains of a slug's hearty meal. For distant effect plant "White Lady" freely, but do not look into her face.' In *My Garden in Spring*, he is even more disparaging: 'I quarrel with her name on account of that cup, for no lady would go out with so clean and fresh a white skirt over such a bedraggled petticoat … The distant effect may be a white lady but close at hand the rags

spell white slut.' (G H Engleheart pre-1897) 'Ornatus' x *N. triandrus* subsp. *pallidulus*

DIVISION 4
Double Daffodils

Taste is a strange thing, and double daffodils are not universally loved. Officially, this division includes flowers that have doubling of the perianth segments, or corona, or both. There may also be more than one flower per stem, so it includes some odd bedfellows. Doubles can be beautiful, especially the many modern cultivars that have a formality best appreciated on the show bench. But I also like some of the old doubles, such as 'Sulphur Phoenix', which have informal, 'fluffy' flowers that look so lovely in the garden and also when picked and brought indoors with lilac and bluebells.

People who dislike doubles will argue that, apart from being ugly, the flowers are too heavy for their stems and the blooms often abort before opening, drying in their spathes. Some of the most popular doubles, including 'White Lion' and 'Golden Ducat', suffer from poor stems, but you should not condemn the group because of the behaviour of these two rotters. 'Golden Ducat' and 'Dick Wilden' are double sports of single-flowered daffodils, and it is too much to expect the stems to be able to support the massive increase in tissue weight. But modern doubles have been selected both for their flowers and for their ability to support them, and most will thrust their flowers into your face as you pass, in all but the windiest spot. Give them a try.

'Abba' 4W-O mid–late

This fine sport of 'Cragford' joins the ranks of 'Sir Winston Churchill', 'Bridal Crown' and 'Cheerfulness' as multi-flowered double sports derived from Division 8. Grow it for its strong stems, and for its lovely white flowers with irregular centres streaked with orange. (J M van Dijk 1984)

'Acropolis' 4W-O mid–late (p. 65)

This is a beautiful, large flower of striking contrasts. The white tepals create a flower 11 cm (4.25 in) across, with a few extra tepals interspersed with brilliant tangerine segments. It is strong and good for the garden, and fragrant too. (J L Richardson 1955)

'Amstel' 4W-YPP late (p. 64)

The strong stems and fully double shape, with masses of pink, yellow-based corona segments, make this a fine show flower of good colour and symmetrical shape. (Brian S Duncan 1988)

'Apotheose' 4Y-O mid

The large flowers (10.5 cm/4 in) have golden yellow tepals, the outer rows overlaid, and orange petaloids interspersed in the centre of the flower. A popular, reliable cultivar. (Oregon Bulb Farms, C Breed 1975)

'Baldock' 4 Y-P mid–late (p. 61)

A loosely double flower with tepals that open yellow and age to pink. (M Hamilton, Koanga Daffodils 1992)

'Beauvallon' 4Y-ORR mid (p. 65)

This hybrid of the famous 'Tahiti' daffodil has large flowers, up to 10 cm (4 in) across, with greenish-yellow tepals and heavily frilled corona segments that are orange tipped with red, and half the length of the perianth segments. (D A Lloyd 1969)

'Blushing Maiden' 4W-P mid (p. 64)

This flower resembles 'Replete' but has looser flower form and is less widely available (I bought 'Replete' in a supermarket, albeit a good one). The flowers are big, 11 cm (4.25 in) across, with white tepals and deep, reddish pink corona segments. (Murray W Evans 1970, David Sheppard 1985)

'Bridal Crown' 4 W-Y early (p. 38)

Times change, and so do our favourite plants. When I was a child, the only multi-headed double available was 'Cheerfulness' and its yellow sport. But, at the beginning of the 21st century, their position of supremacy is threatened by 'Bridal Crown'. I think this is largely due to the early flowering of the newcomer, making it perfect for forcing in pots, and I have bought many pots of them just coming into flower in the local market; they now flower happily in the garden. The flowers are 4 cm (1.5 in) across, loose and informal, with several rows of cream tepals with yellow midribs, interspersed with pieces of

pale orange corona segments. There are two or three flowers per stem and they are sweetly scented. You cannot have too many bulbs of this. Despite the mix-up of photos (and possibly bulbs) in many catalogues, it cannot be confused with 'Cheerfulness' because that has an intact corona, or 'Sir Winston Churchill', which has flowers 6 cm (2.3 in) across. See also 'L'Innocence' in Division 8. (J Schoorl pre-1949)

'Butter and Eggs' 4Y-O
(also known as 'Yellow Phoenix') (p. 62)

It is easy to get excited about the latest doubles and forget some of the older daffodils that enchanted gardeners in Victorian times. Surely they have little to offer us today? Well, I would argue that they have much to offer, and the ones I would avoid instead are the common, mediocre

Yellow double daffodils
Top row:
'John Daniel' 4Y-Y,
'Poppy's Choice' 4Y-R,
'Sherborne' 4Y-Y.
Second row:
'Castle Rings' 4Y-R,
'Tahiti' 4Y-O.
Third row:
'Radjel' 4Y-R,
'Merrymeet' 4Y-YOO,
'Golden Bear' 4Y-Y.
Bottom row:
'Kiwi Sunset' 4 Y-R,
'Baldock' 4 Y-P.

Old daffodils
Top row:
'Glowing Phoenix' 4Y-O,
'Sulphur Phoenix' 4W-Y.
Second row:
'Butter and Eggs' 4Y-O,
'Codlins and Cream' 4 W-O.
Third row:
'Fashion' 11bY-Y/O,
'Mitylene' 2W-Y.
Bottom row:
'Firebrand' 3WWY-R,
'Lucifer' 2W-YOO.

garden-centre doubles. Go for the latest for perfection of form, but also look at some of the older ones: they are so different to most common doubles that they might as well be new. 'Butter and Eggs' is one of these, a frilly flower with narrow segments in two shades of yellow that will totally enchant you and take you back to your childhood with its scent. E A Bowles described them as 'doubles that were garden favourites in the seventeenth century and are still grown where gardeners are wise enough to value old plants of reliably vigorous constitution'. (pre-1777)

'Calgary' 4W-W mid
This is a double form of 'Thalia' and has pure white flowers with numerous tepals but no sign of a corona. It is far more elegant and pleasant than 'White Marvel'.

'Candida' 4 W-Y mid
This large (10.5 cm/4 in) flower has white tepals interspersed with large, creamy segments. It is not too full, and looks cool and elegant. (J L Richardson 1956)

'Castle Rings' 4Y-R mid (p. 61)
This has round flowers created by the breadth of the golden outer perianth row. The flower builds with another two or three rows laid above these, with a ruffled centre of broad tepals interspersed with red corona segments. Good poise, strong stems and some fragrance add to its charms. A regular show winner. (R A Scamp 2002)

'Cheerfulness' 4W-Y late
One of the most popular of all garden daffodils, available everywhere. It flowers late and each strong stem has two or three double, creamy flowers, 2 cm (0.75 in) across, the extra tepals confined within the corona. Above all, it is late and fragrant. It has sported to 'Yellow Cheerfulness', which is identical except for the colour. See also 'Bridal Crown' and 'Elvira', Division 8. (J B van der Schoot, pre-1923; AGM-RHS 1995)

'Codlins and Cream' (also known, wrongly, as 'Sulphur Phoenix') mid (p. 62)
Like 'Butter and Eggs', this is another fine old plant with narrow tepals creating a frilly flower on much thinner stems than most modern doubles. The tepals are creamy white, and the short corona segments are yellow. (pre-1820)

'Crackington' 4Y-O mid (p. 46)
This is a reliable orange and yellow. The corona segments are frilled, and are half the length of the yellow tepals; they open orange and fade a little as they mature. It increases well, and the fine flowers are weather resistant. It wins on the show bench and has neat, low foliage. (D Lloyd, J W Blanchard 1986; AGM-RHS 1998)

'Delnashaugh' 4W-P late
Bringing the season to its conclusion, this popular dull-pink-and-white double has large (10.5 cm/4 in) flowers with pure white, broad

tepals, interspersed with rose-pink corona segments. It is increasingly available as a commercial plant. (J S B Lea 1978)

'Double Event' 4 W-Y mid
The moderately sized (9 cm/3.5 in) flowers have broad white tepals interspersed with short, frilled corona segments. It is a vigorous plant and has good form. (J L Richardson pre-1952; AGM-RHS 1993)

'Double Fashion' 4Y-O mid
A white or creamy flower, 10 cm (4 in) across, with yellow-orange segments interspersed. Good for the garden and similar to 'Extol'. (J L Richardson, G Zandbergen-Terwegen 1965)

'Duet' 4W-OYY early–mid
This sport of 'Golden Castle' has large (10.5 cm/4 in) flowers, its pale yellow tepals having bright yellow segments that are orange at the base. It has strong stems, and is like a richer-coloured 'Unique'. (P B van Eeden 1980)

'Elixir' 4Y-Y late (p. 65)
A rather loose double with flowers 9.5 cm (3.75 in) wide. The tepals are a bright, light yellow and rather incurved, and the corona segments are deeper yellow and less than half the length of the tepals. (G E Mitsch 1976)

'Ensemble' 4Y-Y mid–late (p. 46)
This large (12 cm/4.75 in) flower has golden tepals and slightly deeper corona segments, almost as long as the tepals. A bold, beautiful flower that opens well and has good stems. (Murray Evans 1974, 1986)

'Erlicheer' 4W-Y early (p. 51)
This pretty flower, ideal for cutting and useful because it is so early, has between six and twelve small flowers per stem, each comprising three or four rows of white tepals with short yellow corona segments between. These delicate flowers are sweetly scented. Its synonyms (alternative names) include 'Cheerfulness' (which is very confusing) and 'Gaiety'. (M Gardiner pre-1934)

'Exotic Beauty' 4W-P mid–late
This late flower has rather reflexed tepals and a cup stuffed with pink petaloids.

'Gay Kybo' 4W-O mid
This large flower of neat form has layers of creamy tepals interspersed with orange segments. It has strong stems, ideal for the show bench and the garden. (Mrs H K Richardson, du Plessis Bros 1980; AGM-RHS 1995)

'Gay Time' 4W-R late
This large flower (11 cm/4.25 in) has strong stems and is white, interspersed with short, frilly red segments. (J L Richardson pre-1952)

'Glowing Phoenix' 4Y-O early (p. 62)
These ragged flowers with narrow tepals reach 10 cm (4 in) across and have an old-fashioned charm. The tepals are primrose yellow, while the short corona segments are one third their length, and clear orange. (R O Backhouse pre-1930)

'Golden Bear' 4Y-Y (p. 61)
Combining the form of 'Smokey Bear' and the all-round vigour and some colour of 'Sportsman', this has large (11 cm/4.25 in) flowers with deep yellow tepals and luscious, deep gold, frilled corona segments. A superb and colourful flower with good stems. (Brian S Duncan 1992)

'Golden Ducat' 4Y-Y (p. 76)
This is the best known of all doubles and is readily available. Sports are unusual among daffodils, but they are the source of many doubles and in this case it was a sport of 'King Alfred'. It has large (11 cm/4.25 in) blooms with layers of golden tepals and can be lovely, though it lacks substance. But it tends to flop in the garden and is prone to abort buds when deprived of water. (Speelman & Sons pre-1947)

'Honolulu' 4W-R mid
From the same stable, and the same year, as 'Tahiti', this has bold flowers of red and white on strong stems. (J L Richardson 1956)

'Ice King' 4W-Y mid
This sport of 'Ice Follies' has all the good qualities of that plant but the corona is stuffed full of creamy petaloids that rarely exceed the length of the corona rim. It is distinctive and popular, although not to my taste. (A P van den Berg-Hytuna 1984)

White and pink double daffodils

Top row:
'Kiwi Magic' 4W-Y,
'Blushing Maiden' 4W-P,
'Peach Prince' 4W-O.
Second row:
'Night Music' 4W-P,
'Amstel' 4W-YPP.
Bottom row:
'Sugar Loaf' 4W-P,
'Indora' 4W-P,
'Taslass' 4W-Y.

'Indora' 4W-P late (p. 64)

A fine, full, frilly flower with greenish-white tepals, and pale pink, frilly corona segments that are almost as long as the central tepals. (H Cross, 1974, 1984)

'Jamaica Inn' 4W-YOO late

Named by the producers who gave us many daffodils with a Cornish theme, but this time bred in Ireland, this fine (9 cm/3.5 in) double has pure white perianths and an extra four or five smaller tepals mixed among frilly, broad rich apricot corona segments. A fine flower of loose form and heavy substance. (Brian S Duncan, Dan du Plessis 1993)

'John Daniel' 4Y-Y mid (p. 61)

A full double with golden tepals forming a flower 9 cm (3.5 in) across. The corona segments are evenly spaced between the tepals and are yellow-orange. In the centre of the mature flower is a frilly, entire corona rimmed with orange. (R A Scamp 1993)

'Kiwi Magic' 4W-Y mid (p. 64)

This large (11 cm/4.25 in), substantial flower has white, slightly concave tepals and long, wavy-edged corona segments that open lemon yellow but fade to cream. A superb flower, let down somewhat by poor stems. (Max Hamilton, Koanga Daffodils 1989)

'Kiwi Sunset' 4 Y-R mid (p. 61)

A moderately sized flower, 9.5 cm (3.75 in) across, with bright yellow tepals and bright, deep orange, wavy corona segments, about half their length. (Koanga Daffodils 1995)

'Lingerie' 4W-Y mid

This large (11.5 cm/4.5 in), vigorous flower has white tepals and lemon yellow corona segments on strong stems. (Murray W Evans 1977; AGM-RHS 2000)

'Madam Speaker' 4Y-O early (p. 42)

This is a fine flower with yellow and orange flowers of medium size and show quality, on strong stems. Created to celebrate the work of the Marie Curie Cancer Care charity, and chosen by the Speaker of the British House of Commons, Betty Boothroyd, it is excellent for the garden too. (R A Scamp 1998)

'Madison' 4W-O mid (p. 65)

This double has several rows of white tepals, the inner ones rather creased and folded, and pale orange corona segments in the centre. The components are not well mixed but it is a pretty flower. (unregistered)

'Manly' 4Y-O mid

This good, all-purpose daffodil has small (5 cm/2 in), neat flowers of yellow and orange. It grows well in the garden and has strong stems. (J L Richardson, W Blom & Son 1972; AGM-RHS 2002)

'Mary Copeland' 4W-O mid–late

This old daffodil, bred from the ancient 'Orange Phoenix', is still one to beat for vigour and for garden display. The flowers are large (10 cm/4 in) with white tepals, and frilly orange and scarlet segments interspersed in the loose centre. It may not have the formal style of modern doubles, but it is beautiful in the garden as well as cut, when the delicious fragrance can be appreciated. (W F M Copeland, pre-1913)

'Merrymeet' 4Y-YOO late (p. 61)

The flowers are 10.5 cm (4 in) across, with a few extra golden tepals and broad, ruffled orange corona segments. It has show form and is a strong grower, so good for the garden as well. (Mrs H K Richardson, du Plessis Bros)

***Narcissus poeticus* 'Plenus' 4W-W**

This is the oldest of doubles, but few have bothered to improve upon it – notable exceptions are 'Rose of Mey' (G L Wilson pre-1950) and 'Adoration' (G E Mitsch 1972, a semi-double). It has many names, including simply 'Double White' and *gardenia narcissus*. It is a gorgeous flower with many rows of white tepals and a heady scent. If you rummage in the centre of the flowers you can find traces of red corona, but these are not obvious. It grows well in moist soil but will reward dry soil with dry spathes and dead buds. It is even later to flower than *N. poeticus*, and is worth a try because of its beauty. (pre-1700)

'Night Music' 4W-P mid (p. 64)

This gorgeous flower has broad, white tepals creating a flower 8.5 cm (3.3 in) across. The tepals in the centre are shorter and in-curled, and the corona segments are half their length, frilled and deep salmon pink, quite intense at the edges and rather yellow at the base. A superb bloom. (G E Mitsch 1984)

'Obdam' 4W-W mid (p. 38, 66)

From my experience, this is a rather scruffy double with a very broad corona, golden at the base, and with an irregular amount of doubling. It is another sport of 'Ice Follies', but no improvement. (C J Bakker 1984)

'Odorus Rugulosus Flore Pleno', 'Odorus Plenus'

see 'Odorus Rugulosus', Division 7

'Papua' 4Y-Y mid

These 9-cm (3.5-in) wide flowers have bright, greenish-yellow tepals, and lovely orange-yellow corona segments. (J L Richardson 1961; AGM-RHS 1993)

'Peach Prince' 4W-O mid (p. 64)

This large (10 cm/4 in) flower has white tepals and,

in the centre, a mass of bright, orange-coral, frilly corona segments interspersed with a few white tepals. A flashy flower. (Murray W Evans 1985)

'Petit Four' 4W-PPY mid

This is rather like 'Ice King', but is actually a sport of 'Champagne'. It has a white perianth, 11 cm (4.25 in) across, and salmon pink corona stuffed with petaloids. It is widely available, but in my view nothing special. (R Rijnveld & Sons 1961)

'Pink Pageant' 4W-P mid

A large, round flower of white, with deep pink segments clustered in the centre, and with strong stems. The tepals are thick and clean, and the centre of the flower has a good balance of pink and white. A good show flower. (Brian S Duncan, Rathowen Daffodils 1976)

Double daffodils

Top row:
'Elixir' 4Y-Y,
'Acropolis' 4W-O.
Second row:
'Madison' 4W-O,
'Unique' 4W-Y.
Third row:
'Tahiti' 4Y-O,
'Yellow Cheerfulness' 4Y-Y.
Bottom row:
'Beauvallon' 4Y-ORR.

'Pink Paradise' 4W-P mid

This is an excellent double with a smooth white perianth and broad, frilly, bright pink segments interspersed at the front. It grows and flowers well, and has strong stems and necks. Its main assets are the lack of any orange in the corona segments, and its fine form. (Brian S Duncan, Rathowen Daffodils 1976)

'Poppy's Choice' 4Y-R mid (p. 61)

This strong plant is useful for the show bench and the garden alike, and has 9.5-cm (3.75-in) wide flowers with golden tepals and reddish-orange corona segments. The colour intensifies as the flower matures. In the garden the plant is a bit leafy. (R A Scamp, S Holden 1996)

'Radjel' 4Y-R early–mid (p. 61)

These neat, sun-proof flowers have broad, golden yellow tepals and deep red, wavy perianth segments some 7.5 cm (3 in) wide. It may be small but it is perfectly formed, and a lovely bloom both for cutting and for showing. (R A Scamp 1994)

'Replete' 4 W-P mid (p. 38)

Though this does not have the show form of 'Pink Paradise' and later pink-and-white doubles, it is quite good enough to please in the garden. The large (10.5 cm/4 in) flowers have broad, white tepals at the back and shorter, crumpled tepals at the front of the flower, interspersed with deep, red-pink corona segments. Very showy and impressive. (Murray W Evans 1975)

'Rip Van Winkle' 4Y-Y very early (p. 76)

This is a bit of an oddity, and may be a sport of *N. pumilus* or *N. pseudonarcissus*, but it is so fully double that it is hardly recognizable as a daffodil at all, and for that reason is loved by some but hated by many. It is a short plant with 15-cm (6-in) stems and narrow leaves, and the 5-cm (2-in) flowers comprise innumerable yellow tepals, and corona segments that are narrow and tinged with green. The scruffy flowers are quite cute even if they lack the finesse of most others, and it is worth trying at least once. (pre-1884)

'Serena Lodge' 4W-Y mid–late

With the same parentage as 'Golden Bear', this has flowers 10.5 cm (4 in) wide, of good form, with white tepals and a full centre of golden corona segments. These are held in strong stems and the flowers last well, making it a sure-fire show winner. (Brian S Duncan 1992; AGM-RHS 1999)

'Sherborne' 4Y-Y mid (p. 61)

This has yellow flowers, 10.5 cm (4 in) across with several layers of greenish-yellow tepals, and wavy-edged, orange-yellow corona segments. (D A Lloyd, J W Blanchard 1989)

'Sir Winston Churchill' 4W-O mid

This sport of 'Geranium' has the largest flowers of the several double sports of Division 8 plants. For this reason it has proved popular, and I am sure it will become more common, nudging 'Cheerfulness' from the popularity lists, which would be a shame. 'Sir Winston Churchill' usually has four flowers on the stem, each 6 cm (2.3 in) across, and a delicious scent, so is difficult to ignore. The blooms have white tepals shaded with gold on the midrib, and scattered, orange corona segments. (Unknown, H A Holmes 1966; AGM-RHS 1998)

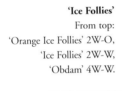

'Ice Follies'
From top:
'Orange Ice Follies' 2W-O,
'Ice Follies' 2W-W,
'Obdam' 4W-W.

'Spaniards Inn' 4W-P late (p. 89)
A fine flower with a pure-white perianth and a few extra, broad tepals, the inner ones small and curled, mixed with broad corona segments in the centre. The combination of pure white and frilly, peachy pink is very pleasing. (Brian S Duncan, Dan du Plessis 1993)

'Sugar Loaf' 4W-P late (p. 64)
This large (10.5 cm/4 in) flower has white tepals, narrower than the modern style, with frilly pink corona segments interspersed with a few other tepals in the centre. A fresh, bright flower that is not very doubled. (Murray W Evans 1968, 1980)

'Sulphur Phoenix' 4W-Y mid–late (p. 62)
A lovely old double with layers of pale yellow tepals that decrease in size near the centre. Between these are small, deeper-yellow corona segments that are hardly visible. It is a shaggy bloom with thin stems. (pre-1820)

'Tahiti' 4Y-O (p. 61, 65)
This is a prolific, neat, orange-red and gold double that has been much used in breeding later generations of flowers. It has strong stems and is not too doubled, so the deep orange segments show up well. The blooms are 11 cm (4.25 in) across. (J L Richardson 1956; AGM-RHS 1995)

'Tamar Fire' 4Y-R mid (p. 46)
Bred from 'Tonga', this flower is similar but longer lasting. The neat blooms are 7 cm (2.75 in) across with broad, bright-yellow tepals, decreasing in size nearer the centre, interspersed with red, frilly, corona segments, A lovely bloom and a fine, bright, garden plant. (Mrs H K Richardson, du Plessis Bros 1976; AGM-RHS 1998)

'Taslass' 4W-Y mid (p. 64)
The rounded flowers are composed of broad, white tepals, interspersed with frilly, pale-yellow corona segments that are deeper yellow at the edge. The blooms are full and beautifully formed. (H G Cross 1974, 1984)

'Telamonius Plenus'
see 'Van Sion'

'Texas' 4Y-O mid
This old double has many layers of yellow tepals, and frilled orange corona segments. (Mrs R O Backhouse pre-1912)

'Unique' 4W-Y early–mid (p. 65)
This popular, vigorous double has strong stems and good flowers, its creamy white tepals being interspersed with prominent, bright-yellow segments. (J L Richardson, G Zandbergen-Terwegen 1961; AGM-RHS 2002)

'Van Sion' 4 Y-Y (also known as 'Telamonius Plenus', 'Vincent Sion', 'Wilmer's Great Double Daffodil')
This was one of the first daffodils I ever noticed, growing in the field around an old house when I was a child. It grew in dense woodland under pines and in openings under shrubs, and its rich gold, double flowers were a wonder, so for sentimental reasons I rate it far higher than its form should logically dictate. But plants are about association and history as well as beauty. This daffodil, according to E A Bowles, was first mentioned by John Parkinson in his *Paradisus* (1629). He wrote that a Fleming living in London, Vincent Sion, had grown it there for many years before it flowered in 1620, and then, before his death, gave bulbs to both Parkinson and George Wilmer, who then appears to have named it after himself. Taxonomist (and splitter) Adrian Haworth (*Narcissorum Revisio*, 1819) invented the name Ajax Telamon for the plant, naming it after the father of the Greek mythological hero Ajax (Ajax was the name given for the genus of trumpet daffodils – and you thought the classification was complex before!). It is a large (10 cm/4 in) and variable flower, with narrow, twisted tepals of pale greenish-yellow, and it is fully double, with alternating layers of tepals and corona tissue, the latter being a deeper yellow. Sometimes the outer corona is split, at other times it is unbroken, giving a trumpet that is stuffed full of bits and pieces. Despite its great age it is still vigorous, and you often see clumps in bloom in old gardens and in fields and woodland, relics of a past civilization. (pre-1620)

'Westward' 4W-Y mid
Like 'Unique', this is a seedling of 'Falaise', and has similar colouring. It is a good, strong, garden plant. (J L Richardson, G Zandbergen-Terwegen 1962)

'White Lion' 4W-WYY mid
One of the most popular of all doubles and available everywhere, it has large flowers with white tepals, interspersed with creamy yellow segments that fade as the flower matures. Despite its popularity and its award, its stems are not strong enough to support the heavy flowers and, not wanting to provide food for slugs, I make room for better things. It does however make a good cut flower. (de Graaff-Gerharda pre-1949; AGM-RHS 1993)

'White Marvel' 4W-W mid (p. 70, 88)
The triandrus 'Tresamble' sported to produce this white double with two or three pendent flowers, their cups stuffed full of white petalloids. It is popular and, amazingly, the stems seem able to cope with the extra weight, so I keep it – but it always looks to me as though someone has tried to suffocate the blooms with tissues. (G Zandbergen-Terwegen pre-1950)

'Yellow Cheerfulness' 4Y-Y late (p. 65)
This sport of 'Cheerfulness' is identical to its parent except in colour, which is primrose yellow instead of cream and is just as late and fragrant. Sometimes blooms show chimaeral streaks, or segments of cream-coloured tissue. (Eggink Bros 1937; AGM-RHS 1995)

DIVISION 5
Triandrus Daffodils

The official classification of these hybrids is that the characteristics of *Narcissus triandrus* are clearly evident, which seems fair enough. This means that they must have two or more pendent flowers per stem, and tepals that reflex, so they should be easy to recognize if you know what *N. triandrus* looks like. Bear in mind, however, that most of these plants are much bigger than the original species, and that poor bulbs may only produce one flower per stem, so if everything else seems right, do not dismiss them because of flower count. They are universally lovely but seem to be more prone to virus than other divisions. Most are sterile, which is no problem for the gardener, but frustrating for the breeder. The earliest-known hybrids were with *N. pseudonarcissus*: 'Queen of Spain' and 'King of Spain', which both had pale-

yellow flowers. But most of the flowers in this division have white or pale flowers. Crossing daffodils of different divisions gives registrars and botanists nightmares, but it gives gardeners great plants. After 'Thalia', 'Hawera' (from the mating of triandrus and jonquil) must be the best known of this division, and a very fine plant.

'Akepa' 5W-P late
This is the first of the pink-cupped triandrus daffodils, and has two flowers per stem. The tepals are broad and the corona is long, cylindrical, and a good, even pink. A desirable novelty and one for the show bench, but without some of the charm of the species. (G E Mitsch 1979)

'April Tears' 5Y-Y late
Bred by combining *N. jonquilla* and *N. triandrus*, this fine plant has four or five 4-cm (1.5-in) wide flowers per stem. They closely resemble the more popular 'Hawera', but this has a more delicate appearance, smaller corona and darker colour, and flowers a week later. It may be a better plant, but the common 'Hawera' is a good substitute. (A Gray pre-1939; AGM-RHS 1996)

'Arish Mell' 5W-W mid
Considered by many to be the benchmark by which others are measured, this fine plant has stems with three or four flowers of pure-white, reflexed, narrow tepals and a long, straight corona. (D & J W Blanchard 1961)

'Budock Bells' 5W-W mid–late
This new triandrus has up to three large (9 cm/3.5 in) flowers per stem. These are pure white with broad, slightly reflexed tepals and long, cup-shaped coronas. It usually produces a second crop of stems. (R A Scamp 1995)

'Hawera' 5Y-Y mid (p. 70)
It is extraordinary that this fine plant is so old; it is perfect for every garden and has real star quality and beauty. The foliage is very narrow and green, and each stem produces up to eight nodding flowers that are lemon yellow with a neat cup and reflexing tepals. Only 20 cm (8 in) tall, it has a long season and usually produces secondary stems. Although said to increase slowly it is good and perennial, and bulbs that I planted along with *Hakonechloa* (Japanese forest grass) have

increased, with no trouble, as I have split the grass. 'April Tears' is similar but less common. You must plant this! (W M Thomson pre-1928; AGM-RHS 1995)

'Horn of Plenty' 5W-W mid (p. 69)
Among many triandrus hybrids that are rather similar, this stands out as exceptional. Though purists will hate it because the corona is uncompromisingly large, it is an outstanding flower with big, cylindrical trumpets under the 6-cm (2.3-in) wide perianth, all in creamy white with a flash of green and yellow on the tube behind the flowers and above the ovary. (C G van Tubergen pre-1947)

'Ice Wings' 5W-W mid (p. 69)
This is among the finest of the group, with clusters of two or three nodding pure white flowers with reflexed tepals on 22-cm (8.5-in) stems. (C F Coleman 1958; AGM-RHS 2001)

'Icicle' 5W-W early
This very fine plant has two to four 3-cm (1.25-in) wide flowers per stem. Each is pure white with reflexed tepals, and a neat corona that is often slightly constricted at the mouth. The blooms open when the stems are only 5 cm (2 in) high, but extend to 15 cm (6 in) as they mature. It is superior to 'Raindrop'. (D & J W Blanchard 1962)

'Lapwing' 5W-Y mid (p. 35)
This seedling of 'Petrel' only has one or two flowers per stem, but these are pretty and have a lemon-yellow corona beneath the white perianth. (G E Mitsch 1975)

'Lemon Drops' 5Y-Y mid
This is another winner from American Grant Mitsch, who crossed *N. triandrus* with 'Fortune' to create this beauty. It has up to three, substantial, pendent flowers per stem, with reflexing white tepals and a broad, pale yellow corona. It flowers freely over a long period. (G E Mitsch 1956; AGM-RHS 2002)

'Liberty Bells' 5Y-Y mid–late
Two or three bright, greenish-yellow flowers are produced on each 30-cm (12-in) stem, with slightly reflexed tepals and long coronas. This daffodil is quite readily available, is showy and

bright, and lasts well. (F Rijnveld & Sons pre-1950)

'Merry Bells' 5W-Y mid (p. 69)
Though not often seen, this is a fine plant with two or three flowers per stem. It has broad, reflexed white tepals, stained yellow at the base, and a broad, funnel-shaped corona in bright, lemon yellow. (Oregon Bulb Farms 1958)

'Mission Bells' 5W-W mid
This has between one and three ivory-white flowers per stem, with long coronas, and is like 'Silver Bells' but more vigorous. (G E Mitsch 1976, R & E Havens 1987; AGM-RHS 2001)

'Niveth' 5W-W mid–late (p. 69)
Old but still valuable, this has lovely, pendent flowers with short coronas that are brilliant white with a silky texture. (H Backhouse pre-1931)

'Petrel' 5W-W late (p. 70)
This is a lovely, small plant with two or more stems from each bulb, often with a second flush,

Triandrus daffodils
Top row:
'Ice Wings' 5W-W,
'Merry Bells' 5W-Y,
'Silver Bells' 5W-W.
Second row:
'Thoughtful' 5Y-Y,
'Horn of Plenty' 5W-W.
Bottom row:
'Tresamble' 5W-W,
'Niveth' 5W-W.

Mixed daffodils
Photographed with
Nonnea and *Leucojum*.
Top row:
'Petrel' 5W-W,
'Hawera' 5Y-Y,
'White Marvel' 4W-W.
Second row:
'Pipit' 7YYW-W,
'Curlew' 7W-W.
Third row:
'Marie-Jose' 11bW-Y/OW,
'Binkie' 2Y-W.
Bottom row:
'Bell Song' 7W-P,
'Stainless' 2W-W.

and each with five or more flowers. These are pure white and pendent with flaring tepals and small, neat coronas. The jonquil in its breeding, adds to its elegance and makes it a strong grower. Delicate and recommended. (G E Mitsch 1970)

'Rippling Waters' 5W-W mid

This profuse plant has stems with three flowers, which are white, touched with yellow at the base of the tepals, and with a funnel-shaped corona. It is taller than 'Tresamble' and has bluer foliage. (Barr & Sons pre-1932; AGM-RHS 1995)

'Shot Silk' 5W-W mid

Another old hybrid, this has three flowers per stem. Each has a starry perianth made of narrow tepals and a long corona, all in white. (de Graaff Bros pre-1931)

'Silver Bells' 5W-W late (p. 69)

This has dumpier flowers than 'Ice Wings', with shorter, broader tepals and a larger corona, but still graceful. (G E Mitsch 1962)

'Tater-du' 5W-Y mid

Looking like pendent lanterns, the yellow flowers of this new cultivar are carried in pairs or triplets on short stems. The blooms have pale yellow, broad, reflexed tepals and broad, ribbed coronas of a deeper yellow. (R A Scamp 1994)

'Thalia' 5W-W late (p. 76)

This may be old, but people still love it – it is possibly the only triandrus daffodil that most gardeners grow. Each stem produces two to four pure-white flowers that nod gracefully, with reflexed, pure-white tepals. It is good for pots and also for general mass planting because of its low cost. (M van Waveren & Sons pre-1916)

'Thoughtful' 5Y-Y early–mid (p. 69)

This has up to three flowers per stem, up to 8.5 cm (3.3 in) across, with pretty, sulphur yellow flowers with broad, funnel-shaped coronas that are ribbed and notched. A distinct and beautiful flower. (A Gray pre-1951)

'Tresamble' 5W-W mid (p. 69)

This resembles 'Thalia' but has better form, with broader tepals that are less reflexed. The corona is creamy white and lightly frilled. There are two or three 9-cm (3.5-in) flowers per stem. (P D Williams pre-1930)

'Tuesday's Child' 5W-Y mid

Like its namesake, this is full of grace, and each of the two or three flowers per stem is 7.5 cm (3 in) across with broad, greenish-white, slightly reflexed tepals and a long, straight, bright yellow corona. (D Blanchard, M J Jefferson-Brown 1964; RHS-AGM 1995)

DIVISION 6
Cyclamineus Daffodils

You cannot mistake *N. cyclamineus* for any other flower, and its hybrids, which make up this division, should show the uniqueness of its shape, with obviously reflexed tepals and one flower per stem at an acute angle and with a short pedicel (the stalk between the flower and the base of the spathe). Hybridizers have pounced on this species to make some marvellous hybrids, and the long, snout-like corona and flicked-back tepals of the species add grace to the hybrids – indeed, when diluted a bit in the hybrids these features can look even more beautiful than in the wild plant. It has also proved to be an easy species to use, being fertile and giving vigorous seedlings. Among the many delightful choices, a few have become staples in the garden, including 'February Gold', 'Peeping Tom', 'Jenny' and 'Jetfire', as well as 'Tête-a-Tête', which cannot sit in this division because of its two flowers per stem.

'Alliance' (or 'The Alliance') 6Y-Y very early

This super, bright, perky flower has golden flowers with swept-back tepals and a stout, strong corona with a flared, frilled mouth. The blooms are held horizontally and are long-lasting. (Rosewarne E H S, M J Jefferson-Brown 1985)

'Bartley' 6Y-Y early

This is similar to 'Peeping Tom' but has slightly smaller flowers. The perianth is 8.5 cm (3.3 in) across with narrow, reflexed tepals, and the corona is long and narrow, a slightly deeper shade of yellow than the tepals. (J C Williams pre-1934)

'Beryl' 6W-YYO early–mid

This is still vigorous and popular, despite its age. The flowers are 7.5 cm (3 in) across and the perianth is pale yellow at first, developing a richer colour as it matures. The corona is cup-shaped and shorter than most of the division, and is yellow with a broad orange rim. (P D Williams pre-1907)

'Carib' 6W-P mid

This is a fine flower with reflexed tepals of pure white and thick substance. Against this sits a broad corona of rich, peach pink. The perianth is 8 cm (3 in) across and the bloom is similar to 'Cotinga', but has a better perianth and flowers earlier. (G E Mitsch 1979)

'Cazique' 6W-W mid

These blooms start pale yellow but they fade to white as they mature. The perianth is 8 cm (3 in) across and slightly reflexed, helping to show off the elegant, white corona. (G E Mitsch 1982)

'Charity May' 6Y-Y mid (p. 73)

This dwarf, free-flowering plant has broad, short, cylindrical coronas with an expanded, frilly mouth and broad, reflexing tepals, all in bright,

clean yellow. This daffodil flowers freely and is vigorous in the garden. (C F Coleman pre-1948; AGM-RHS 1993)

'Coombe Creek' 6Y-O mid–late (p. 42)

A dwarf plant with 8.5-cm (3.3-in) wide, sun-proof flowers. It has ivory tepals, very reflexed and yellow at the base, with a funnel-shaped corona of orange with pink tints, paler at the base. Its short stems suit it to the rock garden but its neat form also makes it suitable for showing. (R A Scamp 1997)

'Cotinga' 6W-P mid (p. 73)

This large flower has wavy, reflexed, ivory white tepals and a long, apricot pink corona that is deeper in colour at the mouth. See also 'Carib', above. (G E Mitsch 1976)

'Dove Wings' 6W-Y early

This is a sister seedling to 'Charity May' and is similar but in yellow and white. The blooms are up to 8.5 cm (3.3 in) across, and the smooth, reflexed tepals are white. The corona is slender, funnel-shaped and bright yellow. (C F Coleman pre-1949; AGM-RHS 1993)

'February Gold' 6Y-Y very early

Despite the fact that this usually flowers in early March rather than in February, it has become one of the most popular small daffodils for naturalizing and garden display. It is a bright flower with swept-back tepals, forming a perianth 7.5 cm (3 in) across, and a long corona that has six lobes and is slightly flared and notched. It lasts well and is a uniform, golden yellow. (de Graaff Bros pre-1923; AGM-RHS 1993)

'February Silver' 6W-Y early

This daffodil is basically the same as 'February Gold', though slightly larger and with white tepals and a primrose yellow corona. (de Graaff Bros pre-1949)

'Foundling' 6W-P mid

This has 'Jenny' as one parent, and it was the first pink cyclamineus I ever grew. It is no longer expensive and is a pretty flower. It is 7 cm (2.75 in) wide with broad, white, recurved tepals and a short, ribbed pink corona that is paler at the base. It is a good garden plant, the flowers augmented by the blue-green leaves. It has been an important parent, giving rise to more recent commercial cultivars such as 'Kaydee' and up-to-date novelties such as 'Kathy's Clown', 'Betsy MacDonald' and 'Coombe Creek', all with similar colouring. (Carncairn Daffodils 1969; AGM-RHS 1995)

'Frostkist' 6W-W mid (p. 51)
This 'Charity May' seedling is similar but has larger (10 cm/4 in) flowers. The corona opens pale yellow and fades to white as it matures. (G E Mitsch 1968)

'Georgie Girl' 6W-GWP mid
Another new cultivar that has 'Foundling' in its ancestry. It is a dwarf plant with broad, white tepals that are reflexed and overlap in the lower half to form a perianth 8.5 cm (3.3 in) across. The short corona is pale yellow when the flower first opens, but changes entirely after a few days, becoming white with green at the base and a broad rim of sun-proof reddish pink around the mouth. (Brian S Duncan 1989)

'Inca' 6YYW-WWY early
Reverse bicolour colouring comes to the division in this super flower, which has an 8-cm (3-in) perianth composed of broad, reflexed tepals that are a biting lemon yellow and white at the base. The corona is long and cylindrical with a slightly rolled mouth, and is greenish-white with a yellow rim. An elegant flower with cool colouring. (G E Mitsch 1979)

'Itzim' 6Y-R mid (p. 38, 76)
This is similar to 'Jetfire' but is slightly taller. The flowers have slightly longer coronas and the tepals are narrower and overlap less. It is a bright flower: the tepals are golden and the long corona is yellow on opening, changing to orange-red after a few days. It is less common than 'Jetfire' but just as worthy of a place in the garden. (G E Mitsch, Rathowen Daffodils 1982; AGM-RHS 1995)

'Jack Snipe' 6W-Y early
This is an easy, free-flowering daffodil with blooms 7 cm (2.75 in) across with reflexed, creamy tepals that are slightly incurved at the edges and a medium-length, cylindrical corona in yellow that is darker at the mouth. A good garden

plant with elegant, bright, nodding flowers. (M P Williams pre-1951; AGM-RHS 1995)

'Jenny' 6W-W mid (p. 73)
This white sibling of 'Charity May' and 'Dove Wings' has large (9 cm/3.5 in) flowers with strongly reflexed, white tepals that are curved and twisted, and a long corona that opens pale yellow and fades to white. The blooms hang their heads gracefully, but it grows strongly. (C F Coleman pre-1943; AGM-RHS 1993)

'Jetfire' 6Y-O early (p. 38)
This superb cultivar is from the same breeder as 'Itzim', but despite obvious similarities, it has a different parentage. Its strengths are the bright yellow, reflexed perianth, 7.5 cm (3 in) across, and the cylindrical, ribbed, bright orange corona. It is neat and ideal for window-boxes and containers, and the flowers have a light scent. The stems elongate as the flowers open and, to add to the length of the display, secondary stems are usually produced from good bulbs. I have bought stocks that were badly virused but still flowered freely before they were culled. (G E Mitsch 1966; AGM-RHS 1995)

'Kaydee' 6W-P mid
This seedling of 'Foundling' has the same colour pattern but the white tepals are broader, and the bright pink corona is cylindrical, flared and beautiful. This daffodil is a striking garden plant with fine form, and it is highly recommended. (Brian S Duncan, Rathowen Daffodils 1984; AGM-RHS 1998)

'Larkwhistle' 6Y-Y early
Though not as popular as some, this is a free-flowering, all-yellow, reliable daffodil with slightly nodding flowers, 7.5 cm (3 in) across, with slightly darker coronas. (L Palmer 1960; AGM-RHS 1993)

'Lavender Lass' 6W-GPP mid
This daffodil, and its sister seedling 'Lilac Charm', have swept-back tepals of pure white and coronas of rich pink. The lilac and lavender is a little fanciful but they are definitely a step away from the salmon colours of most pinks. See also 'Snoopie'. (Brian S Duncan, Rathowen Daffodils 1976)

'Lilac Charm'
see 'Lavender Lass'

'Little Witch' 6Y-Y early
This dwarf plant has yellow flowers with reflexed tepals and narrow, strongly ribbed coronas. (Mrs R O Backhouse pre-1921)

'Mite' 6Y-Y early
This small daffodil, thought to be a hybrid of *N. obvallaris* and *N. cyclamineus*, blooms very early and has 5.5-cm (2-in) yellow blooms with tepals that are strongly reflexed. The all-yellow flowers are similar to 'Jetage'. (J Gore-Booth 1965)

'Peeping Tom' 6Y-Y early
This is supposedly a seedling of *N. cyclamineus*, but it must have had pollen from a trumpet daffodil as father to give it extra substance and size. Though it is almost a century old, it is still a superb flower of deep yellow with slightly reflexed, twisted tepals and a long, narrow corona that flares at the end. The blooms are 9.5 cm (3.75 in) across on vigorous plants. This flower is a real character, and well-named. (P D Williams pre-1918; AGM-RHS 1995)

'Penril' 6W-POO mid (p. 73)
With such fine parents as 'Roseworthy' (2W-P) and 'Foundling', both with pink coronas, this has wide, coppery-orange coronas beneath broad perianths (7 cm/2.75 in) of creamy white. (Brian S Duncan, du Plessis Bros 1989)

'Peppercorn' 6Y-WWY mid (p. 73)
This super flower has reflexed tepals of pale, sulphur yellow and a long, slender corona that is elegantly flared at the mouth. At first the colour is an even, pale yellow, but as the flower matures it becomes white with a yellow rim. (R A Scamp 2002)

'Rapture' 6Y-Y early (p. 73)
This free-flowering cultivar has perfect, golden, cyclamineus flowers with swept-back tepals and a long, cylindrical corona that is slightly narrower behind the mouth. (G E Mitsch 1976; AGM-RHS 2001)

'Reggae' 6W-GPP mid
This seedling has 'Foundling' as pollen parent, and is similar to it, but has tepals that are more reflexed, and a smaller corona that is deep pink with a green base. It has neat foliage and strong stems, making it a good garden plant. (Brian S Duncan, Rathowen Daffodils 1981; AGM-RHS 1998)

'Rival' 6YYG-Y mid
Large (9 cm/3.5 in) flowers of bright yellow with slightly wavy, reflexed tepals, and lightly ribbed trumpet with notched rim. (G E Mitsch 1976, 'Jenny' open pollinated.)

'Roscarrick' 6W-R/P late
Good for the garden and for showing, this brightly coloured flower has pure-white, reflexed tepals and a funnel-shaped, lightly ribbed corona with a frilly, straight mouth in deep pink, paler at the base. (Brian S Duncan, R A Scamp & du Plessis Bros 1989)

Cyclamineus daffodils
Top row:
'Peppercorn' 6Y-WWY,
'Penril' 6W-O,
'Surfside' 6W-Y.
Second row:
'Charity May' 6Y-Y,
'Cotinga' 6W-P.
Third row:
'Wang Hi' 6Y-O,
Rapture' 6Y-Y,
'Jenny' 6W-W.
Bottom row:
'Tracey' 6W-W
(young and older flower).

'Satellite' 6Y-O early

The blooms are 7.5 cm (3 in) wide and have a cylindrical corona with a straight mouth. It was one of the first from Mitsch with bright yellow and orange colouring, followed by 'Jetfire', 'Shimmer' (1978) and 'Soft Touch' (1983). It increases well. (G E Mitsch 1952, 1962)

'Snoopie' 6W-GPP mid

This large (8 cm/3 in) flower from 'Lilac Charm' has broad, white tepals that overlap by at least half, and a deep, cupped corona that is ribbed and bright, rose pink with a green base. (Brian S Duncan, Rathowen Daffodils 1979)

'Surfside' 6W-Y mid (p. 73)

This bright flower has reflexed white tepals with a green tinge, and cylindrical, pale yellow coronas that age to cream. (G E Mitsch 1972; AGM-RHS 1998)

'Swift Arrow' 6Y-Y early

This bright, gold flower has broad, overlapping, swept-back tepals and a long, cylindrical corona, often tinged with orange, with a flared mouth. (G E Mitsch 1977, R & E Havens; AGM-RHS 2001)

'Tracey' 6W-W mid (p. 73)

'Tracey' hangs its head at first, when the long corona is pale yellow, but lifts its face as it ages to white, matching the swept-back tepals. The corona is wider than some, and is beautifully expanded and rolled at the rim. (Miss M Verry 1968; AGM-RHS 2001)

'Trena' 6W-Y early

The 8-cm (3-in) blooms have white tepals that overlap to create a broad, reflexed perianth and a funnel-shaped, flaring, yellow corona. This daffodil is a wonderful, balanced bloom of poise and substance. (Miss M Verry 1971; AGM-RHS 2001)

'Whang Hi' 6Y-O mid (p. 73)

This unusual flower is similar to – but larger and brighter than – 'Beryl', and has broad yellow tepals creating a perianth 7 cm (2.75 in) across that is strongly reflexed. Its bright orange, ribbed, flattish corona is yellow at the base. (C F Coleman 1948, 1960)

DIVISION 7
Jonquils

Because there is not just a single jonquil species, but several closely related ones, the jonquil and apodanthus daffodils are varied. But *N. jonquilla* has made the greatest impact on the division, and plants usually have one to five flowers (to a maximum of eight) with spreading or reflexed tepals and a cup-shaped, funnel-shaped or flared corona that is wider than it is long. The flowers are usually fragrant, a feature that endears them to gardeners. They vary in height dramatically, from the tall 'Stratosphere' to dwarfs like 'Baby Moon' and 'Bobby Soxer'. The earliest jonquils were yellow and very fragrant, but other colours are now appearing, including ones that are pink in the cup, as can be seen in the marvellous 'Bell Song'. Not all the newer cultivars in odd colours have great fragrance, as the influence of the species is diluted, but they are still worth planting for their grace and colour.

'Baby Moon' 7Y-Y late

This dwarf and dainty plant, ideal for the rock garden, has three to five small, bright-yellow flowers per stem. Bred from *N. jonquilla var. minor* and *N. jonquilla*, it is strongly scented. (J Gerritsen & Son 1958)

'Bell Song' 7 W-P late (p. 52, 70)

Not only is this a fine pink jonquil, it is one of the prettiest and best small garden daffodils and is increasingly available at reasonable cost, so should be added to every garden. It has a pure-white perianth, 6.5 cm (2.5 in) wide, which opens pale yellow, while the neat corona is short and bright pink. There are usually two flowers per stem, but may be three, and the bulbs increase well. The flowers are among the last to open and are very durable – sometimes I wonder if they will ever fade! 'Pink Angel' is a sister seedling with creamy tepals and green-based corona, rimmed with pink. (G E Mitsch 1971)

'Bobbysoxer' 7Y-YYO late

This dainty plant grows prolifically and has *N. rupicola* in its ancestry. The flowers are rather like the more common 'Sundisc', but are held on taller stems. They are rounded and pale yellow with a flat corona that is usually a deeper shade and sometimes suffused with orange. (A Gray pre-1949)

'Boscastle' 7Y-Y late

This seedling of 'Aircastle' has two or three flowers per stem with broad, overlapping tepals creating a perianth 8 cm (3 in) across. The shallow corona is a slightly deeper yellow and the bulbs produce a second flush of flowers, creating a long-lasting display. It is very fragrant, and its good form makes it ideal for showing. (R A Scamp 1996)

'Buffawn' 7Y-Y (p. 40)

This is a stocky plant with two or three blooms that have a buff-yellow perianth 7.5 cm (3 in) wide, and a deeper-coloured, smooth, funnel-shaped corona. Not as graceful as some, but it has good fragrance and full flowers.

'Bunting' 7Y-O mid

This bright orange and yellow, fragrant flower resembles 'Kinglet' but has better, smoother flowers, and was released a few years later. (G E Mitsch 1965; AGM-RHS 1998)

'Chit Chat' 7Y-Y late

This has two to four flowers per stem, of bright yellow, the corona being slightly darker. It is similar to 'Pixie', but more vigorous. The name was also given to an old (1927) Division 1 daffodil that is no longer grown. (M Foulds c. 1960, G E Mitsch 1975; AGM-RHS 1996)

'Curlew' 7W-W mid (p. 70, 88)

There are not many white, multi-flowered jonquils, but this fills the gap admirably with one to three flowers per stem. The perianths are 7.5 cm (3 in) wide and creamy white, and the long corona is the same shade. It is stocky and vigorous and a good garden plant. (G E Mitsch 1972)

'Dickcissel' 7Y-W mid

This is a very free-flowering bulb that carries its flowers well above the foliage and is good for all purposes. Bred from 'Binkie', it has two or three lemon-yellow flowers with pointed tepals, while the coronas fade almost to white. (G E Mitsch 1963; AGM-RHS 2002)

'Double Campernelle'

see 'Odorus Rugulosus'

'Eland' 7W-W late

This white jonquil is bred from 'Aircastle' and is similar to 'Avocet', with two or three flowers that open white or pale lemon and fade to white. The perianth is 7.5 cm (3 in) wide, and the shallow corona is lightly frilled. (G E Mitsch 1968)

'Goldfinch'

see 'Pet Finch'

'High Note' 7Y-W mid (p. 35)

This is bred from the important 'Quickstep' and is a sister seedling to 'Cloud Nine' (single flowers of yellow with a white corona). It has a wide, deep lemon perianth and large coronas that fade to white. Each stem carries one to three 9-cm (3.5-in) flowers, and it is a strong grower, ideal for the garden. (G E Mitsch 1974)

'Hillstar' 7YYW-YWW mid

Another chameleon flower, this has two or three 7-cm (2.75-in) blooms per stem with tepals that open lemon yellow but fade to white at the base. The flared and frilled corona opens ivory and

Jonquil daffodils
Top row:
'Wheal Coates' 7Y-O,
'Walton' 7Y-YOO,
'Sweet Blanche' 7W-W
(two blooms).
Second row:
'Pipit' 7YYW-W,
'Penstraze' 7Y-GRR.
Third row:
'Kinglet' 7Y-OG,
'Indian Maid' 7O-R,
'Logan Rock' 7Y-Y.
Bottom row:
'Intrigue' 7Y-W,
'Rosemoor Gold' 7Y-Y.

becomes white at the edge and lemon in the centre. The lemon colouring of this flower is incredibly intense, and a clump of them is unmissable in the garden. (G E Mitsch 1979)

'Hoopoe'
see Division 8

'Indian Maid' 7O-R (p. 75)
This daffodil is similar to 'Suzy' but has a deeper-coloured corona. It has two or three flowers per stem with orange-gold tepals making a perianth 7.5 cm (3 in) wide, and a frilled, red corona. (W G Pannill 1972)

'Intrigue' 7Y-W late (p. 75)
This has two or three acid yellow flowers per stem, and coronas that change, with maturity, to creamy white. The perianth is 7 cm (2.75 in) wide and often has more than six tepals. These

are paler at the base, and the flowers are sweetly scented. (W G Pannill 1970; AGM-RHS 2001)

'Kinglet' 7Y-O late (p. 75)
This has one to three flowers per stem. These are large and have bright yellow tepals that are slightly twisted and only overlap at the base. The bright orange corona is straight and has a notched mouth. (G E Mitsch 1959)

'La Belle' 7Y-O mid
This old cultivar still has its merits. It is short with green leaves and has masses of flowers, with a second flush following the first. Each stem carries two or three yellow and orange flowers. (Barr & Sons pre-1938)

'Logan Rock' 7Y-Y early (p. 75)
This golden yellow flower has slightly reflexed tepals, and a deep, slightly angled corona that has a split and flared mouth. It is similar to 'Sweetness'. (R V Favel pre 1953)

'Martinette' 7 Y-O early (p. 18, 38)
I have enjoyed this early jonquil in my garden for many years and am always surprised at how early and prolific it is. It has up to five flowers per stem, of brilliant lemon yellow with a short, dark orange corona. It is bright and flashy, ideal for cutting, and commonly available. (H I Tuggle Jr, Cornwall Area Bulb Growers' Association 1985)

'Mountjoy' 7Y-Y late
This is a large, rich gold jonquil of good texture and heavy scent. The name has also been used for a Division 2 plant. (Barr & Sons pre-1950)

'New-Baby' 7W-Y late
This cute little flower is a sport of 'Baby Star' and has up to four flowers per stem. These are 2 cm (0.75 in) wide, and have pale tepals and a bright yellow corona. (J Gerritsen & Son 1963)

'Odorus Rugulosus' 7Y-Y mid (p. 76)
It is difficult to know where to put this, or what to call it. The ones I bought went under the name of 'Double Campernelle', but the stock was mixed and grew with both single and double flowers. The single-flowered plants ('Odorus Rugulosus') produce fine flowers with a deeply scalloped corona, and are bright gold with a

Dafffodils and tulip
Photographed with willow.
Top row:
'Odorus Rugulosus' 7Y-Y,
'Odorus Rugulosus
Flore Pleno',
'Thalia' 5W-W.
Second row:
'Minnow' 8Y-Y,
N. canaliculatus 10,
'Lemon Glow' 1Y-Y.
Third row:
'Avalanche' 8W-Y,
'Rip Van Winkle' 4Y-Y
(two blooms),
'Itzim' 6Y-R.
Bottom row:
'Golden Ducat' 4Y-Y,
T. praestans 'Unicum'.

wonderful scent. The double flowers are called 'Odorus Rugulosus Flore Pleno' or 'Odorus Plenus' (Mauger & Son pre-1900), and should be in Division 4. They are packed with golden petals, and the corona segments are not obvious. Though not neat, they are beautiful in an old-fashioned way. I have not sorted my bulbs of this stock into singles and doubles and quite like to see them mixed, to remind me what doubling does to a flower. Both double and single are vigorous, have up to three flowers per stem and are wonderful for cutting. (AGM-RHS 1993)

'Oryx' 7Y-W mid

This has three or four flowers per stem that open pale yellow. Bred from 'Aircastle', it increases well and the small cup fades to white, while the tepals get darker. (G E Mitsch 1969; AGM-RHS 1998)

'Penstraze' 7Y-GRR mid (p. 75)

This fine new jonquil has two flowers per stem. The blooms are bright yellow and have a rich orange-red corona with a green eye. It has shorter stems than some, making it ideal for the garden where it withstands rough weather. However, it is also a good show flower and very fragrant. (R A Scamp 2002)

'Pet Finch' 7Y-O early

This is a small, free-flowering plant that produces one flower per stem. These are gold with a bright-orange corona and, though very early, it produces a second flush of blooms, extending the display. It was previously called 'Goldfinch'. (M J Jefferson-Brown 1959, 1975)

'Pink Angel' 7W-GWP mid–late

This pretty but less common sibling of 'Bell Song' has two or three flowers per stem with ivory tepals forming a 7-cm (2.75-in) perianth, and a white corona that is green at the base and bright pink at the mouth. (G E Mitsch 1964, R Havens 1980)

'Pipit' 7YYW-W mid–late N7 (p. 70, 75, 88)

This is a hybrid of 'Binkie' and *N. jonquilla*, and has up to four 7-cm (2.75-in) flowers per stem. They are similar in colour to 'Dickcissel' but are paler, and the base of the lemon-yellow tepals is white. The rather frilled corona is pale yellow and fades with maturity. (G E Mitsch 1963; AGM-RHS 2001)

'Pixie' 7Y-Y mid

This is a small daffodil, bred from *N. jonquilla*, and has up to six small, bright-yellow flowers with wavy-edged coronas. (M Foulds, G E Mitsch 1959)

'Pixie's Sister' 7Y-Y mid

This has up to five well-formed, golden yellow, 2.5-cm (1-in) flowers on short stems, but needs dry summer dormancy to thrive and is perfect for a pan in the alpine house or the rock garden, being small in stature. (G E Mitsch 1966; AGM-RHS 1996)

'Pueblo' 7W-W mid

Bred from 'Binkie', this has two or three flowers per stem with creamy white, 7.5-cm (3-in) perianths and long coronas that open pale yellow and fade to ivory as they age, but remain darker than the tepals. (G E Mitsch 1966)

'Quail' 7Y-Y mid (p. 24, 41)

One of the most common jonquils, this is sturdy and free-flowering, with two or three fragrant flowers of rich gold per stem. The perianths are 6 cm (2.3 in) wide and the funnel-shaped coronas are slightly darker gold. It is strong growing and ideal for the garden or containers. (G E Mitsch 1974; AGM-RHS 1998)

'Quickstep' 7W-P mid

Many jonquil hybrids are sterile, and 'Quickstep' is historically important because it is fertile and useful for breeding. It is not common but is, itself, a pretty plant with up to three, beautifully poised and fragrant flowers on each stem. The perianth is 7 cm (2.75 in) wide and ivory white, while the small, broad corona is a similar colour but is flushed with a hint of pink – inherited, as it is in many other pink jonquils, from 'Wild Rose' (2W-P 1936). (G E Mitsch 1955, 1965)

'Rosemoor Gold' 7Y-Y (p. 75)

If you only plant one jonquil, make it this! Many jonquils are popular garden plants, but I expect this to become the most famous of all because it is such a good plant. The flowers are large and bright golden yellow, the corona is broad and beautifully flared, and each stem has two or three. Even better, the bulbs produce a second flush of flowers, but it is the fragrance of the flowers that makes this plant exceptional – you will not find a jonquil with a headier scent. Add to this its great vigour, and you have an exceptional plant. It is a hybrid of 'St Keverne' and *N. jonquilla* – obviously a match made in heaven. (Rosewarne E H S, Cornwall Area Bulb Growers' Association 2003)

'Rugulosus'
see 'Odorus Rugulosus'

'Stratosphere' 7Y-O mid–late
This fine and bold plant has two or three fragrant, 6.5-cm (2.5-in) flowers per stem. They open pure gold but the corona, which has a pretty, wavy mouth, can assume an orange hue. When I saw this at the Keukenhof it was an extraordinary 75 cm (30 in) high, but without any sign of orange colouring. (G E Mitsch 1968)

'Sugarbush' 7W-YYW mid
A pretty flower, 6.5 cm (2.5 in) wide, carried two per stem. The flowers open yellow and fade, so the perianth ends white, and the corona acid yellow with a white rim. (A Gray pre-1954)

'Sun Disc' 7Y-Y mid–late
It is impossible not to fall in love with this cute flower, which has tepals that overlap so much that the 5-cm (2-in) perianth appears almost round. The corona is almost flat and the same, bright yellow. Though vigorous and perfectly at home in the garden, because it is dwarf it begs to be planted in a pot or picked so you can appreciate its pretty blooms. (AGM-RHS 1996)

'Suzy' 7Y-O mid
Though not of perfect form, with rather pointed tepals, this bright yellow flower with a small bright orange corona is still popular because it increases fast. Each stem carries up to three 6-cm (2.3-in) flowers that are bright and fragrant. (R A Favell or P D Williams pre-1954; AGM-RHS 1993)

'Sweet Blanche' 7W-W mid (p. 75)
Although each stem has only one, fragrant flower, these are large (10 cm/4 in), and the bulbs send up secondary stems, so there is a succession of flowers. The beauty of a clump of them is augmented by the way the flowers change colour, opening pale yellow and becoming white with maturity. The tepals are narrow and smooth, and

the corona is narrow and ribbed. A fine plant. It was not highly rated by Ron Scamp as a seedling, but a lady who came to pick flowers at the nursery kept returning to this row, and its merits were discovered. (R A Scamp 1995)

'Sweetness' 7Y-Y mid
To prove that sometimes old flowers can hold their own amid the plethora of new daffodils, 'Sweetness' is still loved both for the garden and for showing. It has golden, 6.5-cm (2.5-in), starlike flowers of good shape with a flat, bright, scalloped corona. Though the stems usually have just one flower, the bulbs are prolific and a clump of them will produce many flowers. (R V Favell pre-1939; AGM-RHS 1993)

'Tittle-Tattle' 7Y-GYY late
It is useful to plant this to extend the season of flowers. It has two or three pale yellow flowers per stem with a shallow corona of a deeper shade, tinged with green at the base. (C R Wootton pre-1953)

'Trevithian' 7Y-Y mid
With two or three soft yellow, fragrant flowers 7 cm (2.75 in) across, this is still very popular, and valued for its vigour and wonderful perfume. (P D Williams pre-1927; AGM-RHS 1995)

'Walton' 7Y-YOO mid (p. 75)
This has two flowers per stem, similar to 'Wheal Coates' but with a slightly deeper orange corona that is attractively frilled at the mouth. (R A Scamp 1999)

'Waterperry' 7 W-YPP mid
One of the first of the pink jonquils, this has pastel colouring with up to three 7-cm (2.75-in) flowers per stem with ivory white tepals and a cylindrical corona that is a pale, creamy, salmon-pink at the base, shading to deeper pink at the mouth. Though not as vibrant in colouring as newer cultivars, or of as good form or substance, it is a useful and pretty garden flower. (R V Favell pre-1953)

'Wheal Coates' 7Y-O late (p. 75)
With two 6-cm (2.3-in), perfectly formed orange and yellow flowers per stem, this is a superb garden and show jonquil. The broad tepals make

a fine golden perianth and the shallow, flaring corona is bright orange. Strongly scented, it sends up a second crop of stems to extend the floral display. (R A Scamp 1996; AGM-RHS 2001)

DIVISION 8
Tazettas

With a few notable exceptions such as 'Geranium', the tazetta daffodils are largely ignored by gardeners. This is a serious mistake, because they are exceptionally free-flowering, available in a good range of colours, and are sweetly scented. It is true that many of the true tazettas are rather tender and need good summer heat to do well, while tolerating little winter frost. However, the poetaz cultivars, which are bred by combining tazettas with *N. poeticus* to add more colour, have also inherited hardiness from *poeticus* and cannot be recommended too highly (these are identified below). Given the right garden, some of these grow as luxuriantly as weeds; their stems are so strong and thick, with huge clusters of flowers, that their bases look more like leeks than daffodils. Many also produce a second flush of stems.

My visit to Ron Scamp in Cornwall opened my eyes to the potential and beauty of this wonderful division. The definition of the group states that the plants must show characteristics of the botanical Section Tazetta, and have three to twenty flowers on a stout stem. The flowers, which are usually fragrant, should have spreading but not reflexed perianth segments.

Because these vary so much in their cultivation needs, the flowering time varies from November (under glass) to April (outdoors in a mild climate).

There is something exciting about these flowers, perhaps because each stem carries so many blooms and their fragrance is so rich and syrupy. If you cannot grow any of these outside because of cold winters (poetaz varieties are generally tougher) try at least a few each winter in pots to enjoy indoors.

'Admiration' 8Y-O poetaz (p. 79)
This fine old plant, which E A Bowles describes as 'especially good in the gardens of the French Riviera', has many flowers per stem of pale yellow with broad, creased tepals and a neat, ribbed

corona of orange-red. The flowers are, of course, sweetly scented. (A Vis [van der Schoot] pre-1912)

'Avalanche' 8W-Y early (p. 76, 79)
With up to ten flowers per stem officially but often with considerably more, this exceptionally vigorous plant, with massive stems, is a powerhouse of fragrance. The 3.5-cm (1.4-in) flowers have white tepals and a bright yellow corona that is constricted at the mouth. (pre-1906, T M Dorrien Smith 1955; AGM-RHS 1995)

'Bridal Crown'
see Division 4

'Bright Spot' 8W-R mid (p. 79)
This seedling of 'Matador' has only one to three flowers per stem, but they are large for this division (6.5 cm/2.5 in) and of heavy texture, with creamy yellow tepals and a wide, orange-red corona. (Sidney DuBose, W R P Welch 1993)

Tazetta daffodils
Top row:
'Admiration' 8Y-O,
'Bright Spot' 8W-R
(young flowers).
Second row:
'Early Splendour' 8W-O,
'Dan du Plessis' 8Y-O.
Bottom row:
'Avalanche' 8W-Y,
'Polly's Pearl' 8W-W,
'Hoopoe' 8Y-O.

'Cheerfulness'
see Division 4

'Chinita' 8Y-YYR poetaz mid–late (p. 81)
The tall stems carry two 5-cm (2-in) flowers with broad, slightly unruly, primrose yellow tepals surrounding a flat corona that is yellow with a fine rim of red and a green eye. (F H Chapman pre-1922)

'Cragford' 8W-O early
This very early cultivar was once popular as a pot plant that can easily be flowered for Christmas in the home, and in mild localities even flowers outside in the garden in late autumn. It is a sturdy plant with four to six 5.5-cm (2-in) flowers per stem, each with white, overlapping tepals stained yellow at the base, and with a bright orange, shallow, ribbed corona. It is a fine plant for the greenhouse and conservatory. It is a hybrid of the ancient (1883) 'Gloriosus' (8W-O) not to be confused with 'Glorious' (8W-O 1923) bred by J C Williams (cousin of the raiser of 'Cragford'). It has sported to 'Abba' in Division 4. (P D Williams pre-1930)

'Dan du Plessis' 8Y-O poetaz mid (p. 79)
This hybrid of *N. jonquilla* and the important, fertile, 'Matador' has a rich scent. There are three to six flowers per stem, 5 cm (2 in) wide, with acid yellow tepals and a wonderful, ribbed, brilliant orange corona. An exceptionally fine, fragrant cultivar. (Rosewarne E H S, Cornwall Area Bulb Growers' Association 1996)

'Early Splendour' 8W-O poetaz early (p. 79)
Each stem produces many 6-cm (2.3-in) wide flowers with pure-white tepals that are creased and obviously tinted yellow at the base. The orange coronas are ribbed and bowl-shaped, split and frilled. A large and fragrant flower. (A C van der Schoot pre-1938)

'Elvira' 8 W-YYO early (p. 39)
This has three or four fragrant flowers per stem (occasionally more). Each is about 5 cm (2 in) wide and has white tepals, flushed golden yellow at the base, with a shallow, ribbed orange-yellow corona. It is rarely grown now but is important because it sported to produce 'Cheerfulness' (Division 4), which is still an important commercial plant for cut flowers and bulbs. (R A van der Schoot pre-1902)

'Falconet' 8Y-O poetaz early
This bright and fragrant flower is a sister seedling to 'Hoopoe', which it resembles but is smaller and more vibrant, with three to five well-spaced, tidy flowers 4 cm (1.5 in) wide per stem. It is also earlier than 'Hoopoe'. (G E Mitsch 1979; AGM-RHS 1998)

'Geranium' 8W-O poetaz mid–late (p. 41)
Most of the plants in this section have vigour and big, heavy bulbs, but few are available in high-street stockists. So there is something very satisfying about selecting bulbs of this common cultivar – they are so big and heavy that you actually need a big pot if you are to fit in more than three. It is a sturdy plant, ideal for pot culture, but flowers late (usually in April), and each stem carries up to six flowers about 6 cm (2.3 in) wide. These have pure white perianths with slightly creased and rolled tepals and a shallow, frilled corona of a strong, contrasting orange. It is reliable, fragrant and good for cutting. It has sported to 'Sir Winston Churchill' in Division 4. (J B van der Schoot pre-1930; AGM-RHS 1995)

'Golden Dawn' 8Y-O poetaz mid
This has two or three flowers per stem, each 4.5 cm (1.75 in) wide with broad, greenish yellow tepals and a spreading, ribbed, frilled, deep-orange corona. It is late, fragrant and produces a second flush of stems. (Oregon Bulb Farms 1958; AGM-RHS 1993)

'Grand Monarque' 8W-Y early
Like many early tazettas, this was raised in the Netherlands, and it is still vigorous and adorns gardens throughout Cornwall in March, scenting the air and bringing brightness with its large heads of white and pale yellow flowers. It is the largest of this colour pattern, and very beautiful. It has, inevitably, been given many names in the past, such as 'Nosegay', 'Czar Monarque', 'Floribunda' and 'Grand Monarque de France'. 'Grand Primo Citroniére' is a similar variety, and 'Primo' and 'Scilly White' differ mainly in having white coronas. (Dutch pre-1798)

'Highfield Beauty' 8Y-YYO poetaz (p. 81)

This is an exceptionally beautiful flower with a broad, lemon-yellow perianth, 6.5 cm (2.5 in) wide, and a broad, wide corona that is yellow, edged with orange. The two or three beautifully round flowers are held on strong stems. Although officially only slightly scented, it seems well so to me. (H R Mott 1964; AGM-RHS 2001)

'Hoopoe' 8Y-O poetaz early (p. 79)

This colourful, fragrant cultivar – like 'Dan du Plessis', a hybrid of 'Matador' and *N. jonquilla* – blooms early, and has masses of flowers over a long period. The stems carry two to three (often more) 5.5-cm (2-in) flowers with rounded tepals that are bright gold, while the small corona is a rich orange. See also 'Falconet'. (G E Mitsch 1977; AGM-RHS 2002)

'Hugh Town' 8Y-O early

This hybrid – produced using the good parent 'Matador' pollinated with 'Grand Soleil d'Or' – is becoming popular. The stems carry four to six bright, pale yellow flowers with bright orange, frilled coronas. This does need a warm garden, and bulbs that I have grown for indoor display and then put into the garden have gradually dwindled away (unlike some other tazettas). This is perhaps because it is naturally early, although 'Paper White Grandiflora' and 'Avalanche' survive in similar circumstances. But where conditions suit it is a gorgeous flower and highly scented. (Harry I Tuggle Jr 1974, Rosewarne E H S 1987)

'Jamage' 8W-Y poetaz mid (p. 81)

With more subtle colouring than most, this has stems with two to four 6.5-cm (2.5-in) fragrant flowers per stem, each with a creamy yellow perianth and lemon yellow corona. (G W Tarry, G W Tarry & du Plessis Bros 1990)

'L'Innocence' 8 W-Y poetaz early (p. 38)

This is not a commercial cultivar and I have never seen it for sale, but it does crop up – or it has at least once, because I found it among a pot I planted with 'Bridal Crown'. I consider myself fortunate that I had a bulb that had sported back to the cultivar from which it arose. The single flowers are strongly scented and have white tepals and short, orange coronas. (C P Alkemade pre-1930)

'Martha Washington' 8W-O poetaz (p. 81)

With some of the largest flowers of the division, more than 8 cm (3 in) across, this is a dramatic plant. If each stem only had one flower it would still be worth growing, but each carries two or three flowers. These have creased, white tepals, stained yellow at the base, and a frilly, wide corona in bright orange, slightly paler at the eye. (A Frylink & Sons pre-1927)

'Matador' 8Y-GOR poetaz early

This is thought to have been produced from the seed of 'Admiration' and, unlike most poetaz, is fertile; it has been an important parent in this division. It has three to five flowers per stem and each is pale yellow with a shallow, bright orange corona. (Oregon Bulb Farms 1958)

Tazetta daffodils

Top row:
'Martha Washington' 8W-O,
'Highfield Beauty' 8Y-YYO.
Second row:
'Chinita' 8Y-YYR,
'Jamage' 8W-Y.
Bottom row:
'Mike Pollock' 8Y-O,
'Saint Keane' 8W-O.

'Mike Pollock' 8Y-O poetaz mid (p. 81)
Another from the popular mating of 'Matador' and *N. jonquilla*, this has up to eight flowers per stem, each 5 cm (2 in) wide with bright, yellow tepals and bright orange, bowl-shaped, ribbed coronas. (Rosewarne E H S, Cornwall Area Bulb Growers' Association 1996)

'Minnow' 8Y-Y mid (p. 76)
This is a delightful dwarf that hardly seems at home in this division. It has two or three flowers per stem and these are 2.5 cm (1 in) wide with broad, primrose yellow tepals, and a corona that is shallow and a slightly deeper colour. It is only about 15 cm (6 in) high and is very cute, ideal for the rock garden. It is supposed to grow better in mild climates, but I have never had trouble with it, though perhaps it would flower better with a hotter summer. (A Gray 1962; AGM-RHS 1998)

'Paper White Grandiflorus' 8W-W early
This name identifies one of a group of plants that will keep botanists amused for hours but which, to the gardener, are very similar. 'Paper White Grandiflorus' has larger flowers than 'Paper White', which should probably be called *N. papyraceus*. E A Bowles (in *The Narcissus*) writes that what I assume to be 'Paper White Grandiflorus' (he calls it *N. papyraceus grandiflorus* or *N. papyraceus major*, 'The Paper White') is native through Spain, Portugal and the French Riviera into Italy. But with such a wide natural distribution, why has it been given a cultivar name? Some suppliers sell 'Paper White Grandiflorus' (apparently the same as 'Paper White New Large Flowered') while others sell what they simply call 'Paper White', and I have never planted a mass to see if there is any difference.

Whichever you plant, it will produce stems with about a dozen, pure-white flowers with neat coronas, and perianths with rather starry outlines and bright green ovaries and leaves. As soon as you see a bulb you will fall in love with this plant – the skins are a rich, shiny chestnut brown – and the flowers have a wonderful, rich scent. To be honest, the scent can actually be rather sickly, and anyone who feels ill at the sight of magenta flowers – or would rather starve than enter a hamburger establishment – may prefer to avert their nose, but I rejoice in the smell, especially as it is so easy to enjoy for weeks on end. This is a plant that is not

hardy throughout much of the UK and is bought almost entirely for indoor cultivation. The bulbs, once planted, need no cold, dark period, and you can simply place them in gravel in a bowl and then on the windowsill to flower. In a warm place they can be in flower in five or six weeks but, by planting many pots and keeping them in the greenhouse I can time them so there are flowers for Christmas and on through to March.

Conventional wisdom has it that bulbs thus treated, grown in water, are of no further use, but I have planted them out after flowering and, not only have they survived an inland climate, but have flowered the following year. If nothing else, this illustrates that you should not believe all you read and it shows the importance of allowing foliage to die down naturally to allow time for the bulbs to be fed. Buy this and plant pots liberally, but stake them because, if grown indoors, the stems always fall over just as the first flower starts to open. (pre-1887)

'Polly's Pearl' 8W-W early (p. 79)
This selection from 'White Pearl' has up to 20 3–4-cm (1.25–1.5-in) flowers per stem that open with a creamy corona but age to white to produce an all-white head of fragrant flowers. (H Koopowitz 1979)

'Saint Keyne' 8W-O poetaz early–mid (p.81)
Each flower has white tepals, slightly tinged with yellow at the base and rather creased, and with a frilly, deep orange corona. The wonderfully fragrant flowers are 6.5 cm (2.5 in) wide and there are two or three per stem. (P D Williams pre-1927)

'Scarlet Gem' 8Y-O poetaz mid
This is a cheerful flower with four to six flowers per stem, a rounded perianth of bright primrose, and a broad, ribbed, bright orange corona. (P D Williams pre-1910)

'Silver Chimes' 8 W-W mid
This innovative hybrid, from a cross between 'Scilly White' and *N. triandrus*, is a beautiful plant that was, for a while, included in Division 5. The stems carry from five to eight 5-cm (2-in) flowers with pure-white tepals that reflex to give each bloom a flyaway look. The first flowers are rather upright, but later blooms take after the pollen parent and hang gracefully. The coronas

are longer than most tazettas, and are pale yellow and lighter in colour at the mouth. It has a good scent and is useful in mild areas for the garden and for showing. (E & J C Martin pre-1914)

'Sir Winston Churchill'
see Division 4

'Soleil d'Or' 8Y-Y(O) early
Like 'Paper White', this has a long history in cultivation and its naming is confusing. To start with, it is often called 'Sol d'Or' or just 'Sols'. Then, to make things worse, there is also a 'Grand Soleil d'Or' which has larger flowers that have a brighter colour. Both are ancient, and it is not impossible that the main differences between them could have been caused by a virus. Whatever the name, the plant you will get will have rich, golden tepals around a bright orange corona, topped off with a wonderful scent. It can be treated in just the same way as 'Paper White' and is similarly unsuccessful in cold gardens, but as a treat, either as a bunch of flowers flown in from warmer climes, or as a pot full of bulbs, it is hard to beat. (pre-1731)

'Yellow Cheerfulness'
see Division 4

DIVISION 9
Poeticus

Universally called narcissi by the gardening public, and distinguished by its small cup and white tepals, this division is based on *N. poeticus* and its subspecies and varieties. Officially, the division is defined as having (usually) one flower per stem, and the characteristics of the *N. poeticus* group. The tepals must be white and the corona is very short or disc shaped, usually with a green and/or yellow centre and a red rim, but sometimes of one colour. The flowers are usually fragrant, and though this is not an important group commercially, it is well loved by gardeners, even if they are only familiar with the old pheasant's eye. The division deserves a closer look. Modern cultivars have lost none of the charm of the old flowers, partly because of the restrictions of the Division, and they have more beautiful, finely honed blooms and often better

resistance to the sun, which all too often burns the red rim of the coronas. As a group, they bring the daffodil season to its conclusion, but with finesse and fine fragrance. Try some. See page 93.

'Actaea' 9W-YYR mid
The great daffodil and lily breeder and expert, Michael Jefferson-Brown, wrote that the popularity of this variety 'illustrates the relative lack of breeding and meagre possibility of advance that this cultivar should have dominated commercial poets for so long and that, after a first class certificate awarded in Haarlem in 1923, it should have been judged worthy of an Award of Garden Merit in 1950 after a trial at Wisley'. One can only wonder what he thought of the later award in 1993! At least some more modern flowers received the accolade too. While it is true that this is a flower that leaves show people distinctly cool, it is a good garden plant and sells in huge volumes. Most gardeners are content with it, but I am sure that they would buy something more modern if it were readily available. But it would be a brave grower or distributor who made the change.

It is the classic poet variety, with 8.5-cm (3.3-in) wide blooms that are pure white but rather wavy, and a tiny corona, greenish-yellow at the base, passing to yellow and then red at the rim. Like all, it has wonderful fragrance. (G Lubbe & Son pre-1927; AGM-RHS 1993)

'Angel Eyes' 9W-GYO late
This is rather like 'Quetzal' but has more subtle colouring. The 7-cm (2.75-in) flowers have white tepals, and a small yellow corona that is green at the base and orange at the rim. It grows strongly and flowers well, and the flowers have a neat and precise shape. (G E Mitsch 1976)

'Benbane Head' 9W-GYR late
This seedling of 'Cantabile' has a fine white perianth and a neat corona that is green in the lower half. (Ballydorn Bulb Farm)

'Cantabile' 9W-GYR late
This became the 'modern' standard when it was introduced, with tepals of better substance and form than 'Actaea'. It became an important parent and has small, flat coronas that are very green at first, becoming yellow, with a red edge. (G L Wilson pre-1932; AGM-RHS 1996)

'Chesterton' 9W-GYR late
This fine flower has white tepals, slightly reflexing, and a green, yellow and red corona. It is strong and resistant to weather. (Brian S Duncan, Rathowen Daffodils 1979; AGM-RHS 1999)

'Double White'
see 'Plenus', Division 4

'Dimple' 9W-O late
This cute flower has a flat, neat perianth, a pure-orange corona and fine fragrance. Among the latest to bloom, the flowers are 7 cm (2.75 in) across. (B S Duncan 1992)

'Dulcimer' 9W-GYO late
This old plant with tall stems has rather oblong, white tepals, and a broad orange band around the rim of the corona. (G H Engleheart pre-1913)

'Emerald' 9W-GOR late
This bright flower, 8 cm (3 in) wide, has white tepals and a corona that is largely green with a thin rim of orange and red. (G E Mitsch 1968, 1979)

'Felindre' 9W-GYR very late
An old cultivar with a flat corona that is notched and crimson at the edge. (A M Wilson pre-1930)

'Flora Pleno'
see 'Plenus', Division 4

'Greenpark' 9W-GGO very late
This superb, fragrant, show flower has a smooth, 7.5-cm (3-in) wide perianth, and a corona that is mostly dark green, with an orange rim. (Ballydorn Bulb Farm 1988)

'Green Pearl' 9W-GWW late
This lovely flower has delicate and cool colouring, pure white with a green eye, and the beautiful blooms face upward, so you can appreciate their beauty. (P de Jager & Sons 1974)

'Hellenicus' (*N. poeticus* **var.** *hellenicus*)
see Division 13

'Lyric' 9W-GYR mid–late
This resembles 'Milan', but has better shape and smoother tepals. (Brian S Duncan, Rathowen Daffodils 1977)

'Milan' 9W-GYR late
This famous cultivar is still worth growing, with its 8.5-cm (3.3-in) wide perianth, and its ribbed corona that is split and wavy at the bright red edge. (A M Wilson pre-1932)

'Patois' 9W-GYR very late
One of the very best of its kind, this superb show-quality flower has a solid, smooth perianth, and a fine, flat corona with broad red rim. (Brian S Duncan 1992)

'Pheasant's Eye' (*N. poeticus* **var.** *recurvus*)
see Division 13

'Plenus'
see Division 4

'Praecox' 9W-GYR mid (p. 51)
This is one of the earliest poets and has flowers with typical colouring, but it is not as sweetly scented as most. (pre-1900). See page 93.

'Quetzal' 9W-GYR late
This is not a pure poet, but descended from 'Cantabile'. The 8.5-cm (3.3-in) wide flowers resemble its parent, but have better form. (G E Mitsch 1952, 1965)

'Recurvus' *(N. poeticus* **var.** *recurvus)*
see Division 13

DIVISION 10
Bulbocodium

This is a small group of hybrids, based on the Bulbocodium section of the genus. They usually have one flower per stem, with insignificant tepals and a dominant corona. The anthers are attached to the filament in the centre. They are small plants, at their best in the alpine house, rock garden or well-drained places in the garden. For a fuller description of the species, see Division 13.

**'Golden Bells' (also known as 'Sylvania')
10Y-Y (p. 41)**
This is supposed to be a sport and has typical bulbocodium flowers, but is incredibly vigorous and free-flowering. Each bulb produces as many as 15 flowers, and these are golden yellow, facing

upwards among the grassy, green leaves. It grows to about 15 cm (6 in) high and, because of its vigour, is suitable for containers and the open garden. It is the best introduction to the group, but is not representative because of its ease of growth. It would be wonderful for naturalizing, creating a much bolder display than others in the group. (pre-1995)

'Kenellis' 10W-Y (p. 51)

This is an unusual plant, produced by crossing *N. bulbocodium* var. *citrinus* with 'Snowflake' (1W-W). It was one of Alec Gray's early hybrids, and is small, though big enough for the front of the border. It has narrow white tepals, and a corona that is the same length or longer, in pale yellow – paler inside – that fades almost to white with age.

'Tiffany' 10Y-Y

This is one of many *N. bulbocodium* hybrids produced by Douglas Blanchard. It has larger flowers than most, up to 7.5 cm (3 in) across, in pale yellow, fading to white and blooming later than most. It resembles a large, frilled *N. romieuxii*. (D & J W Blanchard 1960)

DIVISION 11
Split Coronas

These daffodils are simply defined as having a split corona, usually for more than half its length, but there is far more to them than that. Firstly, they are divided into Collar daffodils (11a) and Papillon daffodils (11b). Collar daffodils have their flowers arranged so that the pieces of corona lie directly over the tepals and sometimes almost obscure them. This is officially described as 'corona segments opposite the perianth segments', which I find a somewhat confusing description. The Papillon daffodils have corona segments that lie between the tepals, covering the join of two tepals (described as 'alternate to the perianth segments'). The official description states that Collar daffodils have two rows of three corona segments, and Papillon daffodils have a single whorl of six.

This sounds like nonsense, but there is a difference because the six segments in a Collar daffodil often lie so closely over the tepals that those over the outer tepals are in a different rank to those over the inner three. Collar daffodils usually have a 'harsher' look than the Papillons, which usually have ruffled corona segments.

This division was born in 1929, but it still attracts attention because of the bizarre appearance of some of the flowers. Some of the early cultivars had long anthers and styles. If their coronas had been entire, they would be pleasantly modest, but the slashes down the corona caused them to expose their sexual parts in a rather unpleasant manner, like drunken teenagers in a Mediterranean resort. I do feel that modern cultivars, with stamens of more modest dimensions, are a great improvement. The splitting of the corona also reveals the very centre of the flowers – nothing can escape our gaze, and this can lead to interesting colour effects because the yellow or green of the base of the flower can be seen.

Some of the most common are rather brash flowers with bright colouring. But you can now choose from pinks, whites and every other daffodil shade. Some are subtle and feminine, others are just mad! Among the most weird is 'Trilune', which attracts attention because the corona segments that would have lain over the outer tepals are missing – only the inner three tepals are overlain with the bright yellow corona segments. Split coronas are still something of a novelty and, though I must confess that they do not look much like daffodils, they are beautiful in many cases. They are often recommended as cut flowers, as though we should rush into the garden with scissors as soon as they expose themselves to prevent laughs of derision or 'tut tuts' from the neighbours. But they are just as good for garden display as any others. Try some – but don't follow the practice of so many catalogues and call them 'orchid-flowered'. I have seen an orchid that looked like a bee, and one that looked like a monkey, but never one that looked like these!

'Apricot Lace' 11aW-P mid–late

If you think that split corona daffodils are just a bit too vulgar, look out for this subtle beauty. Each stem carries one or two flowers that are small and creamy white. The corona is pale apricot pink and is slashed into ribbons that lie against the perianth. The tall stems would make it ideal for cutting, and it seems weatherproof. All in all, a superb new addition to the group that should make a big impression. (unregistered)

'Articol' 11aW-YPP mid

From Gerritsen, the original home of 'splits', this large flower (measuring 10 cm/4 in) has ivory white tepals of less than perfect form, and a corona that is heavily frilled and salmon pink, shaded yellow at the base. A pleasant introduction to the group, being showy and inexpensive. (J Gerritsen & Son 1979)

'Astropink' 11aW-P mid (p. 89)

I hope I will not be criticized if I say that I still find pink in daffodils rather artificial. This is not to say I do not like them – I think they are beautiful – but they show the hand of humanity. So I have the feeling that some of the most beautiful split coronas are pink because the odd shape of the flowers suits the colour. Just forget what a daffodil should look like and enjoy this fabulous flower. Each bloom is 8.5 cm (3.3 in)

across, with a white perianth and broad, flat tepals. Against this is set a mid-pink corona that is split into six rather irregular parts. Its colour does not fade in the sun. (G E Mitsch 1981, R & E Havens 1993)

'Belcanto' 11aW-Y late

This early introduction lacks the refinement of later cultivars, but still packs a punch. The 10-cm (4-in) flowers have white tepals, but these are virtually obscured by the bright yellow corona segments. (J Gerritsen & Son 1971)

'Boscoppa' 11aY-O mid (p. 86)

A sun-proof flower, 9.5 cm (3.75 in) across, with broad, overlapping, bright yellow tepals, this has an orange corona – shading to yellow at the base – that almost covers the perianth. (R A Scamp 1996)

'Boslowick' 11aY-O mid (p. 86)

Among the best and most brilliant of the many yellow and orange 'splits', this has 9.5-cm (3.75-in) flowers with golden yellow, ace-of-spades tepals and a slightly ribbed, frilled, deep-orange corona that is just the right size to contrast with the perianth. It has tall stems and is good for showing. (R A Scamp 1991; AGM-RHS 2002)

'Bossiney' 11aW-WPP mid (p. 89)

This has rather short stems, and is a good plant for the garden, though it is difficult to resist picking it. The white perianth is 10 cm (4 in) across and the frilly, split corona is bright pink at the edges, fading to paler pink and then yellowish-pink at the base. To see it is to love it. (R A Scamp 1996)

'Bosvale' 11aW-P mid–late (p. 89)

This large flower has much charm, with its white ace-of-spades tepals almost hidden by the beautiful, pale peachy-pink of the six corona segments. It is nice for cutting and has won at shows. (R A Scamp 2000) 'Chenoweth' x 'Rainbow'

'Broadway Star' 11bW-O/W late

This will appeal to everyone except the purists, who may find it rather scruffy; the rest of us will enjoy the informality of the blooms. These are 8 cm (3 in) wide, with broad white tepals, and the corona is split into six segments that lie across the gaps in the tepals. Each segment is white and frilly with a bright orange streak through the centre. (J W A Lefeber 1975)

'Cassata' 11aW-W early
Even without the novelty of the split corona, this is a good garden plant because of its vigour and the size of its white flowers. These are 10 cm (4 in) across, and the tepals are rather greenish-ivory, but this is neither here nor there since the segments of the corona, which are pale yellow at first and age to white, almost completely cover them. It has a pleasant scent and the corona segments are frilled. (J Gerritsen & Son 1963)

'Changing Colours' 11aW-W mid
As you might expect, the colour of the lovely, round, deeply bi-lobed frilly corona changes as it matures, from pale yellow to white and then to pink. All this activity is set against a pure-white, 10.5-cm (4-in) perianth. The inner segments are narrower than the outer three but this hardly spoils the flower, which is made more lovely because the corona only covers half the perianth. (J Gerritsen & Son 1993)

'Chanterelle' 11aY-Y mid
One of the most popular splits, this has subtle colouring that no one could find brash, the bright yellow corona segments overlapping the pale yellow tepals by about three-quarters. The flowers are fragrant and 8.5 cm (3.3 in) across. (J Gerritsen & Son 1962)

'Colorama' 11aY-O (p. 86)
This is a bright flower that stands out from most others by the width of the corona segments, which are bright orange but have two paler lobes at the base that fill out the flower. These are set against a bright yellow perianth 9 cm (3.5 in) across. (J Gerritsen & Son 1973)

'Congress' 11aY-O mid
This acid yellow flower, with a corona that opens yellow orange and develops its colour as it ages, is 9.5 cm (3.75 in) across. (J Gerritsen & Son 1965)

'Dolly Mollinger' 11bW-O/W mid
This is another informal flower with rather creased white tepals behind an intricate corona that is split into six rather irregular and curled segments that are orange at the base and up the

centre and edged in white. A lovely cut flower. (J W A Lefeber 1958)

'Fashion' 11bY-Y/O early (p. 62)
Though this does not have perfect form, and the lemon yellow perianth segments are not very flat, I love this. The flowers are 10 cm (4 in) across and the corona segments are three-quarters of the length of the tepals, bi-lobed, and a similar shade of yellow, streaked gold and touched with orange at the notched apex. These create a loose, frilly effect. (F Leenan 1966, 1977)

'Jack Wood' 11aY-YYO
This is a fine show flower, a fitting tribute to the eponymous show reporter who gained huge respect and was to be seen at almost every show throughout the UK. It has 10-cm (4-in) flowers with golden tepals and a flat, smooth corona of slightly deeper yellow, with a hint of orange at the edge. (R A Scamp 1997)

'Jantje' 11aY-O early–mid (p. 86)
This is a magnificent, large (10.5 cm/4 in) flower of bright yellow, with bright orange ruffled corona segments that are heart-shaped and are edged by a band of perianth. It is vigorous, and has been successful on the show bench. It is named after Jan Dalton. (R A Scamp)

'Lemon Beauty' 11bW-Y/W mid
This has flowers in much the same mould as the more common 'Broadway Star'. The 10-cm (4-in) flowers have broad white tepals and corona segments that are half as long and bi-lobed, with a yellow streak through the centre and edged with white. I really like these flowers, even though each bloom is slightly different. (J W A Lefeber 1948, 1962)

'Marie-Jose' 11bW-Y/OW mid (p. 70, 88)
Sometimes called 'White Butterfly' which is confusing since it is not the same as 'Papillon Blanc', which was its pod parent, this is a showy flower with blooms 9.5 cm (3.75 in) across. The tepals are broad and ice white, and the corona segments are two-thirds of their length. They are deeply bi-lobed and shaded orange for most of their length, with thin, white, wavy margins. A great flower for cutting and nice in the garden too. (J W A Lefeber 1974)

Daffodils and tulips
Photographed with
Ribes x gordonianum and
Primula 'Katy McSparron'.
Top row:
Narcissus 'White Marvel'
4W-W,
Tulip 'Gavota',
Narcissus 'Pipit' 7YYW-W.
Second row:
T. clusiana var chrysantha,
Narcissus 'Binkie' 2Y-W.
Bottom row:
Tulip 'Aladdin',
Narcissus 'Marie Jose'
11bW-Y/OW,
Narcissus 'Curlew' 7W-W.

'Menehay' 11aY-O mid (p. 86)
An excellent show flower, this has rigidly flat tepals, strong stems, and a cocky, look-you-in-the-eye pose that is lacking in many of this division. The tepals have a wonderful shape and are deep yellow, while the corona segments are bright orange and lie flat against the 8.5-cm (3.3-in) perianth, making an almost perfect circle of orange, leaving the outer two thirds as a contrast. (R A Scamp 1991; AGM-RHS 2001)

'Mondragon' 11aY-O mid–late (p. 86)
Readily available, this has huge (10.5 cm/4 in) flowers for its division, with broad tepals that are bright, lemon-yellow, slightly creased and wavy. The corona segments are broad and bright orange, ribbed and frilled to create a showy bloom that achieves a happy compromise between being too tailored and too fussy. (J Gerritsen & Son 1973)

'Orangery' 11aW-OOY early–mid
This large flower has broad white tepals that are rather creased and in-curled. Its bright orange corona segments are deeply bi-lobed and frilly. In some cases these can show paler areas of yellow or white. It is a bright, pretty flower for the garden. (J Gerritsen & Son 1973)

'Palmares' 11aW-P mid–late
This division is dominated by yellow and orange flowers, but some of the best have pastel colouring, and not all are new. 'Palmares' is readily available and has 9-cm (3.5-in) flowers with ivory tepals that overlap to half way. The corona is split into six segments that are frilly and almost as long as the tepals. They are peachy pink, though much paler at the centre. (J Gerritsen & Son 1973)

'Pampaluna' 11aY-Y mid (p. 86)
This is a rather sophisticated flower because the tepals and corona segments are the same, deep gold. It has great form, with even tepals, and the corona lies flat against the perianth. (R A Scamp)

'Papillon Blanc' 11bW-W late
This has 8.5-cm (3.3-in) flowers with broad, white tepals and frilly corona segments that are white with a yellow streak at first that ages to cream. (J W A Lefeber 1940, 1960)

'Parisienne' 11aW-O mid
This has shorter corona segments than some and though they are heavily frilled and ribbed, the bright orange segments are not overpowered by the white perianth, which is 10 cm (4 in) across. It has been described as a very frilly 'Professor Einstein'. That is appropriate and helps explain how, in my eyes, this differs from most others. It is readily available. (J Gerritsen & Son 1961)

'Pentire' 11aY-R (p. 86)
If you think small is beautiful you will love this bloom, which is about 6 cm (2.3 in) across. It has beautifully rounded, golden tepals, and the corona segments are orange, shading to the same golden yellow at the base. A perky, pretty flower that is a real charmer. (R A Scamp 2002)

'Pink Formal' 11aW-P mid (p. 89)
Despite its name, this daffodil is not a formal

flower at all, but a frothy confection with heavily frilled and ribbed corona segments. These are soft pink and set off against the 11-cm (4.25-in) white perianth. (G E Mitsch 1979, R & E Havens 1993)

'Pink Glacier' 11aW-P (p. 89)
This sister seedling of 'Pink Formal', raised from 'Recital' and 'Phantom' – the latter a popular parent – has more precise form and whiter tepals than its sibling. The inner three tepals are more triangular than the outer, creating a 9 cm (3.5 in) perianth, and the frilly, flat corona segments are a pleasant light pink, shading to yellow in the eye. (G E Mitsch 1979, R & E Havens 1993)

'Pink Holly' 11aW-P
It is the corona that makes this flower so special. The perianth is white, and the slightly reflexed inner three tepals are more triangular than the others. The corona is flat and ruffled, and as good a pink as you will find in any daffodil. This flower should be one with which to astound the neighbours! (R & E Havens 1991)

'Pink Tango' 11aW-P (p. 89)
This striking flower is similar to 'Phantom', part of its ancestry, and has large flowers with white tepals that are often rather inrolled and do not lie flat. Against this, the deep-pink corona segments are very obvious and are rather thin, creating a starry effect, with frilly ends. One to divide opinion. (G E Mitsch & R & E Havens 1975, R & E Havens 1991)

'Printal' 11aW-Y early
This has such ruffled corona segments that it appears to be double. The perianth is ivory white, 8.5 cm (3.3 in) across, and the tepals are creased and in two rows. The corona segments are pale yellow with a deep yellow edge, and they are heavily ruffled and have overlapping lobes. (J Gerritsen & Son 1966, 1976)

'Rosado' 11aW-P late
This was raised from 'Articol' and has white tepals that are almost covered, apart from the tips, by the bi-lobed corona segments. These are salmon pink, shading to greenish-yellow at the base. A pretty flower of delicate colouring. (J Gerritsen & Son 1986)

'Sorbet' 11bW-Y/OW late
These flowers are 10 cm (4 in) across with white tepals of good substance that are only slightly creased. The corona segments are about half the length of the tepals. They are golden yellow with a touch of orange, edged with white, and notched at the tip. It is a fine flower and would make an ideal companion to a planting of 'Broadway Star' and 'Lemon Beauty'. (W F Leenen 1966, 1977)

'Sparnon' 11aW-GYY mid (p. 51)
Raised by Ron Scamp, this is one of several of his seedlings that he was reluctant to name but which, over the years, showed its merits and attracted the attention of visitors. It is a cool flower with white tepals and a ribbed, frilly, pale yellow corona that lies back against the perianth. Vigorous and free-flowering. (R A Scamp 1998)

'Sunnyside Up' 11Y-Y mid–late
This is a gorgeous flower, with the corona split into segments that lie flat against, and cover, the tepals. The segments are frilled and ruffled, creating a strange flower that looks more like a tropical cucurbit than a daffodil.

Pink splits and doubles
Top row:
'Bosvale' 11aW-P,
'Pink Tango' 11aW-P,
'Bosvale'.
Second row:
'Pink Glacier' 11aW-P,
'Bossiney' 11aW-WPP.
Bottom row:
'Astropink' 11aW-P,
'Spaniards Inn' 4W-P,
'Pink Formal' 11aW-P.

'Tiritomba' 11aY-O early–mid (p. 86)
This yellow and orange flower has a 9-cm (3.5-in) perianth that is almost covered by the segments of the corona. These are deep orange, bi-lobed and frilled. The flowers have good pose and even seem to look up as you pass! (J Gerritsen & Son 1974)

'Tricollet' 11aW-O mid–late
This flower, and the following entry, 'Trilune', fascinates some and repels others. As if split coronas were not mad enough, these only have three corona segments. The result is distinctly odd. 'Tricollet' has a white perianth of good form and three orange corona segments that lie over the inner three tepals. The segments are ribbed and lightly frilled. Neighbours will either love this or buy you something to kill caterpillars. (J Gerritsen & Son 1969)

'Trilune' 11aW-Y mid
This companion to 'Tricollet' has a white perianth and three corona segments of bright yellow against the inner tepals. (J Gerritsen & Son 1983)

'Tripartite' 11aY-Y late (p. 131)
This delightful, pale yellow daffodil should convince anyone that splits can be delicate and beautiful. Each stem carries two or three small (6.5 cm/2.5 in) flowers that have a deeper yellow corona split into six segments, three of which reflex more than the others. True, the perianth reflexes as it ages, but it blooms late and lasts well, and is a charming garden plant with grace and beauty. It is rapidly becoming one of my favourite of all daffodils, and it successfully combines novelty with beauty. Its late flowering is useful too. (R L Brooks 1980; AGM-RHS 2001)

'Valdrome' 11aW-Y mid
This tall flower is still popular among the new cultivars, and has a creamy white perianth and lemon-yellow corona segments that cover two-thirds of the tepal. (J Gerritsen & Son 1965)

DIVISION 12
Miscellaneous

This catch-all division includes those daffodils that do not fit into the other divisions. It would

not be of much importance were it not for the work of Alec Gray, whose good luck or dedication presented us with 'Tête-à-Tête'.

'Cornish Chuckles' 12Y-O early (p. 42)
This hybrid of Division 8's 'Matador' and *N. cyclamineus* is a sister seedling to 'Eaton Song', but is a shorter plant with a deeper-coloured corona. It is dwarf and blooms early, and has several golden flowers per stem with reflexed tepals and a darker, lightly ribbed corona. It produces secondary stems to extend the season of flowers. A fine rival to 'Tête-à-Tête'. (Harry I Tuggle Jr 1973, Cornwall Area Bulb Growers' Association 1996)

'Eaton Song' 12-Y-O early
This sister seedling of 'Cornish Chuckles' has slightly taller – though still short – stems, and has two or three 7-cm (2.75-in) flowers per stem, and secondary stems with one or two flowers. (Harry I Tuggle Jr 1973, Cornwall Area Bulb Growers' Association 1989; AGM-RHS 2001)

'Jumblie' 12Y-O mid
This small plant has two or three yellow flowers per stem, with orange coronas that are crowded and have a rather jumbled effect. The tepals are reflexed and the corona is cylindrical, rather constricted at the mouth. The bulbs sometimes produce secondary stems. It is smaller than its sibling, 'Tête-à-Tête', and has been eclipsed by that cultivar. (A Gray pre-1952; AGM-RHS 1995)

'Quince' 12Y-Y early
This is the least commercially successful of the three seedlings raised from 'Cyclataz' (the others are 'Tête-à-Tête' and 'Jumblie'). It has two to four flowers per stem with soft yellow tepals and a deeper-coloured corona. (A Gray pre-1953)

'Tête-à-Tête' 12Y-Y very early (p. 17, 38)
This superb plant must be the most successful of all dwarf daffodils and is available everywhere in spring, from garden centres to garage forecourts and supermarkets. It is the result of one of those genetic quirks that happen from time to time. Its parent was 'Cyclataz', an odd hybrid of *N. cyclamineus* and 'Soleil d'Or'. It has two to four flowers per stem with reflexed tepals and orange

coronas. It is not particularly hardy, or vigorous. Alec Gray grew the plant and one year it set one seed pod, an unusual occurrence. This contained just three seeds, which he sowed. The chances of anything good coming from these was remote, but all three resulted in fine plants and all were released: 'Jumblie', 'Quince' and 'Tête-à-Tête'. 'Tête-à-Tête' is a super garden plant and often the first to flower. Each stem produces one or two flowers, and these open almost as soon as the buds are clear of the soil, the stems extending to 20 cm (8 in) as they age. Usually there are secondary stems, and the bulbs flower for more than a month altogether. The flowers are 6.5 cm (2.5 in) across with bright yellow tepals and a slightly darker, straight or slightly flared mouth. It is now extremely common, but it is impossible not to love it. It is tough enough to thrive in any border, yet cute enough for pots and containers. (A Gray pre-1949; AGM-RHS 1993)

'Toto' 12 W-W mid

This vigorous, small plant, bred from 'Jenny' and *N. jonquilla*, has up to three, starry, 5.5-cm (2-in) wide, white flowers per stem, with slightly reflexed tepals and a cylindrical corona. The corona is yellow at first but ages to white. (W G Pannill 1983; AGM-RHS 1997)

DIVISION 13
Species

There are about 50 species of *Narcissus*, mostly from Europe, especially the Mediterranean, with some species in North Africa. But botanists have not been able to decide whether many are species or subspecies, and the number fluctuates whenever someone tackles the difficult task of sorting out what nature has given us. The majority of species are not plants for the average gardener, requiring either specialist conditions or being too small to satisfy the need for something colourful in the border. Fascinating though they all are, I have not attempted to delve into the world of species *Narcissus*, but have tried merely to skim the surface and describe a few that are either easy to grow, easy to buy, or have been found worthy of the RHS Award of Garden Merit. Specialists will find this selection wanting, but I include it only to illustrate from what plants

the garden daffodil has developed, and to give a snapshot of the diversity of the genus, without any intervention from the hand of the hybridizer.

Narcissus asturiensis (the small clipped trunk daffodil)

It is reassuring to know that however small your garden, you will have room for this golden or pale yellow trumpet daffodil. Not all small flowers deserve to be called cute – some are merely stunted – but *N. asturiensis*, named after the Asturias mountains of north-western Spain, is a little charmer. Despite its diminutive size, it is not too delicate, and it was still growing, after 30 years of minimal maintenance, when I took over at E A Bowles's garden to begin restoration in the mid-1980s. It had endured overgrown conditions in well-drained, gravelly soil that was dry in summer. It is an early flower, opening its blooms on 10-cm (4-in) stems before many daffodils have started to show. It is a perfectly proportioned miniature with a sloping stem, and flowers that have narrow, forward-facing tepals and a corona with a slightly flared, toothed mouth, slightly constricted halfway down the tube.

It prefers acid soil but, as long as it is not wet, it is not difficult to grow, either by dividing clumps or from seed. Obviously, its diminutive stature makes it ideal for a rock garden or a pan in the alpine house, and it deserves protection from slugs. *N. minor* (AGM-RHS 1994) is similar but slightly larger and flowers later, though still early.

N. bulbocodium L. (hoop petticoat daffodil)

The bulbocodium daffodils are found, in the wild, in Spain (apart from the east), southwest France, and patches of North Africa to the south and west of Spain, as far south as Marrakech and Agadir. Though best known as *N. bulbocodium*, there are many subspecies, and I will also deal with four other species here (*N. cantabricus*, *N. hedraeanthus*, *N. obesus* and *N. romieuxii*) because they are similar in overall appearance. The 'bulbocodiums' are instantly recognized by their diminutive overall size, their flowers having disproportionately large, inflated coronas and narrow, tiny tepals that do not add much to the overall appearance of the flower. Other characteristics are the anthers, which are attached to the filaments at right angles (unlike all other *Narcissus*, in which they are more or less in line with the filaments), and the style, which curves upwards to give the flowers a characteristic zygomorphic shape.

Where they grow wild they cover a wide range of altitudes and flowering periods, blooming from November through to May at high altitudes in Spain. The African, winter-flowering species are definitely plants for the alpine house, to protect them from excess winter wet and cold, but *N. bulbocodium* itself is happy in the garden if it has acid soil that is moist in spring, similar to the conditions it enjoys in the wild. In all but *N. hedraeanthus*, the narrow, grassy leaves appear before the flower stems start to grow.

N. bulbocodium subsp. *bulbocodium* var. *bulbocodium* is the overlong name for the typical plant that has bright yellow flowers with dark green leaves and horizontally held blooms about 2 cm (0.75 in) across and leaves 1 mm wide and 10 cm (4 in) long. *N. bulbocodium* subsp. *bulbocodium* var. *conspicuus* has larger flowers, 2.5 cm (1 in) across, in golden or pale yellow, and is probably the kind most often sold. *N. obesus* is similar to *N. bulbocodium* but that it grows on alkaline soils.

The name *N. cantabricus* covers most white-flowered bulbocodiums (apart from *N. bulbocodium* subsp. *bulbocodium* var. *graellsii* and *N. romieuxii* subsp. *albidus*) and is from southern Spain (not from the Cantabrian Mountains of northern Spain, as the name seems to imply). *N. cantabricus* subsp. *cantabricus* var. *cantabricus* (AGM-RHS 1994) flowers for me (in a greenhouse) in November and has beautiful flowers with a 3-cm (1.25-in) wide, broad, pleated, snow-white corona. *N. cantabricus* subsp. *cantabricus* var. *foliosus* (AGM-RHS 1994) produces creamy white flowers in late autumn. But the most beautiful of all is *N. cantabricus* subsp. *cantabricus* var. *petunoides*, which has flowers on 6-cm (2.3-in) stems and enormous coronas 4 cm (1.5 in) wide.

N. romieuxii (AGM-RHS 1993) is from North Africa and has two subspecies, both of which are hardy but benefit from an alpine house to protect them from winter wet. *N. romieuxii* subsp. *romieuxii* var. *romieuxii* has flowers in pale yellow with a broad corona 3 cm (1.25 in) in diameter. *N. romieuxii* subsp. *albidus* has white flowers. *N.*

hedraeanthus has pale yellow flowers, and tepals that are much more obvious than in all other bulbocodiums.

The bulbocodiums have not made a great impact in the general garden, although in recent years 'Golden Bells' has become common (see Division 10). *N. romieuxii* subsp. *romieuxii* var. *romieuxii* hybridizes with *N. cantabricus*, and Douglas Blanchard raised and named some seedlings, introducing 'Muslin', 'Taffeta' and 'Nylon', but these are not common. (*N. bulbocodium* AGM-RHS 1994)

N. canaliculatus (Hort.) (p. 28, 76)

The true species may not be in cultivation and is supposed to have narrow tepals. The plant we can buy under this name is probably more attractive and has in the past (in the UK at least) been sold as the 'Chinese Sacred Lily', one of those stupid names of obscure origin that is supposed to tempt gullible gardeners into parting with their cash (not being Chinese, sacred or even in the lily family, it is an astonishing bit of naming – on a par with 'Japanese Wonder Flowers' for mirabilis roots). It is commonly available and grows to about 20 cm (8 in) high with narrow grey-green leaves and small clusters of flowers with reflexing white tepals and a golden orange corona. It is fragrant, but it is not an ideal plant in most climates because it is not totally hardy and needs a good summer ripening to stimulate flowering. Even fresh bulbs I have grown and planted for greenhouse display have often been disappointing, producing only one flower stem from ten bulbs. It's worth trying in a rock garden, or in mild areas.

Narcissus cyclamineus DC

This familiar plant, which has had such a profound effect on garden daffodils, had a controversial beginning in cultivation. In the 1840s Dean Herbert declared it 'an absurdity which will never be found to exist' after observing illustrations. Yet it was known in the 17th century, but then forgotten until rediscovered in 1885 in Oporto, Portugal. It is, unfortunately, rare in the wild, increasingly so as developments have encroached on the lowland areas it prefers. But it is not a difficult plant to grow, especially in heavy, moist soil, and it flowers early in the year.

The remarkable flowers – which caused all the fuss – have small tepals that are 4 mm (0.2 in) wide but up to 2 cm (0.75 in) long, and they reflex so far that they lie at 180 degrees to the corona, which is long (longer than the tepals) and narrow with a barely flared mouth. The blooms hang slightly from the horizontal and are clear golden yellow with bright green stems and leaves. It is not easy to describe or isolate the charm of these flowers, but E A Bowles did it better than most in his oft-quoted 'wide-awake expression rather like that of a kicking horse with its ears laid back'. (AGM-RHS 1993)

Narcissus jonquilla L.

The jonquils, as a group, can be recognized by having several flowers on a stem, with tepals that never reflex and with coronas that are wider than they are long. All have yellow flowers apart from the odd, green *N. viridiflora*. They are mostly native to Portugal, Spain and a few Mediterranean islands. They are generally lowland plants that grow in moist soil. *N. jonquilla* grows to 40 cm (16 in) high with up to six golden yellow flowers per stem, and the leaves are frequently taller than the flower stems. The blooms are about 3 cm (1.25 in) across and sweetly scented, blooming later than most species. Some stocks flower freely, while others increase vegetatively but rarely bloom. (AGM-RHS 1994)

Narcissus moschatus L. (*N. pseudonarcissus* subsp. *moschatus*) (p. 39)

This, the drooping white Spanish daffodil or swan's neck daffodil, has been cultivated for more than three centuries, but its wild origins are obscure because it has not been found in the wild. It is not uncommon, and is beautiful, with nodding flowers that have white, twisted tepals and a slightly darker, creamy corona 4 cm (1.5 in) in length – longer than the tepals. It is not difficult to grow, and the flowers nod almost vertically. (AGM-RHS 2001)

Narcissus obvallaris Salisb. (*Narcissus pseudonarcissus* subsp. *obvallaris*) (p. 39)

This is the Tenby daffodil, so called because, until recently, it has been found only around the town of Tenby in Wales. However, this association dates only to the 1880s, and seed does not breed true, so it may not be a true species. Recent expeditions have found similar plants in Spain. It is easily grown and commonly available, popular because it naturalizes well, and its small size makes it perfect in grass in even a small garden. It has grey foliage, and the flowers have flat yellow tepals that stand at 90 degrees to the broad, golden coronas on 20-cm (8-in) stems. (AGM-RHS 1993)

Narcissus poeticus L. (p. 131)

This is one of the most recognizable of all wild *Narcissus* and the one that most gardeners refer to as 'narcissus' as opposed to daffodil, the distinction being based on the short coronas of 'narcissi'. Though easily recognized by gardeners, it is a botanical minefield because of the mass of variations caused by the widespread distribution of the plant in the wild, from northern Spain in the west, through southern France and northern Italy, and south-east through the Balkans.

But all have a flat, broad perianth of white tepals (often creamy on opening) and a tiny corona that is flat and ribbed and rimmed with red, the only species to show this coloration. This has been used to breed red and pink cups in hybrids, and not only has the colour been inherited, but also the habit of this red tissue to burn in bright sunlight.

No one seems sure why this should be the 'poet's' *Narcissus*, but it has always been popular and has been cultivated since at least 1570. Each stem produces a flower (occasionally two) about 7 cm (2.75 in) across, and they are the last to bloom in the garden, well into May. The plant has greyish foliage and tall, thin stems, but it is loved most for its sweet perfume, which has been inherited by poet hybrids. From experience I have discovered that late planting results in the bulbs needing several years to settle down to flowering. They are perfect for naturalizing, but be aware that the first cut of the grass will only be possible in July because of the late flowers.

Although the species is frequently called 'pheasant's eye', the name really applies to *N. poeticus* var. *recurvus* (AGM-RHS 1993), which has twisted tepals of the purest white. The corona has a green eye, edged with yellow and a red rim, and its fragrance is strong and sweet. It is found in the western part of the species' distribution and prefers a moist spot. *N. poeticus* var. *hellenicus* is from Greece and has smaller flowers than most (4.5 cm/1.75 in). Its tepals are reflexed, but they are rounded and of good texture, and it has been used in breeding both because of its form and also because it is tough and reliable. *N. poeticus* var. *physaloides* has an inflated spathe.

Narcissus pseudonarcissus L. (p. 58)

This is the typical wild daffodil with which everyone is familiar. It is well worth growing, even though it is eclipsed in size by most hybrids. It has horizontal or slightly nodding flowers with a bright yellow, narrow corona and thin, twisted tepals of a paler colour that do not manage to open much from the line of the trumpet. The foliage is blue-green and the flowers stand on stems 25 cm (10 in) high. It has been known in England since at least 1570 but it may not be native. However, if introduced, it has found conditions to its liking and is at least naturalized in many parts of the UK, including Herefordshire and Yorkshire and, of course, the Lake District, where it forms the 'hosts' that Wordsworth would have seen. It is very likely that in many places it is a garden escape. Easy to grow and delicate, it is ideal for naturalizing in grass and woodland, but is not always easy to obtain. (AGM-RHS 1994)

Narcissus rupicola

This pretty little plant, one of the jonquils, is a Spanish native and grows to about 10 cm (4 in) high with just one (unusual for jonquils) bloom per stem. These are rounded and bright yellow, and about 2 cm (0.75 in) across. It is a good plant for the alpine house, where it can be given a warm, dry summer. (AGM-RHS 1994). *N. rupicola* subsp. *marvieri* (AGM-RHS 1994) is larger in all its parts, and native to Morocco.

Narcissus serotinus L.

I include this because it is an oddity that I have seen on several occasions on holiday in Mallorca, and it is likely to be encountered by any gardener on a non-botanical holiday. It is a charming little plant and one I find exciting because it flowers in autumn – not something that will cause a rapid pulse in daffodil specialists, but enough to tickle me. The autumn rains, or lower temperatures, in October, when I feel I can safely leave the garden for a week, stimulate the small, dark-skinned bulbs to produce flowers, and these are held on narrow stems up to 15 cm (6 in) high above crushed rocks and dry grass. It is common along coastal areas around the Mediterranean and on the islands, and its flowers are only 1–1.5 cm

(0.4–0.6 in) across and pure white, with narrow tepals and a short white corona. Most stems have just one flower, but there are frequently two and sometimes three, and they have a sweet scent. Flowering sized bulbs do not produce a leaf but the flowering stem increases in length after flowering to produce food to bulk up the bulb. It is not suitable for growing outside in the UK but is a nice plant for a cold or cool greenhouse, and easy to grow from seed. This species is not the only one to flower in autumn, and the most desirable is probably the green-flowered *N. viridiflorus*, which is a scented jonquil. With its narrow tepals, tiny lobed corona and deep green colour, it is remarkable, but not easy to cultivate.

Narcissus triandrus L.

This is a distinctive species for gardeners, though it is really a confusing mess of subspecies and varieties for botanists. Things seem to have settled down in recent years, and of the most common variants, var. *triandrus* has white flowers and broad leaves, var. *cernuus* has white or pale flowers and narrow leaves, and var. *concolor* has bright yellow flowers. None of these are very common in cultivation, having been replaced by their hybrids, but *N. triandrus* var. *triandrus* is a pretty plant with up to six nodding flowers. They have reflexed perianths about 6 cm (2.3 in) across and a 1.5-cm (0.6-in) wide corona. It grows to about 30 cm (12 in) high and is best on acid soil. A Spanish species, it is most common in the north-west and centre of that country, where it grows in shady spots. It is in the section Ganymedes, and that was once its generic name too.

In fact, its names are almost as fascinating as the plant itself. 'Triandrus' means 'three stamens' – a ludicrous idea, but Linnaeus named it after seeing an illustration by the botanist Clusius that only showed three stamens. The common name 'Angel's Tears' has an even more interesting origin. The species was introduced to the UK, through wild collections, in the 1880s and 1890s by Peter Barr and his son (also Peter), who collected it in north-west Spain with the help of local boy Angel Gancedo. Angel had to climb steep and rough terrain in blistering heat to reach and remove the bulbs of the plants that Peter Barr had seen, and he returned tired, hot and in tears – apparently of anger. The bag of bulbs was marked 'Angel's tears', and the name stuck. (AGM-RHS 1994)

Chapter 4
Tulips

Wild tulips are found in dry areas in southern Europe, the Middle East and eastern and central Asia, and there are about a hundred species. They vary in height between just a few centimetres and about 40 cm (16 in), and have flowers ranging from the small and dull to large, scarlet blooms blotched with black. Many have more than one flower per stem. The wild species show huge variation, and seem the perfect plants to begin a great dynasty of garden flowers. A few species have obviously led to their own groups of cultivars, such as *T. greigii*, but one of the extraordinary mysteries of the tulip is that it has been impossible to determine just which species created the Turkish tulips that, when brought to Europe, so captured the imagination of gardeners. The mystery is further compounded by the fact that Europe has tulips that appear to be native. *T. clusiana* is odd because it is found wild in Spain but it is sterile and does not set seed, reproducing by stolons. Most wild plants have to be fertile in order to survive, and sterility and vegetative propagation tend to be signs of domestication. So is *clusiana* truly indigenous to Spain, or was it introduced? Doubt also surrounds the yellow, nodding *T. sylvestris*, which is sometimes considered a rare British native. But however it arrived in the UK, like most other tulip species it seems to have played no part in the development of the garden tulip.

The name 'tulip' is said to be an allusion to the resemblance of the flower to the Turkish headgear – *dulbend* in Turkish, which became *tulband* in Dutch. But the Turkish flowers had long, thin tepals and did not resemble a turban at all. The name can be traced back as far as 1578, but until the end of the 16th century European botanists often called it *lilionarcissus*. It was Ogier Ghislain de Busbecq who coined the name *tulip* or *tulipan* when his Turkish guide tried to describe the flowers. In Turkish itself the name is *lale*.

The main tulip species are described in the next chapter, but most tulips follow the same basic plan.

Tulips are perennials that form bulbs. In the first year after germinating, the seed forms a narrow leaf and rapidly forms a small bulb that is pulled down into the soil by its contractile root. This is a thick root that grows vertically, attaches itself to the soil at the base and then contracts to pull the bulb away from the surface. Most bulbs use the same mechanism. When mature, the bulbs produce a stem, with several leaves that are usually restricted to the lower part of the stem, and a flower or flowers at the top. These flowers are simple in construction, with six tepals arranged in two rows. The outer tepals are similar to the inner but may be wider and are frequently streaked with green. Inside are six stamens, and a central ovary with three segments (locules) that contain the seeds.

T. clusiana '**Cynthia**' thriving in a hot, dry spot in the author's garden.

History of the Tulip

Turkish Delight

To the Ottomans – the Turkish people who unseated the Roman Empire from Asia Minor, making it Turkey, and finally captured Constantinople in 1453, making it Istanbul – the tulip was a sacred flower. It was considered a good-luck charm, and it featured in their embroidery and other decoration. They even embroidered tulips on their undergarments.

The Ottomans were a fierce, warlike people, constantly striving to increase their empire by battling against Christian states – but they also appreciated beauty. In the newly taken Istanbul, Sultan Mehmed ll (ruled 1451–81) built the Topkapi palace and laid out the fabulous gardens throughout the walled city that gave it a fabled reputation for beauty. The greatest gardener of them all was Suleyman the Magnificent (ruled 1520–66). He enlarged the Turkish Empire from the gates of Vienna to the Persian Gulf and from Gibraltar to the Caspian Sea.

By now, the tulip was loved in Turkey, and it appeared on clothes, vases and tiles, but was still unknown in Europe. The Sultan would have tulips planted in the fourth, most private court of the Topkapi palace, seen only by him, his most important guests and his gardeners. The court had spectacular views of the Bosphorus, and the tulips jostled with other prized plants such as roses, carnations, hyacinths and narcissi. Everything was done to excess, as befitted such an important ruler. Five thousand servants worked in the palace and there were a thousand gardeners, called *bostancis*. Oddly, the duties of the gardeners included executions: condemned women were sewn into weighted sacks and dropped into the Bosphorus, while men were strangled. Senior officials who had upset the sultan would be killed by the head gardener, the *bostanci-basha*. But *bostancis* also cut the heads off tulips for the palace, and the flowers were carefully shown off in glass vases.

It was in Suleyman's time that the first gardeners devoted themselves to cultivating tulips, and a gardener called Seyhulislam Ebusuud Efendi grew a tulip called 'Nur-I-Adin' (the light of paradise). So highly were tulips regarded that they were given beautiful names. Others were called 'Increaser of Pleasure' and 'Instiller of Passion'. It is not clear if these old varieties were of the same type as the slender tulips that we associate with Turkish tulips today, because some feel that the genetic stock for these was not introduced until a century after Seyhulislam Ebusuud Efendi's death in 1574.

Little was known about the science of horticulture, so the production of new tulips was inevitably slow, but the popularity of the flowers increased and, by 1630, there were 80 flower shops and 300 professional florists in Istanbul. It was at this time that the Turks started to breed new tulips. The wild flowers that grew around Istanbul had round flowers, but the Turks loved those with thin tepals. There were eventually 1,500 cultivars of these 'Istanbul tulips'. Although vast numbers of wild-collected tulips were undoubtedly planted in gardens, the most desirable were those with thin, claw-like tepals, similar to those we call *T. acuminata*, a bloom that makes even lily-flowered tulips look obese.

Fosteriana tulip 'Candela' opening wide in the sun.

T. acuminata is not a true wild species, and it is not clear where or how it originated. It is recorded that in 1651, the Austrian ambassador brought 40 tulip bulbs from Europe to Turkey as a gift for Mehmed IV, 15 years after the height of Tulipomania in the Netherlands, and a source written in 1726 says that the Istanbul narrow tulips were raised from these bulbs. If so, it is a strange turnaround and suggests that Europe must have got at least some of its tulips from places other than Turkey if, as this suggests, the Europeans were able to inject new genetic stock into the Turkish tulip a century after they had first found it there. The origins of the 'domestic' tulip are still not clear. While hybrids of *T. greigii* and a few other species can be easily attributed to specific species, the vast majority of cultivars have origins we can only guess at. Though frustrating, this mystery adds to the magic of the garden tulip.

T. acuminata is the nearest we have to the tulips loved by the Turks and recreated on their art and everyday objects. The tepals had to be of equal width, slender, and on thin stalks, and the slender leaves had to be shorter than the flower stalk. If the flower was broken it was better if the ground colour was white rather than yellow, and double flowers were not allowed. These rules are rather similar to those for English Florist tulips in their rigidity, but the Turks loved slender, elegant flowers, while the English and Flemish liked the broad and round varieties.

Many tulips were imported to Turkey from other countries such as Crete, and in 1574 Suleyman's son Selim II instructed 50,000 tulip bulbs to be sent from Syria for planting in the imperial gardens. Collecting wild tulips from other countries was easy at this time because the Turkish Empire was powerful, but Westerners were starting to visit, and found Istanbul a fascinating place. While there, they discovered the tulip.

The Road to Europe

History has it that the tulip was first brought to Europe by Lopo Vaz de Sampayo, who was a governor of the Portuguese enclave at Goa, India until 1529, when he was for some reason disgraced and ordered to return home. The problem with this story is that the route by sea

from Goa to Portugal (via the Cape of Good Hope) would not have taken him anywhere near Turkey, so how did he get the tulips to bring to Europe? Is it possible that the tulip had spread east to India first?

What is clear from the records is that when Europeans did see the flower in 1561 they thought it was very exciting. It is likely that the first European to see a tulip was the splendidly named Ogier Ghislain de Busbecq. He went to Istanbul in November 1554 as the ambassador of the Holy Roman Empire. He stayed in the Ottoman Empire for eight years, and when he returned he published his racy memoirs, including a description of his first sight of a tulip. On his way back to Istanbul after a trip to Vienna

Tulip 'Quebec', a Greigii tulip, blooming with polyanthus 'Guinevere' in the author's garden.

he passed through an area with many bulb flowers. 'There is an abundance of narcissi and hyacinths in Greece, and they possess so wonderful a scent that a large quantity of them causes a headache in those who are unaccustomed to such an odour. The tulip has little or no scent, but it is admired for its beauty and the variety of its colours. The Turks are very fond of flowers, and though they are otherwise anything but extravagant, they do not hesitate to pay several aspres [coins] for a fine blossom.' He wrote this in 1580, describing a journey made in March 1558.

Tulips seem to have been given so freely as tokens of esteem that the son of the Archbishop of York, George Sandys, who was obviously not there to visit gardens, wrote of his visit: 'You cannot stirre abroad, but you shall be presented by the Dervishes and Janizaries with tulips and trifles.'

The Turkish love affair with tulips continued for another 150 years, with more than 1,000 cultivars still listed by the early 1700s. In the 1730s, however, the tulip fell from favour in Turkey, and although it remained a symbol in art, the bulbs were no longer grown or valued as they had been. Today the Turkish tulip is gone and almost forgotten.

Busbecq may have been the first European to see a tulip in Turkey but he was not the person who introduced them to the West, because a tulip was being grown in Germany by 1559 in the garden of Johann Heinrich Herwart in Augsburg, Bavaria. He was visited by Conrad Gesner, who lived in Zurich and was compiling his *Catalogus plantarum*. This was published in 1561, and its engravings of flowers included the first sight most of his readers would have had of a tulip.

He wrote that in April 1559 he saw a plant that had grown from a seed from 'Byzantia' (the former name of Constantinople) or 'Cappadocia' (a region of what is now central Turkey). 'It was flowering with a single beautifully red flower, large, like a red lily, formed of eight petals of which four were outside and the rest within.' We need not worry that his flower had eight tepals, because flowers on strong bulbs frequently have extra tepals in the same way that the flower at the top of the stem in bearded iris frequently has four standards and falls. He called the plant *T. turcarum*. There are reports of tulips in other

parts of Europe at about this time, which suggests that it may have been introduced several times, since it takes a tulip four or five years to flower and set seed. Tulips reached England by 1582 and France by 1598, and they caught the imagination of gardeners there too, but the Dutch had the greatest stock to work with.

The most important name associated with tulips is Carolus Clusius and he obtained tulips from his friend Joris Rye. Rye was invited to see some strange flowers that had grown from bulbs sent to a merchant among a shipment of cloth from Istanbul. The merchant had not wanted the bulbs and most had been pickled and eaten, but a few of the survivors were given to Joris Rye in 1563. Clusius was a traveller and was in Spain when Rye's bulbs first flowered in 1564; he probably first saw them in 1568, though he did not write about tulips until 1570. Clusius was one of the new breed of humanist scientists and, having heard about the fate of most of the first batch of tulips, he decided to investigate the culinary value of the bulbs and had some preserved in syrup.

Tulipomania and After

In 1573 he was asked to establish a botanical garden in Vienna, which was then only 80 km (50 miles) from the Ottoman border, something of a frontier town. Funds and help were slow in appearing, and it was not a total success. Even worse, many of the bulbs – which he grew from seeds sent by Ogier Ghislain de Busbecq – were stolen, and things simply got worse when his patron, the Holy Roman Emperor Maximilian ll, died. So it was with relief that in 1593 he moved to the University of Leiden and the country that would forever be associated with the tulip.

His main job in the Netherlands was to establish a botanic garden, but this time under the patronage not of an Emperor but of a rich university. He not only grew tulips but studied and described them, and became the main authority in Europe about these fabulous flowers. He and his plants were much in demand.

By 1630 there were tulips in Europe with broad tepals that approximate to the English Florist tulips that exist today, and there were categories for Rosen, Violetten and Bizarden tulips. There were 400 Rosen varieties alone. Although the flowers we would call breeders today were appreciated, it was the 'broken' or 'rectified' flowers – infected with virus – that caused a sensation in the Netherlands. Clusius had discovered that some strange phenomenon magically changed a self-coloured tulip into a bloom with intricate patterns; he also noticed that these blooms were smaller though no one knew the cause.

The fact that as soon as tulips flowered in Europe they produced virused flowers suggests that bulbs were imported, not just seed – since seed should produce 'clean' stock. To induce the breaking, concoctions were made and sold, including such ingredients as bird droppings. Sometimes, after watering tulips with pigeon droppings, the flower actually did change colour, though this was not the cause of the broken patterning. Some thought that to produce a red and white tulip it made sense to cut two bulbs in half and stick them together, but this did not work either. But the irony was that, while peach-potato aphids were busy spreading the virus throughout stocks all the time, it was indeed caused by joining affected and clean bulbs together, but at the molecular level. It was not until the research of Dorothy Cayley in 1928, working at the John Innes Institute in Merton, Surrey under its director Sir Daniel Hall, that the mechanism of viral infection through the sap was identified as the cause.

Eventually the demand for Clusius's tulip bulbs became so great that he had to refuse most requests. But the enthusiasts were desperate to have them, and in 1596 and again in 1598 thieves stole most of his stock of bulbs. He gave up gardening.

But these stolen bulbs formed the basis of the Dutch tulip trade. Clusius's collection had been diverse, and the many different tulips allowed exciting hybrids to be produced. Tulips became fashionable just at the time when the Dutch United Provinces were becoming extremely wealthy through foreign trade, particularly in spices. Tulips also grew well in the light, sandy soil of the country. By 1620, the tulip had become famous but was still not common, and wealthy merchants had plenty of money. Ostentatious shows of wealth were not permissible in the protestant culture of the time, but flowers were God's creations, so surely could not be criticized?

Among the many tulips that emerged at this time, the most famous was 'Semper Augustus', a Rosen that had some blue at the base of the tepals. It had been bred by a French florist who did not rate it highly and disposed of it in 1614. When it became famous, people were sent to search for other, similar flowers in Flanders. The demand for 'Semper Augustus' was huge but could never be met, and in 1624 it is said that only 12 bulbs existed, all owned by Adriaen Pauw, Lord of Heemstede and one of the Directors of the East India Company. He refused to sell any of his bulbs, even though, in that year, he was offered at least 2,000 guilders for a single bulb, twice the average annual earnings of a merchant. But even he could not get enough bulbs to fill his garden and impress his guests, so he arranged mirrors around his flowerbeds to give the impression of having more tulips than he actually possessed – and that he was wealthier too. He must have been obsessed with the flowers, since to own one of these tulips was more than most could afford, let alone a dozen.

Professional bulb growers realized the fortunes that could be made and started production, usually growing bulbs on a small scale, while other pioneers travelled the continent looking for unusual flowers to sell. Most of the growers were based around Haarlem. It seemed a good way to make money from a small plot of land.

Tulip flowers are beautiful, but tulips should be, and initially were, sold while dormant. Selling dull brown tulip bulbs was not always easy, so colourful catalogues were produced to show what was being sold. The first was produced by Emanuel Sweert in 1612, but later versions had up to 500 pages and were lavishly illustrated. They were not just catalogues of what was for sale but advertisements of what tulips a grower possessed – a fine way to show off even when your tulips were not in bloom.

The very rare tulips were still desirable, but more were becoming available. If anything is so rare that you stand little chance of owning it the demand soon wanes, but tulips were soon available, at least to the rich. This all fuelled the price of tulips and they started to spiral after 1634.

The astonishing thing about the 'tulip boom' is that it all happened so quickly. At the end of

Parrot tulip

'Green Wave', one of the most beautiful tulips of all, and exceptionally long lasting.

ridiculous sums did little harm at first, so long as people were buying bulbs that actually existed. But soon people started to sell the offsets before they were certain they had even formed. In late 1635 the practice of selling bulbs that growers and traders actually had in their hands changed to selling 'bulb IOUs'. This allowed the trade to take place all year round rather than just in the summer when the bulbs could be lifted, but it meant that the buyer was giving money for a bulb he had not seen or even knew existed. It was a 'futures' market. The trade then became more complicated because the offsets were sold by weight (azen) and it was possible for less wealthy florists to buy a part share in a bulb.

By February 1637 prices had risen to ridiculous levels, and at an auction in Haarlem on 3 February a batch of bulbs did not reach the expected price. (According to other sources, the crash began on 23 February at Amsterdam.) People's interest in bulbs had become exhausted. For the first time in decades, a batch of tulip bulbs failed to sell. The news spread like wildfire.

Perhaps even the richest people could no longer afford the tulips, or the fine tulips had become so adulterated by poor seedlings that anyone with sense realized that demand had outstripped supply and the tulips then on sale really were not worth as much as their predecessors. Whatever the reason, panic set in. In just three months the price of tulips dropped by 95–99 percent. Sellers were desperate to get their money, and buyers tried to renege on their purchases and avoid handing over the money on their 'futures'. People lost their homes, their livelihoods and their love of tulips for a while. The tulip industry contracted but it did not die.

The Dutch regained their love of tulips. In 1665 the first double tulip in the West was recorded, and in 1680 the first tulip vases were made. It is sometimes said that these were used to grow the bulbs but I cannot see how the bulbs could have been fitted into the narrow necks of the openings. Clearly, cut flowers would be elegantly displayed in the ornate, pyramid-shaped structures.

In 1690, the tulip changed its personality again when the first parrot tulip appeared. At about this time, French florists began to produce wide-cupped flowers called baguettes. It is possible that these growers were remnants of the tulipomania

1634 the prices started to rise. I suppose that panic buying pushed up the price even more through 1635. By the winter of 1636 the price of bulbs doubled in a week. The height of tulipomania was in December 1636 and January 1637. Everyone wanted tulips.

The price of 'Semper Augustus' rose from 5,500 guilders in 1633 to 10,000 guilders in January 1637, the same cost as a large house in Amsterdam. Another, 'Admiral van Enkhuijsen', sold for 5,400 guilders at a time when the average wage for a labourer was 400 guilders a year. Anecdotes about the price of tulip bulbs may not be true, but they are amusing. One tale tells of a merchant who bought a Rosen tulip and put it on the windowsill for a moment to find it gone when he turned round. After a search it was found that a sailor had picked it up, thinking it was an onion, and he was discovered chewing the last pieces of the bulb. The sailor was jailed.

The fantastic trade in tulips went wrong because of speculation. Selling bulbs for and grew the bulbs to satisfy the Dutch market. While florists in England and France may have been growing good tulips, however, they did not have the business acumen of the Dutch. The bulb-growing areas moved from Haarlem to the north-west of the country at around this time, and the Netherlands have been the world centre of tulip production ever since.

British florists were changing the tulip to a flower of great perfection, and among the finest of their productions was 'Miss Fanny Kemble'. This was raised by William Clark of Croydon, one of the top breeders of his day, and when he died in 1832 his one bulb of this tulip was bought by Thomas Davey of King's Road, Chelsea for 100 sovereigns. This was the great era of tulip fanciers, and between 1840 and 1855 there was a British 'tulip war', with different standards being set between the growers in the north and south of the country. Northern growers thought that southerners did not pay enough attention to the patterns on the flowers, and were too obsessed with the shape of the blooms instead.

While the British were admiring the fine nuances of broken blooms, in the US the idea of using tulips for bedding was starting with a massive display of 600 different sorts on Long Island in 1845. Tulips were hardly a novelty by this time, though such lavish displays probably still were. Bulbs had been advertised in American newspapers since 1760, presumably having crossed the Atlantic with Dutch settlers. Dutch bulb sellers also travelled through the United States in early Victorian times, taking orders and supplying tulips to keen gardeners; it became one of the most important Dutch markets.

E H Krelage was just as daring in 1889 when he bedded out with his Darwin tulips around the Trocadero palace near Piccadilly Circus, London. The gardeners at Kew, on the Thames, south-west of London, were also right on the ball as far as fashions were concerned when they bedded with 'Couleur Cardinal' outside the Palm House, or on opposite sides of the Broad Walk – in beds that I have dug myself, many years ago. Peter Barr (of Covent Garden, London) introduced his own bedding tulips based on English breeders, and he was joined in competition against the Dutch by Colchester-based Robert Wallace. The Krelage plants were better and more successful, however. Tulip growing spread throughout the world, and

was particularly important in the north-west US, the UK (centred around the Lincolnshire town of Spalding, which still has a tulip parade each May), Australia, New Zealand, Japan and parts of South America. There are now tulip gardens and festivals throughout the world, with a major festival in Ottawa, Canada every May. But the Netherlands still dominates world production, with about 20,000 hectares devoted to the crop. Every tulip lover should visit the wonderful display at the Keukenhof Gardens in Lisse at least once; the garden at the Hortus Bulborum is another must-see.

The volume of bulbs produced by the tulip industry is not currently increasing, and the area planted may have peaked, but modern methods mean that production times are decreasing and bulbs can be produced more quickly and efficiently, so total sales may still increase. Tulipomania may be long past, but the public's love of this magical flower is still strong.

Greigii tulip 'Corsage' combines bold flowers and patterned foliage.

Types of Tulip

More information about the different groups of tulips is given in the next chapter. The modern classification of the genus, as established in 1955, is as follows:

Single Early Tulips

These have short stems and flower early in the season. Single Early tulips are one of the most ancient groups and include ancient tulips such as 'Duc van Thol', which dates back to 1620. The flowers of this group are not important garden plants today, but are still produced in large numbers for forcing as early cut flowers. (p. 112)

Tulip 'Charmeur', a Triumph tulip with bold variegated foliage.

Double Early Tulips

These are similar in height, colour and flowering time to the Single Earlies but have flowers with more than six tepals. (p. 115)

Triumph Tulips

These are of moderate height, have single flowers, and bloom in mid-season. The official definition states they were bred by hybridizing Single Early and Single Late tulips, but the term was born in 1923 after N Zandbergen of Rijnsburg raised varieties from a batch of seedlings bought from the Zocher company of Haarlem five years earlier. (p. 118)

Darwinhybrid Tulips

These large, bold tulips with a rather restricted colour range were bred by crossing Darwin tulips with *T. fosteriana*. They flower mid-season and are tall. They now include some of the most common commercial tulips. These are sometimes referred to as 'Darwin Hybrids'. (p. 130)

Single Late Tulips

Possibly the most varied of all the groups, this includes tall, late-flowering tulips that were previously called Darwin and Cottage tulips. The Darwins were named by E H Krelage and were tall, strong, rounded tulips that he had bought from French florists, who called them baguettes and who had first shown them in 1886. Cottage tulips were those that did not conform to the high standards of English florists, being either too long in the flower or the wrong colours. They were also generally shorter than the Darwins. But they had an ancient pedigree and were prone to breaking. Soon Cottage and Darwin tulips became interbred, and it made sense to make a new group to house them. (p. 135)

Lily-flowered Tulips

These have single flowers with narrow, reflexed tepals. The first were raised by Rengert Cornelis Segers in 1919. They generally flower quite late and may have short or tall stems, though most are tall. (p. 143)

Fringed Tulips

These have single flowers and bloom mid-season. The edges of the flowers are fringed with small, tooth-like structures. (p. 143)

Viridiflora Tulips

Comprising plants of various heights, and flowers with round or pointed tepals, these all have green streaks through the tepals. (p. 153)

Rembrandt Tulips

These are no longer commercially available and cannot be sold because the virus that causes the colours to 'break' is so destructive to other tulips. Typically the flowers are deep purple and brown with yellow streaks. (p. 156)

Parrot Tulips

These are usually late to flower and have tall stems. They are generally sports with deeply cut tepals, often tinged with green. The first known was discovered in 1665. (p. 156)

Double Late Tulips

These generally have rather long stems and flower at the end of the tulip season. The rounded, heavy flowers are usually fully double. (p. 161)

Kaufmanniana Tulips

This group comprises all the varieties that are clearly bred from *T. kaufmanniana*; they have early flowers, and grow to about 20 cm (8 in). Some have mottled foliage, derived from crosses with *T. greigii*. (p. 165)

Fosteriana Tulips

These are all clearly derived from *T. fosteriana* and have large foliage that is grey or green and sometimes mottled. The flowers are huge in comparison with the size of the plant. (p. 168)

Greigii Tulips

These are hybrids that show clear affinity to *T. greigii*, with spreading foliage that is mottled or striped with purple, and which flower later than Kaufmanniana tulips. (p. 171)

Miscellaneous Tulips

This comprises all the species and varieties of these that do not fit into any other group. (p.175)

Registration of Tulips

Since 1955, the International Commission for Horticultural Nomenclature and Registration for

tulips has been the KAVB (Koninklijke Algemeene Vereeniging voor Bloembollencultuur, or in English, the Royal General Bulbgrowers' Association), based in Hillegom, to the west of Amsterdam. This body is also responsible for the registration of other bulbous plants except *Dahlia*, *Narcissus*, *Lilium* and large-flowered gladiolus.

English Florist Tulips

We are fortunate that the English Florist tulip still exists, thanks to the dedication of a few enthusiasts. They survive now thanks largely to members of the Wakefield and North of England Tulip Society, created in 1835 as the Wakefield Tulip Society. The tulip was converted from a rich person's status symbol to a florist flower of great levels of perfection in the early 19th century. Florist's flowers (as opposed to the bunches of chrysanthemums sold by commercial florists today) were a select band that were highly prized and bred to levels of perfection rarely seen today. The main flowers were pinks, auriculas,

Unfortunately, 'Rex Rubrorum Bontleaf' is not commercially available, but shows what riches could be grown.

polyanthus, tulips and ranunculus, and we are fortunate that it is only the quality of the ranunculus that seems lost forever. These plants could all be grown in pots and all had the potential for great finesse, so they were adopted by working-class gardeners who had little money and little space but an abundance of skill and dedication. Since meetings and shows were frequently held in inns or accompanied by dinners, in certain areas it was probably 'social death' *not* to be a tulip grower.

Like Rembrandt tulips, the beauty of the English Florist tulip depends on the effects of virus. The English were not the only people to grow such plants, and the Flemish Florist tulips (which were the basis for the early Triumph tulips) were similar. The same virus that transforms a plain tulip into such a beautiful work of art weakens the bulb, but fortunately it is not spread from one generation to the next by seed, so to begin with, the tulips have solid colouring. These are called Breeders.

The flower of a good breeder tulip traditionally had a shape like a ball cut so that the top half or two-thirds is removed, but modern taste allows the flower to be rather taller, and the shape of a claret glass. The base should be broad and rounded. It must be symmetrical, and the tepals must have good, strong texture and overlap.

All is straightforward so far, but it gets a lot more complicated. There are three main colours:

Rose breeders are white at the base of the tepals. The upper part of the flower may be pink, scarlet, crimson or red.

Bybloemen breeders also have a white base to the tepals (ground colour), but the rest of the tepal is mauve, purple or as near black as possible.

Bizarre breeders have a yellow base to the tepal (ground colour) and the rest of the tepal is orange, scarlet, brown or black.

To add to the problems of creating a good breeder, the base of the tepals must not have any other colour present – no blue ring, no smudge of grey; the filaments of the stamens must be white or yellow to match the ground colour; and the anthers must be black.

Once you have created your breeder you wait for the virus to work its magic. There are at least two viruses that cause the colours to 'break', and one of them creates flowers that are useless. Not all breeders make good flowers when they break, and

the health of the bulb affects just how the flower will look. If the bulb is strong and fighting off the virus the flower may not show the symptoms as obviously as a weak bulb, but a weak bulb means the flower will be small, and consequently the bulb will be weak again the following year. You can see where the excitement and skill comes in, and why the Dutch got so excited over their broken tulips.

The virus can produce many effects, but the two that are allowed by the English Florists were feathered and flamed flowers. Flowers that show these characteristics are referred to as 'broken' or 'rectified' flowers. Feathered flowers have their colouring around the edge of the tepals, so for instance a Feathered Rose would have pink around a ground colour of white. The effect of the virus is rather like what you see when you release a drop of detergent into a patch of oil floating on water. In an iris, this colour pattern might be called plicata, but it does look rather as though a big, white feather has been placed on the pink tepal. The finest flowers have no colour on the tepals apart from at the edge, but it is a common fault to find it down the centre of the tepal, while a 'skip' is where the coloured edge is broken.

Flamed flowers have the tepal colour around the edge and up the centre of the tepal, and there are diagonal lines of the tepal colour running between these. It is less extreme a change than feathering as far as the disappearance of the tepal colour goes, but it is just as striking because of the busy patterning.

This is not the place to go into too much detail about this fascinating aspect of tulip-growing, but what makes the whole thing so complicated is that, for instance, 'Mabel' – a rose breeder with pink flowers – can produce flowers that are rose feathers or rose flames. Not all breeders will produce rectified flowers of both types, but it happens sometimes.

The garden historian and plantsman Timothy Clarke of Cambridgeshire, UK, grows many of these historic flowers, and recommends that they are in the ground for as short a time as possible. All tulips can be planted late in autumn, coming to no harm if they are planted in November or December, but this seems to be exaggerated with the Florist's tulips. Out of the ground and stored dry and cool they are free from slugs and less prone to fungal diseases that can cause problems such as tulip fire.

The Wakefield and North of England Tulip Society, the best-known growers today, recommend planting in December and into January. The bulbs are planted 10 cm (4 in) deep in soil that is neutral to alkaline, well-drained, and in full sun.

These Florist's flowers are true antiques (or heirlooms) and the flowers that are exhibited today span two centuries. Among the oldest are: 'Cyrano' (Bizarre, raised by Sir A D Hall, 1920), 'James Wild' (Bizarre, raised by J Walker, 1890), 'Sir Joseph Paxton' (Bizarre, raised by Willison, 1845), 'Columbine' (Bybloemen, raised by Sir A D Hall, 1920) and 'Julia Farnese' (Rose, raised by John Slater, 1853). Among modern cultivars are: 'Agbrigg' (Bybloemen, raised by Hubert Calvert, 1970), 'Rory McEwen' (Bybloemen, raised by James Akers, 1990), 'Akers' or 'Akers Flame' (Rose, raised by Jim Akers, 1960) and 'Ruth Duthie' (Rose, raised by James Akers, 1999).

Commercial Production

Tulips are now a major Dutch export but the industry is dominated by family firms, many of which specialize in growing just a few cultivars, or a small range. In fact, it is difficult for a new grower to break into the business, because good stocks of tulips are jealously guarded, and it takes a long time to build up a big stock. This is because tulips increase only slowly. Unlike hyacinths and daffodils, which can be persuaded to rapidly produce a stock of 20 or more bulbils from a single bulb, tulips have to be allowed to increase naturally, and some bulbs only produce a few offsets each year. Tulips also differ from the other two genera in that their bulbs are not perennial. The bulb you plant one autumn will not be there the following summer. Instead, it will be consumed by the flower and replaced by another large bulb, which will be of flowering size if all is well, and there will be one or more offsets, which can be grown on as new bulbs to flower the next year or some time in the future.

This is how tulips are produced. Bulbs are planted and they produce a wonderful display in the Dutch bulb fields. They are allowed to flower and the growers then walk through the rows and cull any that are not up to standard either because they are rogues – the wrong cultivar that has accidentally become mixed up with the stock, or because they are virused. As with hyacinths and daffodils, a leaf of these rejected plants is painted with glyphosate herbicide, which is taken back into the bulb and kills it. This process of walking through the fields and looking at the plants is also how sports are identified and preserved. Most variegated tulips are sports, and they appear at random in the tulip fields. A watchful eye is needed to spot the variegated foliage or a slightly different shade or shape of flower that just might be the next great success. The advantage with sports of existing cultivars is that they share all the other characteristics apart from the one that has changed, so if the original form is a good commercial cultivar, the chances are good that its sports too will grow well and be viable for commercial production.

Once fully open, the flowers have to be removed, or the tepals may fall into the leaves and cause mould to kill the stems and weaken the developing bulbs. This is now done by machine – great lawnmower-like contraptions that trundle

This English Florists' tulip, a flamed bybloemen, relies on the magical effect of virus infection for its beauty.

over the rows, cutting off the heads and dumping them in piles at the ends of the rows. At the end of spring, the bulbs are ready to be harvested just as the leaves have almost died down. The bulbs are cleaned and sorted, the old bulb scales discarded, and the largest bulbs graded and sent for sale. The sorting is now also mechanized. The smaller bulbs are then replanted in November or December and will, depending on their original size, bloom the following spring and provide a new set of bulbs for sale. A 6–7-cm (2.3–2.75-in) bulb, planted in autumn, should produce a 12-cm (4.75-in) bulb that can be sold the next year, plus two 6–7-cm offset bulbs for replanting. (All bulb measurements are of circumference, not diameter.) So although there is no need to have large fields of tiny bulbs that will take many years to reach flowering size during which there may be no bulbs for sale, as is necessary with hyacinths and daffodils, the increase is still gradual.

The main bulb-growing areas in the Netherlands are in the north-west, where the soil is sandy and light, but in the recent past they were also grown in the centre of the country, where the soils are heavier. Tulips will grow well on clay soils, but they need to be well drained, and in the central Netherlands the bulbs are frequently grown in raised rows to prevent waterlogging of the roots. Environmental concerns mean that chemical fertilizers and herbicides are used far less now than in the past, and tulip crops are rotated every three or four years to prevent the build-up of disease. To prevent soil erosion the empty fields are sprayed with a slurry of recycled paper in winter that dries to form a papier-mâché covering that slowly decomposes. It also gives the fields a rather gloomy, grey appearance, in startling contrast to the land in spring when the bulbs are in bloom. In fallow years the fields are sown with organic manures to improve the soil structure and add some nutrients, and the planted fields are sprayed with manure slurry in late winter to feed the bulbs. Despite all the mechanization, the tulip-growing industry is still dependent on casual labour and until 15 years ago it was common for labourers from England to work on the fields; now the majority are from Poland.

Spectacular tulip fields near Keukenhof, Lisse, in the Netherlands.

Cut Flowers

Cut flowers are an increasingly important crop, and, to force the flowers to bloom early, the bulbs are heat-treated. They are stored at high temperatures until about 10 August each year (the exact date depends on the cultivar) to make sure the flower bud has developed in the bulb, and then the temperature is reduced to below 10° C (50° F) for six weeks before planting in trays. Most cut flowers are now grown in greenhouses, but at one time there was a big industry in parts of France, where they were grown outside in fields with soil-warming pipes under the soil surface.

Breeding

Breeding new tulips from seed is a long business. Once you have made your cross and sown the hundreds of seeds, it can take up to seven years before the bulb flowers. You then need to decide if the plant is novel enough to be worth growing on. If it does show promise, the next hurdle is whether it has a commercial future. A good new cultivar must not just look good and be different enough to create a demand; it must also grow well. Some interesting but failed cultivars have fallen by the wayside because they do not produce enough offsets, making them difficult to produce in sufficient numbers to be commercial; or they may increase too freely, making masses of small bulbs that do not easily reach flowering size. In the garden the latter are particularly frustrating, though they may sometimes suit commercial growers if they are able to grow them well. Once a tulip has been selected it can take another 20 years before the bulbs are available in sufficient numbers for it to be launched on the domestic market.

Cultivation

Tulips are easy to use in the garden: plant bulbs in the autumn and they will flower the following spring. Choose small tulips for containers, pots and the fronts of borders, and taller tulips for the backs of borders, and you can be sure of a good display. But tulips have a reputation for flowering well the first year and then being less satisfactory,

either disappearing altogether or failing to flower. Good cultivation can correct this, and it is possible to keep your tulips going for many years – as can be seen by the small, but thriving, band of growers of English Florist tulips.

Bulb Size and Condition

Most tulips are sold in colourful packs, and you may not have much choice of sizes. The biggest bulbs – this is a consideration relevant only to the cultivars, not the species – are usually size 12, meaning that the bulbs have a circumference of 12 cm (4.75 in). Sizes 10 and 11 are cheaper but still usually flower well. I would always recommend that you buy single-cultivar packs rather than cheap mixtures that may well contain far more of one colour than another. Cheap bulbs of any kind are rarely a good investment, and in my experience such packs do not even consistently contain what they promise.

Bulbs should be solid, firm and have skins that show no signs of mould. Sometimes bulbs

Old Rembrandt tulip 'Insulinde' with Joop Zonneveld at the Hortus Bulborum.

become infested with aphids, and these should be rubbed off before planting if they arrived while you had them – never buy bulbs with aphids attached. If bulbs do have mould on the bulb rather than the skins, soak them in a fungicide solution or dust them with sulphur before planting. In recent years, pairs of bulb cultivars, with exotic names that bear no relation to the cultivar names, have become popular. These are usually a good buy if you need help with your selection and they are two tulips that look good together, but you usually pay a premium – and I think it takes some of the fun out of gardening.

It always pays to buy the biggest bulbs you can, and bulb size is usually the difference between good and great tulip displays. Tulip prices, even for the same cultivars, vary widely. Small, flowering-size bulbs will give reasonable flowers but the blooms are often smaller than usual and the stem heights can vary. This may be acceptable if the bulbs are planted in the border in a drift, but it is not good enough for formal bedding where you need large, showy flowers at a uniform height. Anyone who has seen displays of superb tulips at flower shows, such as Chelsea Flower Show in late May in London, will wonder why their own tulips are never as good. The main reason is that the specialists who exhibit at these shows – the best known is Bloms Bulbs – grow and sell only the largest bulbs. If you pay a little extra you get far better flowers.

Tulips like sunshine, well-drained soil and a hot dry summer. More than hyacinths or daffodils, they appreciate being lifted every year. The reason for this, as mentioned above, is that unlike daffodils and hyacinths, the tulip bulb replaces itself completely every year, rather than simply growing larger. It naturally breaks up into two or three new bulbs after it has flowered and, if left undisturbed, the three bulblets may not have room to develop into flowering-sized bulbs.

Planting in Beds

The most common use for tulips is still for bedding, and they are typically planted with a trowel, and between other bedding plants (particularly wallflowers). It is not possible to plant bulbs more than 15 cm (6 in) deep with a trowel, and it is a curious fact, common to many

bulbs, that planting at this relatively shallow depth causes the bulbs to break up into a greater number of smaller bulbs than if planted deeply. This is probably due to the higher temperatures experienced near the soil surface, the soil having an insulating effect from the heat of the sun. (The reticulate iris, especially *Iris danfordiae*, suffers in the same way, and is famed for flowering once in the garden and then disintegrating into a mass of tiny bulblets that never flower.)

Deep planting prevents this. If planting tulips in the garden border, where you wish them to remain undisturbed for many years, they should be planted with a spade, so they are 20 cm or more below the soil surface. In this way, they are less prone to divide into bulblets, maintaining flowering-sized bulbs and they usually flower for many years without any attention. I have planted tulips with a spade for many years, and it does make a difference, though it may work partly through protecting the bulb from later soil cultivation. Whatever the reason, deep planting does work, even on heavy soils. Another reason why bulbs may not thrive when left in the soil for prolonged periods is because they are a tasty morsel for slugs. The general advice when growing tulips is that they should be in the soil for as short a time as possible, and reducing exposure to slugs and other pests and diseases is one of the main reasons for this. Most gardeners do not worry about keeping the bulbs for another year, but many consider this wasteful, and if you have gone to the effort of finding something special, you will want to grow your tulips well.

If you do intend to use tulips for bedding, and want to keep the bulbs for another year, select a sunny spot in good soil. Tulips may come from sunny parts of the world that are baked dust-dry in summer, but today's garden tulips are domesticated and prefer good living. Improve the soil with organic matter such as garden compost or well-rotted manure if you wish. Plant them as deeply as possible, between 15 and 20 cm (6–8 in) deep for most tulips, spaced 10 cm (4 in) apart for the small species, and up to 20 cm (8 in) apart for the larger types. Tulips are ideal for bedding because they are intrinsically formal and look good in rows, like hyacinths but unlike daffodils. Once the tulips show above the soil in spring you can give them a dressing of a general fertilizer that contains trace elements and a high

proportion of potash (K). The plants will not need much attention now until they flower. If you are cutting some flowers for the home, try to cut them so you leave as many leaves on the plant as possible. These leaves will produce food to nourish the bulbs once the flowers have died down. Do not be misled by cut flowers you have bought. When you buy a bunch of tulips they will have all the leaves attached and may even have soil at the base. This is because they have been forced in trays and cut off at soil level, but the growers of cut flowers discard the bulbs once the flowers have been harvested, so are not so careful about the future of the bulbs as you will be in the garden. If left to bloom for garden decoration, the flowers will then drop their tepals and leave a developing seed pod. This should be snapped off as soon as possible after the tepals have dropped (unless you intend to harvest the seeds). The production of seeds is an unnecessary strain on the bulb, and the pods are easy to remove by placing your index finger at the base of the pod and pushing the top of the pod back with your thumb. It will come off with a satisfying snap. I do not always believe what I read (a policy I recommend!) and have conducted small-scale experiments to see if deadheading does make a difference. Common sense, and the fact that commercial bulb growers bother to do it, suggests it does have an effect, and I have found that there is a noticeable difference in bulb size in a given

cultivar between those plants that have been deadheaded and those that have not. But there is another important difference. I have noticed that when plants have been deadheaded, the foliage dies back much more quickly than when the pods are left to develop.

Although some people lift the bulbs at this stage, as soon as flowering has ended, and allow them to dry off, it is not going to result in good new bulbs. If you have to get the bulbs out of the way you can lift them and replant them in soil in an out-of-the-way spot to die down. But it is difficult to lift the bulbs without breaking off the stems which have yet to finish feeding the developing bulbs with nutrients, so I would recommend that the bulbs are left a little longer in the soil. Commercial growers lift their bulbs just before the foliage has died down completely, and there is no need for you to wait for the leaves to go crispy and yellow. You can safely lift the bulbs and clean them when the flower stem begins to wither. The easy way to gauge this is to wrap the top of the stem around your finger. If the stem is pliable enough for you to make a complete circuit around your digit, the bulbs have probably got as big as they are going to get, and you can safely lift them. If the stem still has some stiffness in it, however, the bulb still has some nourishment to take in.

Once lifted, they should be laid in an airy, dry spot to dry off, and then cleaned and sorted, keeping the largest for replanting and either

Fringed tulips
have a special fascination. 'Matchpoint' is one of the few double Fringed tulips.

Tulip 'Ballerina'
at the Keukenhof.

discarding the smallest or growing them on in the garden to flower the next year. When storing tulips, or any other bulbs, the conditions should be dry and airy. Placing them in shallow trays is ideal, and paper bags are suitable for short periods, but plastic bags are not suitable for storage. Short tulips are ideal for containers but because they are usually crammed in with other bedding plants and not planted deeply, they cannot be expected to form such good replacement bulbs. But you may find that some are worth saving for the following year in the garden. Because of the great variations in tulip flowers, you can find one for every type of garden. Small and species tulips are perfect for rock gardens, and although the taller cultivars are most often used in bedding, they also look beautiful with herbaceous plants. White tulips with variegated hostas and ferns always look beautiful. Red or yellow tulips can be combined with the brassy tones of early doronicums and euphorbias, while dark purple tulips are, perhaps, at their best when combined with silvery grey foliage such as artichokes.

Tulips in Pots Indoors

Tulips are not as popular for flowering in pots as hyacinths and daffodils, but there is no reason why they should not be grown either in the cool greenhouse or for display in the home. Many of the choicest species make colourful additions to the alpine house, where they should be grown in pots of loam-based compost with extra grit.

When growing for indoor display, choose the shorter cultivars and those that flower naturally early, such as the Single Early group. Among the best to try are 'Brilliant Star', 'Christmas Marvel' and 'Joffre', all of which are short and early. Plant the bulbs in pots so that the top of the bulb is roughly level with the top of the pot. Cover the bulbs with compost and water well. Ideally, because you want early flowers, you should plant these in late August or September, much earlier than you would plant tulips in the garden. Water the pots and place them in a cool place in the dark, as you would for hyacinths or daffodils. The bulbs will need about 10 to 15 weeks in these conditions, until the shoots grow to about 5 cm (2 in) in height. I prefer to cover the potted bulbs with 10 cm (4 in) of bark or spent compost (as a way of protecting the shoots from the light and frost), and to leave the pots outside in a cold-frame. When the shoots have grown, bring the pots into gentle heat and light, avoiding a huge change of temperature, which can cause the developing flowers to die. Do not try to 'force' the bulbs to flower too early – they are not as easy to manipulate as hyacinths – and do not be too disappointed if they flower just a few weeks earlier than in the garden. At least you will be able to enjoy their beauty at close quarters.

Problems

Tulips are generally free from serious pests and diseases, but there are a couple of problems you may experience.

Aphids

Although they may seem a nuisance rather than a serious pest, aphids can wreak havoc among your tulips. The most common is the green-pink peach-potato aphid, and it is this little beast that, centuries ago, lay in wait in the gardens of Istanbul, ready to infect each new batch of tulips with virus. While it was a novelty for flowers to appear with streaks and blotches, we generally do not want to see the signs of virus in our plants. But, apart from the spreading of viruses, aphids feed on the stems and flowers and cause distortion. It is not uncommon to see aphids feeding on the dry bulbs under the skins, and these must be squashed before planting. If left, all may seem well until the flower buds appear, and then they increase at a devastatingly fast pace and cause the flowers to open small and stunted. Some tulips seem more vulnerable than others, and I have yet to grow 'Black Parrot' without seeing at least some aphids.

Virus

You will know when your tulips are infected with virus because of the breaking of the flower colour. There is no cure, and I would advise you to dispose of them to avoid other plants being infected, unless you are growing Florist tulips.

Squirrels

I suppose I should mention squirrels, mice and pheasants, all of which, along with sundry other creatures, will feed on tulip bulbs. Mice and rats can ruin stored bulbs, so you should put bait or a trap in the storage area. If you find these or other creatures digging up and eating the bulbs, try pegging down some chicken wire over the area where the bulbs are planted and covering this with a little soil. It need not look unsightly, and it usually stops the creatures from digging down to the bulbs.

Tulip Fire

The most common disease of tulips is tulip fire. This is a form of grey mould, and it is called fire because it causes the leaves to look as though they have been scorched – and because it spreads like wildfire. Like most forms of grey mould (*botrytis*) it flourishes in damp, cool conditions, and in the spring of a dry year you may never see it. In the spring of 2004, it ruined many of my flowers. If you are not sure what it looks like, buy a grotty bunch of tulips that are obviously past their best. Wrapped tightly in plastic and kept in a bucket of water as they have been, the poor air circulation and damp conditions are sure to have caused dead areas, starting as spots, on the flowers and foliage. This is tulip fire.

In the garden, if plants are infected at an early stage, the shoots will look yellow and stunted and will not develop. Give them a tug and they will be found to have rotted off at the base. If they become infected at a later stage, usually if the weather at flowering time is wet, the petals (and in the worst cases, the leaves) will also show symptoms. At this stage there is little you can do except remove the affected flowers to prevent the disease spreading to other plants. You can prevent tulip fire by soaking the bulbs in fungicide before planting, and spraying the plants soon after they emerge through the soil in spring. If you have had tulip fire before there will be resting spores in your soil, so the use of fungicide is advised.

Why do Tulips Change Colour?

One last problem that is often raised is why tulips change colour. A clump of tulips that was red one year is supposed to miraculously change to yellow the next. Tulips are known to sport, and if you grow a cultivar that arose as a sport it is always possible that it might revert to its original colour. But this will not happen to a whole clump. The reason is usually down to the size of bulbs, and is most common when a cheap mixture is planted. Being a rag-bag of bulbs and not a good mixture, it may be that only the bulbs of the red tulips are of flowering size, while the yellow tulips are only producing leaves in the first year. These red tulips then break up and, because they have flowered and perhaps were not deadheaded, do not produce a bulb of flowering size. But the yellow tulip bulbs increase in size and the following year they bloom. A miracle!

Chapter 5
Species and Varieties of Tulips

In this chapter, I have brought most of the common commercial tulip cultivars together with some ancient but historically important plants, and some others that are new and may yet make an impression. To this selection I have added a sprinkling of oddities that I just like. The result will be a list that is perhaps unsatisfactory because it is a compromise. I just hope that, for a few years at least, it will include most of the pre-packaged bulbs you find in your local garden centre, or in the beds you pass at major gardens such as the Keukenhof.

Tulips are divided into classes, which makes them easier to manage, though it is odd that some of the classes are based on specific species whose ancestry shows in the plants, some on flower shape, and others on their flowering period. While it is easy to see where some tulips belong, others are less straightforward. But, like other classification systems, it keeps things neat and tidy and does tell you something – a Kaufmanniana tulip is not likely to be good for cutting for example. The current system has taken years to develop, and some old classes such as Mendel and Cottage tulips have been absorbed by others, while important and distinctive classes such as Viridifloras have been formed more recently, as the number of cultivars has increased.

The major classes are:

1 Single Early (p. 112)
2 Double Early (p. 115)
3 Triumph (p. 118)
4 Darwinhybrid (p. 130)
5 Single Late (p. 135)
6 Lily-flowered (p. 143)
7 Fringed (p. 148)
8 Viridiflora (p. 153)
9 Rembrandt (p. 156)
10 Parrot (p. 156)
11 Double Late (p. 161)
12 Kaufmanniana (p. 165)
13 Fosteriana (p. 168)
14 Greigii (p. 171)
15 Miscellaneous – species (p. 175)

Notes to Entries

After each entry the average height is given, followed by details of the raiser and then, if different, the introducer and the date of introduction/registration where known. This is followed by any awards. Details of the awards are given on page 180. Synonyms (other names by which the variety is also known) are given in brackets following the official name.

Notes to Pictures

All picture captions start at the top row, from left to right. The numbers following the tulip names refer to their class.

CLASS 1
Single Early

Single Early tulips are not as important for gardeners as they are for the production of cut flowers, because they can be forced to flower early for cutting – people will always prefer to buy cut flowers out of season, when they cannot pick them from their own gardens. So the chances are that any cut-flower tulips bought in early spring will be Single Earlies. They generally have stems that, in the garden, are about 40 cm (16 in) long, but when forced in boxes, where they are planted with the bulbs on the surface and harvested right down to the bulb, this is long enough to provide a good stem. In the garden they are generally pretty tough and can survive the early spring weather, and most flower around mid-April, which is not as early as the Kaufmannianas and Fosterianas.

Single Early tulips were some of the first to be cultivated, and many of the most beautiful historical cultivars belong here, including 'Keizerskroon', which dates back to 1750 and is still going strong. But it is not alone among ancient survivors. 'Bright Star', 'Diana' and 'Generaal de Wet' are all a century old but still head the popularity list.

The most important of all, from a historical perspective, is 'Duc van Tol', which produced a whole series of tulips that are all dwarf (15–20 cm/6–8 in high) with bright, rather starry flowers. They are no longer available commercially, but they were once prized for forcing and were bred by the Dutch over a long period, from about 1700 to 1920. The oldest has red flowers edged with yellow, and it is interesting that they were still being introduced early in the 20th century even though they were condemned by writers such as Sir Daniel Hall (author of *The Book of the Tulip*).

The Single Early tulips are not the most persistent tulips in the garden and a few, such as 'Apricot Beauty', in my experience seem to want to be annuals, but they are worth planting, especially as a treat in containers, even if they cannot be expected to last for more than a year or two. Because of their short stems and their comparatively early flowering, they are not ideal with wallflowers, but they should be planted with pansies, bellis, polyanthus and myosotis in bedding, and they can be used to brighten up herbaceous borders.

'Apricot Beauty' (p. 113, 147)

This beautiful cultivar should always be considered when buying early tulips because of its large, elegant flower shape and its subtle, pastel colouring in shades of salmon and cream. An added bonus is the sweet scent. It is a sport of the crimson 'Imperator' (Krelage & Son pre-1934), and has produced the sports 'Beauty Queen' (salmon/red), 'Bestseller' (copper orange) and 'Jenny' (orange/yellow). 45 cm/18 in (C v d Vlugt van Kimmenade 1953, EFA-KAVB 1961, AGM-RHS 1999)

'Beauty Queen'

This sport of 'Apricot Beauty' has blooms that are salmon in colour, flared with coral red, with the same attractive flower shape and fragrance. 45 cm/18 in (A L van Bentem & Sons 1979, TGA-KAVB 1979)

'Bellona'

This elegant flower is a bright, golden yellow, but has no exceptional features to reward close inspection except its enticing perfume. Where it excels is as a real pick-me-up in the garden, looking superb with deep blue myosotis and muscari. It has sported to produce the red-streaked 'Montparnasse', 'Red Bellona' and 'Striped Bellona'. 50 cm/20 in (H de Graff & Sons 1944)

'Bestseller'

A bright, copper-orange and gold sport of 'Apricot Beauty', the colours nicely feathered and with a golden centre. Good scent. 45 cm/18 in (Vlugt van Kimmenade 1959)

'Brilliant Star' (p. 147, 169)

There is nothing subtle about this vivid red tulip with pointed tepals that open to reveal a star-shaped bloom with a yellow and black base. 'Brilliant Star Maxima' is synonymous. It flowers early and can be forced to flower for Christmas. It has sported to produce 'Joffre' (yellow), 'Jullklapp' (gold and orange) and 'Sint Maarten' (orange). 30 cm/12 in (1906, FCC-KAVB 1908)

Orange tulips

Top row:
'Oxford's Elite' 4,
'Ballerina' 6.
Second row:
'Apricot Parrot' 10,
'Apricot Beauty' 1.
Bottom row:
'Fly Away' 6,
'Orange Princess' 11.

'Burning Love'
A brightly coloured tulip in shades of blood red with a bright yellow base and dark anthers. 45 cm/18 in (H G Huyg 1981)

'Christmas Dream'
This sport of 'Christmas Marvel' has crimson red flowers that are carmine inside with a white and yellow base. 35 cm/14 in (L J C Schoorl 1973)

'Christmas Marvel'
Like many early tulips, this variety and its sports are most important as commercial cultivars that can be forced for cut flowers, but its cherry-pink flowers have their place in the garden too. It has produced many coloured sports including 'Christmas Beauty' (red), 'Merry Christmas' (crimson) and 'Queen of Marvel' (double). 35 cm/14 in (L J C Schoorl 1954, EFA-KAVB 1954)

'Coquette'
White with a cream flush, and a cream edge to the tepals. The base and anthers are yellow. 45 cm/18 in (Konijenburg & Mark 1973)

'Crown Imperial'
This old tulip has rather interesting colours of purple-brown with a yellow edge. 35 cm/14 in (Zocher & Co pre-1929)

'Diana'
White tulips are always desirable, and this is not only good for commercial forcing, but the large pure white flowers are good for the garden too. The short stems make it a good choice for container planting. 30 cm/12 in (A van den Berg Gzn 1909, AM-KAVB 1914)

'Flair'
A recent tulip that brings some different colour to the Earlies is 'Flair'. It is bright yellow with bright red streaks, especially on the outer tepals. The base is black. 35 cm/14 in (Jac van den Berg 1978)

'Generaal de Wet'
This is a sport of 'Prince of Austria' (1860), which is a dark orange-red colour and strongly scented. It was once considered the finest of Early tulips because of its attractive shape and scent and, 'Generaal de Wet' has inherited that sweet fragrance. But this is bright orange, a combination of scarlet on golden yellow; a perfect contrast with yellow polyanthus and blue myosotis. It is common and very fine. 40 cm/16 in (1904, AM-RHS 1904, AM-KAVB 1921)

'Ibis'
A pretty tulip in rich, deep-rose pink, the edges of the tepals fading to white to give them definition when the flowers are closed. It is a sport of 'White Hawk'. 30 cm/12 in (1910, AM-RHS 1914)

'Joffre'
This is a sport of 'Brilliant Star' and has the same pointed tepals and black base, but is otherwise yellow. 30 cm/12 in (1931, AM-KAVB 1931, EFA-KAVB 1934)

'Keizerskroon'
A tulip has to be rather special if it gets a major award 240 years after its introduction and 'Keizerskroon' is worth growing for its beauty as well as its historical interest. The flowers are brilliant red with a rich yellow edge to all the tepals. In addition, the flowers are weather-resistant, and it is vigorous – as might be expected from a tulip that is still grown in commercial quantities after several centuries. It was one of the first tulips I ever grew, although it was no longer a novelty! It has only produced one recorded sport, 'Rex', a parrot tulip of the same colouring. 35 cm/14 in (1750, AGM-RHS 1993)

'Lac van Rijn'
This beautiful tulip is not commercially available but is held at Hortus Bulborum. It is one of many of the old, forgotten tulips that really should be re-introduced. It is a small plant with bright, starry flowers that are pointed in bud and are purple, edged with white. Inside, the white flowers have a bright yellow centre. With the increasing interest in small plants for containers and pots, this would be a really useful plant; slender and not as dumpy and stiff as many others. One of two historical cultivars at Hortus Bulborum that I really fell in love with (see also 'Rex Rubrorum', Double Early). 30 cm/12 in (1620)

'Merry Christmas'
This sport of 'Christmas Marvel' has crimson flowers that are pale at the base. 35 cm/14 in (Th & W B Reus 1972)

'Mickey Mouse'

This is a sport of the lemon-yellow 'Wintergold', and has golden flowers that are streaked with red. 35 cm/14 in (Kooi 1960)

'Prins Carnaval'

This fragrant tulip has deep yellow flowers, flamed with red, and is a sport of 'Prince of Austria' (1860, orange scarlet). 40 cm/16 in (1930, AGM-RHS 1997)

'Purple Prince'

There are not many purple early tulips so this recent addition is very welcome. The flowers are lilac in shade with a duller flare on the centre of the outer tepals. The purple colour does not refer to the open flower, which is maroon. 30 cm/12 in (L J C Schoorl 1987)

'Red Paradise'

A bright red tulip with a black base, surrounded by yellow. 30 cm/12 in (AGM-RHS 1997)

'Striped Bellona'

This 'Bellona' sport has buttercup yellow flowers with bright red stripes through the tepals. 50 cm/20 in (A Berbee 1973)

'Winter Gold'

A good, deep lemon-yellow tulip with egg-shaped flowers. 35 cm/14 in (0 Huiberts 1942)

'Yokohama'

This is commonly grown as a cut flower and has pointed buds that open to elegant flowers in a rich, deep yellow. 35 cm/14 in (J F van den Berg & Sons 1961)

CLASS 2
Double Early

Double tulips have always been controversial but, without wishing to impose my own views, I think they should be given a chance. Admittedly, not all double flowers are beautiful: the double hibiscus, in which the carefully patterned and sculpted centre is reduced to something resembling a discarded paper napkin, deserves no place in the garden. But tulips, though they have great beauty when they expose their heart to the sun as single blooms, can be attractive when doubled, albeit in a different way.

Not everyone agrees. Writing in 1929, Sir Daniel Hall (in *The Book of the Tulip*) is scathing in his attack: 'It may be agreed that double tulips are more lasting, but it is no gain that a nightmare should endure for two nights instead of one. Were permanence the great virtue, flowers might be made of pottery or enamelled iron.' I never have polyester flowers in my house, convincingly realistic though they may be, but I embrace most double tulips. However, I have a greater fondness for the later doubles than the early ones, because their heavy flowers open at a time when there is a greater chance (though no guarantee) of better weather.

Their great virtue is their large, cheerful flowers, often scented, which bring colour to the garden in April. Most have short stems, which in the past were seen as a disadvantage since they left the flowers so close to the soil. This same characteristic can now be an advantage, due to the rising popularity of gardening in containers. Most are short enough for pots and even window boxes, where they will create a dazzling display. They are also relatively cheap to buy, though they are not always the most long-lived of tulips in the open garden.

Plant Double Early tulips in sheltered parts of the garden and in full sun. You can combine them with attractive foliage plants, but few bedding and herbaceous plants will be stirring by the time the tulips are in flower. And even if you can get the timing right, the tulips will dominate the display unless you choose a brassy companion such as doronicum. Foliage often works best, and *Valeriana phu* 'Aurea' with red tulips, bronze *Carex* with white tulips and blue *Festuca* with pink ones all look good.

One cultivar dominates the range of early doubles: 'Murillo', a pale pink double that was raised in 1860. It might not have received much attention were it not for the fact that it had a prodigious ability to mutate into different colours. There are now in excess of 100 sports, in every possible tulip colour, giving a clue as to how the marvellous range of tulips of all kinds has been achieved, through history, from a limited genetic base. Since they have the same underlying genetics, and identical habit and flowering time, you can mix two or more of these 'Murillo' sports

Sports of 'Murillo'
Top row:
'Ghandi' 2,
'Harlequin' 2,
'Herman Broeckaert' 2.
Second row:
'Electra' 2,
'Johan van Vlaanderen' 2.
Third Row:
'Mr Van der Hoef' 2,
'Murillo' 2,
'Rheingold' 2.
Bottom row:
'Schoonoord' 2,
'Theeroos' 2.

together, and they are commonly available as a mix. Having an aversion to seeing pink and yellow together, however, I prefer to buy separate colours and blend my own.

'Abba' (p. 143)
This sport of 'Monte Carlo' has bright, tomato-red flowers with some fragrance. Though these may have yellow feathering, I have not observed it, and it is one of the brightest early tulips with great garden presence. 30 cm/12 in (Bakker Bros 1978)

'Baby Doll'
Rich, buttercup-yellow flowers. 25 cm/10 in (J F van den Berg & Sons 1961, AGM-RHS 1995)

'Cardinal Mindszenty'
This is a pure-white sport of 'Madame Testout', itself a lilac sport of 'Murillo' that was registered in 1942. 25 cm/10 in (Van Reisen & Sons 1949)

'Carlton'
A deep-red double. 40 cm/16 in (C P Alkemade Cz 1950)

'Electra' (p. 116)
This 'Murillo' sport has flowers of deep, cherry pink, and is still popular and common. 25 cm/10 in (pre-1905, FCC-KAVB 1912)

'Garanza'
This sport of 'Peach Blossom' has deep-pink flowers. 25 cm/10 in (Segers 1944)

'Ghandi' (p. 116)
This 'Murillo' sport has flowers of glowing orange. Non-commercial. 25 cm/10 in (P J de Groot)

'Harlequin' (p. 116)
The ivory flowers of this 'Murillo' sport are feathered with pink, though it is officially described as crimson. Non-commercial. 25 cm/10 in (pre-1912)

'Herman Broeckart' (p. 116)
The vibrant flowers of this 'Murillo' sport are orange-scarlet, and each tepal is edged with creamy yellow to create a busy, bold display. 25 cm/10 in (Van Reisen & Sons 1942)

'Jan W van Reisen'
see 'Willemsoord'

'Johan (van) Vlaanderen' (p. 116)
This 'Murillo' sport has flowers of deep, pinkish mauve with paler petal edges. 25 cm/10 in (Van Reisen & Sons 1944)

'Monsella' (p. 124)
This is another sport of 'Monte Carlo', bright yellow and feathered with deep red. It is a superb tulip that lasts well in the garden. 30 cm/12 in (Bakker Bros 1981)

'Monte Carlo' (p. 122, 164)
This is my favourite yellow double tulip, and well deserves its many awards. The flowers are large

and bright, buttercup-yellow with a pleasant fragrance, but its most notable feature is the longevity of the blooms, which open early and last for many weeks, despite bad weather. They even seem remarkably resistant to tulip fire. Some flowers show hints of red, giving hints of its sport to 'Monsella'. Other sports are 'Abba' (red), 'Monte Femme' (pale yellow), 'Viking' (scarlet) and 'Monte Parrot' (not quite feathery enough for inclusion in the parrot group). 30 cm/12 in (Anton Nijssen & Sons 1955, TGA-KAVB 1969, AGM-RHS 1993)

'Montreux'
This fragrant, pale yellow tulip is deeper in shade when open, revealing the inner side of the petals. The flowers develop a red 'tan' in the sun as they mature. It is bound to become popular for its beautiful colour and useful height. 45 cm/18 in (Hybris 1990)

'Mr Van der Hoef' (p. 116)
This is a yellow sport of 'Murillo' that is still commercially important. The blooms are rich yellow and it has itself sported to other cultivars, though these have not become commercially important. 25 cm/10 in (AM-RHS 1911)

'Murillo' (p. 116)
Many tulips produce sports, and these are often valuable, sharing certain good features of the parent plant but with different coloured flowers or, more rarely, parrot or fringed flowers, or variegated leaves. But 'Murillo' has produced more sports than any other tulip: in excess of 100. 'Murillo' itself has white flowers that are flushed with pink, and it is fragrant. All its offspring have the same, rather pointed, ragged petals, some scent, and are short. These characteristics are useful for the gardener because a mixture or blend of several of these sport cultivars will all bloom together and will be of the same height. Some of the most popular 'Murillo' sports (and some sports of sports) are: 'Electra', 'Mr Van der Hoef', 'Schoonoord' and 'Oranje Nassau'. Others that are less common but may appear in mixtures include the peachy-yellow 'Sungleam', violet purple 'David Teniers' (1960), orange and yellow 'Bruno Liljefors' (1983) and deep-pink 'Rembrandt' (pre 1900). 25 cm/10 in (Gerard Leembruggen 1860)

'Oranje Nassau' (p. 164)
One of the most popular Double Early tulips, this has fragrant, vibrant flowers of deep orange and red. It is a sport of 'Murillo'. 25 cm/10 in (pre-1912, registered 1930, AGM-RHS 1993)

'Paul Crampel'
This is a deep scarlet tulip with a yellow centre. It is a sport of 'Oranje Nassau'. This tulip is named after the French explorer who was killed in Africa in 1891 – most plants named after him seem to have bright red flowers. 25 cm/10 in (C J Zonneveld & Sons 1936, AM-KAVB 1937, FCC-KAVB 1938)

'Peach Blossom'
This is probably the most popular of all Double Early tulips and is, unsurprisingly, another sport of 'Murillo' – indeed it was one of the earliest. The flowers are rose pink. It has itself sported to produce 'Garanza' (deep pink), 'Robert Spencer' (deep pink) and 'Willem van Oranje' (orange). 25 cm/10 in (1890, AM-KAVB 1913)

Purple tulips
Top row:
'Lilac Perfection' 11,
'Atilla' 3.
Second row:
'Queen of Marvel' 2,
'Maytime' 6.
Bottom row:
'Paul Scherer' 3,
'Arabian Mystery' 3.

'Queen of Marvel' (p. 117)

This flower is one of the many sports of 'Christmas Marvel'. It has the same rich cherry-pink flowers, tinged with red. 35 cm/14 in (C J Dekker 1982)

'Rex Rubrorum Bontleaf' (var.) (p. 103)

Look through many lists of tulips and you will find many that look similar. Do we need more yellow Darwinhybrids, for example? This makes me wonder why this unique tulip is not grown commercially. Even if it does not make many good offsets, I am sure that gardeners would pay the increased price for something so special. The buds start as a green and white pompom of bract-like tepals above the variegated leaves and, as the flowers mature, a tuft of red tepals appears as a topknot. As the flowers open, they transform into pretty, double, bright red blooms, and the green bracts disappear under the colour. Two flowers for the price of one! I would pay almost anything for this so let's hope some grower takes up the challenge and a distributor takes the risk. 30 cm/12 in (1830)

'Rheingold' (p. 116)

This is a sulphur yellow sport of 'Murillo'. 25 cm/10 in (Van Reisen & Sons 1942)

'Scarlet Cardinal'

Although not as doubled as some, this is a fine tulip where the bright red of a British postbox is needed. 25 cm/10 in (J de Ruyter 1914, AM-KAVB 1915, FA-KAVB 1941)

'Schoonoord' (p. 116)

This tulip is a pure-white sport of 'Murillo' with yellow bases to the tepals. 25 cm/10 in (FCC-KAVB 1909)

'Stockholm'

Slightly taller than most of this group, this has vivid scarlet flowers with a yellow heart. 30 cm/12 in (Anton Nijssen & Sons 1952, EFA-KAVB 1954, AGM-RHS 1993)

'Theeroos' (p. 116)

Translating as 'tea rose', this 'Murillo' sport has cream flowers flushed with salmon pink that increases as the flowers age, the outer tepals streaked with green. 25 cm/10 in (1890)

'Verona'

This recent addition to the group has globular flowers of pale cream, flecked with green and with white midveins. It is a welcome sight for its fine flower shape, taller stems than most, and sweet fragrance. 40 cm/16 in (Boots 1991)

'Viking'

This sport of 'Monte Carlo' has orange-scarlet flowers with green flares, often feathered with red and a yellow base. Like its parent, it is fragrant. 30 cm/12 in (J W Reus, 1984)

'Willemsoord'

'Electra' sported to produce this attractive tulip with carmine pink tepals that are heavily edged with white. It has itself sported to 'Jan W van Reisen', which is purple, edged with white. 25 cm/10 in (Paul Roozen 1930)

'Willem van Oranje' ('William of Orange')

An orange and copper sport of 'Peach Blossom'. 25 cm/10 in (P Bakker, AM-KAVB 1933)

CLASS 3
Triumph

This is a very diverse group that arose by crossing Single Early tulips with Single Late tulips (originally Darwin, Cottage and Dutch Breeder tulips). The name dates back to 1923, and was coined by N Zandbergen to differentiate some seedlings he bought from a breeder.

This practice of buying seedling stock from other breeders still continues. With such a wide genetic base, we could expect virtually any colour in this group, and would not be disappointed. There is also a wide range of flower shapes. They flower earlier than the Single Late, Darwinhybrid and most Lily-flowered, Viridiflora or Parrot tulips, but overlap with them. Most bloom in mid-April and last well into May. They also vary in height, though most are 'mid-height' and some of the most recent are short. I am no lover of plants that have been stunted by breeders, but some of these, such as 'Strawberry Swirl' and 'Ted Turner', really are superb garden plants, enhanced by their short, but not grotesque, stature.

Triumph tulips include some of my favourite tulips, simply because there is such a variety.

Though any choice is bound to be personal, I make no apologies for recommending the following: 'Blue Ribbon', 'Carola', 'Charmeur', 'Couleur Cardinal' and its sports, 'Don Quichotte', 'Dow Jones', 'Gavota', 'Ice Follies', 'Jerry Davids', 'Orange Flight', 'Strawberry Swirl' and 'Yellow Present'.

'Abra'

This plant is a very popular tulip because it is valuable as a forced cut flower. The blooms are a rich, mahogany red, which changes to golden yellow at the edges of the tepals. The base is yellow inside. It is similar to, but shorter and less dark than, 'Abu Hassan' (see below). It has sported to produce 'Geanka' (red and yellow, 1984), 'Gold Crown' (red and yellow, 1986) and 'Vulcano' (red and yellow, 1985). 40 cm/16 in (Hybrida 1959)

'Abu Hassan' (p. 124)

This always attracts attention because of its rich colouring. The tepals are a deep, mahogany red with a bright yellow edge, and are always curled round to create a sculpted bloom that never quite opens to reveal the pale yellow base and purple anthers. It is often confused with 'Abra' and 'Gavotta'. This tulip has sported to produce 'Rowest' (yellow, edged with mahogany, 1996) and 'Slim Whitman' (variegated). 50 cm/20 in (J F van den Berg & Sons, C Roet & Sons 1976, TGA-KAVB 1976)

'Advance'

see 'Mirella'

'Agrass White'

A nice, compact, white tulip with a slight lily shape. The base is bright yellow and the leaves are grey. 40 cm/16 in (Yokohama Seedling)

'Alfi' (p. 141)

A gentle, pale yellow/cream, globular flower with rounded tepals and pale yellow anthers. 60 cm /24 in (Bik, Jac, Tol 1970)

'Allegria'

This is an attractive tulip with long, tomato-red flowers with a yellow edge and yellow base. These are held on dark stems, and the anthers are black. 45 cm/18 in

'Amazone'

This sport of the salmon pink 'Palestrina' appears to be apricot orange at first but is really a confection of salmon and pink shades with touches of cream and green. The interior of the bloom is brighter red, the base is yellow grey, and the anthers are purple. 40 cm/16 in (Jan van Bentem 1987)

'Anna Jose'

This tulip is a pretty and subtle flower with dusky pink tepals bordered with creamy white. The base and anthers are yellow. 50 cm/20 in (P J Nijssen 1977)

'Annie Schilder'

An elegant and bright flower in orange and scarlet shades. The base is yellow and grey, and the anthers are black. 45 cm/18 in

'Antonio Moro'

A pretty tulip of delicate colouring with a white base inside and out, and pale pink tepals with yellow anthers. 60 cm/24 in (Konijnenburg & Mark 1966, AGM-RHS 1995)

'Arabian Mystery' (p. 117)

Tulips with contrasting colours around their tepals are always popular, and the combination of deep purple with a piping of white has ensured the success of this cultivar. The flowers are rather boxy, with square bases. 40 cm/16 in (P Hopman & Sons 1953)

'Arie Hoek'

This is a bright red tulip in various shades, with a greenish base and black anthers. It has sported 'Arie Design', which has dark green leaves edged with yellow. 55 cm/22 in (Konijnenburg & Mark 1977)

'Arlo'

This is a glorious, rich purple tulip with a white base, bordered with blue. It stood out on a rainy day at the Keukenhof. 45 cm/18 in

'Astarte'

This tulip is a really beautiful plant that blooms in a blend of purple and deep red with a bluish base. 40 cm/16 in (Visser Czn 1983, AGM-RHS 1995)

'Atilla' (p. 117)

This is really a rather unremarkable, though reliable and long-lasting, pale purple tulip, with a white base marked with blue. It is a tulip for bedding rather than gazing at lovingly, and is very popular. It has, however, produced many sports that may be more likely to set the pulse racing, the most interesting being 'Attila Design', which has leaves edged with yellow. Others are 'Attila Graffiti' (crimson and ruby, 1986), 'Attila's Elite' (red and crimson, 1985), 'Attila's Favourite' (pink, edged lilac, 1979), 'Attila's Glory' (violet purple, 1992), 'Attila's Record' (reddish purple, 1979), 'Purple Atilla' and 'Rotilla' (purple and red respectively, both 1993). 50 cm/20 in (G van der Mey's Sons 1945)

'Barcelona'

This delightful flower, pear-shaped in bud but reflexing and spreading its tepals as it matures, is bright mauve-pink with a pale yellow base. A cheerful, bedding tulip. 60 cm/24 in (Hybris 1989, AGM-RHS 1999)

'Bastogne'

A good choice where a knockout red tulip is required. Big, blood-red flowers with a yellow and blackish base and dark anthers open in the warm sun. The outside of the flowers is darker. 60 cm/24 in (Koedijk & Sons 1980)

'Beau Monde'

The world must have seemed very beautiful indeed for the raisers of this gorgeous tulip. It has the most subtle combination of rosy pink on white outside, but the interior of the flower is almost pure white. The base is pale yellow, and the huge blooms are carried on massive stems. A very special flower. 65 cm/26 in (IVT, J & C Reus 1986)

'Ben van Zanten'

A lilac-purple flower with a yellow and cream base. The anthers are purple. 50 cm/20 in (Van Zanten Bros 1967, AGM-RHS 1997)

'Bill Clinton'

A giant among tulips, this has huge flowers on tall stems that are notably devoid of leaves apart from at the base. The blooms are long and vibrant, lipstick pink outside, while inside the base is white with a blue ring and the anthers are black. 65 cm/26 in

'Bing Crosby'

A bright scarlet bloom that is good for bedding. Its sports are 'Glowing Pink' (1983) and 'Pretty Woman' (Lily-flowered). 50 cm/20 in (B P Heemskerk 1947)

'Blenda'

This is a standard, glowing, rich pink with a white base. It has two sports: 'Inzell' and 'Sjakamoro' (purple 1979). 45 cm/18 in (L A Hoek 1947)

'Blue Bell'

A majestic, purple and lilac flower with a white and turquoise base. 50 cm/20 in (Bik. Jac. Tol. 1968, AGM-RHS 1999)

'Blueberry Ripple'

A striking flower with white tepals, heavily flamed with purple-blue. This unusually beautiful flower lasts well. 50 cm/20 in

'Blue Champion'

The only blue you will find in this tulip is an ethereal ring around the pale yellow base. The rest of the flower is pinkish-purple. The tepals are broad and the flowers stocky and bright on strong stems. 50 cm/20 in (J F van den Berg & Sons, C Roet & Sons 1979)

'Blue Ribbon'

This is not the bluest of tulips and so is fancifully named – perhaps it refers to an award. The flowers have the colours of blackcurrants and cream with deep purple tepals edged with white, which is stained pink where the two colours meet. The base is blue. A lovely flower, especially when backlit. 35 cm/14 in (M H Immerzeel, Th Langeveld 1981)

'Brigitta'

A combination of yellow and scarlet streaks, edged with yellow and with a bright lemon-yellow base. 50 cm/20 in (P J Nijssen 1978)

'Calgary'

A short bedding tulip of creamy white, with yellow flames up from the base of the tepals, and with yellow anthers. 20 cm/8 in (Vertuco, Veul Bros 1995, TGA-KAVB 1990, AGM-RHS 1995)

'Capri'
Red and carmine flowers with an interesting purple base, edged with white. 40 cm/16 in (Bok, Jac Tol 1974, AM-RHS 1982, AGM-RHS 1993)

'Carnival de Rio'
This has rounded blooms of white, flamed with red and yellow at the base, and the leaves have bold cream edges – spectacular if a bit overdone. 45 cm/18 in

'Carola'
A beautiful bloom with deep, neon-pink tepals that are paler at the edge. The flowers are very full and round, and the base is white with yellow anthers. 45 cm/18 in (Vertuco 1986)

'Cassini' (p. 132)
This is a strong-growing, common tulip with deep-red flowers and a yellow base. It is short and ideal for bedding because it lasts well. It has two sports, the red and yellow striped 'Casino' (1978) and 'Orange Cassini'. 45 cm/18 in (Segers 1944)

'Charles'
A bright scarlet tulip with a yellow base – often listed as a Single Early. It has sported to the Double Late 'Charles Peony' (1995). 40 cm/16 in (C P Alkemade Cz 1954)

'Charmeur' (p. 132)
This splendid sport of 'Princess Victoria' has deep, pinky-red flowers edged with white. These are good enough on their own, but the leaves are boldly edged with cream and have wonderfully wavy edges, so the wait for the blooms to open is scarcely a hardship. Recommended. 45 cm/18 in (J A Borst & Sons 1992, TGA-KAVB 1990)

'Coby's Spirit'
Slender in bud, the base of the tepals is bright yellow while the rest is a deep, currant red. A vibrant, shorter-than-average tulip. 35 cm/14 in (Van den berg-Hytuna, C G van den Berg & Sons 1993)

'Couleur Cardinal' (p. 150)
This important old tulip has sported to present us with some of the most popular and beautiful of all garden tulips. It is an attractive, short plant with blue-grey leaves and deep scarlet flowers, shaded with purple – a feature that seems to be consistent in all its sports. Its age should not dissuade you from planting this, one of the finest bedding tulips. It has sported to 'Arma' (Fringed), 'Prinses Irene' (Triumph) and 'Rococo' (Parrot). 35 cm/14 in (1845, AM-RHS 1906)

'Cruquius'
A bright flower of red shaded on pink. It is a brighter red inside, with a blue base and black anthers. 35 cm/14 in (Vooren, C and A Bentem 1989, AGM-RHS 1995)

'Debutante'
This is a bright and broad tulip, with cherry-pink tepals edged with white. 50 cm/20 in (IVT, H Roozen Niczn 1984)

'Demeter'
A bright, blackcurrant-purple flower, with a small greenish-yellow base. 60 cm/24 in (Tubergen, AM-KAVB 1932, AGM-RHS 1993)

'Don Quichotte' (p. 132)
One of the latest to bloom in my garden, this is an exceptionally beautiful, clear-pink tulip with yellow anthers and a white base, touched with blue. The outer tepals open further than the inner ones, which remain upright. Recommended. Its sports are: 'Anastasia' (salmon, 1994), 'Rosalie' and 'Roxette' (red and pink respectively, both 1991). 50 cm/20 in (Konijnenburg & Mark 1952, AGM-RHS 1995)

'Doris' (p. 141)
This colourful bedding tulip has short stems, and large flowers with pointed tepals, creating an elegant outline. The tepals are bright orange, shaded with bronze – the inside of the flowers is very bright, and the anthers black. 40 cm/16 in (Van Zanten Bros 1967)

'Dow Jones'
When you want something devastatingly showy, pick this. It is a sport of the red and white 'Leen van der Mark', but has scarlet tepals edged with yellow, blending to orange between. The tepals are broad and the blooms open into fiery bowls

Yellow tulips
Top row:
'Monte Carlo' 2,
'Golden Melody' 3.
Second row:
'Golden Oxford' 4,
'Fidelio' 3.
Bottom row:
'Olympic Flame' 4,
'Wendy Love' 3.

the tepals. The base is also bright yellow. 40 cm/16 in (J F van den Berg & sons, J A Borst 1977, AGM-RHS 1999)

'Fats Domino'
A large, fragrant tulip of clear, lemon yellow with yellow anthers. It is not common but is large and showy – and its name should ensure popularity. 50 cm/20 in (Van den Berg-Yokohama, C G van den Berg 1991)

'Fidelio' (p. 122)
This is an elegant tulip with vase-shaped buds in rich apricot, opening to yellow-centred flowers of stippled orange. Rather special. 55 cm/22 in (G R Tromp 1952, TGA-KAVB 1956, AM-RHS 1978, AGM-RHS 1993)

'Fire Queen'
'Prinses Irene' is made even more special in this variegated sport. The flowers are identical, but the leaves have a narrow white edge. 35 cm/ 14 in (A L van Bentem & Sons 1980, AGM-RHS 1997)

'First Lady'
This is a fine bedding tulip of good shape with elegant, pear-shaped buds. The colour is a rich, rather vibrant, bluish-pink, while its white base has a hint of blue inside. 55 cm/22 in (Hybrida 1951, FCC-RHS, AGM-RHS 1993)

'Fontainebleau'
A tall, majestic tulip with rich, blackcurrant-purple flowers that have a thin, creamy-yellow margin around the upper part of the tepals. 60 cm/24 in

'Frances Bremer'
A beautiful, broad, deep-pink flower with a rosebud-like shape when partially open. The base is white and the anthers blue, while the stems are short and stiff. Another exceptionally fine pink, and a super choice for small beds and pots. 25 cm/10 in (Vertuco, J & J van den Berg-Botha 1990, TGA-KAVB 1990)

'Friso'
The blood-red flowers have a yellow base that can be seen on the outside of the flowers. 45 cm/18 in (Van Zanten Bros 1988, AGM-RHS 1999)

to worship the sun. Absolutely wonderful. 50 cm/20 in (De Geus-Vriend 1993)

'Dreaming Maid'
A popular cultivar with delicately coloured flowers of rosy violet, edged with white. The base is white too. 55 cm/22 in (Kerbert 1934)

'Dynamite'
This short tulip is brilliant red with a white base, and a touch of blue inside and out. The anthers are black. 30 cm/12 in (Hybris, J N M van Eeden 1994, TGA-KAVB 1993, AGM-RHS 1995)

'Early Glory'
Blooming earlier than most Triumph tulips but lasting well, this has mauve-pink flowers with ivory bases. 45 cm/18 in (H G Huyg 1981)

'Etude'
This bold, square-based flower is blood red with a bright yellow edge around the top two-thirds of

'Frohnleiten'

This is a short tulip with bold orange flowers, brushed with red. It has a yellow base and black anthers. 30 cm/12 in (Van den Berg-Yokohama, J S Pennings 1993)

'Gander'

This is a bright, magenta-pink tulip with a white base, and is popular for bedding. It has many sports: 'Gander's Ouverture' (pale cream with slight pink flush, 1986), 'Gander's Rhapsody' (white, edged with cherry, 1970), 'Gander's Sensation' (red, flushed purple, 1966), 'Gander Special' (bright red), 'Gander's Symphony' (richer colouring than 'Gander's Rhapsody'), 'Kaiserin Maria Theresia' (mauve, stippled red, 1982), 'Othello' (bright red, 1969), 'Pink Lady' (pink, flushed purple, 1969), 'Red Gander' (red, white base, 1969) and 'Rose Tendre' (ruby red, 1969). 60 cm/24 in (Segers 1952)

'Garden Party'

A popular tulip with white tepals that have very distinctive broad, glowing carmine-pink edges. Its sport 'Garden Beauty' has narrower pink edges, while 'Garden Picture' (1980) is similar in colouring but taller. 40 cm/16 in (P Hopman & Sons 1944, AM-KAVB 1944, AGM-RHS 1997)

'Gavota' (p. 88, 124, 169)

In a relatively short time this has become immensely popular, and has purplish tepals edged with primrose yellow. It is similar to 'Abu Hassan', but is more purple than brown. A good tulip to plant with purple or primrose wallflowers, or to enjoy on its own. 45 cm/18 in (Václavik, Cebeco 1995)

'Golden Melody' (p. 122)

A big, beautifully shaped, bright buttercup-yellow tulip with a good fragrance. It has sported to produce 'Washington'. 55 cm/22 in (P Hermans 1961, FA-KAVB 1963)

'Golden Show'

This is a big, scented yellow flower. 45 cm/18 in (Jac Tol Jr 1953)

'Happy Generation' (p. 155)

This sport of 'Ida' (yellow and flamed red, 1954) has white flowers with red flames rising from the base, which is flushed with yellow. The foliage is also edged with white. Though this all sounds exciting, the tepals have a thin texture and are damaged by wet weather. 50 cm/20 in (J de Vries & sons 1988)

'Havran'

This is a deep-purple, almost black tulip with tepals that recurve at the ends to create an almost Lily-flowered shape. The base is white, and the blooms tall and elegant. 45 cm/18 in (Letland)

'Helmar' (p. 124)

This is a beautiful striped tulip with bright red streaks on a golden yellow ground. The blooms open wide and cup-shaped, and the base is yellow with black anthers. It is a sport of 'Yellow Mask' (yellow, tinged purple, 1964). 55 cm/22 in (D & A Noort Bros, P Kortekaas 1986)

'Hermitage' (p. 150)

One of the many sports of 'Prinses Irene', this is a very fine tulip, with flowers of a beautiful mandarin orange, in many shades, and a distinctive flare on the outside of the tepals. 35 cm/14 in (J de Wit & sons, 1986, TGA-KAVB 1986)

'Hibernia'

This is a superb, large, elongated white bloom with nothing to detract from its purity. It looks superb with a new fresh growth of ferns or fennel. 45 cm/18 in (Jac Tol Jr 1946)

'High Noon'

From slender buds, the white, pink-edged blooms unfurl. The centre is pure white, completing a serenely elegant flower. 45 cm/18 in (K Wiedijk 1953)

'High Society'

This sport of 'Orange Wonder' (bronzy orange, 1954) has blooms of deep, reddish orange, with an edge of pure mandarin. Like many orange tulips, it is fragrant. 45 cm/18 in (Jac Tol 1958, AM-KAVB 1958, TGA-KAVB 1960)

'Holberg'

A purple flower with a yellowish base and yellow anthers inside. 50 cm/20 in (Konijnenburg & Mark 1987, AGM-RHS 1999)

'Hollandia'

This is a blood-red tulip with a yellowish base. It is triploid, which should result in greater vigour and means it is sterile. 40 cm/16 in (Van Zanten Bros 1988)

'Ice Follies' (p. 124)

This is a glorious tulip with huge flowers that open fully to greet the sun and to show off the white tepals, striped with bright red. It is showy and spectacular. It is a sport of 'Van der Eerden' (red, 1933) and has itself given the sport 'Linda de Mol'. 50 cm/20 in (Van der Laan Bros, J A van Noort 1975)

'Ile de France' (p. 143)

This is a glorious red tulip that is deep-red inside and darker on the exterior of the tepals. One of the finest red Triumph tulips. 50 cm/20 in (Blom & Padding 1968, QC-TGA-KAVB 1973)

Two-tone tulips
Top row:
'Olympic Flame' 4,
'Ice Follies' 3.
Second row:
'Gavota' 3,
'Abu Hassan' 3.
Bottom row:
'Helmar' 3,
'Monsella' 2.

'Inzell'

This is the ivory-white sport of 'Blenda'. They look well when planted together above blue myosotis. 45 cm/18 in (N Koster & Sons 1969)

'Jan Reus'

A deep-red tulip with typical black basal marks, edged with yellow. 50 cm/20 in (Hybris, Reus Bros 1986)

'Jerry Davids'

One of the most beautiful tulips, with rich, neon-pink tepals that are white and purple at the base, coloration that can be seen from the outside on a sunny day. Exceptional for bedding. 50 cm/20 in

'Jimmy'

This is a short, orange tulip with tepals that are brushed with reddish-pink in the centre. The base is yellow, edged with green, and the anthers are purple. 35 cm/14 in (J van Hoorn & Co 1962)

'Judith Leyster'

This is a large tulip with flowers shaded in coral-pink tones, with a broad ivory flare up the centre of each tepal. It is very subtle, despite the huge size of its blooms. It has sported to produce 'Prins Claus' (yellow and red, 1994). 55 cm/22 in (IVT, G H van Went & Sons 1980, TGA-KAVB 1980)

'Kaiserin Maria Theresia'

see 'Gander'

'Kees Nellis'

You cannot fail to be cheered by this dazzling bloom. The tepals are bright blood-red, edged with golden yellow, and when the blooms are open they expose their bright yellow centre and rim to give a large, bowl-like zoned flower. This fantastic flower has three sports: 'Bright Parrot' (red and yellow, 35 cm/14 in, 1994), 'Patilmo' (red, 1993) and 'Santana' (red, 1993, often multi-flowered). 45 cm/18 in (H 't Mannetje 1951)

'Leen van der Mark'

Whether open or in bud, this is a pretty tulip, with tepals that are bright red and an ivory white top. Though the red colouring extends to the base on the outside, inside there is a crisp, white base that contrasts with the suffusion of white into red at the top of the tepals. A great tulip and almost as wonderful as its sport, 'Dow Jones'. 45 cm/18 in (Konijnenburg & Mark 1968)

'Leo Visser'
The blooms are reddish-pink with a subtle white edge along the length of the tepals, except at the top. The base is white with a green blotch. 50 cm/20 in (P J Nijssen, Boots 1992)

'Lily Schreyer'
A tall, bright yellow tulip, combining several shades when mature. 55 cm/22 in (Konijnenburg & Mark 1983, AGM-RHS 1999)

'Lilystar'
This is a short tulip that I think could easily be moved to the Lily-flowered class. It has tomato-red blooms and pointed tepals that are edged with white as the flowers age. The base is white too and the leaves are wavy. 35 cm/14 in

'Linda de Mol'
A glorious, large flower with pale lemon-yellow flowers that have irregular lines of bright red, primarily along the main vein of the tepal. The tepals are rather narrow and open, making it a gappy flower, but the colouring is so bold this fault can be overlooked. It is a sport of 'Ice Follies'. 50 cm/20 in (Groot-Vriend 1994)

'Lucky Strike'
This has deep-red flowers edged with pale yellow. 55 cm/22 in (P & J W Mantel 1954)

'Lustige Witwe' ('Merry Widow')
Although not as popular as it once was, this is still a common tulip, with deep reddish-pink flowers and white-edged tepals. As well as a fistful of awards, it has a stadium-full of sports, several of which have been produced by radiation treatment: 'Destiny' (carmine with white base, 1980), 'Frederica' (purple, 1958), 'Giuditta' (red, edged yellow, 1959), 'Hanna Glawari' (cherry with white base, 1972), 'Ivette' (rose and white, 1980), 'Lustella' (pink with lilac flame, 1978), 'Paganini' (deep rose, 1963), 'Rimo' (red, edged white, 1987), 'Santina' (cherry and purple, 1982), 'Success' (purple with white edge, 1971), 'Yvonne' (purple with red, 1985) and 'Zarewitch' (red, edged yellow, 1969). 40 cm/16 in (G van der Mey's Sons 1942, AM-KAVB 1943, FA-KAVB 1948, HC-RHS 1978)

'Lydia'
A deep-pink tulip with paler margins and a green base. 35 cm/14 in (P Vooren, Boots 1988)

'Madame Spoor's Favourite' (p. 141)
The tepals are a combination of vermillion and pale yellow, with yellow at the edge and centre of the tepals. It is a paler sport of 'Madame Spoor' (mahogany, edged yellow, 1951). 50 cm/20 in (W Zandbergen Nzn 1979)

'Makassar'
This is a deep, butter-yellow flower with bright green foliage. 45 cm/18 in (De Mol & A H Nieuwenhuis 1942)

'Mamasa' (p. 141)
A bight yellow flower with pointed tepals and yellow anthers. 55 cm/22 in (De Mol & A H Nieuwenhuis, 1942)

'Margot Fonteyn'
A bright tulip with red tepals, edged with red, having a yellow base and black anthers. It has one sport, 'Mary Belle' (1995) of similar colouring. 40 cm/16 in ('t Mannetje, Leo Bisschops 1962, TGA-KAVB 1962)

'Meissner Porzellan'
The name of this tulip suggests something special and sophisticated and you will not be disappointed with this white flower, edged with bright rose pink. The colouring of this lovely bloom increases as the flower ages, and it is a tall plant. Its sport, 'Lucas van Leyden' (1986) has more distinct colouring. 55 cm/22 in (Konijnenburg & Mark 1952)

'Mirella'
This elegant flower is in shades of salmon (cooked, smoked and raw) with paler edges as the flower matures. It is a sport of 'Advance' (Tubergen 1920, scarlet). 60 cm/24 in (P Bijvoet & Co 1953, AM-KAVB 1960, FCC-KAVB 1961, AM-RHS 1967, AGM-RHS 1995)

'Mistress'
This superb new tulip has slender buds that open into funnel-shaped flowers with narrow bases and wide-open tops. The colour is a bright, clear pink with a pale base. 55 cm/22 in

'Monte Rosa'

This beautiful, chunky, pastel flower has pale, pinky-white tepals that are suffused with a central band of pink on the outside of the outer three tepals. Inside, the flower is pale pink with brown anthers. 60 cm/24 in (De Geus 1984, TGA-KAVB 1984, AGM-RHS 1999)

'Most Miles'

A bright, currant-red tulip with a yellow base. 60 cm/24 in (De Mol & A H Nieuwenhuis 1944, FA-KAVB 1951, FCFA-KAVB 1952, FCC-RHS 1977, AGM-RHS 1993)

'Musical'

A glossy red tulip with a black and violet base, and purple anthers. 50 cm/20 in (Bik, Jac. Tol 1972, AGM-RHS 1999)

'Nairobi'

A bright, deep-red tulip with a purple base, edged with white. 55 cm/22 in (Tulip Flower, K Otjes & Son 1995, TGA-KAVB 1994)

'Nashville'

Another deep-red tulip with creamy-yellow edges. The base is cream with black anthers. Though tall, the flowers have rather weak necks and do not hold up well in wet weather when fully open. 55 cm/22 in

'Negrita'

This is a popular purple tulip, made more interesting by its veins of deep maroon complemented by a greyish base. The base is blue, edged with white. It has two sports: the darker-shaded 'Negrita Favourite' (1992) and 'Gabor' (ruby red, 1996). 45 cm/18 in (Bik, Jac Tol 1970)

'New Design'

This premium variety has large flowers that are creamy yellow at first, but soon develop their pink colour with cream around the base and the main vein. The tepals have rather ragged edges, but the leaves are edged with creamy white, often flushed with pink. A sport of 'Dutch Princess' (orange, edged yellow, 1959). 50 cm/20 in (Jac Tol 1974, TGA-KAVB 1974)

'Ninja'

This is a tall, vibrant tulip with large flowers of bright, neon pink that have dark centres and a yellow base. 55 cm/22 in

'Olaf'

This is a deep-red tulip with noticeable yellow basal blotches and black anthers. It has two sports: 'Bristol' (bright pink, 1968) and 'Sweet Memory'. 40 cm/16 in (Kerbert 1930)

'Orange Bouquet' (p. 172)

This is a multi-flowered tulip with bright tangerine scarlet flowers that are bright yellow at the base of the blooms. Stems usually produce three or four flowers. Its sport is 'Red Bouquet' (1984) which makes a good companion in a border for a really vibrant show. 50 cm/20 in (Konijnenburg & Mark 1964, AM-RHS 1977, AGM-RHS 1993)

'Orange Cassini'

This sport of 'Cassini' has orange flowers that are shaded with red on the outside, and bright orange interiors with a lemon-yellow base. Combine it with 'Cassini' and polyanthus for a long-lasting and bold display. 45 cm/18 in (J van der Burg 1981)

'Orange Flight'

This may be a sport of 'Orange Monarch' and has similar flowers of orange, tinged with reddish purple. It has striking leaves that are variegated, but not simply edged, with primrose yellow, the variable but largely broad stripes running along the leaves near, but not at, the edge. 45 cm/18 in

'Orange Monarch'

The large blooms are deep orange, tinted with reddish purple on the exterior, while the inside is a paler, bright orange with a golden base and purple anthers. A bold flower. 45 cm/18 in (G Lamboo, Eggink Bros 1962)

'Orange Surprise'

This is among the darkest of orange Triumph tulips, with a shiny texture, but for some reason described in the catalogues as tomato red! Inside, the base is yellow and the anthers are black. 50 cm/20 in (Raven Bros, 1991, TGA-KAVB 1991, AGM-RHS 1995)

'Orléans'

This is basically a white tulip, with flowers that

are egg-shaped at first. They are ivory white overall, shading from yellow at the base, both inside and out, to creamy white. The anthers are yellow. (IVT, G H van Went & Sons 1981, AGM-RHS 1999)

'Oscar' (p. 172)
A big, bold, beautiful red tulip with a yellow base and purple anthers; all a red tulip should be. 40 cm/16 in (Bik, Jac Tol 1975, AM-RHS 1982)

'Othello'
see 'Gander'

'Page Polka'
This is a large, colourful tulip with a broad white triangular flare from the base of the tepals, surrounded by deep, rosy pink. The colour spreads as the flowers age, but the base is white and the anthers are yellow. 40 cm/16 in (Konijnenburg & Mark 1969)

'Passionale' (p. 155)
A pleasant, if not very exciting, purple bedding tulip with a yellowish base. 40 cm/16 in (L J C Schoorl 1983, TGA-KAVB 1983)

'Patriot'
A bright scarlet flower with a slight white edge and yellow base. 45 cm/18 in

'Paul Richter'
This is a large tulip of bright, pelargonium red that makes a good bedding tulip where something bright is needed. It has two sports, 'Accent' and 'Red Sensation' (1975). 50 cm/20 in (Rijnveld & sons 1943, AM-RHS 1978)

'Paul Scherer' (p. 117)
This is a welcome addition to the group with large, deep blackcurrant flowers on sturdy stems. 50 cm/20 in

'Pax'
This pure-white tulip is not an important cultivar but has sported to produce: 'Adriana' (red, 1974), 'Advice' (cream, 1986), 'Alfred Heineken' (amber on cream, 1986), 'Golden Peace' (bright yellow and pale blue shade, 1988), 'Silent Peace' (grey on cream, 1982), 'Snow Parrot' (white parrot), 'Vaticaan' (ivory and

yellow, 1988) and 'Yellow Pax' (yellow, 1961). 45 cm/18 in (P van Kooten 1942)

'Peach Blush' (p. 52)
I have included this although I know little about it: apparently it was developed for the American market as a container plant. The chunky flowers are white, with a small, dark-bluish base and black anthers. The flowers are flushed pink on the outside. It is pretty and is a novelty because of its height. 25 cm/10 in

'Peer Gynt'
This commercial pink tulip has elegant blooms that open to reveal pure pink flowers with a white base. Outside, the tepals are blended with a deeper shade and have a mauve edge. 50 cm/20 in (Konijnenburg & Mark 1973)

'Peerless Pink'
Though an old tulip, this is still popular because of the clean, pink flowers and their satiny texture. It has two sports: 'Peerless Beauty' (pink and yellow, 1962) and 'Peerless Flame' (primrose with red, 1971). 45 cm/18 in (Carlee, 1930)

'Pink Lady'
see 'Gander'

'Primavera'
A pinkish-red, very tall tulip with paler edges to the tepals and a yellow-green base. It has one sport, 'Primavista' (1994), which has deeper-coloured blooms. 60 cm/24 in (Konijnenburg & Mark 1969)

'Princess Victoria'
This is a super flower with cherry-red/rose tepals that have a bright white edge along the top, and sides that define the classic shape of the tulip with their pointed tepals. The base is white. Good in itself, I think its sport 'Charmeur' is even better. 50 cm/20 in (J F van den Berg & Sons, Van den Berg-Yokohama 1979, AGM-RHS 1995)

'Prinses Irene' (p. 150, 172)
This sport of 'Couleur Cardinal' has become one of the most popular tulips. It is distinct from early in spring, when its grey/blue foliage appears. The flowers are burnt orange, flared with greyish purple, while the centre is yellow. Its sports are

'Fire Queen', 'Hermitage', 'Orange Princess' (Double Late) and 'Prinses Margriet'. 35 cm/14 in (Van Reisen & sons, 1949, AGM-RHS 1993)

'Prinses Margriet' (p. 150)

This sport of 'Prinses Irene' is similar but the flowers are golden yellow with the typical bronze-purple flare on the outside of the tepals. The two could be planted together with great effect. 35 cm/14 in (Van Reisen & sons, 1960)

'Prominence'

This dark red tulip with black base edged with yellow is unexceptional, but forces well for cut flowers so its many, varied sports have been welcomed. These are: 'Beauty of Prominence' (yellow, flushed and flamed red, 1985), 'Libretto' (yellow, shaded red, 1964), 'Prominence Dream' (red with yellow base, 1994), 'Prominence Exotic' (slightly parroty red, 1994), 'Promirande' (red, edged white, 1985), 'Red Nova' (Double Late red, 1989), 'Rochester' (cherry red, 1968), 'Romance' (ivory with pink blush, 1978), 'Sacramento' (yellow and salmon red, 1990), 'Wibo' (pale yellow, flushed purple, 1968), 'Winterberg' (similar to but paler than 'Romance', 1895) and 'Yellow Star' (yellow, 1985). 40 cm/16 in (P van Kooten 1943)

'Rocky Mountains'

Although it starts ivory with a primrose yellow flame while young, the mature flowers are white and round with yellow anthers and greyish leaves. 40 cm/16 in (Vertuco, J A Borst & Sons 1991)

'Rosalie'

This sport of 'Don Quichotte' has pale pink flowers with a yellow base and yellow anthers. 55 cm/22 in (G Groot-Vriend 1986)

'Rose Tendre'

see 'Gander'

'Salmon Pearl'

The rose-pink flowers are edged with coral pink on the outside and the open flowers show a brighter red shade, with a yellow base and yellow anthers. 40 cm/16 in (H G M Huyg 1985)

'Seadov'

A bright, deep-red tulip of great intensity and compact height. 30 cm/12 in

'Sevilla'

This red tulip is carmine red inside with a greenish white base. 55 cm/22 in (Hybris 1991, TGA-KAVB 1991, AGM-RHS 1999)

'Shirley' (p. 136)

This readily available tulip has rather dumpy flowers with broad tepals. These are ivory white, speckled around the edge with purple, forming a narrow edge. This increases and 'stains' the tepals as they age. The base is white, spotted with purple. Its sport, 'Shirley Dream', has more pronounced purple colouring. 50 cm/20 in (Bik, Jac Tol 1968)

'Silver Dollar'

A white tulip that is ivory and pale yellow when immature, with a yellow base. 55 cm/22 in (IVT Van Dam 1984)

'Singapore'

This is a very short tulip with deep-violet flowers and a white base. 30 cm/12 in

'Sjakamaro'

This sport of 'Blenda' is purple, with reddish shading at the edge of the tepals. The base is white with a purple edge and the anthers are purple. 45 cm/18 in (N B Munster 1979)

'Slim Whitman' ('Amaranth')

This sport of 'Abu Hassan' has the same flowers, but the leaves are edged with pale yellow. It really is a fine plant. 50 cm/20 in (Boots, D P de Graaf 1987)

'Snowstar'

This flower is pure white in colour. 45 cm/18 in ('t Mannetje 1955)

'Strawberry Ice'

A bright red tulip with a white base. 45 cm/18 in

'Strawberry Swirl'

This beautiful tulip has grey-green leaves that perfectly complement the blooms. These are pink with a basal white flare on the outside of the tepals, and a deep pink bar on either side before fading to mid-pink at the edge. The base is white and the blooms have scent. A superb bedding tulip with enough going on to make it interesting, though I have to say that I think the colour is more raspberries than strawberries. 35 cm/14 in

'Strong Gold'
A golden yellow tulip with orange shading on the outer tepals. 40 cm/16 in (J F van den Berg & Son, J A Borst & Son 1989, AGM-RHS 1999)

'Swinging World'
A pretty pink tulip with broad tepals to give a chunky, substantial bloom. The outer tepals are shaded with deep pink, while the inner ones are pale pink, fading almost to white at the edge. 50 cm/20 in (Peer Gynt & Walcure)

'Synaeda Amor'
The pale pink flowers are an attractive shape, with a square base that is white inside. 45 cm/18 in (Synaeda)

'Synaeda Blue'
Not blue, the flowers are actually purple, edged with white. 55 cm/22 in (Synaeda)

'Ted Turner'
Perhaps my favourite short yellow tulip, this has large, chunky flowers on short stems and seems completely weatherproof. The colour is a refreshing lemon yellow, unsullied by the bright yellow interior and pale brown anthers. Worth searching out. 30 cm/12 in (A Nijssen & Sons, Vertuco 1995, AGM-RHS 1999)

'Telecom'
A salmon-orange tulip of rounded shape that is shaded with pinkish red and opens to reveal a scarlet flower with a yellow and green base and purple anthers. 50 cm/20 in (Konijnenburg & Mark 1983, AGM-RHS 1995)

'The Cure'
Showy is a barely adequate description for this big bloom in brilliant lipstick pink. The base is white with a blue ring and the anthers are cream. 50 cm/20 in (Klaver Bros)

'Thule'
Basically red, edged with yellow, this is rather more than that, and the same marginal yellow flares out from the base of the tepals. It is a sunny flower that reveals its yellow centre when fully open. Very attractive. It has three sports: 'Fortissimo' (yellow, 1981), 'Sally' (yellow, 1991) and 'Thule Exotic' (yellows and red, 1995). 45 cm/18 in (Anton Nijssen & Sons 1954, QC-(bc)-TGA-KAVB 1969, AM-RHS 1978)

'Typhoon'
This has wavy leaves and rather slender tepals that are bright scarlet. The blooms have a yellow base. 45 cm/18 in

'Valentine'
This is a mauve/lilac flower with a paler, almost white edge to the tepals. The base is pale yellow. It has one sport, 'Ladylike' (pale pink and cream, 1993). 45 cm/18 in (Bik. Jac Tol 1970, AGM-RHS 1999)

'Veronique Sanson'
The blooms are almost Lily-flowered in shape and are orange inside, with a rather darker shade on the outside of the tepals. The base is yellow. 45 cm/18 in (C G v/d Berg)

'Washington'
This sport of 'Golden Melody' has yellow flowers with irregular red stripes through the tepals and around the edge. It is fragrant and attractive, but for a yellow and red striped tulip, 'Helmar' or the paler 'Linda de Mol' are more evenly patterned, and are of similar height. 55 cm/22 in (J Lighthart 1981)

'Wendy Love' (p. 122)
A pale yellow tulip with slight pink flushing on young flowers. 50 cm/20 in (Bentum Bluefields)

'White Dream'
A pure-white tulip, ivory at first, with rounded shape and yellow anthers. It has two sports: 'Crème King' (ivory, 1995) and 'Mont Ventoux' (ivory and primrose, 1995). 50 cm/20 in (J F van den Berg & Sons, J A Borst 1972)

'Wildhof'
A lovely, rounded, blocky flower of pure white, shading to a yellow base, inside and out. 45 cm/18 in (L A Hoek 1947, AGM-RHS 1995)

'Yellow Flight'
A short, bright yellow flower with very little

shading, and yellow anthers above bright green leaves. 35 cm/14 in (Hybris, Boots 1994, TGA-KAVB 1993)

'Yellow Present'

While it is understandable that purple tulips might be called blue, the term 'yellow' for this fine tulip is stretching the point just a bit too far. Really a delicious cream colour, the base is lemon yellow and shows through the base of the tepals. The official height is 35 cm (14 in) but in my experience it is much taller than this. It is a magnificent, large flower, and the colour is useful, with pale blue bedding where a bright white would be too harsh a shade. Recommended. It has two sports: 'Golden Present' (which is genuinely yellow, 1989) and 'Red Present' (bright red, 1972). 35 cm/14 in (Golden); 50 cm/20 in (Red). (Hybrida 1853)

'Zurel'

There are not many purple tulips with white streaks and edges, so this is a useful addition and slightly taller than 'Blueberry Ripple'. The blooms are a very bright purple, with a white, feathered edge and a white centre with yellow anthers. It is a sport of 'Hans Anrud' (purple, 1953). 55 cm/22 in (Vertuco 1994, TGA-KAVB 1994)

CLASS 4
Darwinhybrid

A relatively new group of tulips, Darwinhybrids were introduced in 1943 and bred by D W Lefeber at Lisse in the Netherlands. They are derived from crossing Darwin tulips with *T. fosteriana*. *Tulipa fosteriana* has brought not only vigour to the hybrids but its seeming immunity to many viruses. As a result the Darwinhybrids were immediately popular, and they remain some of the most common tulips, dominated by 'Apeldoorn' and its sports, which increase rapidly so are easy for suppliers to produce.

Most Darwinhybrids are rather tall tulips, and the blooms tend to be rather triangular in shape when they begin to open, and have a flat base. But they soon become cup-shaped, and open into large blooms with tepals that overlap because of the broad base. Despite 60 years of development, this section still has a rather limited colour palette, with red, yellow and orange dominating, though there are pinks and some bicolours, but no whites. Neither is there the range of shapes and colour blends seen in the Single Late and Triumph tulips. But as long as people want big, vibrant tulips that are vigorous and increase well, the group will remain popular, and it includes some of the brightest reds of all.

'Ad Rem'

This is a bold, bright tulip with scarlet tepals edged with orange/yellow. The base is yellow and black. It has several sports: 'Marit', 'Royal Ad Rem' (deeper colouring, 1994) and 'Sahara Rally' (red, changing to yellow, 1996). 60 cm/24 in (Konijnenburg & Mark 1960)

'American Dream'

This has flowers that are white, with a bright scarlet edge to the tepals. The flowers are creamy when young. 60 cm/24 in

'Apeldoorn' (p. 132)

Because of its rapid rate of increase, this has become the most popular of red tulips. But this habit of splitting into several, small bulbs does not make it a good garden plant – a situation where the bulbs are kept for more than one year. Deep planting in borders is the best way to treat 'Apeldoorn' to attempt to reduce this splitting.

From Lefeber, the company that brought us the first Darwinhybrids, it is a bold bloom in cherry red, shaded scarlet and with a yellow base to the outside of the bloom. Inside, the base is black, edged with yellow, while the anthers are black. In addition to being so popular itself, it also has an astonishing number of sports, presumably because of the vast numbers that have been grown. These are: 'Apeldoorn's Elite', 'Apeldoorn's Favourite' (scarlet, flushed purple, 1963), 'Apeldoorn's Glory' (red and orange, 1968), 'Apeldoorn's Record' (cherry red, edged apricot, 1963), 'Beauty of Apeldoorn', 'Crystal Beauty' (see Fringed tulips), 'Exotic Bird' (see Parrot tulips), 'Fringed Apeldoorn' (red, Fringed, 1971), 'Fringed Golden Apeldoorn' (yellow, Fringed, via 'Golden Apeldoorn', 1982), 'Golden Apeldoorn', 'Holland Happening' (see Parrot tulips), 'Orange Apeldoorn' (red and orange, 1968), 'Orange Queen' (mandarin and yellow, 1985), 'Phoenix Memory' (orange and red, 1993), 'Springfield' (gold, streaked red, 1976) and 'Striped Apeldoorn'. 55 cm/22 in (D W Lefeber & Co 1951, AM-KAVB 1963, FCC-RHS 1954)

'Apeldoorn's Elite'
The large blooms are bright mandarin, flushed on yellow. The base is black with a yellow edge. A lively tulip with some finesse. Its two sports are 'Bienvenue' (yellow, flushed rose, 1984) and 'Surprise' (red with yellow edge, 1986). 55 cm/22 in (J S Verdegaal 1968, TGA-KAVB 1968, AM-KAVB 1969, AM-RHS 1978, *AGM-RHS 1993*)

'Apricot Impression'
All the 'Impressions', including one called 'First Impression' that I have grown but cannot trace, are big, oval flowers on tall, strong stems that last for ages, perhaps because they seem reluctant to open fully. They are showy and robust, with large leaves at the base of the stems. 'Apricot Impression' has dark, salmon-pink flowers shaded with tangerine. The base is black, edged yellow, and the anthers are yellow. 55 cm/22 in (World Flower 1996)

'Banja Luka'
This is a distinct tulip, resembling 'Princess Margaret Rose' (a Single Late) more than anything else. The blooms are rich yellow, with a band of bright red around the edge, feathered with yellow. 55 cm/22 in

'Beauty of Apeldoorn'
A large golden yellow flower flushed with magenta. The interior is yellow with a black base. It is a sport of 'Apeldoorn'. 55 cm/22 in (Bentvelzen 1960, TGA-KAVB 1961, AM-KAVB 1962, HC-RHS 1969, AM-RHS 1978)

'Big Chief'
The name does not suggest the pastel colouring of this tulip, though it is quite a brute in stature. The flowers are salmon red with a broad creamy flare up the outside of the tepals that decreases as the flowers age, but never disappears. The base is pale yellow and the interior is flushed with orange. 60 cm/24 in (Frijlink & Sons 1959, AM-KAVB 1960, FCC-RHS 1969, *AGM-RHS 1993*)

'Blushing Apeldoorn' (p. 131)
This sport of 'Beauty of Apeldoorn' is yellow, edged with orange. 55 cm/22 in (Balder 1989)

'Burning Heart'
This sport of 'Ivory Floradale' is pale yellow with blood-red stripes from the base of the tepals, most marked on the inner tepals. The base is yellow and the anthers purple. 55 cm/22 in (J N M van Eeden 1991, TGA-KAVB 1991)

'Daydream'
This sport of 'Yellow Dover' is bright yellow flushed with orange to give an apricot colour overall. 55 cm/22 in (J N M van Eeden 1980, AGM-RHS 1997)

'Dover'
This was one of the first of the Darwinhybrids and is still a good, bright red with a typical black base, edged with yellow and black anthers. It opens wide in the sun and looks brilliant. It has several sports: 'Beauty of Dover' (buttercup yellow, flushed red, 1961), 'Dutch Fair', 'Yellow Dover' (AGM-RHS 1997)and 'Striped Dover' (yellow, flamed red). (D W Lefeber & Co 1945, AM-KAVB 1953, AM-RHS 1978, AGM-RHS 1993)

Daffodils and tulips
Photographed with cytisus and erysimum.
Top row:
Tulip 'Queen Ingrid' 14,
Tulip 'Oratorio' 14,
Narcissus poeticus.
Second row:
Narcissus 'Tripartite' 11aY-Y,
Tulip 'Quebec' 14.
Bottom:
Tulip 'First Impression' 4,
Tulip 'Blushing Apeldoorn' 4.

Daffodils and tulips
Photographed with athyrium.
Top row:
T. clusiana 'Tubergen's Gem' 13,
'Hans Mayer' 4,
'Golden Apeldoorn' 4.
Second row:
Daffodil 'Baby Moon' 7Y-Y,
'Cassini Apeldoorn' 4.
Third row:
'Ballerina' 6,
'Georgette' 5.
Bottom Row:
'Don Quichotte' 3,
'Queen of Night' 5.

'Dutch Fair'

This sport of 'Dover' has buttercup-yellow flowers streaked with scarlet outside. The inside is flamed with tomato red, with a black base and purple anthers. 55 cm/22 in (Van Eeden Bros 1974)

'Elizabeth Arden'

This is a popular pink tulip with a slight lilac tint, and a pale base inside. At one time there were very few pinks, so this was important. There are far more now but this is still a pretty, elegant tulip that should not be overlooked. 55 cm/22 in (De Mol & A H Nieuwenhuis 1942, AM-RHS 1957)

'Empire State'

This bright red tulip is similar to 'Oxford' but taller and larger. It has two sports: 'Golden Empire State' (yellow, flushed red, 1963) and 'Striped Empire State' (yellow, striped red, 1963). 60 cm/24 in (D W Lefeber & Co 1956, AM-KAVB 1959, FCC-KAVB 1960, AM-RHS 1967, FCC-RHS 1969)

'Garant'

This variegated sport of 'Golden Apeldoorn' has bright yellow flowers with a black base, and the foliage is broadly rimmed with butter yellow. A good colour combination and a beautiful plant. 45 cm/18 in (J Dignum & Sons 1993, TGA-KAVB 1993)

'General Eisenhower'

This was once a very popular red tulip but is not seen much today. That is a pity because it is a vigorous plant with large blooms that have a black base, edged with yellow and black anthers. It has one sport, 'Royal Pearl' (lemon yellow, 1957). 55 cm/22 in (D W Lefeber & Co 1951)

'Golden Apeldoorn' (p. 132)

One of the most popular yellow tulips, this has golden flowers with a black star on the base, and black anthers. It has, as might be expected of an 'Apeldoorn' sport, plenty of sports of its own: 'Fringed Golden Apeldoorn' (see 'Apeldoorn'), 'Garant', 'Hans Mayer', 'Lemon Apeldoorn' (pale yellow, 1989), 'Rainbow Warrior' (yellow, edged red inside, 1987), and 'Yellow Pomponnet' (a Double Late, 1995). 55 cm/22 in (C Gorter Gzn and A Overdevest Gz, TGA-KAVB 1960, AM-KAVB 1960, HC-RHS 1969)

'Golden Oxford' (p. 122)

This sport of 'Oxford' is yellow with the faintest red margin to the tepals. The base is yellow in colour with black anthers, and it has some fragrance. 55 cm/22 in (A Overdevest Gz 1959, HC-RHS 1978)

'Golden Parade'

This is paler than most other 'golden' tulips, although the inside of the tepals is a deeper shade. The base and anthers are black. It is a sport of 'Parade' (red, 1951). 60 cm/24 in (A Overdevest Gz 1963, HC-RHS 1969)

'Gordon Cooper'

This is a large, rounded, beautifully coloured flower that is pink outside with a red edge, and

bright red inside. The base is blue and yellow, and the anthers are black. 60 cm/24 in (Konijnenberg & Mark 1963)

'Gudoshnik'

This was one of the first non-red varieties introduced to the category, and is yellow, spotted and flushed with rose red. The base and anthers are black. The blooms are remarkably variable, not only with time but from plant to plant. Still popular despite its age, it has two sports, 'Jewel of Spring' and 'Polka' (tomato red, 1987). 60 cm/24 in (D W Lefeber & Co 1952)

'Hans Mayer' (p. 132)

This is a superb sport of 'Golden Apeldoorn', with buttercup-yellow flowers that are flamed with vermillion inside and out, and with a brown base and anthers. This flower is a showy, beautiful tulip, especially when it is fully open. 55 cm/22 in (C Gorter 1972, TGA-KAVB 1972, AM-KAVB 1973)

'Hollands Glorie'

This was one of the first Darwinhybrids, along with 'Lefeber's Favourite', 'Dardenelles' (cherry red, 1942) and 'Red Matador' (scarlet, 1942). It has rich carmine flowers edged with bright red, while inside they are scarlet orange – a really vivid colour. In addition the flowers are huge, and held on strong stems. You can well imagine the excitement these early cultivars caused when they were introduced, despite the lack of Dutch awards; it is still one of the finest. Its sport, 'My Lady', is also successful. 60 cm/24 in (D W Lefeber & Co 1942, AM-RHS 1957, FCC-RHS 1978, AGM-RHS 1993)

'Ivory Floridale'

This is the nearest we have to a white Darwinhybrid, and the fact that it is cream in colour rather than snowy does not detract from its beauty – pure white can be a difficult colour to use in the garden anyway. The flowers are cream and flushed with green through the centre of the tepals at first, but later change to ivory, developing a few red spots as they mature. Inside, the flower is creamy yellow, with purple anthers. A large, sophisticated bloom. It is a sport of 'Floradale' (red, 1954). 60 cm/24 in (Doornbosch Bros 1965, AGM-RHS 1997)

'Jaap Groot'

This new tulip has large flowers that are cream-coloured with a broad yellow flame up the outside of the tepals. The base is black and the flowers are fragrant. In addition, the rich green leaves, which are all low on the stems, have a thin but well-defined white rim. A cool and classy tulip. 60 cm/24 in (Mut. 'Golden Apeldoorn')

'Jewel of Spring'

This sport of 'Gudoshnik' has pale, sulphur yellow flowers that are rimmed with red, and have a greenish-black base and black anthers. Its sports are 'Flaming Jewel' (yellow, flamed red, 1972) and 'Fringed Elegance' (see Fringed tulips, below). 60 cm/24 in (A Overdevest Gz 1956, TGA-KAVB 1959, AM-KAVB 1960, AM-RHS 1965, FCC-RHS 1978, AGM-RHS 1993)

'Juliette'

This sport of 'Golden Oxford' has regained some of its original red colouring, but only around the edge of the tepals and as some flames from the base. The base is yellow, the anthers are purple, and the flowers are noticeably fragrant. 55 cm/22 in (Q van den Berg & Sons 1985)

'Koningin Wilhelmina'

Few tulips are brighter than this amazing sport of 'Lefeber's Favourite'. The tepals are scarlet, edged with orange, but this description hardly does justice to the bright luminescence of the flowers as they glow in the sun. The base is yellow and can be seen from the outside of the flower, the anthers black, and the flowers are fragrant. There is also a variegated form with broad, primrose edges to the leaves. 55 cm/22 in (C Nieuwenhuis 1965, FCC-RHS 1969, AGM-RHS 1993)

'Lefeber's Favourite'

This was one of the first Darwinhybrid tulips, and it is among the last to bloom. The fragrant flowers are deep carmine red, edged scarlet and with a yellow base. It has several sports: 'Koningin Wilhelmina', 'Miracle' (red and yellow, fragrant, 1961), 'Olympic Gold' (gold, fragrant, 1962), 'Striped Favourite' (yellow, flushed red, fragrant, 1960). 55 cm/22 in (D W Lefeber & Co 1942, AM-KAVB 1852, FCC-KAVB 1853, AM-RHS 1957)

'Lighting Sun'

This sport of 'Oranjezon' is pale orange, flushed with pinkish-red in the centre of the tepal, while inside, the flower is scarlet red and orange. It is a beautiful flower, especially when backlit. 50 cm/20 in (Nic van Schagenb 1985)

'London'

Along with 'Dover' and 'Oxford', this is a good red Darwinhybrid, with deep red flowers that open to scarlet with a black base, and the inevitable yellow ring and black anthers. Neither unusual nor sophisticated, it is an excellent choice for bedding. 55 cm/22 in (D W Lefeber & Co 1950, AM-RHS 1978)

'Marit'

This sport of 'Ad Rem' is exceptionally beautiful. The tepals are peachy yellow with a large raspberry-red flame up the centre, and inside the base is pale with black anthers. It is scented, and many of those I have seen produced several flowers per stem. It is a big plant with large leaves, and very striking. 50 cm/20 in (AGM-RHS 1997*)*

'My Lady'

This sport of 'Holland's Glorie' is a smoked-salmon colour on the outside and bright orange inside, with a bronzy green base. 60 cm/24 in (John van Grieken 1959, TGA-KAVB 1960, AM-KAVB 1961, HC-RHS 1969, FCC-RHS 1978, AGM-RHS 1993)

'Ollioules'

Despite the pastel colouring of this tulip, it has great presence in the garden because of its size – it is enormous. The flowers are rosy pink but paler at the edges of the tepals, and there is a hint of green and lilac. Inside, the flower is pale-yellow and pink with a pale-yellow base touched with blue, and the anthers are dark. It has the colours of blackcurrant cordial in milk. 55 cm/22 in (Van Zanten Bros 1988, TGA-KAVB 1988, AGM-RHS 1999)

'Olympic Flame' (p. 122, 124)

This bright and colourful flower is pale, bright yellow with deep red flames, mostly at the sides of the outer tepals and the centre of the inner ones. Inside, the colours are the same with black anthers. 55 cm/22 in (A Verschoor Jr 1971, AGM-RHS 1997)

'Orange Goblet'

This orange flower is among the largest of tulips, and has a bright yellow-coloured base inside the bloom. 60 cm/24 in (Frijlink & Sons 1959, AM-KAVB 1960, TGA-KAVB 1960, FCC-KAVB 1962)

'Oranjezon' ('Orange Sun')

This was the first non-red Darwinhybrid, though it was introduced as a Triumph tulip and has true mandarin-orange flowers with a bright yellow base. Its sport, 'Lighting Sun', is just as beautiful. 50 cm/20 in (Hybrida 1947, AM-KAVB 1964, AGM-RHS 1995)

'Oxford'

This beautiful, bright scarlet tulip is similar to, but earlier than, 'Apeldoorn'. The exterior of the flower has a slight flush of maroon that lifts the colour, and if you look inside the open flower you will notice the yellow base and the scent. It has a rash of sports as you would expect from a bulb that has been grown in vast numbers. These are: 'Beauty of Oxford' (yellow, spotted red, A Overdevest Gz, 1961), 'Comic' (red, edged gold, A Overdevest Gz, 1959), 'Golden Oxford', 'Kingwood Centre' (red, flushed yellow, A Overdevest Gz, 1959), 'Oxford's Elite' and 'Striped Oxford'. 55 cm/22 in (D W Lefeber & Co 1945, AM-KAVB 1953, HC-RHS 1957, FCC-RHS 1978, AGM-RHS 1993)

'Oxford's Elite' (p. 113)

In a colour pattern common to many 'Elite' sports, this 'Oxford' sport is cherry red with an orange edge to the tepals on the exterior. Inside, the flower coloured is bright red on orange with a yellow base. 55 cm/22 in (G G Kol, 1968, TGA-KAVB 1968)

'Parade'

This is a large, red tulip that opens wide in the sun with a black base, edged with yellow and black anthers. Like many red Darwinhybrid tulips, it has a set of orange and yellow sports: 'Beauty of Parade' (orange on yellow, 1963), 'Golden Parade', 'Parade Elite' (deep red on orange, 1996) and 'Parade Record' (red on orange, 1972). 60 cm/24 in (D W Lefeber & Co 1951, AM-KAVB 1953, FCC-RHS 1978, AGM-RHS 1993)

'Pink Impression'

The 'Impressions' are all big, imposing flowers with elongated, oval blooms that last well. 'Pink Impression' has pale pink flowers, flushed on the outside with darker pink and edged with shrimp pink. Inside are black anthers and a small black base, but the flowers seem reluctant to open fully, which probably leads to their long life in the garden. Its sports are 'Apricot Impression' (World Flower 1996) and 'Red Impression' (Van der Wereld 1994, AGM-RHS 1997). 'Design Impression' has yellow-edged leaves and 'Salmon Impression' has soft, salmon-pink flowers. A tulip bought as 'First Impression' (p. 131) does not seem to be one of these sports, because its flowers are smaller. 55 cm/22 in (IVT, Van der Wereld 1979, TGA-KAVB 1979, AGM-RHS 1997)

'President Kennedy'

This is a buttercup-yellow flower, stippled with red. Inside, the base is bronzy green with black anthers. It is a sport of 'Doctor Philips' (orange red, D W Lefeber & Co 1950). 60 cm/24 in (P J de Groot, D W Lefeber & Co 1961, AM-RHS 1965, FCC-RHS 1978, AGM-RHS 1993)

'Queen Wilhelmina'

see 'Koningin Wilhelmina'

'Red Impression'

see 'Pink Impression'

'Salmon Impression'

see 'Pink Impression'

'Spring Song'

A bright flower that is red, shaded with salmon. Inside, the base is blue, edged with white. 55 cm/22 in (J H Veldhuyzen van Zanten Az 1946)

'Springtime'

A large, deep-red flower with a yellow base inside. It has two sports, 'Golden Springtime' (pure yellow, D W Lefeber & Co 1957) and 'Striped Springtime' (yellow, striped red, A Overdevest Gz 1963). 55 cm/22 in (D W Lefeber & Co 1956)

'Striped Apeldoorn' ('Solstice', 'Turmoil')

Inside and out the tepals are yellow, striped and speckled with red. The base and anthers are black. 55 cm/22 in (A Overdevest Gz 1963)

'Striped Oxford' ('Central Park')

Red flushing and striping on yellow, with a yellow base and black anthers inside. As with all the 'Oxford' sports, the blooms are fragrant. 55 cm/22 in (A Overdevest Gz 1963)

'Tender Beauty' (p. 172)

This universally revered tulip has large blooms of white with a broad pink edge to the tepals, and a yellow base. It is slow to increase and expensive. It is one of the few tetraploid Darwinhybrids. It has one sport, the 'Ljudmila Zagamulova' (broad red margin on white, Khondyrev 1993). 50 cm/20 in (Hybrida, AM-RHS 1954, TGA-KAVB 1972, AGM-RHS 1999)

'Vivex'

This orange flower is, on close inspection, carmine edged with gold and orange. It is bright and rich in colour. 60 cm/24 in (Konijnenburg & Mark 1960, AGM-RHS 1999)

'World's Favourite'

This is a large red flower with a golden edge to the tepals. 45 cm/18 in (IVT, World Flower 1992, TGA-KAVB 1992)

'Yellow Dover'

see 'Dover'

CLASS 5
Single Late

This large group was created to absorb a wide range of plants, including those formerly classified as Darwin and Cottage tulips. They all flower from late April onwards, and most have tall stems so are ideal for bedding. The two groups inevitably became interbred and it was impossible to differentiate them. The Darwin tulips arose from old Flemish Florist tulips called Baguettes, or Baquettes, which usually had rounded tepal tips and a rather squat shape with a rounded or square base, but none had yellow colouring – in compliance with the requirements of Flemish florists – and were mostly violet and pink with white or blue bases. E H Krelage bought a collection of these tulips from Jules Lenglart of Lille in 1885: 20 different breeders and 800 broken tulips, making a total of 10,000 individual

White and pink tulips
Top row:
'Gerbrand Kieft' 11,
'Snow Parrot' 10.
Second row:
'Libretto Parrot' 10,
'Akela' 5.
Bottom row:
'Flaming Purissima' 13,
'Shirley' 3.

The Cottage tulips were a miscellany of old tulips that did not meet the high standards of the English Florist tulips, particularly if they lacked the one-third or one-half ball shape required. They were also shorter than the Darwins. Because both the Darwins and the Cottage tulips are closely descended from the old Florist tulips, which were bred for form and colour and then selected for their ability to produce broken colours when infected with virus, these seem to be among the most prone to 'breaking' in the garden, and 'Bleu Aimable' regularly does so in my garden. It is from the Darwins in particular that those sold as Rembrandt tulips were derived, with new names.

You can find superb tulips among these, including modern wonders alongside old favourites such as 'Mrs John T Scheepers' – which remains one of the few tetraploid tulips – and triploids such as 'Maureen', bringing to gardeners great size and vigour – and to breeders, frustration.

'Akela' (p. 136)

This is white with ivory flushes, shaded with bright pink around the edge of the tepals. The base and anthers are yellow. This is a lovely subtle tulip. 45 cm/18 in (J F van den Berg & Sons, J A Borst 1980)

'Alabaster'

A pure white flower, enhanced by greyish foliage. 55 cm/22 in (1942)

'Aristocrat'

A sophisticated bloom of pale violet edged with white. 70 cm/28 in (Segers 1935, AM-KAVB 1938, AGM-RHS 1993)

'Atlantis'

This is a beautiful tulip with rounded, chunky blooms of lilac purple with a white edge (cream at first) to each tepal. The base inside is blue and the anthers are yellow. 40 cm/16 in (J F van den Berg & Sons, J Lighart 1981)

'Avignon'

This is a strong, tall tulip with bright colouring. The tepals are deep red with more orange edges, and the inside is tomato red with a yellow base and yellow anthers. It is a sport of 'Renown' and

bulbs. Amazingly, no one else bid for these bulbs, which formed the basis for what became the Darwin tulips. Krelage therefore preserved some of the last of these important flowers and brought them to the attention of the gardening world. His aim was to convince gardeners of the value of these varieties, because at that time only the early tulips were regarded as suitable for bedding displays, while late tulips were grown only as breeders, and then infected with virus for competition. English tulip fanciers may have criticized the lack of perfection in the flowers or brilliancy of colour, but the range of shades was wide and made a good starting point for better things. The early Darwins included pink 'Suzon', white 'Zwanenburg' and 'White Queen', cerise 'Pride of Haarlem', dark purple 'The Bishop', and several other 'blacks' such as 'La Tulipe Noir' as well as the famous 'Clara Butt'. Krelage was ahead of his time promoting these fundamentally good but rather plain tulips for mass planting, but he was, ultimately, right. He named these tulips after the great British naturalist Charles Darwin, with the permission of Darwin's son Francis.

itself has two sports: 'Rochelle' (red and orange, 1983) and 'Batavia' (orange and purple, 1994). 65 cm/26 in (W Dekker 1966, TGA-KAVB 1970, AM-KAVB 1970)

'Bacchus' (p. 137)

A deep burgundy, egg-shaped tulip with paler base. Not commonly available. Its age is uncertain, but it was known (and considered old) in 1929. 70 cm/28 in

'Baronnesse'

This is a beautiful, fragrant, pink tulip with paler edges to the tepals and a milky-white base with blue and white blotches. The anthers are dark brown in colour. 55 cm/22 in (J F van den Berg & Sons 1981)

'Bartigon'

This is an old bright red tulip that has a mass of sports including the fine 'Queen of Bartigons' (salmon pink, 1944, AGM-RHS 1995), none of which are very common. The best known is 'Cordell Hull', which is widely seen. 'Bartigon' was once a major cut flower variety, but is not common now. 55 cm/22 in (Krelage & Son 1894, AM-KAVB 1916, FA-KAVB 1922)

'Belcanto'

This is a rich red tulip with a golden yellow edge to each tepal. The interior is blood red, edged with yellow, and it has a yellow base and purple anthers. 50 cm/20 in (J F van den Berg & Sons 1965)

'Big Smile'

This has blooms that are bright yellow and elongated in bud. The wide-open flowers are pale yellow at the base. 60 cm/24 in (IVT, W van Lierop & Sons 1990, TGA-KAVB 1990)

'Bingham' (p. 141)

This sturdy, bright yellow tulip is not common but has much to commend it for general bedding. 60 cm/24 in (Segers, 1960, AM-KAVB 1950)

'Black Beauty' (p. 137)

This rare tulip is bigger and darker than 'Queen of Night', and with squarer flowers. It is possibly the darkest of all tulips. 65 cm/26 in (M v Waveren & Sons, 1955)

'Black Diamond' (p. 137)

A tall tulip that has burgundy brown flowers with a paler central flare on the exterior. 70 cm/28 in (Rijnveld & Sons 1962, *AGM-RHS 1995*)

'Black Pearl' (p. 137)

This rare, dark tulip has matte blooms that are slightly larger and deeper in colour than 'Queen of Night'. 60 cm/24 in (M v Waveren & Sons, 1956)

'Black Swan'

This is a giant of a tulip, towering over most others. The blooms are deep, darkest maroon with a faint white base on the outside of the tepals. Inside there are deep brown anthers, and the base is a fascinating blue shade. 70 cm/28 in (Rijnveld & Sons 1963)

Single late, black tulips
Top row:
'Queen of Night' 5,
'The Sultan' 5,
'La Tulipe Noir' 5.
Second row:
'Black Beauty' 5,
'Black Diamond' 5.
Third row:
'Fra Angelico' 5,
'Black Pearl' 5,
'Phillipe de Comines' 5.
Bottom row:
'Wienerwald' 5,
'Bacchus' 5.

'Bleu Aimable' (p. 147, 155)

Everyone should grow this superb tulip, or its Parrot sport, 'Blue Parrot', at least once. The flowers are lilac but lose some of their pinkness as they age, and the tepals are beautifully sculpted and curved and of great substance, so they last well. Look inside the flowers and you will find the pale base is true blue. Note: photo shows atypical, small blooms. 60 cm/24 in (Krelage & Son, AM-KAVB 1916)

'Blushing Beauty'

With so many tulips to try it is difficult to make a shortlist but this, or its parent 'Temple of Beauty' or some of the other sports, must be included. Held on lofty stems, the huge flowers are almost the shape of trumpet lilies, with narrow bases and wide-open mouths. The tepals are pointed and splay wide open and are apricot yellow with rosy red shading from the base, especially on the outer tepals. The inner ones are paler and all have a distinct stripe up the centre. Sometimes the flowers loll over to one side, but even this does not detract from the splendour of this tulip, which must be grown to be appreciated. See also 'Blushing Lady'. 75 cm/30 in (D W Lefeber & Co 1983)

'Blushing Bride'

A creamy white tulip with a delicate, red edge to the tepals. The base and anthers are yellow. 50 cm/20 in (P H Beelen, 1959, HC-RHS 1970)

'Blushing Lady'

This is another, exceptionally lovely tulip, rather like 'Blushing Beauty', but with more yellow blooms, shaded with rosy red. 75 cm/30 in (D W Lefeber & Co, J N M van Eden 1991)

'Bronze Queen' (also known as 'Biscuit', Clio', Duc de Orleans' and 'Sensation') (p. 140)

With its string of synonyms, this must have been an important tulip in its time, but no longer. The attractive flowers are golden orange, with a purple tint to the outer tepals. (date unknown)

'Caravelle'

A deep, ruby-red tulip with slightly darker edges to the tepals, and with a black base and purple anthers. Rather plain but good for bedding. 55 cm/22 in (Konijnenburg & Mark 1981)

'Cherbourg' (p. 141)

Despite its Dutch awards, this fragrant orange tulip is no longer a commercial cultivar, although it displays an attractive suffusion of yellow and bronze. (AM-KAVB 1915, FCC-KAVB 1920) (note: photo shows green streak that is not typical)

'Clara Butt'

This is one of the best known and loved of all tulips, though it is not as popular as it was, perhaps because of stiff competition. The blooms are salmon pink with a white base, tinged with grey, and the flowers are rounded and attractive. It is less often seen now than its Parrot sport 'Fantasy'. 55 cm/22 in (Krelage & Son 1889, AM-RHS 1904, AM-KAVB 1950)

'Cloud Nine'

This is a white tulip that is edged and speckled with deep pink. The base is blue and the anthers are dark. It often produces more than one flower per stem but may not be reliable. (Jan Ligthart)

'Colour Spectacle'

This sport of 'Georgette' has bright, rich yellow flowers, heavily flamed with bright red from the base of the tepals. Like its parent it is multi-flowered, with four or five blooms on each stem, and lasts well. It is a good bright bedding tulip, though usually rather shorter than the official height. 50 cm/20 in (Visser CZN 1990, TGA-KAVB 1990)

'Companion'

This is a tall, bold tulip with large blooms of carmine that have a lighter edge. The base is white with a blue edge and the anthers are yellow. 70 cm/28 in (Van Zanten Bros 1962, AGM-RHS 1995)

'Cordell Hull'

This showy sport of 'Bartigon' has creamy-white flowers that are striped and stippled with blood red. The base is white with a touch of blue. Though old, it is still worth growing because of the bold colouring, and it is widely available. 55 cm/22 in (P Bakker Mz 1933, AM-KAVB 1933, FCC-KAVB 1939)

'Cri de Coeur'

see 'Renown'

'Cum Laude'

A 'blue' tulip with flowers of dark violet, and with a blue and white base inside. 60 cm/24 in (Grullemans & Sons 1944)

'Dillenburg'

This is a large, fragrant, orange bloom that benefits from copper and terracotta shading to prevent the colour being too plain. 'Dillenburg's Parrot' (1966) is a sport. 60 cm/24 in (Tubergen, AM-KAVB 1916, FCC-KAVB 1937)

'Dordogne'

The colours of this large, orange tulip change as the flowers age from pinkish red, to red with an orange margin on the tepals. The base is yellow. It is a sport of 'Menton'. 65 cm/26 in (W Dekker & Sons 1991, TGA-KAVB 1991)

'Douglas Bader'

This subtle flower is pink with a cream base. The centre is ivory with purple anthers. 45 cm/18 in (J F van den Berg & Sons 1976)

'Dreamland'

This popular tulip has creamy white flowers that are broadly edged with pink. The base is white with yellow anthers. It has two sports: 'Holland Pink' (1994) and 'Holland White'(1994). 60 cm/24 in (H G Huyg 1969, AM-KAVB 1960, TGA-KAVB 1962, FCC-KAVB 1962, AGM-RHS 1995)

'Esther'

This sport of 'Pink Supreme' has bright pink blooms with a paler edge and a blue base. 50 cm/20 in (C J Keppel 1967, TGA-KAVB 1967, AM-KAVB 1970)

'Fra Angelico' (p. 137)

With large flowers of blackcurrant black, this flower is not commercially available at the moment. (The name 'Fra Angelico' is also used for a *Greigii* hybrid.) 60 cm/24 in (Krelage & Son pre-1895)

'Georgette' (p. 132, 147)

This is a multi-headed and multi-coloured tulip that is sometimes sold as the 'chameleon tulip'. Each stem produces three to five flowers. The central one opens first and is the largest. The blooms are pale yellow and have a subtle red edge

at first, but this extends as the flowers age so that eventually the flowers are almost coral red with a yellow base. I find it is usually shorter than the official height and although not exactly beautiful, it is showy. I have also bought bulbs that produced leaves with an insignificant white edge. It has three sports: 'Colour Spectacle', 'Red Georgette' and 'Lucette' (yellow, 1990). 50 cm/20 in (Hybrida 1952)

'Grand Cru Vacqeyras'

see 'Renown'

'Grand Style'

This is a big, tall bedding tulip with pink and red-suffused flowers that are purplish inside, The base is yellow in colour, edged blue with yellow anthers. 65 cm/26 in ('t Mannetje 1962, AGM-RHS 1995)

'Halcro'

Big, bold and long-lasting, this is a fine bedding tulip of bright scarlet red. The base is yellow, edged with green. One of the finest for a brilliant show of red. 70 cm/28 in (Segers 1949, AM-KAVB 1949, FCC-KAVB 1964, AM-RHS 1977, AGM-RHS 1993)

'Heart's Desire'

This is a tall and pretty flower in shades of pink and purple, with a greenish-white base. 60 cm/24 in (Nieuwenhuis Bros, C W van der Huist 1981, AGM-RHS 1995)

'Helga' (p. 141)

This is a huge, pale yellow tulip that opens its face to greet the sun. It has a deeper shade inside, and yellow anthers. 65 cm/26 in (Rijnveld & Sons, 1963)

'Hocus Pocus'

Another fabulous sport of 'Temple of Beauty', this one has large, lily-shaped blooms of yellow and red. The outer tepals are lemon yellow with a slight red flush, but the inner tepals are streaked with deep red, though the colouring is rather variable. The inside of the flower is mainly yellow. 75 cm/30 in (D W Lefeber & Co 1983)

'Hofstra University'

This is a tall, majestic tulip that is ivory white at

first, ageing to white with a pale-yellow base inside and out, and with yellow anthers. 65 cm/26 in (IVT, Van der Wereld 1986)

'Inglescombe Yellow'
see 'Princess Margaret Rose'

'Kingsblood'
This is a good cherry red tulip with scarlet around the edge of the tepals and a yellow base. 60 cm/24 in (Konijnenburg & Mark 1952, AM-RHS 1977, AGM-RHS 1993)

'Koningin Juliana' (p. 141)
A beautiful orange tulip that is a richer shade inside, with a yellow base and anthers. Fragrant. 65 cm/26 in (F Roozen, 1974)

'La Courtine'
This is a tall, striped tulip with a golden yellow ground colour and a red stripe up the centre of the tepals, with smaller stripes on either side. The anthers are yellow. It is a sport of 'Renown' and has its own sport, 'Roi de Midi' (pure yellow, 1991). 65 cm/26 in (W Dekker & Son 1988)

'Landseadel's Supreme'
As the string of awards suggest, this is a fine, deed-red tulip with strong stems that is a perfect companion for wallflowers in traditional spring bedding. The blooms are cherry red with a pale base and purple anthers, and very long-lasting. Its sport is 'World Expression' (AGM-RHS 1999). 60 cm/24 in (D W Lefeber & Co 1958, AM-KAVB 1959, FCC-KAVB 1961, TGA-KAVB 1967, AM-RHS 1970, FCC-RHS 1977, *AGM-RHS 1993*)

'La Tulipe Noir' (p. 137)
Not really a black tulip and not even the blackest, a title that must belong to 'Black Beauty' to my eyes. But we must rate these in context and, as an ancient cultivar, it must have been exciting when first introduced. It is deep blackcurrant, of moderate size, and its flower profile is egg-shaped. 55 cm/22 in (Krelage & Son, 1891, AM-RHS 1901, AM-KAVB 1939)

'Magazine Prima'
A deep-pink tulip with a white base inside, and black anthers. 55 cm/22 in (Elt Brouwer)

'Magier' ('Magician')
This beautiful cultivar has stood the test of time and is still popular. The chunky flowers last for ages and have milk-white tepals that are stippled around the edges with lilac and there is a cream stripe up the centre of the outer tepals. As the flowers age the cream disappears and the lilac colouring spreads down over the flower until it is almost entirely lilac. Anthers purple. 60 cm/24 in (Hybrida 1951)

'Maureen'
While red tulips are hard to beat, white tulips also have a purity that is exceptional in the garden, and 'Maureen' is one of the best. The huge, oval blooms, a shape inherited from its parent 'Mrs John T Scheepers', are pure white (with an ivory flush in youth) and tower over most others. This triploid flower is beautiful with the fresh fronds of ferns. 70 cm/28 in (Segers 1950, AM-KAVB 1949, FCC-KAVB 1956, AM-RHS 1960, AGM-RHS 1993)

'Menton'
This sport of 'Renown' is triploid, and has interesting flowers of deep pink with an orange edge, while the inside is red with a central, thin white stripe, and a yellow and white base. 'Dordogne' is its sport. 65 cm/26 in (W Dekker & Sons 1971)

'Mrs John T Scheepers'
One of only a few tetraploid tulips, this is a real beauty with large, oval blooms of pale yellow. Its extra vigour shows in its large blooms. Because it is tetraploid (and so, if crossed with a 'normal' diploid tulip will give rise to sterile triploids) it is both a valuable and frustrating parent. Old but highly recommended. 60 cm/24 in (Tubergen, AM-KAVB 1930, FCC-KAVB 1931, AGM-RHS 1993)

'Niphetos' (p. 141)
Though not common, this is one of the most beautiful pale-cream tulips, slightly deeper inside, with yellow anthers. It was used to great effect in bedding at the Royal Botanic Gardens, Kew in the 1980s with bronze fennel, a combination I will never forget. It has two sports, 'Golden Niphetos' (deeper yellow, 1955) and 'Silver Wedding' (see 'Sweet Harmony'). 65 cm/26 in (Grullemans & Sons 1933)

'Orange Wings'
see 'Rosy Wings'

'Palestrina'
This is shorter than most but has massive flowers in salmon-pink shades, with a slight green flush on the outside when the flowers are young. 40 cm/16 in (Captein Bros 1944)

'Perestroyka' (p. 169)
Yet another magnificent sport of 'Temple of Beauty' that always attracts gasps of admiration – it literally stands head and shoulders above the competition with large, lily-shaped blooms, but this time in mango with soft scarlet flushing on the outside, and a yellow base. No awards yet, but it's only a matter of time. 75 cm/30 in (D W Lefeber, W van Lierop & Sons 1990)

'Phillipe de Comines' (p. 137)
From the same stable and era as 'La Tulipe Noir', this has darker and slightly larger flowers. Not common but it is a commercial cultivar. It sported to produce 'Black Parrot' in 1937. (Krelage & Son, 1891)

'Picture'
This cultivar stands (almost) alone due to its strange flower shape. The tepals are broad at the base but curl inwards in the upper half, and their ruffled edges twist out to give the blooms a sculpted look. They are the same lilac pink as its parent 'Princess Elizabeth' (1898), with a white base and blue ring, but have a thick texture. To my mind it looks too much like weedkiller damage for me to really enjoy, but I can see it might appeal to some. 'Witty Picture' is its pale pink sport. 60 cm/24 in (G Baltus 1949, AGM-RHS 1995)

'Pink Diamond'
This tulip is a paler sport of 'Pink Supreme', and has feminine flowers of delicate pink, which become slightly paler at the edge of the tepals. Its sport 'Silverado' is paler still – ivory flushed with pink. 50 cm/20 in (Verbruggen 1976, TGA-KAVB 1976)

'Pink Jewel' (p. 155)
This sport of 'Queen of Bartigons' is ivory, shaded with pink – a delicate shade. Inside, the tepals have a pronounced white stripe in the centre extending from the white base. 55 cm/22 in (J J Duif 1980, TGA-KAVB 1980)

'Pink Supreme'
Another of the group of pink sports originally derived from 'Utopia' (red, 1935). This is light, bright pink with paler edges to the tepals. Its own sports are 'Esther' and 'Pink Diamond'. 50 cm/20 in (Captein Bros 1947, AM-KAVB 1949)

'Princess Margaret Rose' ('Colour Beauty')
This is one of several sports of the tough and reliable triploid, British-raised 'Inglescombe Yellow' (W T Ware 1906). It is a superb, long-lasting flower that opens bright yellow with a thin, bright red edge to the tepals, but as the flowers age this colour spreads over the outer edges to give a rich and flashy bicolour effect. Old but recommended with mixed wallflowers for a traditional cottage garden look. 45 cm/18 in (J Bankert 1944)

Golden tulips
Top row:
'Koningin Juliana' 5,
'Helga' 5,
'Bingham' 5.
Second row:
'Cherbourg' 5,
'Bronze Queen' 5.
Third row:
'Niphetos' 5,
'Mamasa' 3,
'Alfi' 3.
Bottom row:
'Doris' 3,
'Madame Spoor's Favourite' 3.

'Queen of Night' (p. 132, 137, 147)
This is the best known 'black' tulip and dark enough for most gardeners, though there are better tulips (see picture of 'black' tulips, p. 137). The rounded flowers have attractive grey/blue bases, black anthers and white stigmas, and some scent. It is commonly called 'Queen of the Night' – presumably after the character in Mozart's *Magic Flute* – but I have seen it called 'Queen of the Knight' – presumably Guinevere! 60 cm/24 in (Grullemans & Sons, AM-KAVB 1944)

'Recreado'
A globular, deep-purple flower, subtly flamed with violet, with a bluish base and purple anthers. 50 cm/20 in (Visser Czn 1979)

'Red Georgette'
This sport of 'Georgette' has clusters of bright red flowers that are mat on the outer surface but open to shining blooms with a yellow and black base. Though not exceptional in form or colour, the mass of blooms of bright colour make this one of the best for bedding. 50 cm/20 in (Visser Czn 1983, AGM-RHS 1993)

'Renown'
With the tetraploid 'Mrs T John Scheepers' in its ancestry, this triploid has large, oval blooms and great vigour. The flowers are pale carmine with a paler, orange edge and a white base outside. Inside the base is yellow, edged blue. It is a strong, bold bedding tulip with interesting colouring. It has many sports: 'Avignon', 'Cri de Coeur' (yellow, flamed red, 1973), 'Grand Cru Vacqeyras' (cherry pink, 1995), 'La Courtine', 'Menton' and 'Renown Unique' (Double Late, 1988). 65 cm/26 in (Segers 1949, AM-KAVB 1949, FCC-KAVB 1951, AM-RHS 1968)

'Rosy Wings'
This is a bright pink, elongated flower with a white base that shows through the outside of the bloom. Its two sports are 'Orange Wings' (scarlet and orange with green midribs, 1977) and 'Roxanne' (red and white, 1983). 60 cm/24 in (Tubergen 1944, AM-KAVB)

'Sorbet'
Inside, the blooms are white, but the outsides of these glorious flowers are white with strong raspberry-pink flames and some pale flushing. It is a large, refreshing, well-named tulip. 60 cm/24 in (Jac J v d Eyken 1959, TGA-KAVB 1960, AM-KAVB 1961, FCC-KAVB 1961, AM-RHS 1970, AGM-RHS 1993)

'Swarovski'
The large flowers of this tulip are a lovely mixture of pink, salmon and orange. However, it is the foliage that is exceptional, being marked with broad and showy lime-green margins. 60 cm/24 in (Mut. 'Renown')

'Sweet Harmony'
This is a popular tulip with unusual colouring. The blooms are lemon yellow with a broad band of white around the top. Apparently the Dutch call this variety 'Advocat met Slagroom' (eggnog with cream) which is appropriate but unnecessarily confusing. The flower is distinct enough not to appear as though it is fading or ageing and it has a bright, fresh look that is welcome in the garden. It is a sport of 'Mrs Grullemans'. 'Silver Wedding' (1950), a sport of 'Niphetos', is the only other Single Late tulip with similar colouring, and is larger but far less common. 55 cm/22 in (Jac B Roozen 1944, AM-KAVB 1944, FCC-KAVB 1947, AM-RHS 1955, AGM-RHS 1993)

'Temple of Beauty'
One of the most magnificent of all tulips, this has towering stems with salmon-coloured flowers blushed with pink. The leaves are slightly mottled, which betrays one of its parents – it is supposedly a hybrid between *T. greigii* and the Lily-flowered 'Mariette'. That such an unlikely pairing produced this beautiful offspring is nothing short of miraculous, and its great stems must be the result of hybrid vigour from new 'blood' in the breeding. It was once classed as a *Greigii* hybrid, which must have surprised unsuspecting gardeners who put it in window boxes. Fortunately it has been blessed with five wonderful sports: 'Blushing Beauty', 'Blushing Lady', 'Hocus Pocus', 'Perestroyka' and 'Temple's Favourite'. 75 cm/30 in (D W Lefeber & Co 1959, TGA-KAVB 1972, AGM-RHS 1993)

'Temple's Favourite'
Like its parent 'Temple of Beauty', but has bright

orange flowers with a carmine flare and a yellow base. 75 cm/30 in (D W Lefeber & Co 1984)

'The Sultan' (p. 137)
A dark blackcurrant-coloured tulip with a paler base. Historical collections only. (Krelage & Son, 1896)

'Toyota'
This is a tall, elegant tulip of bright, crimson red, shaded with scarlet and with a white edge around the tepals. The base is pale yellow with a violet edge, and the anthers are grey. 65 cm/26 in (IVT, Captein Bros and Van Til Hartman 1984)

'Union Jack'
This sport of 'Cordell Hull' has larger flowers than that variety; they are chunky in shape, with ivory-white tepals heavily flamed with raspberry red. The base is white, edged with blue, to complete the patriotic colouring! 55 cm/22 in (P Bakker Mz 1958, AM-KAVB 1960, FCC-KAVB 1961, AM-RHS 1961, AGM-RHS 1995)

'Violet Beauty'
This is a violet purple flower with a white base and purple anthers. 45 cm/18 in (H G Huyg & Son 1993)

'Wienerwald' (p. 137)
A beautiful tulip with burgundy tepals, narrowly edged with white. The base of the tulip is pale green, and the anthers are purple. 50 cm/20 in (Zandvoort, 1971)

'Wisley' (p. 143)
A bright red, glossy tulip with a bright yellow base that shows on the outside of the tepals. Inside there is a large yellow base, and yellow anthers. 50 cm/20 in (IVT, C and A van Bentem 1987)

'Witty Picture'
see 'Picture'

'World Expression'
This sport of 'Lanseadel's Supreme' (AGM-RHS 1993) is a showy bloom of deep cream, ageing to white, with blood-red stripes extending from the base. Inside the flower, the base is yellow. 60 cm/24 in (Worldson Bulbs 1992, TGA-KAVB 1992)

'Zomerschoon'
This is probably the oldest tulip still in cultivation, though it is far from common because it increases slowly. The slender flowers are yellow at first but cream at maturity, with irregular streaks of salmon. Not for everyone – and expensive when available – but a beautiful curiosity. 40 cm/16 in (1620, AM-RHS 1954)

CLASS 6
Lily-flowered

Lily-flowered tulips are among the most elegant of all. Their flowers are typically waisted and have a broad base, with narrow tepals that end in a sharp point. In my opinion, the best flowers have an hourglass shape, the tops of the petals recurving elegantly, though the shapes do vary and some have more slender flowers than others. Some of those with broader flowers have inner tepals that stand upright until the flower is middle aged, when they unfurl like the others.

Red tulips
Top:
'Karel Doorman' 10.
Second row:
'Aladdin' 6,
'Wisley' 5.
Bottom row:
'Abba' 2,
'Ile de France' 3.

They were once included, along with other shapes, in the Cottage tulips, but they were given their own class in 1958. In many respects they are more like the old Turkish tulips than any other – the Turks valued slender tulips with narrow tepals more than the chunky, rounded shape found in most modern varieties.

'Retroflexa' was one of the first of the class, a primrose tulip that was for a long time thought to be a species, along with 'Elegans Alba' (50 cm/20 in), which is creamy white with a narrow red edge and received an Award for Merit from the Royal Horticultural Society in 1895. In Joseph Jacob's book *Tulips* (1912) it is described as 'vase-shaped', so the Lily-flowered term was not used, and 'Retroflexa' is recommended for cutting. In *The Book of the Tulip*, Daniel Hall describes 'Retroflexa' as having 'the most waisted *fleur-de-lis* shape of all tulips. It is a bright buttercup yellow, with no tinge of orange'.

It may have been raised by V van der Winne sometime before 1863, when he sold his stock. It was then hybridized by the Krelage nursery, beginning the race of Lily-flowered tulips, which were introduced commercially from 1914. The work was then continued by Rengert Cornelis Segers, who used 'Bartigon', a red tulip that forces well, making crosses with a wide range of partners possible.

Lily-flowered tulips usually cost a little more than other late tulips, but they are worth the extra money. They are beautiful when just opening, and in dull weather when they are closed, but those with the narrowest tepals are equally lovely when they open fully and present you with wide, starlike blooms. They are supremely suitable for cutting, but they are effective in the garden too. I have noticed that many Lily-flowered tulips have leaves that are attractively wavy, especially the upper leaves on the stems. I would not say that they are worth growing for their leaves alone, but it does make the bed look more interesting. Most are tall and mid-to-late season. Whether you choose something with pastel shades or go for bright colours is a matter of taste; there are no bad Lily-flowered tulips, and all benefit from the shape of their blooms.

'China Pink' has rather more blocky flowers than some, but it is not over large, and it is such a pretty colour that it has long been a favourite of mine, especially with myosotis. But the superb,

bright orange 'Ballerina' also perfectly combines shape and colour. 'Westpoint' is a good yellow because the flowers have perfectly recurving tepals, and 'Marilyn' deserves attention because its pure-white tepals are streaked with red. And one that stands out from the rest is 'Trés Chic', a short tulip in pure white with grey leaves that just oozes class. This is a rapidly expanding group, so look out for new cultivars such as fragrant 'Jane Packer', 'Holland Cherry' and 'Holland Chic' in the future as they become more widely available.

'Adonis' (p. 146)
This may be old, and a primitive Lily-flowered tulip, but it is large and bright, with tomato-red blooms and a yellow base. The tepals are broad but recurve as the flower ages. It is not commercially available at present. 55 cm/22 in (Krelage & Sons pre-1914)

'Aladdin' (p. 88, 143, 169)
Deservedly popular, this vibrant tulip has scarlet-red tepals with a delicate yellow rim around the entire length, except at the base. Inside, the base is yellow and black. The tepals are broad at the base but narrow in the upper half, where they turn back to create a wonderful shape. Brightens up the dullest garden. It has sported to produce 'Aladdin's Lamp' (pale yellow 1970), 'Aladdin's Record' and 'Cabaret'. 55 cm/22 in (De Mol & A H Nieuwenhuis 1942)

'Aladdin's Record'
This has more elegant flowers than 'Aladdin' with wider and more distinct yellow colouring that lines the length of the tepals. The yellow base is also more pronounced. 55 cm/22 in (Lighthart Bros 1984)

'Astor' (p. 146)
Not widely grown but very beautiful, the flowers have broad tepals of apricot salmon with a broad brush of pinkish red on the outside of the bloom. It deserves to be brought into general cultivation. 55 cm/22 in (Tubergen, AM-KAVB 1936)

'Ballade'
This has rather broad-based flowers, with attractively recurving tepals that are narrow in the upper half. They are pale purple with a broad white edge that extends round the upper three-

quarters of their length, while the base is pale yellow. It is very popular and widely available. It has sported to produce many other cultivars, including: 'Ballade White' (1994) with ivory flowers flushed with palest blue; 'Je t'aime' ('Ballade Orange') orange, edged yellow (1995); 'Sonnet' ('Ballade Dream') purple-red, edged yellow (1994); and 'Ballade Gold'. 55 cm/22 in (Nieuwenhuis Bros 1953, AM-RHS 1982, *AGM-RHS 1993*)

'Ballerina' (p. 110, 113, 132)

Like many orange tulips, this is pleasantly scented, but it would be worth a place in the garden even without this bonus. It is a beautiful, bright colour that is not pure orange, as a cursory glance would suggest, but has red flushing on the exterior and a yellow base inside. Tall, elegant, brightly coloured, but not too large, it is one of the best and one of very few orange tulips in this class – see 'Fokker Fan-Fan'. 55 cm/22 in J F van den Berg & Sons, J A Borst 1980, YGA-KAVB 1980, *AGM-RHS 1995*)

'Burgundy'

The deep-purple flowers have narrow tepals. It is a sport of 'Captain Fryatt' (garnet with a paler edge, Tubergen, AM-KAVB 1931). 50 cm/20 in (Grullemans & Sons 1957)

'Cabaret' (p. 146)

This uncommon sport of 'Aladdin' has beautiful, large, narrow-tepalled blooms of cherry red, with a paler stripe up the centre of each tepal. 55 cm/22 in (Nieuwenhuis Bros 1963)

'China Pink' (p. 146)

This old tulip still heads the popularity list because of its medium height and elegant, soft pink flowers, which are elegantly shaped and not too big. They have a white base and pale anthers that are exposed when the blooms open fully to an exciting star shape in full sun. It has sported to produce 'Pearl of China' and 'Stien Kaiser' (white, 1967). 45 cm/18 in (De Mol & A H Nieuwenhuis 1944, *AGM-RHS 1995*)

'Dynito'

This is an elegant, tomato-red tulip with narrow blooms and a bright yellow base. 55 cm/22 in (D van Buggenum Mz 1949)

'Elegant Lady'

Opening from beautiful, slender buds, the flowers are a gorgeous, creamy white, with rosy shading on all the sunny parts of the bloom. It deserves a very special place in the garden, with subdued surroundings to show off the pastel colouring. 60 cm/24 in (Nieuwenhuis Bros 1953)

'Flashback'

A new, bright, rich yellow tulip with elegantly recurved tepals. 45 cm/18 in

'Fly Away' (p. 113)

One of the most elegant of all, with very narrow tepals that form willowy bud and starry flowers. These are bright red, with a broad yellow edge. 45 cm/18 in

'Fokker Fan-Fan'

A new, bright-orange tulip with narrow tepals. 45 cm/18 in

'Gisella'

A good pink tulip that seems to have been eclipsed by 'China Pink', but is rather taller. 55 cm/22 in (Segers 1942, TGA-KAVB 1947)

'Goltu'

This is a welcome addition, not only for its short stems, bringing Lily-flowered tulips to tubs and window boxes, but also for its truly elegant blooms in sulphur yellow. It is not common, but well worth trying. 30 cm/12 in (Vertuco 1986, TGA-KAVB 1986)

'Holland Cherry'

A new, rich pink tulip with slight white patches at the base of the tepals. 45 cm/18 in (Bolroy)

'Holland Chic'

A new, white tulip with red/pink stripes down the midrib of the inner tepals and a yellow base. 45cm/18 in (Bolroy)

'Holland Jewel'

A new, bright, pure-yellow-coloured tulip. 50 cm/20 in (Bolroy)

'Jacqueline'

Taller than 'Gisella', much taller than 'China Pink', and perhaps better than 'Mariette', this is also a much bolder colour: neon pink. The base is white with yellow anthers, and the leaves are strikingly wavy. 65 cm/26 in (Segers 1958, AM-KAVB 1962)

Lily-flowered tulips
Top row:
'Synaeda King' 6,
'Talbion' 6,
'Yellow Marvel' 6.
Second row:
'Lilac Time' 6,
'Maytime' 6.
Third row:
'Martha' 6,
'China Pink' 6.
Bottom row:
'Cabaret' 6,
'Astor' 6,
'Adonis' 6.

'Jane Packer'
A shorter, bright red tulip with a yellow base and some fragrance. The blue leaves are wavy, and it is elegant and colourful. 40 cm/16 in (Huiyg)

'Libera'
The bright-red flowers are edged with yellow. Surprisingly, it is a sport of the Triumph 'Zarewitch', which has similar colouring and height. 40 cm/16 in (P W Straathof 1995)

'Lilac Time' (p. 146)
A popular tulip of elegant shape with purple-pink flowers and a white base. It is more pink than 'Maytime', which is also common. 45 cm/18 in (De Mol & A H Nieuwenhuis 1945)

'Lilyfire'
A new tulip with gorgeous flowers. The tepals are bright yellow with orange borders, while the meeting of the two shades is marked with red. 45 cm/18 in

'Lilyrosa'
A new pink tulip of deep rose with a white base. 45 cm/18 in

'Linette'
A deep purple flower with a white base. Not grown much now. 55 cm/22 in (Tubergen 1942)

'Macarena'
Slender blooms of white, and a cream central stripe through each tepal. 50 cm /20 in

'Mariette'
An important pink tulip because of its many sports, and also because it is such an elegant, beautiful flower on tall, strong stems. Beautiful and slender in bud and in full bloom. Its sports include 'Christina van Kooten' (carmine pink, 1974), 'Marilyn', 'Marjolein', 'Tiko' (yellow and orange, 1974) and 'Windmill' (yellow and pink, 1974). 55 cm/22 in (Segers 1942, TGA-KAVB 1947, AM-KAVB 1949, FCC-KAVB 1950, AM-RHS 1968)

'Marilyn'
This sport of 'Mariette' is a super tulip. It has large blooms with elegant white tepals that have long stripes of red along the midrib and shorter ones either side. The stripes are seen on both sides of the tepals, so the effect is not lost on the fully open blooms. It has produced two sports: 'Mona Lisa' (yellow, striped red, Verbruggen 1988) and 'White Wings'. 55 cm/22 in (Verbruggen 1976)

'Marjolein'
This sport of 'Mariette' has blooms the colour of blood oranges, its mandarin tepals being flushed with crimson red. The base and anthers are yellow. 55 cm/22 in (P Visser Cz 1962, AM-RHS 1982, AGM-RHS 1993)

'Martha' (p. 146)
An old tulip that is no longer in commercial

production, with broad flowers of carmine pink. 45 cm/18 in (Tubergen 1936)

'Maytime' (p. 117, 146)

This is an established and very popular tulip. Its elegant, pointed flowers have tepals of deep lilac-purple, with a pale, almost white, edge. The base is yellow. It is more purple than 'Lilac Time'. 50 cm/20 in (De Mol & A H Nieuwenhuis 1942)

'Mona Lisa'

see 'Marilyn'

'Moonshine'

This is a bold flower, with narrow-tipped, broad-based tepals, bold and bright yellow throughout. 'Moonstrike' is another yellow tulip, but paler in colour, with a bright yellow base inside. 50 cm/20 in (Hybris, P A van Geest 1987)

'Picotee'

This is an old tulip, and one of the first Lily-flowered cultivars. It is white but stippled with pink, and the colouring becomes more intense with age. It was classified as a 'flushing tulip' in the past and Daniel Hall (*The Book of the Tulip* 1929) describes it as 'a comparatively dwarf flower of less than average size, with long and pointed petals that open with a crimson edge and gradually flush with pink'. 'Picotee' is a good grower and cheap, and makes an excellent edging flower. It is rare now, and seems rather tall for edging all but the biggest beds. 55 cm/22 in (1895)

'Pierot'

This extraordinary tulip is a most beautiful bloom that is even more beautiful in early morning or evening light. The flowers are narrow and elegant, and are creamy white at the base and translucent tomato-red above. It is unlike any other and deserves to become available and popular. 50 cm/20 in

'Pieter de Leur' (p. 147, 164)

A really good, short red tulip with deep, cherry-red flowers and a white base. It is earlier than most, but the flowers last well. 30 cm/12 in (INRA, LB Kaptein's Sons 1993)

'Pretty Woman'

This is a sport of the Triumph 'Bing Crosby', and

has deep-red flowers with a green base. It has strong stems and deep-green leaves. 40 cm/16 in (Jan van Bentem 1992)

'Queen of Sheba'

This is a tall, elegant tulip of deep, mahogany red, with an orange edge and blackish base, has a regal quality, thanks to its shape and rich colour. 60 cm/24 in (De Mol & A H Nieuwenhuis 1944, AM-RHS 1968, AGM-RHS 1995)

'Red Shine'

One of the commonest Lily-flowered tulips, and one of the best, though its flowers lack the waisted finesse of some. The blooms are deep, crimson red, and open to glossy red stars that are hard to beat. One to try if you think you don't like the group. 55 cm/22 in (Hybrida 1955, AM-RHS 1982, AGM-RHS 1995)

'Royal Design'

Another red tulip edged with golden yellow, but

Tulips photographed from above to show their inner beauty
Top row:
'Pieter de Leur' 6,
'Doll's Minuet' 8.
Second row:
'Queen of Night' 5,
'Groenland' 8,
'Bleu Aimable' 5.
Third row:
'Quebec' 14,
'Queen Ingrid' 14.
Bottom row:
'Brilliant Star' 1,
'Georgette' 5,
'Apricot Beauty' 1.

useful because it is shorter than 'Aladdin' or 'Sonnet' (see 'Ballade'). 40 cm/16 in (Hybris, Groot-Vriend 1988)

'Sapporo'
A strikingly beautiful flower with pointed tepals, it is basically white with a yellow base, though official descriptions say it is green and pale yellow when young. I also noticed the faintest pink blushing. In any case it is a superb flower, on stocky stems, and stands somewhere between the towering 'White Triumphator' and the shorter 'Trés Chic' and 'White Elegance', which I also rate highly. 45 cm/18 in (P J Nijssen, Boots 1992)

'Synaeda King' (p. 146)
Beautiful flowers with tepals that are rounded at the base and have narrow upper parts. These are bright, currant red with a broad yellow edge. The interior of the tepals has less red. It is not common but very attractive. 50 cm/20 in (Tulip Flower, Oosterbaan 1995, AGM-RHS 1999)

'Talbion' (p. 146)
This has never become common, but it has beautiful blooms with rolled tepals that give an exceptionally elegant profile. The colour is a blend of pale yellows, and the interior is slightly darker. 50 cm/20 in (IVT, Th Timmerman 1982)

'Trés Chic'
The short stature of this superb white tulip would suit it to containers and exposed gardens, but it deserves a place in any garden. The waisted flowers are pure white with a pale green tinge at the base, and the centre is pale yellow. Hard to see the purple tinge in official descriptions. 45 cm/18 in (Hybris, Van Dam 1992, TGA-KAVB 1991)

'Virily Pink'
A new satin-pink tulip. 'Virily Red' and 'Virily Yellow' complete the set. 45 cm/18 in (Vertuco)

'West Point'
This was the first Lily-flowered tulip I grew and is still a favourite because the blooms are so shapely with their gracefully recurved tepals in pure, crisp, lemon yellow. The flowers also have some scent and open to gold stars in the sun. 50 cm/20 in (De mol & A H Nieuwenhuis 1943, HC-RHS 1982, AGM-RHS 1995)

'White Elegance'
A comparatively short tulip and earlier than some others, it has gorgeous flowers with recurved tepals. The blooms mature to white with a yellow base, but begin life as ivory, flushed with cream. The leaves are pleasantly wavy. Recommended. 35 cm/14 in (De Geus-Vriend 1993)

'White Triumphator'
Tall, with big blooms of purest white, you have to love this, even though the flowers are not as reflexed as some others. One of the best white tulips. 60 cm/24 in (Tubergen 1942, HC-RHS 1982, AGM-RHS 1995)

'White Wings'
This sport of the striped 'Marilyn' has the same slender shape, but is ivory white. 60 cm/24 in (Verbruggen 1995)

'Yellow Marvel' (p. 146)
A large, yellow tulip, no longer commercially available. 45 cm/18 in (Tubergen 1934)

'Yonina'
This is a novelty with dark pink blooms on short stems. The tepals are cherry red with pale edges, and elegantly pointed. 30 cm/12 in (Hybris, Holland Bolroy Markt 1994)

'Youri Dolgoruckiy'
This is a very special tulip with slender flowers of deep-pinkish red with black anthers and a blue base. The foliage is attractively wavy. New but destined for great things if the name does not put people off. 45 cm/18 in

CLASS 7
Fringed

Not everyone loves Fringed tulips, and the addition of little teeth or, more accurately, masses of short needles, around the edge of the tepals is not enough to make a bad tulip into a good one. But they are interesting and are usually attractive. Most Fringed tulips that are available seem to have simple flower shapes with rounded tepals, and I think it should stay that way – I would not like to see Lily-flowered or Parrot tulips with fringing (restraint is a virtue in so many areas of life!). The fringing varies from simple small teeth, through rows of needle-like structures at about a 60-degree angle to the petals, to a frenetic mass of needles at all angles.

Some Fringed tulips have occurred as sports, and three of these have arisen from that good red Darwinhybrid 'Apeldoorn'. These are 'Crystal Beauty', 'Fringed Apeldoorn' and 'Fringed Golden Apeldoorn'. Other early fringed sports were 'Sundew' (from 'Orion'), 'Arma' (from 'Couleur Cardinal'), and the double 'Fringed Beauty' (from 'Titian'), which was probably the first. Sports were the only source of Fringed tulips for many years until the Seger Brothers, whose name is dominant among the following cultivars, successfully bred and introduced many fine Fringed tulips between 1950 and 1975 (their later tulips were introduced by others). Their first introduction was 'Swan Wings', which remains the best white and is one of the most beautiful of all white tulips. They now have their own section in the classification of tulips, but the early cultivars were derived from Darwinhybrid, Double Early, Triumph and other groups, so they were rather variable in height and flowering time. But most are now bred as Fringed tulips and they bloom in May (in the northern hemisphere), along with Single Late tulips.

Fringed tulips remain more expensive than most others, presumably because of their novelty value and low volume of sales rather than due to increased costs of production. They are well worth the extra money. They grow as well as other tulips, but they do deserve a rather special place in the garden and I would not recommend mixtures because the busy colours detract from the delicacy of the flower form. These blooms rely for their effect on close inspection, and a vast array of shades only detracts from their finer points.

Your choice will depend on what is available as much as your taste but among the more common cultivars I would recommend 'Blue Heron' for its subtle colouring, 'Crystal Beauty' for its vivid colouring and nice fringing, and 'Warbler' if you want a lot of fringe on your flowers. Among the more modern, which may take some time to become common, I am impressed with 'Matchpoint' because of its toothy, double flowers, 'Cummins' because of its delicate shades of mauve and cream, and 'Huis ten Bosch', which, if it had a name that anyone but the

Dutch could pronounce would surely become the most popular of all with its bright, pink and white flowers.

I fear that, in the future, fringing may become overdone and make the flowers too fussy – 'Barbados' is one of the ugliest tulips I have ever seen, looking like a cactus that has got stuck inside a tomato – and I speak as one who loves growing cacti and tomatoes! For now, Fringed tulips are available in all colours (though I have not seen striped flowers, thank goodness), and most are attractive in the garden. Many have paler coloration at the edge of the tepals, and this only accentuates the fringing. Their beauty can best be appreciated when they are cut and brought into the home, and it is as cut flowers that they really excel.

'Aleppo'
A beautiful pale red tulip with light fringing that benefits from the apricot-gold-coloured edge to the tepals. The interior of the flower is orange with a yellow base, making a beautiful bloom at every stage. 50 cm/20 in (Segers 1969, TGA-KAVB 1973)

'Amsterdam Arena' (p. 150)
This new sport of 'Arma' is similar to it except for the foliage, which is variegated with a narrow, white edge.

'Arma' (p. 150)
This has links to the great 'Prinses Irene', because it is also a sport of 'Couleur Cardinal' but in this case it is not the colour that has changed but a delicate fringing around the edge of the deep-red tepals. It is not the most obviously Fringed tulip, but it is worthy because of the great merits of the original plant. 35 cm/14 in (Knijn Bros 1962, AGM-RHS 1997)

'Barbados'
To prove that you can have too much of a good thing, this remarkable tulip takes fringing to unacceptable limits. The flowers are not improved by being an intense pink with hints of orange – the sort of colour that used to be limited to diascias. The tepals are not just fringed: they are puckered all over, in the same way as laced bearded iris, the worst of which look like plastic with pins pushed through. It is a remarkable

breeding achievement, but it is not a great beauty. 60 cm/24 in (Vertuco)

'Bellflower'

This has become one of the most common of all Fringed tulips, and has pink flowers with a white base. 60 cm/24 in (Segers 1970)

'Blue Heron' (p. 152)

I would like this flower even without the fringed edge because of the violet colour, which is paler at the tepal edge. The flowers have an attractive flaring shape, and the fringe is pale and shows up well. Closer inspection the flowers reveals a white base and black anthers that add to the charm of the flower. It is a good grower too. 60 cm/24 in (Segers 1970, TGA-KAVB 1973, *AGM-RHS 1995*)

'Burgundy Lace'

Most catalogues that offer Fringed tulips will include this established cultivar with deep-red, egg-shaped flowers that have a delicately fringed edge. 70 cm/28 in (Segers 1961, AM-RHS 1970, TGA-KAVB 1973)

'Calibra'

Although this blood-red tulip does not have the most obvious fringing, it is notable because of its Lily-flowered shape and striped foliage. The outer tepals are only fringed at the top. 50 cm/20 in (H G Huyg & Son, 1993)

'Canasta'

This is a sturdy, new tulip with large, globular flowers of bright red, and a white edge that is nicely fringed. The base is white. One to look out for. 30 cm/12 in (Vertuco)

'Canova'

This violet tulip has paler, almost white edges that are nicely fringed. The base is white, edged with blue. 60 cm/24 in (Segers 1971)

'Crystal Beauty' (p. 169)

This is a sport of 'Apeldoorn' and has the same vermillion-red colouring with a black base, edged in gold. The tepal edges are lightly fringed and open wide. It is a beautiful variety and a good one to choose if you are not sure you will like Fringed tulips. I was really delighted with this when it first flowered in my garden. 'Fringed Apeldoorn' is another red, fringed sport of 'Apeldoorn', and 'Fringed Solstice' is a yellow-and-red sport of this. 55 cm/22 in (P van Dijk & Sons 1982, TGA-KAVB 1982, AGM-RHS 1999)

'Cummins'

This is rather special, with beautiful mauve flowers that are darker at the base. The colour fades to the tepal edges where it is almost white, and the edges are furnished with ferocious fringing, like shark's teeth, right down to the base. Young flowers have a cream tint. 50 cm/20 in

'Davenport'

This has red flowers edged with yellow. (Vertuco)

'Exotica'

A creamy white, sometimes multi-flowered, short tulip with light fringing. 40 cm/16 in

'Fancy Frills'

One of the most common Fringed tulips, this has rose-pink flowers that are ivory at the base of the tepals and around the edge, where the hairy fringing is abundant. 45 cm/18 in (Segers, W A

M Pennings 1972, TGA-KAVB 1973, AGM-RHS 1995)

'Farness'
This beautiful, Fringed tulip is glowing red with a pale orange fringe and orange inside, with black anthers. 55 cm/22 in (Segers 1974)

'Fringed Beauty'
This sport of 'Titian', which is a Double Early tulip, has scarlet orange flowers, edged with yellow and yellow fringing. Early. 25 cm/10 in (AM-KAVB 1931, AGM-RHS 1999)

'Fringed Elegance'
Being a sport of the popular yellow 'Jewel of Spring', this is a widely available and reliable Fringed tulip. The large flowers are sulphur yellow and dotted with red, increasingly so as the flowers age, and the fringe is pale yellow. 60 cm/24 in (Johan C van Reisen, Breed, 1974, TGA-KAVB 1974, AM-KAVB 1974, AGM-RHS 1999)

'Fringed Rhapsody'
This is a big, tall tulip with pale yellow flowers, variously speckled with red and with a neat, needle-like fringe. 60 cm/24 in

'Frosty Dawn'
A beautiful, clean, crisp flower in pale yellow, with a creamy fringe and yellow base and anthers. 55 cm/22 in (Segers 1974)

'Hamilton'
Among the many Fringed tulips, this stands out because of its beautiful, egg-shaped flowers in rich buttercup yellow, neatly edged with teeth. 50 cm/20 in (Segers 1974, TGA-KAVB 1974, AGM-RHS 1995)

'Hellas'
Not as popular as it once was, the earlier 'Red Wing' becoming the best-known red. Deep red blooms with brighter edges and a showy fringe. The base is bronze-green and yellow. 55 cm/22 in (Segers 1973, TGA-KAVB 1973)

'Henley' (p. 152)
This is a beautiful, bicoloured tulip with red tepals that are edged with creamy apricot, a colour that extends down the inside of the flowers. The jagged fringe is attractive. 55 cm/22 in (Segers 1970)

'Huis ten Bosch'
This is my favourite pink in this group, being mid-pink with white flares and darker streaks on the tepals, and a white base. The fringing is very pronounced and needle-like, and just the right amount to avoid being too peculiar, but make sure that no one can miss it. 55 cm/22 in

'Lambada'
This is a striking new tulip with blooms of bright orange and a raspberry flush to the outer tepals. The tepals are rimmed with very long and showy spine-like fringing. An exceptionally lovely flower. 50 cm/20 in (W van Lierop & Sons 1991, TGA-KAVB 1991, AGM-RHS 1995)

'Lavendel Dream' (p. 152)
A mauve-pink tulip with a white base, inside and out, and a pretty white fringe. 50 cm/20 in

'Madison Garden' (p. 152)
This is a large, carmine-pink tulip with a creamy pink fringe. The base is cream with blue tints. 50 cm/20 in (Segers, W A M Pennings 1986)

'Maja' (p. 152)
A delicate, egg-shaped tulip of a creamy yellow shade, with a finely fringed edge. The interior is a darker shade. 65 cm/26 in (Segers 1968)

'Matchpoint' (p. 109)
A very showy and distinct short tulip, this plant has double flowers of lilac mauve with a white base, tinted with blue, that can be seen in fully open flowers. The outer tepals are often streaked with green, and the fringing looks almost like hoar frost; a valuable addition to the range. 30 cm/12 in (Vertuco)

'Mon Amour'
A bright, double, golden yellow with good fragrance. (Vertuco)

'Noranda' (p. 152)
This is a deep-red tulip with a paler base and an orange fringe. 50 cm/20 in (Segers 1971, TGA-KAVB 1973)

'Palmares'
Tomato-red flowers with a gold-and-white edge that is nicely fringed. 30 cm/12 in (Vertuco)

Fringed tulips
Top row:
'Regulus' 7,
'Blue Heron' 7,
'Lavendel Dream' 7.
Second row:
'Madison Garden' 7,
'Pasadena' 7.
Third row:
'Sagitta' 7,
'Noranda' 7,
'Henley' 7.
Bottom row:
'Maja' 7,
'Warbler' 7.

'Parabole'
A pale pink and purple flower with purple fringing and a pale base that is edged blue with black anthers. 60 cm/24 in (Segers 1970, AGM-RHS 1995)

'Pasadena' (p. 152)
An attractive, rose-pink tulip with a pale base, with tints of blue and delicate, paler fringing. Some flowers show green streaks when young. 55 cm/22 in (Segers 1970)

'Red Wing'
A striking tulip of deep, rich red, with a black base. The fringe is attractive and the same shade. 50 cm/20 in (Segers 1972, TGA-KAVB 1972, AGM-RHS 1995)

'Regulus' (p. 152)
The violet flowers are pale at the edge and the fringe is almost white. The base is also white. 60 cm/24 in (Segers 1970, TGA-KAVB 1974)

'Royal Sphinx'
This tulip is shorter than most and very attractive, with creamy yellow flowers, flushed primrose. 40 cm/16 in (H G Huyg 1988)

'Sagitta' (p. 152)
The square-based flowers are red, with an orange edge and fringe; the base is yellow. 60 cm/24 in (Segers 1974)

'Starfighter'
A showy bloom, this has tepals of rich red, broadly edged with white at the top, and a crystalline fringe. 50 cm/20 in (Segers, J A Borst & Sons 1995, TGA-KAVB 1990)

'Sundew'
This sport of the Single Late 'Orion' has bright red flowers. It sported to produce 'Sothis', a blue-based, blood-red-fringed tulip introduced by Segers in 1942. 40 cm/16 in (AM-KAVB 1930)

'Swan Wings'
A wonderful flower with an appropriate name, this has pure-white flowers with a beautiful fringe. The base is white but the anthers are black. (Segers 1959, AM-RHS 1970)

'Warbler' (p. 152)
This is one of the most strongly fringed tulips, and the bright, lemon-yellow colour and sturdy stems make it a good choice for the garden. 45 cm/18 in (Seger, W A M Pennings 1987, TGA-KAVB 1987)

'Za-za' (p. 52)
This is a new tulip for the American market, where it will be promoted for containers. It has short stems and tomato-red flowers with fringing around the edge, particularly the inner tepals. It is shorter than most Fringed tulips, but I was not impressed. 25 cm/10 in

CLASS 8
Viridiflora

All tulips are beautiful, but Viridiflora tulips are in a class of their own. Once again, they are a varied group, and the flower shapes vary from rather rounded blooms to those that are similar in shape to Lily-flowered tulips, which I much prefer. Their common characteristic is that the flowers have some green in the mature flower, usually as a broad green flame up the centre of each tepal.

They can, perhaps, be traced back to 'Viridiflora' (*Tulipa viridiflora*), an assumed predecessor species with yellow and green flowers, which has never been found in the wild. They all seem to have been produced from seed. They do not appear to have arisen as sports, which have been the source of many Parrot and Fringed tulips, but Viridiflora tulips have themselves sported to produce others of the same kind, though in different shades. 'Viridiflora' dates from at least 1700 and is 45 cm tall (18 in). 'Viridiflora Praecox' presumably flowers earlier, and is larger at 50 cm (20 in), but is not in commercial cultivation (a tulip called 'Viridiflora' *is* available, but I am not certain it is the original plant). The first commercial hybrid was 'Formosa', a yellow and green flower with elegant, waisted lines, followed by 'Groenland', which is pink and green and rather dumpy, and 'Pimpernel', which is crimson and green and has a reflexed shape. Perhaps because of the leafy nature of the tepals, the flowers often last longer than the average tulip and most, but not all, are late, often bringing the tulip season to a close.

Many are short because they are descended from the prolific 'Artist', which is only 30 cm (12 in) high, and has produced three good sports: 'Golden Artist', 'Green River' and 'Hollywood', which are among the most popular varieties and have, between them, produced others. But there are taller Viridifloras such as 'Groenland' and 'Green Spot'.

'Adrian T Dominique'

Although the flowers are not huge, they are elegant and fluted, with rounded tepals that have a small point. They are a blend of pink and cream with a broad green band rising from the base of each tepal. 55 cm/22 in

'Artist' (p. 154)

'Artist' has been one of the most successful of this group, and is also a fairly early introduction, but it has all the elegance and subtlety we expect. The blooms are shapely, with pointed tepals that have a broad, deep-green band, edged with salmon pink, and some lilac shading on the outside. The green stripe on the tepals extends to the tip. It is shorter than most, which is useful for containers. Raised by the pioneering work of Adriaan and Jan Captein, from two flowers without any green in the tepals, it has produced several useful sports with the same habit: 'Golden Artist', 'Green River' and 'Hollywood'. 30 cm/12 in (Captein Bros 1947, AM-KAVB 1947, *AGM-RHS 1995*)

'China Town' (p. 154)

'Artist' sported to 'Golden Artist', and this has in turn produced 'China Town', a beautiful tulip with the same elegant shape, but this time the colour on either side of the green band is rich pink that gradually fades to the edge. To add extra value, the leaves have a thin white margin. It is a top-notch tulip. 30 cm/12 in (A W Captein & Son 1988, TGA-KAVB 1988, AM-KAVB 1989, AGM-RHS 1995)

'Dancing Show' (p. 154)

This beautiful tulip is not commercially available, but deserves to be. The flowers are very elongated, with long, narrow, pointed tepals that are bright yellow with a thin, green band that extends up the whole length of the outer tepals, but is less pronounced on the inner ones. 45 cm/18 in (Konijnenburg & Mark 1969)

'Deirdre'

This is one of the most subdued of Viridiflora tulips. The tepals have a mid-green band, and this fades to creamy green at the edges, with a hint of apricot shading. The flowers have reflexed tepals. It is best for cutting because of its subtle colouring. 50 cm/20 in (P L Braaksma 1990)

'Doll's Minuet' (p. 147, 155)

A fine tulip with discreet green stripes from the base of the tepals, this looks more like a Lily-flowered tulip. The colour is bright, rosy purple, and the flowers last for many weeks. They are beautiful when just mature and equally so when fully open. 55 cm/22 in (Konijnenburg & Mark 1968)

Viridiflora tulips

Top row:
'Artist' 8,
'Golden Artist' 8,
'Hummingbird' 8.
Second row:
'China Town' 8,
'Esperanto' 8.
Third row:
'Dancing Show' 8,
'Eye Catcher' 8,
'Formosa' 8.
Bottom row:
'Florosa' 8,
'Hollywood' 8.

'Esperanto' (p. 154)

This sport of 'Hollywood' has elegant flowers with pointed tepals, each of which is deep, pinkish-red with a green band up the outer surface. In addition, the leaves have a thin, white edge which is not very showy. I always plant this and wait with great anticipation, but it has never quite fulfilled my expectations. 30 cm/12 in (J Pranger 1968, TGA-KAVB 1977, AM-KVB 1979, AGM-RHS 1999)

'Eye Catcher' (p. 154)

A superb tulip with rather narrow, fluted tepals that are deep, bright scarlet with a deep green, wide band along their length. The narrowness of the tepals gives the blooms a starry effect when fully open. It seems to glow in the garden. 55 cm/22 in (Konijnenburg & Mark 1968)

'Florosa' (p. 154)

This elegant tulip is mostly green, but the edges of the gently recurving tepals shade from deep green to cream, and then pink at the edge. It has tall stems and is ideal for cutting. 65 cm/26 in (P B van Eeden, W A M Pennings 1979)

'Formosa' (p. 154)

This has comparatively 'normal' flowers, with flat tepals to give an open goblet-shaped bloom. But the blooms are an attractive yellow colour with a broad green band through the blooms. It was one of the first of the group, and still popular. 30 cm/12 in (Polman Mooy, AM-KAVB 1926)

'Golden Artist' (p. 154)

This sport of 'Artist' is identical except for the colour, which is amber gold. 30 cm/12 in (Captein Bros 1959, AM-KAVB 1959, FCC-KAVB 1962)

'Green Eyes' (p. 164)

An elegant flower with narrow tepals. These have a slender green stripe, while the rest of the tepal is yellowish-green. The inside of the flower is similarly coloured, with yellow anthers. 55 cm/22 in (Konijnenburg & Mark 1968)

'Green River'

This is one of the most recent of the many sports of 'Artist', and has tepals that are green, edged with rich red and margined with yellow. The leaves are also edged with yellow. 30 cm/12 in (C Nielen & Son 1993)

'Green Spot'

A primarily green-and-white flower, with a bluish base and yellow anthers. 55 cm/22 in (Bik Jac Tol 1969, AM-RHS 1982)

'Green Valley'

The blooms are bright pink with a white and green band. 50 cm/20 in (Janis R)

'Groenland' (p. 147, 155)

The blooms of this popular cultivar are rather rounded and not as elegant as some. They open rather too green but the pink-mauve colour at the edge of the tepals extends as the flowers mature to create a showy flower that is suitable for ordinary bedding as well as when a special plant is required. Because of its dumpy shape I try not to like it, but I have to grudgingly admit that because of its exceptionally long-lasting flowers, it is one of the best. It is one of the latest tulips to bloom. 55 cm/22 in (J F van den Berg & Sons 1955, AM-KAVB 1960)

'Hollywood' (p. 154)

This sport of 'Artist' has bright red flowers with a strong green band, often looking bronze where overlaid with red, up the tepals. It has sported to produce the tulips 'Esperanto' and 'Hollywood Star'. 30 cm/12 in (Captein Bros 1956, AM-KAVB 1958, TGA-KAVB 1969, FCC-KAVB 1969, AM-RHS 1970)

'Hollywood Star'

This sport of 'Hollywood' differs mainly in the cream variegation around the leaf edges but this is also visible in the flowers that may show white or greyish streaks. A beautiful tulip. 30 cm/12 in (C Nielen 1987)

'Hummingbird' (p. 154)

A useful, taller tulip with yellow flowers that are marked with broad bands of bright green, especially when the flowers are young. 50 cm/20 in (D W Lefeber & Co 1961)

'Pimpernel'

The flowers have pointed tepals that reflex a little to create a graceful outline, while the tepals have a very broad green flare at the base and are deep, purplish red above. 40 cm/16 in (D W Lefeber & Co 1956, AM-KAVB 1961)

'Spring Green'

A common cultivar with ivory-white flowers that have a broad green feather through the centre of the tepals. There are also variants called 'Flaming Spring Green', which has red streaks in the lower part of the tepals, and 'Red Spring Green' and 'Yellow Spring Green', which both seem to have the same flower shape and may be sports. 50 cm/20 in (P Liefting 1969, AGM-RHS 1993)

'Tricolored Beauty'

This is a tall tulip with moderate-sized blooms that are not obviously marked with green except in bud. When fully open they are pinkish-orange, with a darker streak through the centre of the tepals and a yellow base with black anthers. The

top of the tepals is paler. An interesting new tulip that has some *Greigii* genes. 55 cm/22 in

'Violet Bird'

It is odd that this, the only violet Viridiflora, is not more widely available. It is certainly attractive, with pointed tepals that recurve slightly and a lovely deep, violet shade. The whole width of the lowest third of each tepal is green, and this extends up the tepal, almost to the top. 50 cm/20 in (J F van den Berg & Sons 1968)

'Viridiflora'

The granddaddy of them all, this has blooms with rounded tepals that are yellow, with a green flame from the base that extends about halfway along their length. 45 cm/18 in (1700)

Mixed tulips
Photographed with purple hazel.
Top row:
'Groenland' 8,
'Doll's Minuet' 8.
Second row:
'Pink Jewel' 5,
'Passionale' 3.
Third row:
'Happy Generation' 3,
'Wirosa' 11.
Bottom row:
'Bleu Aimable' 5 (two blooms),
'Blue Parrot' 10.

CLASS 9
Rembrandt Tulips

As previously discussed, the effect of tulip breaking virus has more than its fair share of mystery, and it is easy to wax lyrical about it, comparing its effect to 'living on the edge' – the familiar idea that putting one's life in danger through hazardous sports or taking drugs makes existence sweeter (not something I can speak of with great experience). But you do not need to free-fall from a helicopter to see that there is a dangerous beauty to 'broken' or 'rectified' tulips. The virus weakens the plant, but is also responsible for the beautiful feathering of colour on the flowers as the diseased tissue cuts through the colour. Ideally the tulip will be receptive to the virus and create a beautiful flower, but tough enough to maintain its vigour and produce a good flower. Sometimes the plant is not strong enough and is fatally wounded by the virus, but may produce one, supreme flower before it succumbs, reinforcing that the beautiful really do die young. To gaze at these beautiful flowers is to contemplate the ephemeral nature of beauty.

Though Rembrandts do not have the sophistication or bright colours of the English Florists tulips, they are still beautiful enough to enchant most gardeners, and they are now rare. Their sale has now stopped because of the danger the virus poses to the stocks of other varieties of tulip, and they are only preserved in a few gardens; at Hortus Bulborum they are separated from all others by at least 25 m (80 ft), and are carefully sprayed to prevent aphids, which spread the virus, from infecting neighbouring plants.

You are unlikely to be able to find Rembrandt tulips for sale, though the virus does pop up in gardens from time to time. It should be treated with caution because it is a killer, and it can spread to almost any other tulip. The effects are not always pleasant – the old florists did not spend centuries selecting the best breeders that 'break' beautifully for nothing! I have had some broken tulips that looked beautiful but others where the effect was very ugly.

Instead, we must content ourselves with striped tulips in which the patterning of the colours is genetic, not viral. Tulips such as 'Mickey Mouse', 'Cordell Hull' and 'Sorbet' are poor imitations of the flowers that made grown men risk all – but they are pretty, inexpensive and risk free!

See the section on English Florists tulips in chapter 4 for further information (picture p. 107).

CLASS 10
Parrot Tulips

Parrot tulips are the most spectacular of all tulips and, being among the most expensive, are reassuringly luxurious. Few, if any, have been produced by conventional breeding, and most are mutants: sports of existing cultivars, either by natural means or by such techniques as treating bulbs with X rays. As such, they usually share the flower colour and general characteristics of the parent, but have distorted, curled, twisted and cut tepals.

In most cultivars, the tepals are ruffled and the edges slashed into rounded lobes, but they may also have extra tissue, forming feathers that grow from the flat surface. Most also have green streaks and 'feathering', and this is most prominent on the outer tepals and either side of the main, central vein. Because of the extra tissue and the ruffling and twisting of the tepals, the flowers are not able to close in wet and cool weather, which gives the flowers extra presence in the garden. But it also means they are more vulnerable to bad weather and are often weighed down by rain. Personally, I do not mind that the flower stems bend and present the blooms at quirky angles, though I can see that purists might find it infuriating. Small bulbs, on the other hand, which are only just of flowering size, may not display typical flowers, and the blooms may look rather ordinary.

Early Parrots, such as 'Markgraaf', 'Cramoise Brillant' and 'Sensation', had large flowers on rather slender stems, and hung their heads. In Joseph Jacob's *Tulips* (1912), it is recommended that they are grown in hanging baskets in the greenhouse. 'Each one will make a very pleasing object, the great uncouth and ragged blooms hanging down in charming confusion, and displaying their quaint colouring and weird shapes.' With 60-cm (24-in) stems, a basket would be at least 1.2 m (4 ft) across in flowers, so you would need a lot of room for this, and it is not necessary for modern cultivars!

Parrot tulips are fine for the garden, but they really earn their stars as cut flowers. It is impossible to choose the best and most have their charms. Some of the following are either new and not yet easily obtainable, while a few are antiques, suffering from the same problem. Any shortlist of commercial cultivars must include 'Estella Rijnveld' and 'Blue Parrot'; I would also recommend 'Apricot Parrot', 'Libretto Parrot', 'Flaming Parrot', 'Snow Parrot' and, the finest and weirdest of the lot, 'Green Wave'.

'Air'

A new tulip with globular flowers, it has ruffled bright pink tepals, marked with green. 50 cm/20 in (V dam Triflor Mut. Rai)

'Amethyst'

A beautiful Parrot with ruffled and slashed tepals that are mauve/lilac, paler at the edges and with a white base inside, edged with pale blue. 50 cm/20 in (IVT, Boots 1975, TGA-KAVB 1975)

'Apricot Parrot' (p. 113)

A string of awards is a hint that this might be rather special – and it is. A sport of 'Karel Doorman', a yellow-edged, red Parrot, this is everything a Parrot should be: big, blowsy and extravagant at every stage. The tepals are large and ruffled and a gorgeous blend of apricot and cream, with occasional pink and green flashes and a pale streak down the centre of the tepals. The stems are hardly strong enough to support the huge blooms – which open flat before the tepals fall – and they tend to nod over. I can forgive this in such a beautiful tulip, but it suggests that a sheltered position in the garden is desirable. 50 cm/20 in (H G Huyg 1961, AM-KAVB 1964, TGA-KVB 1964, AM-RHS 1982, *AGM-RHS 1993*)

'Bird of Paradise' (p. 158)

A sport of the mahogany-red Triumph 'Bandoeng', this strong Parrot has bold flowers of the same colour, edged orange, with a gold interior. The tepals are pleasantly ruffled and slashed, and it is bold without being too ridiculous. 40 cm/16 in (De Goede, Valkering Jzn 1962, AM-KAVB 1962)

'Black Parrot' (p. 158)

Because of its combination of deep colouring with bizarrely ruffled and very feathered tepals, this is a sought-after tulip and usually in short supply, at least when I have ordered it. A sport of 'Philippe de Comines', it is the same, deep purple, but is sometimes flecked with green. I have to admit that I find it disappointing. If any tulips in my garden are going to get an attack of greenfly, it is these. In addition, the tepals are rather mean in width. It can look splendid, especially in magazines and catalogues, but my love affair with it is over; perhaps, as in so many infatuations, I expected more than it could give. 50 cm/20 in (C Keur & Sons 1937, AM-KAVB 1941, AGM-RHS 1995)

'Blue Parrot' (p. 155, 158)

This is a rather subtle Parrot, the tepals only modestly ruffled and feathered, but it owes its beauty to the delightful colour of its parent, 'Bleu Aimable', a wonderful confection of violet/lilac with a blue base. It is tall and strong, with rather square-based flowers that are large and long-lasting. It has sported to produce 'Caland' (purple), 'Caprice' (violet purple, 1951), 'James Last' (violet on mallow purple, 1974) and 'Muriel' (deep violet). 55 cm/22 in (1935 Jan Dix Jr)

'Blumex' (p. 150)

This sport of 'Rococo' has similar colouring to 'Prinses Irene', in shades of orange with purplish feathering, and with the same, chunky flower shape as 'Rococo'. These are among the best Parrots for exposed sites because of their short stature and chunky flowers. 35 cm/14 in (Yuyn, Van Dam, 1992)

'Caland' (p. 158)

This sport of 'Blue Parrot' has the same, restrained flower shape, but the blooms are purple, with the same blue base. 55 cm/22 in (Segers 1958)

'Carmine Parrot'

This sport of the Triumph 'Carmine Charm' has blooms of cherry-red and purple, with a blue and green base. The tepals are waved and ruffled. 55 cm/22 in (G A Preyde, 1988)

'Cramoise Brillant' (p. 158)

A large, ruffled, scarlet flower. Not commercially available. One of the oldest Parrots. 50 cm/20 in (pre-1912)

'Diana Ross'

A sport of the bright red Parrot 'Erna Lindgreen', this has beautiful blooms that are lightly ruffled

Parrot tulips

Top row:
'Caland' 10,
'Cramoise Brilliant'
('Sparkler') 10,
'Double Fantasy' 10.
Second row:
'Estella Rijnveld' ('Gay
Presto') 10,
'Fantasy' 10.
Third row:
'Blue Parrot' 10,
'Black Parrot' 10,
'Bird of Paradise' 10.
Bottom row:
'Markgraaf' ('Markgraaf
van Baden') 10,
'Orange Favourite' 10.

in shades of pale purple and pink, with a more orange interior that shows at the edge. As flamboyant and exciting as its namesake. 50 cm/20 in (Th N Grooteman 1985)

'Doorman's Elite'
see 'Karel Doorman'

'Doorman's Record'
see 'Karel Doorman'

'Double Fantasy' (p. 158)
As might be expected, this is a double sport of 'Fantasy', though it is only loosely double. The flowers are very similar, and are interchangeable for general garden decoration, though the difference is noticeable as a cut flower. They often have additional, narrow green tepals at the base of the flowers. 60 cm/24 in (1943)

'Eagle Wings'
This beautiful, large Parrot has ruffled tepals of deep, golden yellow, flaked with red. It opens to reveal a small blackish base. It is robust and weather-resistant – I saw it in a gale! 55 cm/22 in

'Erna Lindgreen'
This sport of the Triumph 'Korneferos' has globular blooms of bright red, lightly ruffled and subtly flared with green. 50 cm/20 in (Alb Lindgreen 1951)

'Estella Rijnveld' ('Gay Presto') (p. 158)
Ranking high on my list of top tulips, I always look forward to this delightful flower opening. It is quite late, but the large, floppy flowers are bold and very parroty, with masses of extra tissue. Its colouring is rich red and white, with odd green flecks. No two tepals are the same and the base is white, edged with a thin, blue line. Stocks seem to vary, and my latest have been shorter than average and almost too distorted. It is a sport of 'Red Champion'. 50 cm/20 in (Segers 1954)

'Exotic Bird'
Though strictly a Darwinhybrid tulip, this is so odd that I have included it here. It is a sport of 'Apeldoorn', with the same bright red – especially inside the flowers – and with a black basal blotch edged with yellow. However, the tepals are shredded and twisted and some even arise below the flower proper. It is a real oddity, and though a monstrosity in many ways, I find it strangely compelling. 45 cm/18 in (J Ruiter & Sons 1986)

'Fancy Parrot'
This is a sport of 'Salmon Parrot', and has large blooms with moderate ruffling and feathering. The base of the tepals and the midrib is creamy yellow, while the upper part is bright pink. It is a showy and dramatic flower. 50 cm/20 in (De Geus-Vriend 1995)

'Fantasy' (p. 158)
Early Parrots were regarded more as novelties than sensible garden plants because the stems were not strong enough to support the extra tepal tissue that made the flowers so exotic. But 'Fantasy' changed all that, and its string of awards is a testament to the impact it made and the affection it still commands. A sport of the Single

Late 'Clara Butt', it has the same rich pink flowers, but here they have ruffled edges and are streaked with green, primarily on the outer tepals, either side of the main vein. A good choice as an introduction to the group. 55 cm/22 in (1910, AM-KAVB 1919, AM-RHS 1921 & 1982, FCC-KAVB 1922, AGM-RHS 1993)

'Flaming Parrot'
One of the best, this dazzling Parrot is a sport of 'Red Parrot', itself a sport of 'Gloria Swanson'. Each flower, on a tall stem, is bright yellow, and each tepal has a bright red streak along the midrib, with extra feathering, especially near the base. The base is pale and the anthers black. It is always dramatic. 70 cm/28 in (P Heemskerk, C A Verdegaal 1968, TGA-KAVB 1968)

'Giant Parrot'
Only the top half of these blooms show much ruffling, but the huge, elongated size and shape of the bright vermillion flowers, and the light mottling of the leaves, make this a distinctive tulip. When open, the flowers display a black base that betrays its alliance to the *Greigii* group. 45 cm/18 in (D W Lefeber & Co 1972)

'Glasnost'
see 'Karel Doorman'

'Green Wave' (p. 100)
When a Viridiflora tulip (in this case 'Groenland') decides to 'go Parrot', the result can be extraordinary, and 'Green Wave' is perfect for gardeners that want something special, including me! The tepals have the central green stripe of the parent, edged with mauve/pink, but the tepals are jagged and ripped. In early life the flowers are globular, but as they age they open out to form a large, starry confusion of streaked and distorted tepals with small, malformed, dark anthers in the centre. The rather narrow tepals prevent the flowers being as heavy and lumpy as some other Parrots, and they last well in the garden or as cut flowers. One of the best, though not the brightest. 50 cm/20 in (J J Rozenbroek 1984)

'Holland Happening'
The Darwinhybrid 'Apeldoorn' has yet again sported to create a new tulip, and 'Holland Happening' is a pleasant Parrot with lightly ruffled flowers of scarlet, flamed with green. The interior is bright red with the typical black base, edged yellow. 50 cm/20 in (Jan van Bentem 1986)

'James V Forrestal'
see 'Karel Doorman'

'Karel Doorman' ('Doorman') (p. 143)
This is an important Parrot because it has produced a mass of sports. It is itself a sport of 'Alberio', a cherry-red, edged white Triumph tulip. 'Karel Doorman' has bright red flowers, lightly flaked with green and with a faint yellow edge. The tepals, though not madly ruffled, have narrow 'feathers' around the edge. Its sports are: 'Apricot Parrot', 'Blondine' (yellow flamed with red, 1956), 'Comet' (orange, edged yellow, 1952), 'Doorman's Elite' (red, edged yellow, 1969), 'Doorman's Favourite' (blood red, edged yellow, 1971), 'Doorman's Record' (red, carmine and gold, 1975), 'Glasnost' (orange with yellow edge, 1990), 'Harmony' (yellow and pink, 1961), 'James V Forrestal' (orange, edged yellow, 1955), 'Javazee' (purple red, 1963), 'Moderato' (pink, green and white, 1969), 'Onedin' (gold and pink, 1980), 'Red Devil' (red and carmine, 1985), 'Salmon Parrot' and 'Vermillion Parrot'. 50 cm/20 in (John B Meskers & Sons 1946)

'Libretto Parrot' (p. 136)
This subtly coloured tulip is a sport of the Triumph 'Libretto'. The large, globular flowers are pale cream, flushed with pink. The flowers are lightly streaked with green and gently ruffled. It is a beautiful flower of pastel colours that change as the flower ages, and much better than any description. 40 cm/16 in (W J Kok & Sons 1993)

'Markgraaf' ('Markgraaf v. Baden') (p. 158)
This ancient Parrot is not commercially available. The narrow blooms are ruffled and basically red, patterned with bright yellow and overlaid with purple and green. The stems are slender and hardly able to support the fully open heads. 50 cm/20 in (1750)

'Madonna'
This is a huge, globular bloom, with pure white flowers, heavily streaked and flashed with green, particularly either side of the main vein of each tepal. The flowers become whiter as they age. The

base is yellow. 50 cm/20 in (H Verdegaal & Sons 1960, AM-KAVB 1960)

'Muriel'
This is one of several sports of 'Blue Parrot', and has deep-purple flowers that are heavily ruffled. 55 cm/22 in (D Keppel 1961, TGA-KAVB 1969)

'Onedin'
see 'Karel Doorman'

'Orange Favourite' (p. 158)
This is a sport of the Single Late 'Orange King', which is no longer grown commercially. But this Parrot has remained popular because of its elegantly frilled flowers in a pleasant shade of orange, feathered with green and with a yellow base. In addition, the flowers are fragrant. 50 cm/20 in (K C Vooren 1930, AM-KAVB 1934, HC-RHS 1982)

'Parrot City'
A gorgeous tulip in shades of gold and mandarin, with red and yellow edging. The flowers are heavily ruffled and have extra feathers on the tepals, also flashed with green. A great orange Parrot and a sport of 'Doorman's Elite'. 50 cm/20 in (Rozenbroek, Holland Bolroy Markt 1996)

'Parrot King'
This is similar to 'Parrot City', but has more ruffling and feathering, and more pronounced green areas on the flowers. 50 cm/20 in

'Pink Panther'
This superb Parrot is in shades of pink, with flashes of green. The tepals are deeply cut and wavy, and the base is white, edged with purple, which shows on the outside of the bloom. It is a sport of 'Prunus', itself a deep-pink sport of 'Bartigon', a highly variable old, red Single Late tulip (see also 'Red Champion'). 55 cm/22 in (A J de Vries 1983)

'Professor Röntgen'
This globular orange tulip is a sport of 'Salmon Parrot', and the colour is a combination of yellow and scarlet with green flakes on either side of the central vein of the tepals. The flowers are slightly ruffled, with some extra feathering. 50 cm/20 in (C A Verdegaal 1978, TGA-KAVB 1978)

'Quasimodo'
A large flower in rosy red, with purple tints, this is a sport of 'K & M's Triumph', a red Triumph tulip. The tepals are lightly ruffled. 50 cm/20 in (De Geus 1984)

'Rai'
The Triumph tulip 'Frederica' sported to produce this Parrot in pink and lilac with green streaks across the tepals. The base of the flower is white. 35 cm/14 in (Burger & Blank, Van Dam 1986)

'Red Champion'
This bright tulip is a sport of 'Bartigon' and has bold, red flowers with green-streaked frilly tepals. It has produced several sports, including 'Estella Rijnveld'. 50 cm/20 in (H M Ruysenaars 1930)

'Red Sensation'
A red tulip with glossy tepals that are flared with green and heavily ruffled. It is a sport of Triumph tulip 'Paul Richter'. 45 cm/18 in (J G Kok 1975)

'Rococo' (p. 150)
This Parrot is a sport of 'Couleur Cardinal' and has the same colouring, but with splashes and streaks of green. The tepals are thick, inwardly curled and of heavy substance, so they look almost like red peppers. The blooms are robust and weatherproof. Some stocks have strange leaves with jagged teeth that face downwards, towards the base. It has sported to produce 'Blumex'. 35 cm/14 in (H Slegtkamp & Co 1942, AM-KAVB 1944)

'Salmon Parrot'
This is an artificially produced sport of 'Karel Doorman' in shades of salmon pink and cream with green flashes. It is large and beautiful, especially when fully open. 50 cm/20 in (De Mol & C A Verdegal 1956)

'Show Parrot'
A dramatic, heavily ruffled flower of cherry red with a black centre. The tepals are flecked with green. 50 cm/20 in (Mut. Pax)

'Snow Parrot' (p. 136)
This, possibly the most beautiful of all white tulips, is a sport of 'Pax', a white Triumph tulip. It is not pure white, the outside of the outer tepals

being flushed with 'French blue' (a lavender grey shade, a colour that crops up in some other 'Pax' sports). The inside of the flowers is shaded with ivory and pale yellow. It is not the biggest or most bizarrely feathered, but it just shows that even among the Parrots, sometimes sophistication can win out. Some tulips delight from afar; this one rewards quiet, close contemplation. It is not a common tulip, but is commercially available and deserves to be widely grown. 40 cm/16 in (A P Molenaar, Ammerlaan 1986)

'Super Parrot'
A large, white Parrot with green areas around the midrib of each distorted, ruffled tepal.

'Texas Flame'
This sport of 'Texas Gold' has globular gold flowers, with red flames and green splashes. 45 cm/18 in (J de Wit Czn 1958, AM-KAVB 1960)

'Texas Gold'
This has golden flowers with a narrow red edge, and is a sport of 'Inglescombe Yellow'. In addition to the popular 'Texas Flame', it has sported to 'Texas Cocktail' (yellow, striped claret, 1969) and 'Texas Fire' (yellow, edged red). 45 cm/18 in (G van der May's Sons 1944)

'Topparrot'
A red Parrot with a black and yellow base. It is a sport of 'Prominence', a red Triumph. 40 cm/16 in (Triflor, Van Dam 1992)

'Vermillion Parrot'
Yet another sport of 'Karel Doorman', this time with bright red flowers. 50 cm/20 in (Lefeber Bros 1969)

'Weber's Parrot'
This is a sport of 'Weber' (if only all names were so logical!) and has blooms of cream and pink with considerable areas of corrugated green tissue, especially at the base. 40 cm/16 in (Van Graven Bros 1968)

'White Parrot'
A rather old Parrot, and sport of the ancient 'Albino' (Krelage & Son 1911). It has pure white flowers, flared with green, of a pleasant, globular shape. 40 cm/16 in (Valkering & Sons 1943)

CLASS 11
Double Late

Some say that this is the most controversial group of tulips, and they have had some very unpleasant things said and written about them. In 1929, Sir Daniel Hall (in *The Tulip*) wrote of them simply: 'Better dead.'

Joseph Jacobs in 1912 (in *Tulips*) decided that 'there is nothing much to say about late double tulips except that nowadays the section is a very small one, and that they are of no use under glass. Out of doors I have grown a few from year to year, but they have seldom been a success'.

Things have changed and we have a good choice now. I love them and can find no great fault with them, and they are surely no more controversial than Parrots or Fringed tulips. They are often called peony-flowered tulips, and the name is fitting. The flowers usually have rounded tepals and do, indeed, look remarkably like double peonies.

They are among the last tulips to flower, and so miss the worst of the cold, spring weather. Their main failing is that they succumb to May rainstorms that often rapidly follow sunny spells, causing the flowers to fill with water. The flowers are stuffed with tepals and, because of this, cannot close properly once mature. This extra weight results in their beautiful flowers snapping off at the neck, a lamentable disaster that cannot be remedied. There is only one thing for it; to pick up the flowers and float them in water in the house so you can enjoy their sumptuous beauty and, often, sweet perfume.

'Bleu Céleste' was probably the first of the group. Like other groups, they are a disparate lot, varying in height, colour and size. 'Angelique' (a sport of 'Granda') is the best known pink, and very beautiful. 'Lilac Perfection' (in smoky mauve) and 'Maywonder' (in deep rose) remain my favourites at about 45 cm (18 in) tall, but 'Golden Nizza', in brilliant red and gold stripes, is taller and flashier. And it is impossible not to be impressed with 'Uncle Tom', with its huge blooms in rich maroon.

'Allegretto'
Loosely double blooms of deep red, edged with golden yellow. 35 cm/14 in (J F van den Berg & Sons 1963)

Double late tulips
Top row:
'Maartje Kuiper' 11,
'Uncle Tom' 11,
'Lilac Perfection' 11.
Second row:
'Clara Carder' 11,
'Eros' 11.
Third row:
'Gold Medal' 11,
'Rocket' 11,
'Mazurka' 11.
Bottom row:
'Mount Tacoma' 11,
'Carnival de Nice' 11.

'Angelique'

This is, perhaps, the most desirable of all Double Lates, with its taller stems and sumptuous flowers that are a blend of pale and darker pink shades with green streaks on the outer tepals. The double flowers look almost like pink roses. It is a sport of 'Granda', a deep pink double, and has sported to produce 'Annelinde', which is identical to 'Angelique' except that it has foliage edged with a thin white band. 45 cm/18 in (D W Lefeber & Co 1959, AGM-RHS 1999)

'Bell Air'

Semi-double flower, with multi-headed stems. The blooms are pure white, and the loose centres reveal the bright yellow base inside. Though the flowers are not of the highest standard, it is a good bedding plant. 35 cm/14 cm (Hybris)

'Black Hero'

A recent and very popular tulip that is bound to stay the course, being the only 'black' Late Double. It is a sport of 'Queen of Night', and with such an ancestry should be a good garden plant. Awards for this flower cannot be far off. 60 cm/24 in (J Beerepoot 1984)

'Bleu Céleste' ('Blue Flag')

This old cultivar is rarely seen now but did, at least, stimulate interest in the group. It was praised, at the start of the last century, for its beauty, the tall-stemmed blooms being pale lavender. 45 cm/18 in (1750)

'Blue Diamond'

This sport of the Triumph 'Prince Charles' (AGM-RHS 1995) has deep purple, rounded blooms with a pale green base, edged with blue. It is widely available. 40 cm/16 in (J Reus 1990)

'Bonanza'

This bright flower has a rather squat shape with a flat base and is bright red, edged with gold. It has sported to the mandarin, edged white tulip called 'Mary Bonanza', and the scarlet and yellow 'Orange Bonanza'. 40 cm/16 in (1943, AM-KAVB 1943)

'Boule d'Or'

This beautiful tulip is fully double and has bright yellow flowers, slightly paler inside, with a few green flares on the outside. A crisp, clean colour. 45 cm/18 in (Hybris, Van Dam 1992)

'Carnaval de Nice' (p. 162)

This is a popular sport of 'Nizza' and has globular white flowers, striped and feathered with red. The stems are tall and strong and the leaves have narrow white edges. The combination of the two colours creates a beautiful bloom. 50 cm/20 in (Tubergen 1953, AGM-RHS 1999)

'Casablanca' (p. 164)

This is one of the best of the whites, and also one of the tallest doubles. The large, squat blooms are ivory white with a yellow base, and often have green streaks on the outer tepals, especially when the flowers are young. 55 cm/22 in (J F van den Berg & Sons 1981)

'Chato'

This is a tulip with lovely lilac/pink flowers. The

leaves, though not coloured, are attractive because they are wavy and add to the plant's interest. 40 cm/16 in (Jan v/d Salm)

'Clara Carder' (p. 162)
The tall stems carry rounded blooms I would call bright, deep-rose pink, though they are often described as Tyrian purple. 50 cm/20 in (Segers 1943, TGA-KAVB 1947, AM-KAVB 1950)

'Crème Upstar'
Like its pink and white parent 'Upstar', this has large, fragrant flowers, but these are pale yellow, flushed with red, and edged with pink to create a delicate, pastel confection. 35 cm/14 in (J Lighart 1994, TGA-KAVB 1990)

'Daladier'
Bright pink flowers with white and green feathering at the base. 50 cm/20 in (Zocher & Co 1951)

'Double Focus'
This sport of 'Wirosa' has blooms of bright red, with a golden yellow edge. 35 cm/14 in (Van Dam 1992)

'Double Sensation'
This is perhaps the most exciting and controversial double I have seen. It has tall stems and semi-double, Lily-shaped flowers. It resembles a double 'China Pink' but has some bronze/green streaks on the outer tepals. Not in the same mould as others, it may not become very commercial. 60 cm/24 in

'Dubbele Roodkapje'
This double sport of 'Red Riding Hood', the popular *Greigii* hybrid, has the same characteristics but flowers with a few extra tepals . 30 cm/12 in (Mut. Red R H)

'Dubbel Geel'
The flowers are intensely double and primrose yellow. 35 cm/14 in

'Erfurt'
Though this flower can be described as cherry on an ivory ground, the overall effect is of a vibrant, neon pink. This is a bright, showy tulip, for which it would be hard to find suitably coloured companions. 45 cm/18 in (Kroone, P Hopman Kroonjuwelen 1996)

'Eros' (p. 162)
An enormous tulip on tall stems, this has blooms of deep rose, flared with white and some green. It is also sweetly scented, it has sported to produce the vivid red 'Rocket'. This is truly deserving the group name of peony-flowered tulip. 55 cm/22 in (Zocher & Co 1937, AM-KAVB 1937)

'Eternal Flame'
This is deep pink with a white margin to the edge of each tepal. The foliage is also variegated. 40 cm/16 in (Maveridge)

'Finola'
A rival to 'Angelique', this has globular blooms of pale pink. The outer tepals are flared with green. 40 cm/16 in (Finola Vertuca)

'Gerbrand Kieft' (p. 136)
A gorgeous tulip with large blooms that are basically white, but are flushed with cherry red on the outside of the tepals; there are also some green streaks. It fades as it matures to a beautiful pastel bloom. 'Zizanie' is its more intensely coloured sport. 45 cm/18 in (Hybrida 1951, AGM-RHS 1999)

'Golden Nizza' (p. 172)
This bolder coloured sport of 'Nizza' has squat blooms, which develop slowly into wonderful flowers that are bright yellow, striped with red. It is very special and popular. 50 cm/20 in (P Nijssen & Sons 1951, AM-KAVB 1951)

'Gold Medal' (p. 162)
This is a bright golden flower, streaked with green. Not commercial. 40 cm/16 in (C P Alkemade Czn 1946)

'Herman Emmink'
The bright flowers have tepals that are slightly rolled and are deep red, with a broad margin of bright yellow. A bold, flashy flower. 40 cm/16 in (Hybris, Holland Bolroy Markt 1994)

'Holland Candy'
This lovely tulip has bright pink flowers. The blooms, however, are not heavily double. They contrast well with the blue-green leaves. 35 cm/14 in (Bolroy)

Mixed tulips
Photographed with *Ribes x gordonianum*.
Top row:
'Green Eyes' 8,
'Crystal Beauty' 7,
'Pieter de Leur' 6.
Second row:
'Orange Princess' 11,
'Monte Carlo' 2.
Bottom row:
'Oranje Nassau' 2,
'Casablanca' 11.

'Jet Set'
This has red flowers that fade to white at the edges. 35 cm/14 in (Huiyg)

'Lilac Perfection' (p. 117, 162)
It is surprising that this beautiful Double tulip does not have any awards! The large blooms are rather squat and have rounded lilac tepals of a satiny texture. Often the stems, on strong bulbs, have several flowers. One of the best, and beautiful with blue myosotis. 50 cm/20 in (Hybrida 1951)

'Maartje Kuiper' (p. 162)
The face of the bloom is rich, luscious pink, but the exterior of the tepals is purple-pink with an ivory base. It is loosely double but very attractive. 30 cm/12 in (Hybrida 1951)

'Maywonder'
One of the most popular of this group. The large blooms are rose pink, flushed with white, and very beautiful and peony-like. 50 cm/20 in (Hybrida 1951, AGM-RHS 1999)

'Mazurka' (p. 162)
This is a fully double tulip, with brownish-red tepals lightly edged with yellow. 45 cm/18 in (Hybrida 1952)

'Miranda'
This deep, bright red tulip is a sport of the Darwinhybrid 'Apeldoorn's Favourite', and is taller than most. 55 cm/22 in (J A van Gent & Sons, C A Verdegaal 1981)

'Mount Tacoma' (p. 162)
This is a beautiful white tulip with rounded blooms of pure white. It has some green streaks on the outer tepals and, sometimes, a touch of pink. 45 cm/18 in (Polman Mooy pre-1924, AM-KAVB 1926, FCC-KAVB 1939)

'Nizza'
This has tall stems with squat blooms that are yellow, striped with red. It has sported to 'Golden Nizza' which is more popular and has slightly deeper colouring – though to be honest they are similar, and you would not need to plant both in your garden the same year. Other sports are 'Carnival de Nice', which is very beautiful, and red 'Saint Tropez'. 50 cm/20 in (J F van den Berg & Sons 1939, AM-KAVB 1939, FCC-KAVB 1949)

'Orange Princess' (p. 113, 164)
This is a double-flowered sport of 'Prinses Irene' with the same colouring, but with double flowers on stout stems. It is one of the best of all Late Doubles and has sported to 'Red Princess', the colour of the original 'Couleur Cardinal' (see Triumph tulips) and also a winner! Perhaps it will not be long before we get a double sport of 'Prinses Margriet' to complete the set! 35 cm/14 in (C J Zonneveld & Sons and J W B & Th. Reus 1983, TGA-KAVB 1983, AGM-RHS 1997)

'Pink Star'
This is another pink tulip, but is deep, lilac pink. Its ruffled tepals are edged with white, and have some green streaks. It is a sport of 'Wirosa'. 35 cm/14 in (Van Dam 1992)

'Red Princess'
see 'Orange Princess'

'Red Nova'

This is a bright red tulip that is a sport of the Triumph 'Prominence'. 40 cm/16 in (Reus and S Bakker 1989)

'Rembrandt'

Confusingly, this name not only refers to the class of old Rembrandt tulips that are no longer commercially available (see class 9, above), but also to some specific varieties, including this new Double Late with deep-pink flowers that have paler edges and wavy leaves. (It is also the name of a Double Early with pink flowers, and a scarlet Single Early, neither now commercially available.) 35 cm/14 in ('Murillo' sport)

'Renown Unique'

This sport of the Single Late 'Renown' has the same bright colouring, a combination of bright pink with an edge of tomato red. The flowers are globular and fully double but the outer tepals are usually partly green and shorter than the inner tepals. 65 cm/26 in (H C M Overdevest 1988)

'Rocket' (p. 162)

This sport of the tulip 'Eros' has bright, cherry-red flowers. 50 cm/20 in (Rijnveld & Sons 1943, AM-KAVB 1943)

'Rosario Double'

This is a sport of the Triumph 'Rosario', and has blooms of deep, carmine pink with a basal white flare. Unlike its parent, there is green feathering around this area.

'Saint Tropez'

This deep-red tulip is a sport of 'Nizza', and the red is from the streaks in that cultivar. The tepals are brighter inside and flushed with purple on the outside. It has sported to 'Clarion' (Huiberts-Veul 1984), which has deep pink and red flowers. 50 cm/20 in (J W van Saase 1965)

'Sunset Tropical'

Very bright pink double. 40 cm/16 in (Kapiteyn)

'True and Fair'

This is a bold, large flower of rich, buttercup yellow, with ragged-edged tepals. The outer tepals are boldly streaked with bright green, and the flowers have some scent. 40 cm/16 in (Hybris)

'Uncle Tom' (p. 162)

It amazes me that this is not more widely available, because the large flowers open to reveal glossy tepals of rich mahogany red with yellow bases. Its rich colouring and huge size make it one to try. 45 cm/18 in (Zocher & Co, AM-KAVB 1939)

'Upstar'

This flower combines ivory white and bright pink. The pink is usually confined to a broad edge around the tepals, and the base is white. The most important sport is 'Crème Upstar'. The sport 'Mutant Upstar' has watermelon-pink flowers, edged white. 'Up Pink' and 'Up Stripe' are two other, deeper-coloured sports. 45 cm/18 in (J F van den Berg & Sons, J A Borst 1982)

'West Frisia'

A large, glowing flower of rose and deep red, with a rich yellow edge and yellow base. I have seen a wonderful, variegated sport, 'Mutant West Frisia', that may soon be available. 40 cm/16 in (J F van den Berg & Sons, J A Borst & Sons 1978)

'White Pearl'

The white flowers are heavily streaked with green on the outside, and are infused with yellow in the centre of the flowers. 45 cm/18 in (H Roozen Nicz 1987)

'Wirosa' (p. 155)

A popular tulip with large flowers that are crimson pink, edged with creamy white. It has sported to produce 'Double Focus' and 'Pink Star'. 35 cm/14 in (P & J W Mantel 1949, AGM-RHS 1995)

CLASS 12
Kaufmanniana

The waterlily tulip, *Tulipa kaufmanniana*, is one of the earliest and most vigorous tulips, and is a fine garden plant. Because it increases rapidly, it is also cheap to buy. In their first year the bulbs produce a large bloom of creamy white, with pink shading on the outside of the outer tepals, and a golden centre. In the second season these will have increased, and there are usually three or four smaller flowers on thinner stems from the small bulbs that have formed during the previous year. While other tulips usually increase to produce a large number of bulbs that are not large enough to bloom, this tulip seems to be able to produce a flower from all but the tiniest bulb. It seems to naturalize well in borders, and continues to bloom for many years without having to be lifted, though lifting is advisable in climates with wet, moist summers. In my own garden it is the first tulip to bloom, and shrugs off bad weather, though the stems are slender and the flowers can flop in wet weather. Protection from slugs and snails is essential.

It has attracted the attention of hybridizers, and there are now many cultivars. Although a few (such as 'The First') have similar colouring and differ mainly in having larger flowers on stronger stems, most have introduced brighter colours to the group, so we can have bold and brash as well as subtle Kaufmannianas in our early spring gardens. Tempting though the hybrids may be, they lack the grace of the species and, though I am not a 'species snob', I would urge you to try the wildling at least once – it really is a worthy addition to any garden.

Kaufmanniana tulips are all short and compact, most about 20 cm (8 in) high in bloom, though they are so keen to open their flowers that they usually show colour when they are significantly shorter than their stated heights. Most have the plain green leaves of the species, though the influence of genes from the later-flowering *Greigii* tulips has given many hybrids the maroon striping of the latter. The famous bulb company van Tubergen was responsible for much of the early development of the group and their achievements are still among the best of the commercial cultivars. Breeders seem to have concentrated on red and yellow flowers, and there is a bewildering choice in this colour combination. The most popular, and cheapest, is 'Stresa', but you should also consider 'César Franck', 'Corona', 'Giuseppe Verdi', 'Glück' and the superb 'Goudstuk'.

They are ideal for the front of the border, for rock gardens, and for containers such as pots, window boxes and hanging baskets. They are also worth potting to bring into the greenhouse or home, where they will flower a few weeks earlier than in the garden. Their short stems make them less than ideal for cutting, unless for short posies. *Tulipa kaufmanniana*, from central Asia, is certainly worth growing unless you demand vibrant colours in the garden. The flowers are about 12 cm (4.75 in) across when fully open and are cream-coloured, which shades to bright yellow at the base of the open blooms. The anthers are cream. When closed, the flowers are shaded with red on the outer three tepals. The foliage is quite lush and greyish, but the flowers are held above this on stems 15–20 cm (6–8 in) high.

'Alfred Cortot'
This sturdy flower has deep-red flowers that are brighter scarlet inside with a black base. Obviously rich in *T. griegii* genes, it has mottled foliage. 25 cm/10 in (Tubergen 1942, AM-RHS 1966, AGM-RHS 1993)

'Ancilla'
This pretty tulip has the same basic colour as the species but is stockier, and the exterior has a broad, soft pink flush. The interior is white with a red ring around the base, which is very beautiful when the flowers open in sun. It has sported to the uncommon 'Pink Dwarf' (1985). 20 cm/8 in (Tubergen 1955, AGM-RHS 1993)

'Berlioz'
At first sight, this bright tulip appears to be pure gold, but the outsides of the outer tepals are flushed with brown. In bright sunlight these rather starry flowers positively glow, and are enhanced by the purple marbling of the leaves, inherited from *T. greigii*. It is a strong grower and very suitable for pots. 20 cm/8 in (Tubergen 1942, AM-RHS 1939)

'César Franck'
This is a bold and striking flower. The three outer tepals are red, edged with yellow on the exterior, while the three inner ones have only a red smudge on yellow. They open to bright yellow blooms. 20 cm/8 in (Rijnveld & Sons 1940)

'Chopin'
A yellow tulip with densely mottled leaves, which give this otherwise unexceptional cultivar an intriguing twist. The blooms have a dark basal blotch. 25 cm/10 in (Tubergen 1942)

'Concerto'
This is one of the more subtly coloured

Kaufmannianas, with plain green, rather grey leaves and large, ivory-white flowers. When they open they reveal the slightly deeper coloration of the interior, and a black base edged with gold. Though not brash, this is an imposing and beautiful tulip for bedding or containers. 30 cm/12 in (Hybrida)

'Corona'
This bold tulip has slender blooms that, when closed, are bright red with a deep yellow base and edge. Things get even better when the flowers open to reveal the yellow interior, with a bright red ring around the gold centre, and yellow anthers. The leaves are green. This is one to put in containers to bring the fascinating flowers nearer eye-level. 25 cm/10 in (Tubergen c. 1943, AM-RHS 1948)

'Daylight'
If you need something bright in spring, this vibrant and uncompromising scarlet tulip fits the bill. The leaves of this plant are slightly mottled and the base of the interior is black with yellow markings. It has a sport, called 'Golden Daylight' (W Lemmers Cz 1988). 25 cm/10 in (M Thoolen 1955)

'Duplosa'
Unlike any other tulip, this has strange but attractive semi-double flowers in pinkish-red (usually described as raspberry red; I would say strawberry red, a subtle but important distinction). The leaves are green and it is usually one of the earliest tulips to bloom. It deserves container planting so you can appreciate the distinctive flowers. 25 cm/10 in (P Bijvoet & Co 1955)

'Early Harvest'
This is a prolific tulip that seems to have inherited its propensity to bloom from its parent species, and it has beautiful flowers too. These are a mixture of mandarin, red and yellow shades, with the red confined to the centre of the tepals and golden yellow suffused around the edge. The base is yellow and greenish, and the leaves are lightly mottled. It is early, bright and beautiful. 25 cm/10 in (Rijnveld & Sons 1966, TGA-KAVB 1966, AM-KAVB 1973, AGM-RHS 1993)

'Fashion'
This rather pastel-coloured tulip has rosy pink tepals with purple hints. These have a creamy white edge and a yellowish base inside and out. The leaves are green. It has sported to 'Hamlet' (1982). 30 cm/12 in (Tenhagen Bros 1962)

'Franz Léhar'
The pale yellow and red flowers of this tulip are nice enough, but it is almost better before and after flowering, when the foliage display is not interrupted by blossom. The leaves are intense blue-grey and heavily mottled with purple. 30 cm/12 in (J C van der Meer 1955, TGA-KAVB 1958)

'Fritz Kreisler'
This has some of the largest flowers of all, a rich pink with a sulphur yellow edge. The flowers have a mauve hue when closed, and the base inside is yellow with carmine patches. The large number of awards is testament to its beauty. 30 cm/12 in (Tubergen 1942, AM-KAVB 1942, AM-RHS 1948, FCC-RHS 1966)

'Giuseppe Verdi'
In the same style as 'Stresa' and many others, this has rich gold flowers, with red on the outside and a golden yellow interior with red blotches. The leaves are mottled and the flowers thin in bud. It is less vibrant than some. 30 cm/12 in (J C van der Meer 1955)

'Glück'
This short tulip with mottled foliage has sulphur yellow flowers, deeper inside, with red flames up the outside of the tepals, particularly on the outer three. It has sported to 'Little Diamond' (1988). 20 cm/8 in (Tubergen 1940, AM-RHS 1966, AGM-RHS 1997)

'Goudstuk'
This is another yellow and red tulip, with deep red on the exterior of most of the outer tepals, the rest of the flower being deep, golden yellow. It is more expensive than most but is a good choice where you want something dazzling. It is bigger than the popular 'Stresa', though the leaves are not mottled. 30 cm/12 in (Tubergen 1952, AM-RHS 1966)

'Heart's Delight'

This pink tulip has tepals that are deep pink on the outside, with a paler pink, almost cream-coloured, edge, but the colours merge as the flowers age. The interior of the flower is pale pink with a golden, red-blotched base, and the leaves are mottled. It is cheap and popular. 20 cm/8 in (Tubergen 1952, HC-RHS 1966)

'Jeantine'

This pretty tulip has rather starry flowers, typical of the Kaufmanniana shape that is, regrettably, lost in many of these hybrids that have broad flowers, inherited from *T. greigii*. Overall, the effect is apricot pink deepening to red at the base inside, around a yellow base that can also be seen on the outside of the flowers. The leaves are green. 20 cm/8 in (Tubergen 1952, AGM-RHS 1993)

'Johann Strauss'

This has flowers in creamy white with red shading on the outside of the outer tepals in the upper two-thirds. The leaves are mottled and the base of the flowers inside is yellow. 20 cm/8 in (Tubergen pre-1938, HC-RHS 1966)

'Love Song'

This is similar in overall appearance to 'Early Harvest', but is more red. The foliage has subtle striping. 25 cm/10 in (Rijnveld & Sons 1966)

'Scarlet Baby' (p. 52)

Among my favourite early tulips, this is a bright red flower that reveals its bright yellow heart and anthers when open. It grows well, and even small bulbs flower, so if left undisturbed a bulb quickly forms a cluster of elegant flowers. It is perfect for window boxes and pots. 20 cm/8 in (J C van der Meer 1962)

'Shakespeare'

The large flowers are a suffusion of red and orange with a yellow edge and paler inside with a golden base. 25 cm/10 in (Tubergen 1942, AM-KAVB 1942)

'Showwinner'

This relatively modern tulip is possibly the best of the reds, with more substance than 'Alfred Cortot'. The flowers are deep red, and open to scarlet with a yellow base. The leaves are mottled.

25 cm/10 in (Rijnveld & Sons 1966, TGA-KAVB 1966, AGM-RHS 1993)

'Stresa'

Among the most common of all Kaufmannianas, this has yellow flowers with the outer tepals heavily flushed with red on the exterior. The inner base is also marked with red, and the leaves are mottled. 25 cm/10 in (Tubergen 1942, HC-RHS 1966, AGM-RHS 1993)

'The First'

Though last in the list, this is one of the earliest to bloom. Its colouring is just like the species, but it is larger and more robust, perhaps suiting those who dislike flowers that are shy to display their virtues. 20 cm/8 in (F Roozen 1940)

CLASS 13
Fosteriana

The Fosteriana tulips are bred from *T. fosteriana*, a species from Central Asia, and include some of the most brilliant of all garden tulips. They grow up to 40 cm (16 in) high, and have such large flowers that the stems are sometimes unable to support them because they flower in early spring (usually early April) when the weather can be rough. The species has bright red flowers and most have a bold black blotch at the base inside. It is surprising to discover that this magnificent species was not introduced into Europe until 1904, and then again separately in 1914. One of the most popular of all, 'Princeps', is not a hybrid but a selected clone from those early introductions. Hybridizers have found the good attributes of the species – huge, goblet-shaped flowers, a strong constitution, and resistance to virus – too good not to use, and they have crossed it with the Darwin tulips to create the Darwinhybrids which now dominate volume sales of tulips.

Fosterianas should be planted where you want a brilliant show of flowers. Most have vibrant blooms without the subtle shadings of other classes, but this need not put you off. Though pastel shading is lovely, we should not neglect these dazzling flowers that will stop everyone in their tracks. A few, such as 'Dance', show distinct influences of *T. greigii* in their flowers and the group is starting to become more complicated.

The flowers change character more than most as they develop, and have long, tongue-shaped tepals that create a slender bud and an oblong bloom when young. They often have slightly recurved tepals to the closed blooms when mature. They open almost flat in the sun, and can be huge, up to 25 cm (10 in) across when fully open. They are generally strong growing and will survive for several years in the open garden, if in a sunny spot in well-drained soil. The foliage is often bright green but it may also be greyish. They are not as suitable for containers as the other, shorter, early tulips because they tend to flop over when in full flower. This is tolerable in the garden but, because planting tends to be less deep in containers and they are usually placed near the house, they have a tendency to become more drawn than usual.

'Candela' (p. 96)

This is a large, elongated flower in pure canary yellow. It is striking at all stages, but especially when fully open: then the flowers, like many other Fosterianas, can be more than 20 cm (8 in) across. Its black anthers distinguish it easily from 'Yellow Purissima'. 'Soroptimist' (red with yellow base, 1996) is its sport. 35 cm/14 in (K van Egmond & Sons 1961, TGA-KAVB 1961, AM-KAVB 1961, AGM-RHS 1997)

'Cantata'

Sometimes spelt 'Cantate', this is a bright, vermillion red, with a paler flame up the outside of the flowers and a black basal blotch inside with a yellow border. The foliage is bright green and is one of the best early, red tulips. It has sported to produce 'Polo' (yellow and red, 1982). 'Flaming Youth' is similar but slightly taller – you do not need both. 30 cm/12 in (Tubergen, AM-KAVB 1942)

'Dance'

This beautiful tulip is different to most of the group. When in bud the flowers are rose-red with white edges, but open to starry flowers that have intricate black and yellow centres. With a broad red ring, and white in the upper half of the tepals, this makes a striking bloom. 25 cm/10 in (Hybrida 1952, AM-RHS 1954)

'Easter Moon'

A large, yellow flower that is slightly paler on the exterior. 30 cm/12 in (AGM-RHS 1997)

'Easter Parade'

This tulip has red flowers, edged with yellow, and is yellow inside with a patterned base. It has sported to 'Hit Parade'. 40 cm/16 in (Hybrida, AM-RHS 1954)

'Flaming Purissima' (p. 136)

This is probably a sport of 'Purissima' and has similar, ivory-white flowers that are lightly speckled with pink in the upper part of the tepals. This coloration increases as the flowers mature. 45 cm/18 in

'Flaming Youth'

A vermillion tulip with shiny green leaves. The base of the flowers is black with a yellow edge. 35 cm/14 in (Beisenbusch 1949, AGM-RHS 1999)

'Hit Parade'

This sport of 'Easter Parade' has yellow flowers, and the outer tepals have a broad central flare of scarlet. The base inside is brown with a thick ring

Mixed tulips

Photographed with *Sambucus* 'Black Beauty'.
Top row:
'Perestroyka' 5,
'Brilliant Star' 1,
T. clusiana 'Tubergen's Gem' 15.
Second row:
'Gavota' 3,
'Aladdin' 6,
T. vvedenskyi 'Tangerine Beauty' 15.
Third row:
'Red Riding Hood' 14,
T. clusiana 'Tubergen's Gem' 15.
Bottom row:
'Corsage' 14,
'Crystal Beauty' 7.

of bright red. 40 cm/16 in (W Lemmers Cz 1979, TGA-KAVB 1979)

'Juan'

This superb flower deserves to be grown more often, because it is an exceptional orange tulip. The large flowers are intense orange with a bright yellow base that shows even when the flowers are closed. The yellow anthers increase the beauty of the open flowers and – the icing on the cake – the leaves are striped with dull purple, inherited from *T. greigii*. 'Toulon' (Tubergen 1961, AGM-RHS 1997) is similar but darker in colour and has a dark basal blotch. 45 cm/18 in (Tubergen 1961, AGM-RHS 1997)

'Madame Lefeber' ('Red Emperor')

This old tulip has yet to be superseded when it comes to size and brilliance. The flowers are just about the biggest of any tulip – 25 cm (10 in) across on large bulbs – and are dazzling red with a yellow-edged black blotch above greyish foliage. Of course, with great size comes problems, and the stems are not always strong enough to support the massive flowers, so choose a sheltered spot. 40 cm/16 in (Tubergen 1931, AM-KAVB 1931, FCC-KAVB 1932)

'Orange Brilliant'

Probably the brightest, deepest orange in this class, the flowers are deep orange and the interior is flushed almost red. The base inside is yellow with a slight green edge, and the anthers are black. 40 cm/16 in (K van Egmond & Sons, J Kol 1969)

'Orange Emperor'

This fine orange tulip has carrot-orange tepals with a yellow base – though they are not as obvious from the outside as 'Juan' – and young flowers have a green stripe from the stem. The anthers are black. It has strong stalks – a valuable virtue. 40 cm/16 in (K van Egmond & Sons, Segers 1962, AM-RHS 1979, AGM-RHS 1997)

'Pinkeen' ('Rose Emperor')

The elegant flowers are cerise with paler edges on the exterior and a yellow base. It is very early for the group. 40 cm/16 in (Tubergen 1945)

'Princeps'

This is a selected clone from original collections of the species and is significantly shorter than most. Its deep, bright red flowers have a greenish base, edged in yellow and purple anthers. The foliage is grey. 25 cm/10 in (Jan Roes)

'Purissima' ('White Emperor') (p. 52)

This is one of the best white tulips. Its huge, shapely flowers have a yellow base on strong stems. It even has a little scent. The flowers are decidedly creamy at first, but they become milky white with maturity and are augmented by greyish foliage. It has sported to produce 'Yellow Purissima' and red 'Purissima King' (1994). 45 cm/18 in (Tubergen 1943, AM-KAVB 1949, AGM-RHS 1997)

'Red Emperor'

see 'Madame Lefeber'

'Robassa'

This sport of 'Red Bird' differs mainly in its variegated foliage, which is unlike that of almost any other variegated tulip. The flowers themselves are deep pink and vermillion, with paler stripes at the base and a pretty centre that is black, edged with yellow, the whole augmented by purple anthers. But the excitement starts long before the flowers open because the greyish leaves are streaked with cream, and flushed with pink as they emerge. Most variegated tulips have the cream or yellow confined to the edge, but 'Robassa' is much less disciplined, and the cream bands – of irregular width – turn up anywhere. It is usually expensive, and is not to everyone's taste, but there are times when it is best to let your hair down. 30 cm/12 in (H Vreeburg & Sons 1981)

'Rondo'

A relatively 'quiet' cultivar with yellow flowers that have red colouring on the outside of the outer tepals. It is golden yellow inside, with red basal blotches. 30 cm/12 in (Hybrida 1952)

'Rose Emperor'

see 'Pinkeen'

'Rosy Dream'

A superb and interesting tulip with white tepals, the outer three of which are heavily flushed with a carmine/rose colour in the centre. When open, the flowers reveal a bronzy black centre, edged with red. 35 cm/14 in (Rijnveld & Sons, Breed 1971, TGA-KAVB 1972)

'Solva'
This tulip is coral pink with a yellow base. 45 cm/18 in (Rijnveld & Sons)

'Soroptimist'
see 'Candela'

'Spring Pearl'
An elegant tulip of salmon pink with a yellow base and grey foliage. 40 cm/16 in (Rijnveld & Sons 1955)

'Sweetheart'
This is often stated to be a sport of 'Purissima', but is actually a sport of an unnamed white Fosteriana. The large flowers have tepals that are yellow at the base, with flames that lick into a broad white margin. The base and anthers are yellow. I find this flower looks too much as though the edges have been scorched, but I seem to be in a minority on this, since it is a popular plant. Confusingly, or conveniently, the similarly named Single Late 'Sweet Harmony' has similar colouring. 40 cm/16 in (J C Nieuwenhuis 1976)

'Sylvia van Lennep'
This sport of 'Analita' (red, edged white, Hybrida 1952) has bright red flowers with a black base, edged yellow, and black anthers. 35 cm/14 in (Hybrida 1965)

'Toulon'
see 'Juan'

'White Emperor'
see 'Purissima'

'Yellow Purissima'
This sport of 'Purissima' is bright yellow, with a slightly deeper shade at the edge of the tepals and with greenish-yellow anthers. 45 cm/18 in (J N M van Eeden 1980, TGA-KAVB 1980, AGM-RHS 1997)

'Zombie'
This is one of many pink and white Fosterianas raised by C V Hybrida in the 1950s, and is one of the most popular. Its large flowers are distinctly marked with carmine on cream at first, but the colours merge as the blooms age. Inside the tepals are cream and rose with a black base, edged red. 35 cm/14 in (Hybrida c. 1950, AM-RHS 1954)

CLASS 14
Greigii

Tulipa greigii was introduced from the wild, where it is found in Central Asia, in the 1870s, and is so distinctive that it has led to its own group of hybrids. The most characteristic feature of the species is its foliage, which is often wavy and ground-hugging, but is most striking because it is beautifully striped with dull purple. The red flowers are rather chunky and angular, with square bases in profile, and the outer tepals usually recurve more than the inner three. All these characteristics show themselves in the many hybrids, even though these show the influence of other species, such as *T. kaufmanniana* and even the Darwin tulips. Strangely, since it is a beautiful species with obvious and unique features, it did not attract the attention of hybridizers until the 1950s, but there are now more than 200 cultivars. Most have short stems, and though the typical species has deep red flowers with a black blotch in the centre, the colour range is now wide, and there are even multi-flowered cultivars that are good value when you want a bold display. Most flower in April, following the Kaufmannianas and Fosterianas. Like the Kaufmannianas, they are precocious, and open their flowers when they are barely free of the foliage, but the stems elongate as they develop. They prefer light soils, and though the species is shy to produce offsets, this is not a problem with the hybrids. They are admirably suited for window-boxes and containers, flowering at a height of 20–30 cm (8–12 in), and also for the front of borders and the rock garden. But do not smother them with surrounding bedding (which will cover their leaves) or half their beauty will be lost. By far the cheapest and best known tulip in this class is 'Red Riding Hood'. It has bright red flowers and should not be ignored just because it is common. It is a good garden plant.

'Addis'
A popular tulip with sulphur yellow tepals that

blotches in the base. The exterior of the bloom is carmine red, edged with yellow. 25 cm/10 in (Jac. B Roozen 1955, AGM-RHS 1997)

'Calypso'
This recent introduction has orange tepals edged with yellow above attractive foliage. 30 cm/12 in (Jan van Bentem 1992, TGA-KAVB 1992, AGM-RHS 1997)

'Cape Cod'
This popular cultivar has large flowers that are dull yellow inside with a black base, edged orange, and the outside is apricot orange edged with yellow. 30 cm/12 in (Hybrida 1955)

'Charmeuse'
Taller than most, this pretty tulip has orange-scarlet tepals, edged with yellow. Inside, these are yellow, striped with red, and having a brown and yellow base. 40 cm/16 in (Hybrida 1965, TGA-KAVB 1965)

'China Lady'
This delicately coloured flower reflects the Kaufmanniana pattern, with creamy white tepals with a central streak of pinkish red on the outside of the outer three tepals. The flower's heart is yellow with a greenish base marked with red. The foliage is especially good. 30 cm/12 in (Hybrida 1953, TGA-KAVB 1974, *AGM-RHS 1993*)

'Compostella'
Although not always classified as multi-flowered, good-sized bulbs of this variety usually produce two or three bright flowers in scarlet, edged with orange-yellow. The fiery flowers really glow, and it is a perfect bedding cultivar. 25 cm/10 in (Hybrida 1955)

'Corsage' (p. 101, 169, 172)
The beautiful flowers are a blend of orange and pink edged with yellow. 30 cm/12 in (Hybrida 1960, TGA-KAVB 1960, HC-RHS 1966, AGM-RHS 1993)

'Czar Peter'
This is one of the nicest of the pinks, the tepals deep pink to the tip, with a white edge. The colouring is similar, but more intense inside the flower. This is a really beautiful bloom. 25 cm/

Mixed tulips
Photographed with *Corylus maxima* 'Purpureum' and erysinum.
Top row:
'Oscar' 3,
'Tender Beauty' 4.
Second row:
'Corsage' 14,
'Prinses Irene' 3.
Third row:
'Orange Bouquet' 3,
'Golden Nizza' 11
(and bottom).

have a broad apricot orange flush to the outside, and a bronzed base. 20 cm/8 in (A Overdevest Gz 1955, AM-RHS 1966, AGM-RHS 1997)

'Ali Baba'
The flowers are deep pink at first, fading to rose outside and brighter red inside with a red-blotched, yellow base. 30 cm/12 in (Hybrida 1955, AGM-RHS 1997)

'Bella Vista'
This sport of 'Zampa' has bright pink tepals edged with lemon yellow, while inside the flower is deep yellow with basal blotches of bronze green. 30 cm/12 in (A Verschoor Jr 1972, TGA-KAVB 1972, AGM-RHS 1997)

'Buttercup'
Inside, the flowers are golden yellow with red

10 in (Verwer 1982, TGA-KAVB 1982, AGM-RHS 1997)

'Donna Bella'

Beautiful indeed, this subtle flower is cream inside with a black base, blotched with red, and the outside of the tepals is flushed with carmine. The leaves are, perhaps, even finer than the flowers, heavily striped with purple. 30 cm/12 in (Hybrida 1955, AGM-RHS 1993)

'Dreamboat'

This has salmon flowers, a blend of red and amber with a pale exterior base. Inside, the base is green-bronze with red blotches, and the flowers are held on short stems above attractive foliage. 25 cm/10 in (Hybrida 1953, AM-RHS 1966, TGA-KAVB 1972)

'Early Star'

The tepals of this tulip are bright, lemon yellow, and the outer three are flushed with deep red on the exterior. Inside, the base of the tepals is marked with a large red blotch. 25 cm/10 in (IVT, Van der Wereld 1994, TGA-KAVB 1994, AGM-RHS 1997)

'Easter Surprise'

This sport of 'Tango' (scarlet orange, Hybrida 1952), is bright orange with a golden yellow base. Inside, the yellow base is more extensive, and the bottom of the flower is bronzy green. A bright and refreshing flower with purple anthers. 40 cm/16 in (Hybrida 1965, TGA-KAVB 1974, AGM-RHS 1997)

'Engadin'

This bold flower is deep red on the outside, with a yellow edge that also covers the inside of the flower, where there is a red stripe up from the base. (Hybrida 1955, TGA-KAVB 1973, AM-RHS 1979, AGM-RHS 1993)

'Flowerdale'

A beautiful flower with strong Kaufmanniana influences. The flowers open to a starry shape with tomato-red tepals shaded with yellow on the outside and golden inside, with red flushing and a black base, edged red, and with yellow anthers. The foliage has only light marking. 25 cm/10 in

'Für Elise'

This sport of 'Spring Beauty' (red, edged yellow, 1981), is pale yellow, with the palest hint of pink suffusion. A delicate flower. 30 cm/12 in (C and A van Bentem 1986)

'Grand Prestige' ('Charming Silvia')

This bright red tulip is taller than most in the class, and has a bronze green and yellow base. A bright choice for bedding. 45 cm/18 in (D W Lefeber & Co 1972, AGM-RHS 1999)

'Grower's Pride'

A large red tulip with a black base and purple anthers, and attractive foliage. The inside of the tepals is much brighter than the exterior, and the flowers are at their best when fully open. A star among red tulips. 35 cm/14 in (Captein Bros 1971, TGA-KAVB 1971)

'Julius Caesar'

This is a big, tall cultivar. Its shining, bright red flowers have a dark brown base and yellow anthers. 40 cm/16 in (D W Lefeber & Co, J Verdegaal 1986, AGM-RHS 1997)

'Longfellow'

A big, tall *Greigii* with brilliant red flowers, and a black base inside. 50 cm/20 in (Hybrida 1960, AGM-RHS 1997)

'Margaret Herbst' ('Royal Splendour')

This fine tulip has big vermillion flowers with a black base on strong, tall stems, and very low foliage with exceptional mottling. Even more amazing than 'Grower's Pride' and worth searching for, though it is not common. It has several sports, all benefiting from their parent's size: 'Imperial Giant' (red and yellow, 1987), 'Lemon Giant' (yellow, 1989) and 'Stardom' (red and yellow, 1987). 50 cm/20 in (D W Lefeber & Co 1949, AM-KAVB 1963)

'Marina'

The blooms are primrose yellow, with scarlet shading on the exterior of the outer three tepals. The interesting base is brown, edged with scarlet. 30 cm/12 in (Uittenbogaard & Sons 1962, AGM-RHS 1997)

'Mary Ann'

With flowers similar in colour to 'China Lady',

red on white, and with a pinkish-white interior with a bronzy-green base marked with scarlet, this is a beautiful choice. 35 cm/14 in (Hybrida 1955, AM-RHS 1979)

'Miskodeed'

A rather subtle but bright flower, with yellow tepals flared with apricot on the outside. The interior golden base has bright red blotches. 30 cm/12 in (Hybrida 1955)

'Odia'

A lovely, rounded bloom of pale yellow, flushed outside with red on the outer three tepals. The beauty of the flower really shows when they open to reveal the dark brown base, edged with bright red and augmented by the yellow anthers. 20 cm/8 in (Hybrida, J P van Kooten 1981, AGM-RHS 1997)

'Orange Elite'

This is taller than most, and has apricot-orange flowers with a deep green base inside. The foliage is mottled. 35 cm/14 in (Hybrida 1952, AM-RHS 1966)

'Oratorio' (p. 131)

This lovely tulip has chunky flowers of deep pink, with a hint of apricot and a black base inside, augmented by better-than-average foliage. 30 cm/12 in (Hybrida 1952, TGA-KAVB 1963, HC-RHS 1966, AM-RHS 1979, AGM-RHS 1997)

'Oriental Beauty'

A lovely red tulip that opens to reveal vermillion tepals and a deep brown base. The flowers are elegant and not too large. 30 cm/12 in (Hybrida 1952, AGM-RHS 1997)

'Oriental Splendour'

A string of awards should suggest that this is good. But it is not the most typical of the group, taller than most and with only light mottling of the leaves. The flowers have tepals of carmine red, edged with pale yellow, and the interior of the flower is pale yellow with a green base, edged red. It is big, interesting and lasts well. 50 cm/20 in (D W Lefeber & Co 1961, AM-KAVB 1961, FCC-KAVB 1963, AM-RHS 1967 & 1979, AGM-RHS 1993)

'Pandour'

The flowers are pale yellow, flushed with pale scarlet. 30 cm/12 in (Hybrida 1952)

'Pink Sensation'

This flower is bright scarlet, shaded with pink inside, but the tepals are shaded with greyish-pink on the outside. The base is brown with a yellow border, and the anthers are yellow. 40 cm/16 in (C and A van Bentem 1987, AGM-RHS 1997)

'Pinocchio'

A popular choice, this has elegant flowers of scarlet red, the tepals edged with white to create a startling bloom above marbled foliage. Its sport, 'Perfectionist' (1994, AGM-RHS 1997) has tepals with a broader white margin. 'Pinocchio Coral' is also available. 25 cm/10 in (Bito 1980, TGA-KAVB 1980)

'Plaisir'

An attractive bright red flower, with tepals broadly edged with creamy yellow and with a yellow and black base. The flowers have an elegant shape with recurving tips. 'Californian Sun' is its brighter sport (1988). 25 cm/10 in (Hybrida 1953, TGA-KAVB 1972, AM-RHS 1979, AGM-RHS 1993)

'Princesse Charmante'

This tall, showy tulip has fragrant, orange flowers that are flushed with red. 45 cm/18 in (D W Lefeber & Co 1965, AGM-RHS 1997)

'Quebec' (p. 97, 131, 147)

This sport of 'Toronto' is multi-flowered and has all that tulip's fine qualities, but the flowers are a peachy red, edged with pale yellow when closed, opening to reveal a pale yellow-peach flower with a yellow base. This does not seem to quite match the official description of scarlet edged with chartreuse, but it is how I saw the flowers. 35 cm/14 in (P & M van der Poel 1991)

'Queen Ingrid' (p. 131, 147)

This tulip follows the red on pale yellow pattern of many others, including 'China Lady', and has a lemon-yellow interior with a black base surrounded with red. 35 cm/14 in (Hybrida 1955)

'Red Riding Hood'('Roodkapje')(p. 52, 169)
If you find any *Greigii* tulip in your local stockist, it is likely to be this. It may be common but, sometimes plants are common because they are good, not just because nurseries find them easy to grow! The waisted flowers are carmine red, and when they open they reveal the brighter red interior and black base. The leaves are attractively striped with purple, and hug the ground. All round, an excellent choice for mass planting because of its low price. 'Red Riding Hood Bont' (leaf) has unusual variegated foliage – not necessarily a striking addition, but interesting nonetheless. 30 cm/12 in (Hybrida 1953, FCC-RHS 1979, AGM-RHS 1993)

'Red Surprise'
A bright red tulip with a black base. I am not sure what the surprise is! 30 cm/12 in (Hybrida 1953, TGA-KAVB 1961, FCC-RHS 1979, AGM-RHS 1993)

'Rob Verlinden'
This very special, tall *Greigii* has a massive red flower and slightly mottled leaves with a narrow white edge – very special. Not commonly available, but it stood out from all the rest when I saw it. 50 cm/20 in

'Rockery Master'
This short tulip has pretty, salmon-pink flowers that are slightly more red inside, with a bronze-green base. 25 cm/10 in (Hybrida 1852)

'Rosanna' ('Roseanna')
A pretty flower that is unusual for its violet-pink flowers, edged with pink on the outside. Inside, the tepals are pink with a yellow base, edged with red. 30 cm/12 in (Hybrida 1952, TGA-KAVB 1973, AGM-RHS 1997)

'Sombrero'
Not quite as exciting as its name suggests, this is a bright-red tulip that has a deep-yellow base with bronze spots. 35 cm/14 in (Uittenbogaard & Sons 1962)

'Sweet Lady'
A mid-pink flower that is paler at the base of the tepals on the outside, and has a bronzy-green and yellow base. 30 cm/12 in (J C van der Meer 1955)

'Toronto'
It is difficult to beat multi-flowered tulips when you need a splash of colour. Though it is true that the flowers are sometimes not as perfect, and they can be crowded, the best have them spaced nicely on the stems – and 'Toronto' is among the best. The flowers are coral red and lack any subtle patterning – even the base is simply yellow and bronze – but the leaves are mottled, and it is just a pretty, bright plant. Bulbs usually produce stems with two or three flowers. It has two sports: 'Orange Toronto' (orange and red blend, 1987) and 'Quebec'. 35 cm/14 in (Uittenbogaard & Sons 1963, AGM-RHS 1993)

'Trinket'
This is a showy flower, especially fully open, when it can be seen in all its glory. The pale yellow flower has a brown and yellow base, edged with red. When closed, the red, white-edged tepal backs can be seen. 25 cm/10 in (Captein Bros 1963, AGM-RHS 1997)

'Yellow Dawn'
This is not as yellow as you might imagine, and certainly not at dawn. Only when the sun is higher in the sky and the flowers are fully open do they look yellow, and then with a pretty yellow base, edged purple, black and red. The exterior of the tepals is carmine, edged with deep yellow. It has a sport, 'Trouvaille' (claret and vermillion, 1965), and both are good growers. 35 cm/14 in (Hybrida 1953, HC-RHS 1966)

'Zampa'
The outer tepals of this predominantly primrose-yellow flower are flushed with carmine pink. It is popular and grows well, but is not really exceptional. Its sport is 'Bella Vista'. 30 cm/12 in (Hybrida 1952, AM-RHS 1966, FCC-RHS 1979, AGM-RHS 1993)

CLASS 15
Miscellaneous

This book is confined mostly to garden plants, so this is not a complete list of tulip species, just those that are most likely to be encountered for sale. They include oddities such as *T. turkestanica* that you are bound to want to grow at least once, and other, really good plants that I like to grow regularly, such as the similar but garden-worthy variants of *T. praestans*.

I have marked those that I believe are good garden flowers with an asterisk (*). This does not mean that the others should not be grown – just that they have less obvious garden appeal (unless you like unusual and subtle flowers) or are not likely to perform reliably in their first spring without special treatment, such as a raised bed. The author of the name is given, along with the date of official description or date of introduction to cultivation in Europe.

*Tulipa acuminata** Vahl ex Hornem (p. 176)

Although this is not a true species, and has never been found in the wild, it is important because it has a flower shape that makes it the likely precursor of the tulips favoured and created by the Turks. It

Tulip species
Top row:
T. acuminata 15,
T. tetraphylla 15,
T. hageri 15.
Second row:
T. ostrowskianum 15,
T. orphinidea 15.
Bottom row:
T. primulina 15,
T. bakeri 'Lilac Wonder' 15,
T. clusiana 'Stellata' 15.

was described in Europe in 1813 and was grown in the UK by the 1860s, but was cultivated long before this. Few tulips are more beautiful. The flowers have six thin, long tepals that are at least 12 cm (4.75 in) long, but only 1 cm (0.4 in) wide at the base and, with their irregular edge, and red and yellow colouring, look like licks of flame. They are beautiful at every stage of their development, from their chilli-like buds to spidery stars. 50 cm/20 in

Tulipa aucheriana Baker

This pretty, crocus-like tulip has a mauve-pink flower with a pale yellow centre. A bunch of flowers on short stems appears at the base of the ground-hugging leaves. Similar to *Tulipa humilis*. 10 cm/4 in (Described 1883, Iran, AM-RHS 1970, *AGM-RHS 1993*)

Tulipa bakeri A D Hall (p. 176)

This stoloniferous species from Crete is very similar to *T. saxatilis*, with bright green, shiny leaves, and mauve-pink starry flowers with a bright yellow centre. (Described 1938).

It is most often offered as 'Lilac Wonder'* which is actually mauve-pink with a large, rounded egg-yolk-yellow centre separated from the pink by a pale band. Not my favourite combination of colours, but the flowers are full and rounded and it does make a show. 15 cm/6 in (Visser Czn 1971, TGA-KAVB 1975, AM-KAVB 1976, FCC-KAVB 1977, AGM-RHS 1995)

*Tulipa batalinii** Regel

This lemon-yellow tulip is closely related to the red *T. linifolia* and *T. maximowiczii*, and has been crossed with these to produce the cultivars below. It has narrow grey foliage, edged with red, and the flowers open from a distinctly triangular closed state to beautiful bowls of colour. It is usually easy to grow, and may spread in well-drained soil. It is not commonly available but many catalogues offer at least one of the following cultivars: 'Apricot Jewel' (orange and yellow, G H Hageman & Sons 1961, sport of 'Bright Gem'), 'Bright Gem' (pale yellow, flushed salmon, Jan Roes 1952, many awards including AGM-RHS 1995), 'Bronze Charm' (yellow, feathered bronze, Tubergen 1952), 'Red Gem' (also known as 'Red Jewel', vermillion and scarlet – good but less easy, G H Hageman & Sons, W P van Eeden 1985, TGA-KAVB 1985) and 'Yellow Jewel' (yellow with pink flush, G H Hageman & Sons 1961, AM-KAVB 1961, TGA-KAVB 1961). 'Sunrise' (pre-1958) and 'Sunset' (pre-1914) have also been available. The great plantsman E A Bowles noted (in *My Garden in Summer*, 1914) that the bulbs have an attractive tuft of hairs at the top, and that he had raised seedlings in different colours, something that iris king W R Dykes also achieved at about the same time. These were not commercial, however, and it was Dutch growers in the 1950s who brought the coloured cultivars to the masses. All are perfect for planting in pots to decorate the alpine or greenhouse or to bring into the home for short periods when in bloom. 15 cm/6 in (Described 1889, Central Asia, AM-KAVB 1900, FCC-RHS 1970, AGM-RHS 1993)

Tulipa biflora

With a wide distribution on rocky hillsides throughout the region of Lake Aral and the Caspian Sea and beyond, this small species has rather dull flowers in white with a yellow eye, greenish-grey on the reverse, and is like a dwarf *T. turkestanica* but with no more than five flowers per stem. The reverse of the tepals is flushed with green and grey, and Bowles wrote that they flowered as early as December in Middlesex (North London). I agree with him that the flowers look more like ornithogalums (*O. nutans* in shade), the reason I am not enamoured of *T. turkestanica*. The small flowers are fragrant and it is easy to grow. 15 cm/6 in (Described 1776)

*Tulipa clusiana** de Candolle (p. 88, 169, 176)

This, the lady tulip or candlestick tulip, is one of the prettiest species and grows well with me, lasting for several years in a dry, sunny spot without any disturbance. The small, thick-skinned bulbs produce elegant stems with pretty flowers that are white with a deep carmine streak on the reverse of the outer tepals. Inside, the flowers are white with a violet-purple base and inky anthers. In var. *chrysantha* (1948, 20 cm/8 in, AGM-RHS 1993) the basic flower colour is yellow, as in the slightly taller var. *chrysantha* 'Tubergen's Gem' (Tubergen 1969 – yellow anthers, yellow base, free-flowering) and 'Cynthia' (Tubergen 1959, AGM-RHS 1999 – green anthers, purple base). *Tulipa clusiana* var. *stellata* ('Stellata') differs from the species mainly in its lack of violet colouring in the base. Sometimes the stems produce more than one flower. 25 cm/10 in (Kashmir, Afghanistan, Iran and Iraq, but naturalized in southern Europe; probably first flowered in Europe in Florence in 1607)

Tulipa dasystemon

see *T. tarda*

Tulipa eichleri Regel

This is similar to *T. undulatifolia*, and has superb flowers. They are dull red in bud and give little hint of the brilliant flowers that open to reveal scarlet tepals with black basal blotches and a yellow border. The flowers are dramatic and big for a species, being some 12 cm (4.75 in) across. 30 cm/12 in (Described 1874, Caucasus to north-west Iran)

Tulipa fosteriana Hoog ex W Irving

This large-flowered, scarlet species has been exploited to create a series of beautiful and dramatic cultivars. It was collected on behalf of van Tubergen in 1904 in Samarkand, and named after the famous gardener Sir Michael Foster. 25–40 cm/10–16 in (Described 1906, Central Asia)

Tulipa greigii Regel

This species stands out from all others because of the attractive purple striping of the leaves. The flowers are deep red with a waisted shape and a black blotch at the base, surrounded by yellow. It was first cultivated in St Petersburg in 1871. It has been hybridized with other species, particularly *T. kaufmanniana*, to produce a large group of cultivars, most of which retain the beautiful foliage patterns. 20–30 cm/8–12 in (Described 1873, Central Asia – Aralo-Caspian region)

*Tulipa hageri** Heldreich (p. 176)

This attractive species has starry flowers that are brownish red and green when closed, and open to reveal the dark red inner surface of the tepals with a black base and yellow margin. It is closely related to *T. orphanidea* and *T. whittallii*. There are usually three to five flowers per stem above the rather floppy, narrow, red-edged leaves. It is usually easy to grow in a sunny spot with well-drained soil. 'Splendens' is the most common form, and is coppery bronze, while 'Nitens' is bright red. 20 cm/8 in (Described 1874, Greece and Turkey)

Tulipa humilis* Herbert

This bright and pretty tulip is closely related to *T. aucheriana*. Several flowers are carried on short stems above a flat rosette of narrow foliage. It is ideal for the rock garden, and though the flowers are typically pink with a yellow centre, there are many cultivars and varieties. Most are easy to grow in a sunny spot and should be included in any group of hardy bulbs for the alpine house or frame. In most cases the tepals are flushed with green or brown on the exterior, especially the outer three, which are often much narrower than the inner three.

The variations include the following: 'Eastern Star' (deep pink with bright yellow base, Visser Czn 1975), 'Lilliput' (deep red with violet base, multi-flowered, Visser Czn 1987), 'Magenta Queen' (lilac purple with lemon base, W Kooiman 1975), 'Odalisque' (maroon red with large gold base, Visser Czn 1976), 'Pegasus' (purple with brown base, multi-flowered, Visser Czn 1987), 'Persian Pearl' (cyclamen purple with yellow base, Visser Czn 1975), 'Zephyr' (bright red with black base, Visser Czn 1987), var. *pulchella* (pale purple with deep blue base and white edge), the Albocaerulea Oculata Group (fabulous white flowers with bright blue base), 'Rosea' (light violet with yellow centre), the Violacea Group (purple pink with yellow and dark-green basal blotches, which are black in 'Black Base' and yellow in 'Yellow Base'). 10 cm/4 in (Described 1844, Turkey and Iran)

Tulipa kaufmanniana* Regel

This superb species flowers early in spring and has large, creamy-white flowers flushed with cherry red. It and its hybrids are described on page 165. 20 cm/8 in (Described 1877, Central Asia)

Tulipa kolpakowskiana Regel

Although this varies in nature, with orange, red and yellow flower colours, in cultivation it is seen with yellow flowers that have outer tepals streaked with red on the outside. 20 cm/8 in (Described 1877, Central Asia, AGM-RHS 1993)

Tulipa linifolia* Regel

With its narrow, grey, wavy foliage and broad-tepalled flowers on 10-cm/4-in stems, this is similar to, and often lumped with, *T. batalinii*, but the gorgeous, flaring flowers are scarlet with a large black base, similar to *T. maximowiczii*. 10-cm/4-in (Described 1884, Central Asia, AGM-RHS 1993)

Tulipa orphanidea Boissier ex Heldreich (p. 176)

This species from Greece and Turkey has one or more flowers from each bulb. Each has rather subdued flowers in dull orange with black anthers, and a pleasant form that is egg-shaped at the base but with tepals that are pointed at the top. It is similar to, but not as bright as, *T. whittalli* (*T. orphanidea* Whittallii Group – AGM-RHS 1999), while multi-flowered 'Flava', with its yellow flowers flushed with dark red, is more popular. (See also *T. hageri*.) 20 cm/8 in (Described 1862)

Tulipa ostrowskiana Regel (p. 176)

This is similar to, but usually flowers later than, *Tulipa kolpakowskiana*. It has large red flowers with a small, greeny-black base, edged with yellow. 15 cm/6 in (Described 1884, Central Asia)

Tulipa praestans* Hoog

You get good value for money with this multi-flowered species, which has brick-red flowers and red or black anthers, but usually no black patch at the base of the flower – though there is a paler, almost yellow area on the exterior where the tepals join the stem. The tepals are rather narrow and the tips usually pointed, but the four or five flowers are in proportion to the plant, as far as garden decoration is concerned, and colourful. The flowers often start to open while the leaves are still wrapped around them. The foliage is often softly hairy, and may be rather grey in colour. It grows best in light soil that dries out in summer, and I have bulbs that have flowered undisturbed for many years at the base of a south-facing wall under a coronilla. Catalogues often show it in combination with blue muscari, an association that works very well. There is an interesting choice of cultivars, which all have their merits. 30 cm/12 in (Described 1903, Central Asia). The following cultivars are all derived from *T. praestans*:

'Bloemenlust'

This is a sport of 'Zwanenburg Variety' and has the same bright red flowers, but the leaves have a lemon-yellow margin and a thin edge of red. It is brighter and shorter than 'Unicum', but far newer and less common at present. 15 cm/6 in (Ruyter Bros 1995)

'Fusilier'

This has very grey foliage and pale scarlet flowers with narrow tepals and distinct yellow at the base, all inherited by its sport, 'Unicum'. 30 cm/12 in (Jac B Roozen, AM-KAVB 1939, FCC-KAVB 1942, AM-RHS 1966, AGM-RHS 1993)

'Red Sun'

This has red flowers and the leaves are variegated with cream, but the edge of the leaf is green.

'Unicum' (p. 76)

This sport of 'Fusilier' has beautiful grey leaves with moderately wide primrose-yellow margins. These are beautiful before and after flowering, and I once won a 'Best in Show' with a pot of this, carefully deadheaded because it had flowered too early for the show! The leaves last well after flowering, and are as beautiful as most hostas.

'Van Tubergen's Variety'

This is supposed to be dwarf, but eventually reaches the same height as the rest. The flowers open orange-red, with a starry shape. 35 cm/14 in (van Tubergen *c.* 1914)

'Zwanenburg Variety'

This has red flowers with a starry shape, and is said to be the tallest of all. Ironically, its sport is the short 'Bloemenlust'. 35 cm/14 in (Hoog).

'Ispahan' (orange, 40 cm/16 in) and 'Regel's Variety' (bright red, 40 cm/16 in, AM-RHS 1903) are two others that are not commonly available. *T. subpraestans* Vvedensky is similar to *T. praestans*, but has only one flower per stem. But these are considerably larger and bright tomato red. 40 cm/16 in

Tulipa primulina Baker (p. 176)

This delicate, sweetly scented flower is white with a purplish-brown flush on the reverse of the outer three tepals. It can be reluctant to open its flowers except in warm sun, but is easy to grow and pretty for a special place on the rock garden. 20 cm/8 in (Described 1882, Algeria)

Tulipa saxatilis Sieber ex Sprengel

This Cretan species, which is similar to *T. bakeri*, is very easy to grow in a sunny spot and even survives in clay soils, but it spreads by stolons to form great carpets of glossy, bright green foliage, and it is sometimes shy to flower in the UK. A good, hot summer is often followed by a better display of bloom. The showy blooms are bright pink with a round, large, yellow base. If this had been bred I would not like it, and I see no great virtue that it is nature that created such a vile combination of colours. 20 cm/8 in (Described 1825, but in cultivation since *c.* 1600)

*Tulipa sprengeri** Baker

Not only is this Turkish species one of the last to flower, often extending into June, but it is one of the prettiest. Its elegant stems and scarlet flowers have pointed tepals that are olive green at the base, and on the reverse of the outer three. It has shiny green foliage and will naturalize in grass, and seed itself in dry soils. Bowles wrote that 'it is always rather sad to see the first one open, for it means the close of the Tulip season, and that a day or two onward the hot sun and old age will tell on the Darwin and English Tulips'. During the restoration of his garden I found this tulip growing in several spots where it had survived summer drought and being overgrown. It is curiously expensive to buy, but should be included in gardens with gravelly soils. 40 cm/16 in (Described and introduced in 1894 by Naples Nurseryman C Sprenger, AGM-RHS 1993)

Tulipa sylvestris Linnaeus

This delightful and fragrant species is sometimes offered for sale. It is a stoloniferous species from woodland areas, with bright green leaves and nodding buds that open to yellow flowers. The outer three tepals are flushed with green and they reflex to create an intriguing shape. They are held on rather lax stems, so the whole effect is rather informal for a tulip. Inside, the flowers are bright yellow. In var. major they have eight tepals, and in 'Tabriz Variety' they are lemon yellow and green. 30 cm/12 in (Described 1753, West Africa, Europe and Central Asia)

*Tulipa tarda** Stapf

Cheap and readily available, this is about as adventurous as most gardeners get when it comes to species tulips, but it is a good introduction and should not be despised because it is common. From brownish buds open the starry flowers that are golden yellow and white, the yellow extending two-thirds of the way up the tepals. Each bulb produces about five flowers, and these open wide in the sun. It is supposed to be stoloniferous, but my bulbs, in raised beds, have never made a break for freedom except by seed. *Tulipa dasystemon* is often confused with this species, but the flowers have no white edge to the tepals. *T. urumiensis* is similar but the tepals are only lightly tipped with white. 10 cm/4 in (Described 1933, Central Asia, AGM-RHS 1993)

Tulipa tetraphylla Regel (p. 176)
A pretty, elongated flower, nipped in at the waist with yellow tepals that are flushed red on the reverse of the outer three. 35 cm/14 in (Described 1875, Central Asia)

Tulipa turkestanica Regel
This is similar to, but larger than, *T. biflora*, and has up to seven flowers scattered on each branching stem. Exciting though this sounds, the blooms are dull white, grey on the reverse, with a golden centre and not very colourful. It is often said that the seedpods are interesting, which only emphasizes the failings of the flowers! It is common and popular and quite easy to grow. 20 cm/8 in (Described 1875, Central Asia, AGM-RHS 1993)

Tulipa undulatifolia Boissier
This flamboyant flower is bright red with a black, basal blotch. The flowers seem so keen to open in the sun that the tips of the tepals curl under in the warmth. The leaves have wavy margins. 30 cm/12 in (Described 1844, western Turkey and Greece)

Tulipa urumiensis Stapf
This easy species, which may be extinct in the wild, has bright yellow, starry flowers that are purplish in bud. 'Tity's Star' lacks most of this purple coloration to the buds and flowers very freely. 10 cm/4 in (Described 1932, northern Iran, AGM-RHS 1993)

Tulipa vvedenskyi Botschantzeva (p. 169)
A late-flowering, bright red tulip, with attractive, blue-green leaves. 'Tangerine Beauty' (AGM-RHS 1997) is orange red. 25 cm/10 in (Central Asia)

Awards

Suffixed KAVB = Koninklijke Algemeene Vereeniging voor Bloembollencultuur (Royal General Bulbgrowers' Association)
    TGA = Trial Garden Award
    AM = Award of Merit
    HC = Highly Commended
Suffixed RHS = Royal Horticultural Society
    AGM = Award of Garden Merit
    AM = Award of Merit
    FCC = First Class Certificate

Some Royal Horticultural Society awards are no longer extant and are included for information only. AGMs that are no longer current are italicized.

Multi-flowered Tulips

For the sake of convenience, here is a list of all the multi-flowered varieties of tulip, some listed above, some not.

  'Baden-Baden'
  'Bo-Peep'
  'Candy Club'
  'Colour Spectacle'
  'Fringed Family'
  'Georgette'
  'Hans Dietrich Genscher'
  'Happy Family'
  'Louisa'
  'Madame Mottet'
  'Modern Style'
  'Monsieur S Mottet'
  'Orange Bouquet'
  'Quebec'
  'Red Bouquet'
  'Red Georgette'
  'Rexona'
  'Roulette'
  'Royal Ruby'
  'Sanshimai'
  'Sneezy'
  'Toronto'
  'Wallflower'
  'Weisse Berliner'
  'White Wings'
  'Willy Wong'

Chapter 6
Hyacinths

'Oh, for a time machine!' exclaimed Alan Shipp, commercial hyacinth grower and holder of the UK's National Plant Collection of hyacinths, as we looked through old lists of hyacinths once grown but now long lost. There can be few plants that have suffered the ravages of time as badly as hyacinths. What we grow today – the dozen or so cultivars offered by garden centres and nurseries – may seem extensive but it is only about ten per cent of what could be available, and what is grown by Alan Shipp. But even the extent of his collection is as nothing compared to what gardeners grew in 1798.

History

The name hyacinth has classical origins: Linnaeus named it after Hyacinthus (Hyakinthos), a Spartan youth, charming and handsome, who was loved by both Apollo and Zephyr. But, in one of those inevitable problems with jealousy that result from three-way friendships, Hyacinthus was drawn to Apollo, and Zephyr was out for revenge. So one day, while Apollo was throwing quoits with Hyacinthus, Zephyr came down and blew Apollo's quoit off course, so that it struck and killed Hycacinthus. Apollo was distraught, and from the blood of Hyacinthus he created a purple flower, marked with 'ai, ai' (a cry of woe) so that all would remember. Or you may prefer the version in which Apollo and Hyacinthus were throwing discus; Apollo threw too hard and struck Hyacinthus. Unfortunately, hyacinths are neither commonly purple nor marked with 'ai, ai' and it is probable that the plant to which the myth originally attached was a gladiolus – which frequently have marks on the lower tepals – or iris. Anyway, the plant we know as hyacinth got the name, and it was, for a while, associated with grief and woe, and then with games and sports – all from this myth. To the

Pink hyacinths and violas in a large container.

Greeks, the name is synonymous with youthful male beauty. The name 'jacinth' was used in Elizabethan times but can refer to plants other than the hyacinth we know today.

Hyacinthus orientalis is native to Turkey and Iran, and was known to the ancient Greeks and Romans; Homer and Virgil mention its fragrance. A plant that resembles the white Roman hyacinth is widespread in southern France and is thought to have been brought there by the Romans. It seems odd that Roman influence did not spread these plants further, to northern Europe. Roman hyacinths have small flowers on elegant stems and are not common. 'Albulus', which grows around the north shores of the Mediterranean, is the true, white Roman hyacinth. 'Borah' is not a true Roman hyacinth at all but a hybrid of *H. orientalis* and 'Bismarck' (an additional source of confusion is that the standard photo of 'Borah' reproduced around the world on bulb boxes is in fact a multi-flowering 'Delft Blue'). 'White Festival', from Lithuania, which resembles a true Roman hyacinth, was released in commercial numbers in 2004.

The Dutch Mini-boom

The first bulbs of what we would recognize as a hyacinth in its modern form were probably sent in 1573 by the diplomat Ogier de Busbecq to Carolus Clusius at the garden he was creating in Vienna for the holy Roman Emperor Maximilian II. In 1593, Clusius moved to Leiden, taking his bulbs with him. Clusius is an important name in the history of tulips, and he was largely responsible for the establishment of the bulb industry in the Netherlands, though possibly indirectly because thieves were known to raid the Leiden Botanical Garden for material to hawk to tulip-mad gardeners. For several decades the hyacinth did not arouse much interest, although the occasional double appeared. By 1715, a wide range of colours was available in the Netherlands, and doubles with contrasting eyes. It is said that the doubles were routinely destroyed by growers because they did not set seed, and so were useless for propagation. It seems that the bulb farmer Peter Voorhelm was the first to discover that people wanted to buy the double-flowered plants and were prepared to pay handsomely. In that

same year he introduced one of the most famous varieties of all, 'King of Great Britain', and the family business bred many new varieties. Hyacinths slowly grew in popularity. They never caused the heady frenzy of tulips, perhaps because the memories of the tulip crash of 1637 – or rather, the memories of an earlier generation's reminiscences – were still vivid, even a century later. Nevertheless, the popularity, and price, of hyacinths peaked in 1736. Thereafter prices dropped dramatically: that of white 'Staaten Generaal' fell from 210 to 20 guilders, 'Red Granaata' fell from 66 to 16 guilders, and 'Gekroont Salomon's Jewel' fell from 80 to 3 guilders. Yet in 1753 George Voorhelm's catalogue still listed 351 cultivars, even though prices had dropped dramatically since their peak.

Because bulbs were still anything but cheap, they were not bedded out but, rather, enjoyed in containers, after a French scientist (Henri Louis Duhamel) discovered in 1749 that bulbs could be grown in water alone. Growing hyacinths in glasses and more elaborate ceramic containers became all the rage. By 1780, the British pottery maker Josiah Wedgwood was one of the main manufacturers of these ornate containers and his wares were sold throughout Europe.

In 1798, by which time commercial hyacinth cultivation in the Netherlands had settled down to a steady level, the Haarlem firm of Voorhelm and Schneevoogt offered a range that is more than mouth-watering – it would make today's hyacinth lover want to cry, knowing what was once available but is now gone. There were 32 different varieties of white doubles with yellow eyes, 80 double whites with scarlet eyes and 50 whites with purple eyes, among many others. Prices varied from about 10 to 60 florins (contemporary exchange rates were 11 florins to the pound Sterling, then equal to just over $4, which in turn is the equivalent of just over £60 and $65 respectively in terms of purchasing power today) so these were still very expensive. The differences between these varieties must have been minuscule but we should not condemn the growers of the past for raising, naming and selling so many, since today, too, we have so many fuchsias, roses and indeed daffodils that seem the same when described on paper. Even allowing for exaggeration in descriptions, however, it seems we have lost a great deal.

Hyacinths were also highly fashionable in France at this time, and were bedded out in vast numbers at Versailles, apparently at the request of Madame de Pompadour, mistress of Louis XV; she also had them forced in hyacinth glasses to decorate the palace interiors. How these varieties were created is a mystery. Hyacinths are prone to produce sports, and 'King Codro', 'Pink Royal' and 'Hollyhock' are double sports of single cultivars. But even so, sports do not seem a likely source of so many variations – surely if they were, then with the vast acreages grown today, there would be some sign of doubles emerging with contrasting eye colours. The answer may be in sexual reproduction because doubles do breed remarkably true to type, with little mutation. It is claimed that even single-flowered hyacinths, if they have double-flowered ancestors, can produce double seedlings. This is useful because few doubles make good female, or pod, parents. But since many doubles produce some anther tissue, which in turn produces pollen (the male sexual cells) there is also potential for breeding.

Victorian Mass Cultivation

By 1837, in the *Catalogue of Flower-Roots* of Flanagan & Nutting, Mansion House, London, there are still many hyacinths listed. Of these, 114 are doubles, including 28 whites with various coloured eyes, and there are six double yellows. Singles were actually less common, perhaps reflecting the fashion for showing the flowers as opposed to their use for bedding which is so common now. Of the total of 153 hyacinth cultivars in the catalogue, only 'Grande Blanche Imperiale' is still available today. It is interesting to note that, despite the premium now paid for double-flowered hyacinths, this was not always the case in 1837: the double blue 'L'Amitié' cost just 3d while 'Grande Blanche Imperiale' cost 1s 3d and mixed blue, white or red hyacinths cost 4s a dozen. The hyacinths at this time had between 20 and 30 florets per stem, about as many as can be expected on any modern double.

The Victorians loved hyacinths but none of their favourite varieties survive, and we only have descriptions and illustrations. They did not bed hyacinths out as much as grow them for showing, and doubles were favoured. In *The Gardener and*

Practical Florist of 1843, precise requirements are given. The pips (individual florets) must have broad tepals, and each layer should lie over the next. The stems must be strong enough to hold the flowers at right angles to the main stem and the flowers must be large enough so that, when fully open, there are no gaps between them and the stem cannot be seen. What marks them apart from most of today's cultivars is that the Victorians aimed for a conical flower spike, with more flowers in the lower rows than at the top, and crowned with a single flower facing upwards. With a precise fussiness rarely seen today, doubles that hold their flowers drooping down, or that have recurved tepals, are criticised. The *Practical Florist* concludes: 'The colours should be bright, clear and dense, whatever the shade; and any better approach to scarlet, blue or yellow, than those shades we now possess, would be highly esteemed; flowers with dark eyes, very clear outsides, and those with striped petals, would be held to be better than those selfs in general, but would give no point against form.'

War and Decline

By 1930, the number of doubles listed in catalogues had dwindled to a mere handful, but the worst of it is that, while we do still have hyacinth varieties that first appeared before 1930 – 'L'Innocence' and 'Lady Derby', for example – not one of the doubles that had still survived to that point seems to have made it through World War II. In *Cultuurboek voor den Nederlandschen* by G Kluft (1930), there are many doubles mentioned. These include 'Lord Anson' (double white with rose eye), 'Madame de Stale' (or 'Madame de Staël', double white with rose eye), 'Non Plus Ultra' (or 'Ne Plus Ultra', double white with dark violet eye), 'Princess Beatrice' (double white with purple eye), 'Generaal Antinck' (porcelain blue with dark blue eye) and 'A la Mode', which appears to have sported to produce a series. 'A la Mode' itself seems to have been double with a violet eye, but there were also blues and pinks. But the greatest losses of all from this list, as if the foregoing were not enough, are the yellows. Among those mentioned are 'Bouquet d'Orange' (double yellow-orange with a red eye), 'Croesus' (lemon yellow with a darker eye), 'Louis d'Or' (yellow with a rose eye) and 'William III' (orange-yellow with a rose-pink eye). These are all lost for ever. We do still have one yellow double ('Sunflower'), thanks to the work of Dr Rita Raziulyte in Lithuania and Alan Shipp who holds a tiny stock. Could these old, lost hyacinths be recreated? It seems unlikely since nothing close to their appearance exists today. The old doubles with contrasting eyes are only a dream now, and the only extant hyacinth with a contrasting eye colour is 'Blue Magic', which is deep blue with a white eye. It might be possible to breed double blues with white eyes from this. Alan Shipp has recently received stock of 'Prince Albert', a double red with a white eye. These two plants have potential but it will take a long time to recover anything that has been lost.

Many of the hyacinths we grow today were bred in the 20th century, and some are very recent. A range raised by the Dutch IVT (the Institute for Horticultural Plant Breeding) form part of Alan Shipp's collection and bear classical names such as 'Helena' and 'Helios' but these have not yet become available commercially apart from the dark blue 'Kronos'. Other than this wonderful plant, the rest seem unexceptional, but they may have the merit of great vigour during production. A huge boost to the UK National Plant Collection came as a result of Alan Shipp's correspondence with Dr Rita Raziulyte, Deputy Head of Research at a flower research station near Vilnius in Lithuania. She liked hyacinths and

collected them, and during her research discovered catalogues that listed every variety grown in the botanic gardens and research centres of the former Soviet Union. Because of the USSR's isolation, these gardens consequently proved a treasure-trove of old plants no longer cultivated in the West. Alan Shipp describes his first sight of the list as feeling like a stamp collector 'seeing a whole page of Penny Blacks'. Of about 240 hyacinths thought to exist today, only about 60 are still in commercial production, though the actual number may be smaller since some different names may refer to the same varieties. Probably fewer than 20 varieties are grown in sufficient numbers to be of interest to large commercial concerns.

So what does the future hold? Unfortunately, it does not look bright if you buy your hyacinths from garden centres, where the range available is likely to contract even further, rather than expand. Some hyacinths are grown by single growers in the Netherlands and as they retire, their stocks disappear with them, maintained only in bulb museums and botanic collections. In 2004, the following had just gone out of commercial production: 'Bismarck', 'La Victoire', 'Oranje Boven', 'Grand Monarque', 'Yellow Hammer', 'Lord Balfour', 'Perle Brillante' and 'Menelik'. 'Dreadnought' was dropped a few years before and 2004 was the last year 'Prins Hendrik' and 'Prinses Maria Christina' were grown in commercial quantities.

Hyacinths are easy to grow in pots and go on to give a beautiful display of colour.

It seems a shame that, although daffodils still have growers' societies and shows – as, to a lesser extent, do tulips – hyacinths are ignored. Daffodil societies often distribute bulbs in the autumn for members to grow and show, and it would not be impractical for the same thing to be done with hyacinths. The problem with this idea is that the skill in growing hyacinths, or any other bulb, does not show until the following year. What you see in spring is not the result of your own efforts but what was done while the bulb was growing the year before.

The fact that hyacinths grow and flower so readily, with so little effort, rather counts against them as show flowers. But surely there is a chance here for a category at a show. With a few specialists making unusual doubles available to enthusiasts, and four or five doubles available from good garden centres, there is potential for a show class. The spikes of blooms can be 'dressed', just like other flowers, to mask gaps in spikes; well-grown bulbs, generally bigger than can be bought, would make the strongest spikes; and they could be displayed as cut flowers or as plants in pots, which would expose the strength or weakness of the stems. Almost anyone can grow a hyacinth, but it takes skill to grow them well. Perhaps it is time we stopped leaving hyacinth-growing to children with jam jars and started to treat them more seriously.

Propagation

Hyacinths do not naturally produce many offsets. While daffodils regularly produce offsets and tulip bulbs disintegrate every year, replacing themselves with several more, hyacinths may grow for several years without so much as a small bulblet being produced. This is fine for the gardener but not much use for the commercial grower, so a means of rapid propagation is needed. Obviously, plants can be grown from seed but the results will be variable, and vegetative (clonal) propagation is needed.

Scooping

In the case of hyacinths, the most common method is called scooping. This relies on the ability of the bulb scales to produce buds, and tiny bulbs, on a cut surface at the base. This sounds like magic but it is probably more common than we imagine. I have propagated lachenalias from leaf cuttings and, though they are tender and from distant South Africa, they are partners in the Mediterranean family *Hyacinthaceae*.

In late summer, while we are busy planting hyacinths in the garden, growers are scooping their hyacinths, using a small, curved blade to remove the base plate completely. This exposes

Hyacinth 'Snow Blush'.

Scooped hyacinth bulbs.

the base of all the scales and kills the flower bud. These scooped bulbs are then left in trays, cut side uppermost, at a temperature of about 27° C (81° F) for three months, though if you try this at home the temperature can be lower. By the end of three months the cut surfaces will be studded with small, white, tooth-like bulblets; the bulbs are then planted in rows to grow. The following spring, instead of the familiar five or six leaves and central flower spike, the bulb produces a mass of narrow, grassy leaves, a sign that all those tiny bulbs are growing. The number of bulblets that a single, scooped bulb will produce varies: with small bulbs and less vigorous cultivars it can be as few as 20, but it can be as many as 80, with 40 being average. 'Prins Hendrik' is shy, with about 20 bulblets but 'Lady Derby' is prolific.

At the end of the growing season, the bulblets are lifted as a mass and cleaned from the old bulb. They are then stored in a nylon net and planted in this to make harvesting easier the following year after planting. When planted for their third season, they should be spaced sufficiently to allow growth to flowering size, and they should then be left in the ground for the fourth year. They may be ready for sale after four years, or they may need a further year of growth either to reach flowering size or to produce a large bulb to attract a premium price. The young bulblets are usually planted 6–10 cm (2–4 in) deep to grow on. If not planted deeply enough the bulblets will produce contractile roots and pull themselves deeper into the soil – 'King of the Blues' and 'Carnegie' are particularly sensitive to shallow planting.

Cross-cutting and Coring

An alternative way to propagate hyacinth bulbs is to cross-cut them. Using a straight, sharp knife, the base plate is cut to take out two or three intersecting diagonal grooves, creating a star-shape, cutting through to the scale leaves and damaging the central growing point and flower bud. This treatment results in fewer bulbs being formed than in scooping, but each will be larger, and perhaps reach maturity a year earlier.

Bulbs can also be cored, similar to the way you would take the centre out of an apple with a corer. This results in even fewer bulblets than cross-cutting, but it is the way multi-flora hyacinths are produced. These are often described as a breakthrough in breeding, but the method is simple and long-established; they are merely standard hyacinths treated in a special way. A bulb is cored and planted into the ground where it forms a clump of five to eight smaller bulbs that are lifted after several years and kept together as a whole to attract a premium price. Multi-flora hyacinths are fun, and the large bulbs, which look rather like a clump of barnacles, produce a satisfying clump of flowers. You could easily make your own from your favourite hyacinth with a bit of planning.

The vigour of a bulb is an important consideration for growers, and even a small difference can make the difference between retaining and discarding a potential cultivar. With the fixed costs that a business has to pay during the long years needed to grow a saleable bulb, it becomes of great economic significance if 90 per cent of a plant's bulbs are large enough to sell in five years, rather than just 50 per cent. Which would you grow?

Cleaning and Grading

Once the foliage has died down the bulb grower will lift the bulbs, clean them of outer scales, and grade them according to size. Soil is also removed, especially if they are to be exported, to prevent any disease organisms from travelling between countries. Bulbs are sent in large quantities to packers who either distribute them loose in boxes (identifying the variety by photos) or prepack them so they are ready for display in garden centres and shops. Often, bulbs from just one grower are sold under different brand names, so even if you prefer a certain company's product, you may be getting the same plants from another. Do not be persuaded by price or favouritism alone when you buy.

As a general rule, any hyacinth you buy will be of flowering size. I have never bought a hyacinth that did not flower so if yours doesn't, it is probably a question of the quality of care you have given it – adequate moisture and sunlight, and the proper temperature. The only other situation in which they might fail to flower is if you bought cheap, soft bulbs. It doesn't pay to skimp on the cost of a bulb.

Big bulbs have the biggest flower spikes and sizes vary from a circumference of about 14–15 cm (5.5–6 in) to 18 cm (7 in). This may not seem much of a variation, but it does make a difference to the volume of the bulb. For bedding I would chose 14–15-cm bulbs because they are significantly cheaper than the rest and their spikes are still quite large enough for a garden setting. For containers, or anywhere that needs fewer bulbs, I would choose 15–16-cm bulbs just to give a slightly better display. It is normally recommended that the biggest bulbs – about 18 cm – should be used for pots and bowls indoors, but these produce large spikes that are top-heavy. They can also cost up to twice as much as the

14–15-cm bulbs, depending on how easily the bulbs grow to this size. I stick to bulbs between 15 and 17 cm (6–6.75 in) for indoors.

Disease and DNA

Disease does not seem to be as great a concern in hyacinths as in daffodils and tulips. It does exist, although it may not show itself through obvious symptoms. What disease there is in commercial stocks does not appear to affect vigour. 'Grand Monarque' is strong-growing despite being found to have at least four identifiable viruses when tested (interestingly, the same ones that affect potatoes and tomatoes).

Hyacinths have particularly variable numbers of chromosomes. In tulips most plants are diploids (that is, they have two copies of every chromosome, one from each parent), as nature intended, and are described by the formula 2n = 24 (that is, two copies of each of 12 different types of chromosome). Therefore, the few tetraploids (with four copies of each chromosome, two from each parent) are 2n = 48. By crossing a tetraploid with a diploid you get a triploid (three of each chromosome, two from one parent and one from the other: 2n = 36), which is all quite logical, but with hyacinths the number of chromosomes seems completely

Hyacinths are increased by 'scooping' mature bulbs. These 87 little bulbs were produced from a single bulb, an exceptional harvest.

random. Their 'normal' (diploid) number seems to be 2n = 16, but there are tetraploids with 2n = 24 (rather than the expected 32), and numerous other variations as well. As a rule, plants with higher numbers of chromosomes have larger flowers and larger foliage that is erect at first and then flops after flowering. Those with 2n = 16 and 2n = 24 tend to have small, neat foliage. This wide variety in chromosome numbers is evidence of the hyacinth's long history of cultivation.

Cultivation

Hyacinths are easy to grow but they do require well-drained soil and a sunny spot. Once in the garden they can be left for three or four years before being lifted and divided. They do prefer a rich soil, so apply a slow-release, organic fertilizer at planting time, or a general fertilizer when the plants begin to show through the soil.

The correct planting depth is quite important for hyacinths if you are hoping to keep the bulbs

Three multiflora hyacinth bulbs produce a mass of blooms.

for more than one season. Like most bulbs, hyacinths have the ability to correct their depth if not sufficiently deep in the soil, but a secondary consequence of shallow planting is that, by experiencing higher temperatures than usual (since they are not being insulated by the soil above), the bulbs split rather than remain as one. Presumably, the adaptive advantage of this is that it is easier for the contractile roots to pull a small bulb down into the soil rather than a big, flat-based bulb, but for the gardener, the consequence is that the bulb produces a cluster of small flower stems or breaks up into smaller bulblets that do not flower at all.

Growing in Pots and Bowls

You can grow both prepared and ordinary hyacinths in pots or bowls to enjoy the flowers indoors. Prepared hyacinths have been heat-treated so they will flower earlier than normal if you treat them correctly. They are usually available in mid-August and they need to be planted before the middle of September so that the treatment is not interrupted and the bulbs have ten weeks in a cool, dark place, and then about four weeks to expand their foliage and flowers when brought into a cool light spot before flowering at Christmas.

If planting in pots and bowls, it is always best to stick to one cultivar per pot. Though hyacinths are surprisingly consistent in their flowering time in the garden, they will bloom at different times if grown in a pot together. The idea of having a longer display of flowers from a bowl may seem a good one but, in practice, I find the result visually unattractive, with one flower spike fading as another is at its peak, and no bulb having the chance to shine as it should because of the withering corpse at its side. So I would recommend either buying more bulbs and planting a bowl of each cultivar, or planting each bulb in its own pot – you can then put several plants, at their peak, together.

If you are planting in pots, with drainage holes, you can use any type of compost. I would always use a compost that contains some loam because this will provide stability when the hyacinths are in bloom, and also some nutrients for the bulb, ensuring a good display the following year. You can also use a multipurpose compost or, since hyacinths need only water, you can grow the bulbs in bowls of gravel, expanded clay aggregate, glass beads or any other inert material. Bulb fibre is traditionally used in bowls. Based on sedge peat, it contains charcoal and oyster shell, which are alkaline, preventing the compost becoming stagnant and acidic. When growing bulbs in water alone or with an inert aggregate it is usually recommended that some charcoal is added to the water to keep it 'sweet'. While this may be a good idea I have never had a problem when I have not used charcoal.

Growing in a Glass

Another way to grow hyacinths is to plant them in a (transparent) hyacinth glass or vase; however, I suspect most people try it only once. The attraction is that children can be fascinated by watching the roots of the hyacinth grow through the soil, then burst into shrieks of delight when the flowers open. In practice, after the bulb has been placed in the jar, with water added so it is just below the base plate, the bulb still has to be placed somewhere cool and dark for the obligatory ten weeks or so. But unless he or she is keen, a child will soon forget about the bulb in the cupboard. ('Paper White' daffodils are far better for children.)

If the hyacinth is remembered, it can be brought out into the light and the leaves will unfurl to reveal the flower spike. With some speed, the spike will extend until, just as it reaches its peak of beauty, it will either collapse and flop to one side or, even more dramatically, it will lean over in the night and cause water and broken glass to cascade over the floor. This fate can be at least partially prevented if you keep the hyacinth in a cool room and in good light.

While I am being negative, I should mention gift packs, and especially those designed to be given as Christmas presents. These can be nice gifts, but I dislike buying anything I cannot see and they are rarely good value unless you collect packaging. There is no point in giving a pretty box containing a scoop of dusty compost and a plastic bowl with a few hyacinth bulbs for Christmas. The bulbs will be unlikely to grow well and may even be dead if they have been on display in a shop for a long while. Hyacinths at Christmas can be a lovely gift, but plant them in September and give them when in bloom.

Kept in the Dark

After planting in pots, it is always recommended that hyacinths are kept in a cool, dark place for a while, usually ten weeks in the case of prepared hyacinths. It is usually said that cool temperatures are required to stimulate root development, but if you dig up a bulb from the garden in August you will discover it has started to put out roots – at the warmest time of the year. So roots and cool temperatures do not seem to be linked. Instead, the cool temperature (below 13° C/55° F) is needed to stimulate the growth of stems. Plants grown in pots for indoor decoration are kept in the dark until the shoots are about 5 cm (2 in) tall, partly to ensure that the flower buds grow above the neck of the bulbs and also to prevent the bulbs from forming contractile roots. If bulbs are planted so the shoots turn green as soon as they grow, they immediately form contractile roots that grow straight down through the soil and pull the bulbs into the soil depths. I plant bulbs in pots, spaced so they are just touching and with the nose of the bulbs just above the rim of the pot. They are then given enough water to moisten the compost. I usually then put them in a cold-frame and cover them with bark or used growing bags but you can also put them in a cardboard box in a cool, dark place. If planting in bowls and leaving them outside in a cold-frame, cover the surface with plastic to prevent autumn rains filling the bowls with water and causing rot.

Light and Warmth

When the buds are about 5 cm (2 in) high, the bowls or pots can be brought into the light and warmth to flower. But remember that high temperatures and poor light will reduce the length of the flower display and will cause the foliage to become drawn and the flower spikes to fall over. It is possible for a bowl of hyacinths to last as long as three weeks in a cool room or conservatory, but as little as a few days next to a radiator. A common problem, which often afflicts my

Hyacinth 'Blue Star'
in the home.

prepared bulbs will not flower the following year. I have never found this to be the case and my bulbs usually flower well the second year. I might be tempted to put this down to using a good compost were it not for the fact that even bulbs grown in water and pebbles produce some flowers in the second year; so I think that decent treatment after flowering is the key to success.

As soon as the flowers fade, they should be removed. A hyacinth only has five or six leaves and the central flower stem forms a significant proportion of the green plant, so deadhead your hyacinths by pulling off the individual flowers. This is not as onerous as it may seem and I find that loosely cupping my hand around the base of the stem and pulling my fingers up the stalk will remove most in a single movement.

It is generally suggested that the pots of bulbs should be gradually acclimatized to outside conditions, and I often put them in the greenhouse if there is room. However, I also sometimes stand them outside, and they seem to come to no harm. They must be kept moist and must be allowed to develop and then die down naturally. Drying them off as soon as they have flowered is a cruel and ungrateful way to treat a plant that has just given you its flowers.

hyacinths when grown indoors, is when the flower stems flop over. This is caused by excess heat and poor light, but we do not live outdoors in January, and can be forgiven the luxury of a little heat in the home.

Therefore, staking of the stems is necessary. In bowls this is difficult because the depth and nature of the compost mean that small, split-cane stakes have no chance of standing upright on their own, let alone of supporting the hyacinths. By far the best method, if a little gruesome, is to use a wire (cut from a coat hanger is ideal) or a split cane with a sharp point. This can either be inserted through the top of the flower spike or threaded through the buds and flowers on one side. It is then pushed into the bulb itself and is usually completely effective. I know that this does not harm the bulb unless it is inadvertently pushed through the central growing point, but I confess that I do not like doing it to valuable plants.

After the First Year's Flowers

Once flowering has finished, potted plants can be kept for future years. It is often stated that

Planting Out

The bulbs in these pots can be allowed to dry off gradually and kept for planting later, or they can be planted out in the garden straight away, while still in leaf. I favour the latter simply because it involves less work, though you do have to suffer the inevitably rather floppy foliage of the forced bulbs till they die down. Of course, hyacinths are ideal for use in the garden too. I love them both in containers and in the open garden, so I plant all those I have first grown indoors in two rows beside a path where they form one of the first real spectacles of the gardening year. Hyacinths are especially good in outdoor containers but the compost in pots can become frozen in winter and hyacinths, although generally hardy, will be killed if the bulbs freeze, as I have found from bitter experience. In the Netherlands, hyacinth bulb fields are covered with straw in winter to insulate them – something that is not done with daffodils or tulips.

Pests and Problems

When planted out in beds, hyacinths are surprisingly free from problems. Aphids are rarely stirring in enough numbers to cause a problem so early in the year and – though perhaps I have just been lucky – I have never seen them clustered on shoots in the way that they grip onto tulips. Botrytis (grey mould) often kills flower buds if they are grown in pots in stagnant conditions, but it is rarely a problem outside. I have only really seen it in forced plants sold in pots that are stored in plastic sleeves and watered from above so that water collects in the shoots and lies there without any air circulation.

For bulb growers, swift moth, the grubs of which attack the base plate of the bulbs and slow or even stop the increase in weight of the bulb, can be a serious pest. But it, too, is not a common problem in the garden, which is just as well since, in the UK at least, there are no soil insecticides that can be used to control them.

Planting Partners

Violas and pansies are ideal partners for hyacinths because they too usually have a few early-spring blooms. Wallflowers are usually too tall and flower too late to make good companions, though they could be used to cover the foliage of the hyacinths. Primroses and polyanthus are also good for beds, and *bellis* and *myosotis* complete the traditional line-up. I must admit that in recent years I have not bothered with companion plants in my small raised beds and have just planted 50 hyacinths, about 15 cm (6 in) apart, in one or two cultivars. Pure white 'Carnegie' and deep wine 'Distinction' always make a startling combination, and next year I will veer to the more subtle and choose 'Splendid Cornelia' and 'Fondant'.

Hyacinths also have their place in the herbaceous and mixed border, provided they are not too shaded. Though I accept that some people find the orange shades difficult to live with, I adore 'Gypsy Queen' and her brethren; many years ago I planted some under a sycamore maple (*acer pseudoplatanus*) 'Brilliantissimum', with valerian (*valeriana phu*) 'Aurea'. When I moved house I dug up the whole scheme (the sycamore was still small) because the combination worked perfectly, the hyacinths matching the colour of the young sycamore foliage. The tree eventually died but the hyacinths and valerian pulled through.

Whatever hyacinths you choose, remember that they are just like you. They can make the effort to be posh and formal, or they can be relaxed and slouch about. When we buy them they have been manicured so they give us their best. Even gold-laced polyanthus and auriculas cannot look more groomed. If we plant them and ignore them, however, they fall into bad habits, and their smaller spikes, with fewer flowers, will fit into borders without intimidating other flowers. But lift them and give them a good meal and they will soon be on their best behaviour again. Like so much in life, the results depend on how much effort you want to make.

Hyacinth 'Gypsy Queen'.

Chapter 7
Species and Cultivars of Hyacinth

Blue hyacinths

Columns descending, from top left.

First column: 'Kronos' 4, 'Peter Stuyvesant' 3.

Second column: 'Marie' 3, 'Professor de Hertogh' 4.

Third column: 'Sky Jacket' 4, 'Blue Star' 3.

Fourth column: 'Bismark' 3, 'Blue Magic' 4.

Fifth column: 'Debutante' 4, 'Blue Blazer' 3.

Though there may not seem to be much variation among the hyacinths available today, apart from basic colour, once you start to look more closely you can begin to understand how fascinating they can be. They are ideal plants for a collection because they do not take up much room and are not difficult to maintain. The following selection, arranged by colour, is extensive but not complete. But it does include all those likely to be grown commercially at present or in the near future, as well as desirable plants that may eventually become available.

Most hyacinths grow to about 25–30 cm (10–12 in) high when in bloom, and most flower in late March or early April. I have not made much mention of fragrance. I have never found a hyacinth that had no scent, and I am not aware of a great difference in the fragrance of different cultivars, so I am sure it does not vary as much as in daffodils or tulips. But it varies with weather and ambient conditions. I have never known a hyacinth to smell anything but wonderful outdoors. But in the warmth of the home it can lose its sweetness and become more 'green', and as the flowers start to die it can be very unpleasant. I only mention this to emphasize, again, that hyacinths are hardy plants and, in the home, they should be kept in as cool conditions as possible.

Though I don't wish to get too technical, I have included the chromosome count (for the diploid state), where known for each cultivar – for instance (2n = 27). I have not done this for daffodils or tulips, but this has greater relevance for hyacinths because those with higher chromosome numbers usually have larger flowers and, more particularly, broader foliage. This can make a difference in the garden, but may also be useful for anyone who wants to try their hand at hybridizing. The typical 2n for *H. orientalis* is 16 but numbers vary enormously. The raiser and date of introduction is given where known.

Note to Pictures

The number given in the captions after each name refers to the number of florets shown.

Blue

Few hyacinths are truly blue, most have at least some purple in their colouring, but they encompass shades from the deepest, inky indigo to pale sky blues. Among those that are common, 'Blue Magic', 'Kronos' and 'Marie' are good deep blues, and 'Delft Blue' and 'Sky Jacket' are good pale blues. And 'Blue Peter' is a must if you like pastel colours.

H. orientalis

This is a small plant with up to fifteen flowers per stem, with recurved tepals and a sweet scent. It is really only of historical importance and not available commercially.

'Bismarck' (p. 192)

Once a common cultivar, this is becoming less popular and may soon be difficult to find. The large flowers have recurved tepals with a distinct darker band down the centre. The blooms are augmented by dark stems. (D J Ziegler 1875)

'Blue Blazer' (p. 192)

The deep-blue flowers have broad tepals, especially the outer three. A good, rich blue hyacinth. (C Geerlings 1979)

'Blue Haze'

This dark-stemmed hyacinth has flowers of rich mid-blue, a useful colour in the mid-range of blues. (Langelaan-hulsebosch 1944)

'Blue Jacket' (p. 198)

A good, deep-blue hyacinth. (C J Zonneveld 1953, AGM-RHS) (2n = 27)

'Blue Magic' (p. 192)

This has long been my favourite dark-blue hyacinth because, although the flowers are not large, they are such a deep, inky indigo. This colour is enhanced by a white eye to each flower that develops as the flowers age. The leaves are neat and the flowers are carried on dark stems. It just oozes class. (G van der Mey 1971)

'Blue Peter' ('Delft Lilac') (p. 199)

Despite its name this is hardly blue and its synonym is more accurate. The reddish stems carry the pretty, lavender flowers that change shade as they age, and in different lights. A sport of 'Delft Blue', this deserves a special place in the garden. (W Zanderbergen 1986)

'Blue Star' (p. 190, 192)

'Delft Blue' has produced many sports, and this is one of the best. The flowers are dark blue with an inky tint, and the stems are very dark. (Prins and Topper 1982)

'Borah' (p. 194)

The most common Roman or fairy hyacinth, with pale blue flowers, making a pleasant contrast to the thicker spikes of others. (G van der Veld 1946, AGM-RHS). See also 'Rosalie'.

'City of Bradford'

This is another sport of 'Delft Blue' and has medium-sized blooms of rich, dark blue, paler at the edges, on dark stems. (J Walkerling 1984)

'Concorde'

Described as aster-violet, the flowers are intense, deep blue with a purple tinge, and the florets have a paler edge. A dramatic garden hyacinth that is just beautiful close up. (Walter Blom & Sons 1971)

'Cote d'Azur'

The recurved flowers are pale blue with a deeper stripe down the centre of each tepal. (G van der Meij 1943)

'Crystal Palace' (p. 200)

This recent double is a sport of 'Blue Jacket' and a wonderful addition to the few doubles that are available. The colour is a deep, rich blue, and the stems are dark.

'Debutante' (p. 192)

A fine hyacinth that has rich blue flowers with paler edges and dark centres. The stems are very dark, adding to the rich effect, and the foliage is neat and low, making it excellent for bedding.

'Delft Blue'

This common hyacinth is pale blue, with a hint of lilac. It is an important commercial cultivar and perhaps because of the sheer quantity of bulbs that have been grown, it has produced a large number of sports – see 'Blue Star', 'Blue Peter', 'City of Bradford', 'Diana' and 'Snow Blush'. (J W A Lefeber 1944, AGM-RHS) (2n = 30)

'Diana' (p. 194)

Discovered growing in a bed of 'Delft Blue' by Alan Shipp, this beautiful hyacinth is probably the most important new cultivar of the 20th century. Its colouring is unlike any other, with a picotee pattern on the florets, each of which is pale pink with a soft blue border. The stems are

Blue hyacinths
Columns descending,
from top left.
First column: 'Satana' 4,
'Perle Brilliante' 3.
Second column: 'Duchess
of Westminster' 3,
'Borah' 4.
Third column: 'Myosotis' 4,
'City of Bradford' 3.
Fourth column:
'Gainsborough' 3,
'Koh-I-Nor' 4.
Fifth column: 'Diana' 4,
'Goluboj Elektron' 3.

red. It is a chimera, and commercial propagation has proved difficult to date. If this becomes commercially available it will be worth every effort to obtain and should give a new boost to the popularity of hyacinths. (A K Shipp new)

'Doctor Stresemann'

Steel blue flowers on dark stems. (N Dames 1930) (2n = 31)

'Dreadnought' (p. 200)

Double hyacinths are remarkably varied in form and this has especially lovely flowers with six 'normal' outer tepals, and a centre of small, narrow, 'permed' tepals, making each flower a work of art. The colour is a rich, mid-blue. (pre-1900)

'Duchess of Westminster' (p. 194)

This old cultivar, re-introduced from Lithuania, deserves to be better known. The blooms are large and deep indigo with paler edges, and the stems are very dark. An impressive and colourful garden hyacinth. (M van Waveran pre-1935)

'Gainsborough' (p. 194)

This has large, fleshy flowers of light blue, each tepal paler at the edges, on dark stems. The flowers reflex, and the plant is showy and dramatic. (M van Waveran) (2n = 30)

'General Kohler' (p. 200)

The tepals of this fine blue double are broad and triangular to give the flowers a substantial, starry look. They are rich, pale blue. (1878) (2n = 29)

'Goluboj Elektron' (p. 194)

This Lithuanian cultivar has striking flowers of pale cobalt blue on dark stems. The blooms are large and the tepals are broad, the inner ones are hooked.

'Grand Monarque' ('Blue Ice')

The dark stems carry large flowers with recurved tepals. They are pale, cool blue with some cobalt on the reverse and tube. (V van der Vinne 1863)

'Koh-I-Nor' (p. 194)

An impressive new addition to the range of pale-blue hyacinths, this winning cultivar has mid-blue flowers that are darker on the reverse. The tepals are broad and fleshy and reflex a little. The flowers are carried on attractive, dark stems. (J A Scharma 1985)

'Indigo King'

An attractive hyacinth with flowers that are pale blue when open, but the reverse of the tepals is deep blue. (H Corsten 1920)

'Kronos' (p. 192, 195)

It would be difficult to imagine a darker-blue hyacinth than this modern cultivar. The blooms are large and rather irregular in shape, with narrow tepals, making bold spikes of deep, indigo-blue flowers. Definitely one to look out for. (IVT 1982) (2n = 24)

'Marie' (p. 192)

This very dark hyacinth has deep blue flowers flushed with indigo, the intense colouring enhanced by dark stems. (J Prinsen 1860) (2n = 16)

'Maryon'

This striking hyacinth has dark, inky-blue flowers that are especially dark on the reverse.

'Minos' (p. 195)

The violet-blue flowers have broad tubes to reveal the yellow anthers, and the tepals are broad to give 'full' flowers. The tepals are often splashed with darker shades. (IVT 1980) (2n = 27)

'Miss Molly Gilroy'

Alan Shipp raised this new hyacinth and named it after his granddaughter. It has florets of silvery, deep lilac-blue, with reflexing tepals on attractive dark stems. (A K Shipp new)

'Myosotis' (p. 194)

Like many pale-blue hyacinths, this has blooms that are distinctly true blue on the reverse. The large flowers have long tepals, deeper blue in the centre, and are carried on green stems. (C Rijnsburger 1896) (2n = 30)

'Nestor'

This fine hyacinth has strong spikes of rich blue flowers. (IVT 1983) (2n = 16)

'Ostara'

This standard dark blue has flowers with a hint of violet. (C van Waveren-Kruyff 1942) (2n = 25)

'Perle Brillante' (p. 194)

It is generally considered that newer flowers are bigger and better than the old, but this ancient hyacinth has massive, fleshy flowers on sturdy spikes that would be difficult to beat. The flowers are pale blue with turquoise on the reverse, especially lovely when the flowers are part-opened, allowing you to see the dark stems too. (1895) (2n = 31)

'Peter Stuyvesant' (p. 192)

One of the best dark blues, this has flowers that have paler edges and dark stems. It is apparently being grown in smaller quantities, which is a shame because it was, for a while, one of the best reasonably common dark-blue hyacinths. (M C Zonnenveld 1987)

'Professor de Hertogh' (p. 192)

The inky-blue flowers have hints of violet and purple, creating a wonderfully rich effect. (M C Zonnenveld 1988)

'Queen of the Blues'

The dark stems carry pale blue flowers that recurve. (A J van den Veldt 1870) (2n = 24)

'Satana' (p. 194)

The small florets on this hyacinth have narrow, reflexed tepals that are mid-blue with darker central stripes, on dark stems.

'Sky Jacket' (p. 192)

This exceptionally lovely hyacinth has large, fleshy flowers of a beautiful, pale blue on dark stems. The tepals have a deeper central strip and recurve slightly. This beautiful hyacinth is well worth paying a little extra for. (M C Zonnenveld 1976)

Modern Hyacinths bred by IVT (now Centre for Plant Breeding Research in the Netherlands)

Columns descending, from top left.

First column: 'Odysseus' 3, 'Helios' 4.

Second column: 'Hermes' 4, 'Minos' 3.

Third column: 'Aeilos' 3, 'Perseus' 4.

Fourth column: 'Kronos' 4, 'Helena' 3.

Fifth column: 'Nereus' 3, 'Pallas' 4.

White

White hyacinths are all rather similar, the main differences being in size, as well as the double flowers of 'Ben Nevis', 'Crystal Snow' and 'Madame Sophie'. 'Carnegie' and 'L'Innocence' are the most common whites, and of these I prefer 'L'Innocence' because of its larger blooms. If 'Grand Blanche Imperiale' ever becomes available it should be snapped up because of the huge, blush flowers.

White hyacinths
Columns descending, from top left.
First column: 'L'innocence' 4, 'Polar Giant' 3.
Second column: 'Carnegie' 3, 'Mont Blanc' 4.
Third column: 'Ben Nevis' 4, 'Snow White' 3.
Fourth column: 'Colosseum' 3, 'Madame Kruger' 4.
Fifth column: 'White Pearl' 4, 'Snow White' 3.

'Aeilos' (p. 195)
Large flowers with broad, smooth tepals of pure white. (IVT 1982) (2n = 32)

'Ben Nevis' (p. 196, 200)
Large, double flowers with several rows of long, narrow, straight tepals. The flowers have a yellow centre, and the outer tepals are often tinged with green. (M van Waveren 1942)

'Carnegie' (p. 196)
One of the two common white hyacinths (the other is 'L'Innocence'). This differs in that the flowers are smaller and less fleshy. The tepals are narrow, slightly ribbed, and often hooked. (A Lefeber 1935) (2n = 29)

'Colosseum' (p. 196)
Rather disappointingly small flowers, with ribbed and sometimes twisted tepals of pure white. (George V D Veld 1935)

'Crystal Snow' (p. 200)
The large, double flowers of this hyacinth are rather irregular in form, but the outer tepals are usually broad. The inner tepals are narrower and may be twisted. (new)

'Grand Blanche Imperiale'
This ancient hyacinth has huge flowers that are fleshy and white, with a faint pink blush that fades as the flowers mature. In the Voorhelm and Schneevoogt catalogue of 1798 it sold for 2 florins a bulb. (1798)

'L'Innocence' (p. 196, 198)
One of the two most common whites ('Carnegie' is the other) and often sold as prepared bulbs for Christmas flowering. It has large flowers with broad tepals. (V van der Vinne 1863, AGM-RHS) (2n = 27)

'Madame Kruger' (p. 196)
Large, pure-white, starry flowers; the inner tepals of this plant are often slightly ribbed and incurved. (D J Ziegler 1905)

'Madame Sophie' (p. 200)
This sport of 'L'Innocence' has double white flowers. The blooms are variable in form, and typically have normally formed outer tepals with a cluster of curved tepals in the centre. (J A Bronkhorst 1929) (2n = 27)

'Mont Blanc' (p. 196)
A pretty white hyacinth, its florets have equally sized tepals and it has pale green foliage. (Seger Bros 1944)

'Pallas' (p. 195)
The florets are small but have rounded tepals and

good form. It is an interesting alternative to other, common whites. (IVT 1980)

'Polar Giant' (p. 196)
This exceptional white has large flowers with rounded, smooth, broad tepals. (C J Zonneveld)

'Snow Blush'
This sport of 'Delft Blue' has white flowers with the gentlest pink blush on stems that are tinged with red. This is a pretty, pastel hyacinth. (A K Shipp new)

'Snow Queen'
Medium-sized flowers of pure white. (Verdegaal Bros 1945)

'Snow White' (p. 196, 201)
This is a small-flowered, Roman or fairy hyacinth. The flowers of this plant are pure white and the tepals are hooked and crinkled. (P van Reisen 1950)

'White Pearl' (p. 196, 201)
'Pink Pearl' has produced several sports, and 'White Pearl' is one of these. It has the same, medium-sized florets, with narrow tepals, the inner three usually with hooks. I have known it occasionally to produce pink or partly pink flowers on the spike. (Paardekoper 1954)

Pink, Red and Purple

This is the most varied range of colours, from soft pinks to deep blackcurrant purples and reds that almost achieve scarlet. 'Jan Bos' remains the most common red, but others worth trying where you need a strong red-pink are 'La Victoire' and 'Tubergen's Scarlet'. I would recommend you try some of the lilac or purple shades such as 'Splendid Cornelia', 'Violet Pearl', 'Mulberry Rose' and, if you can find it, striped 'Lord Balfour'. And you must add 'Distinction' or 'Woodstock' to your garden.

'Apple Blossom' (p. 197)
This sport of 'Dr Lieber' has pale pink flowers with narrow tepals to give a starry appearance. The flowers become deeper as they mature. (Leo Roozen pre-1954)

'Amethyst' (p. 199)
This sport of 'Marconi' has flowers of a pretty, violet shade. It is an unusual and attractive colour in the garden. (Langelaan-hulsebosch 1950)

'Chestnut Flower' Double (p. 200)
No double hyacinths are common, but this is often offered for sale and is a lovely cultivar with soft pink flowers that are loosely double. It is rather short in height with a low flower count, the florets being widely spaced on the stems. But the flowers are large and fleshy, and very pretty. (D Bakker 1880) (2n = 30)

'China Pink' (p. 197)
This sport of 'Delft Blue' has pretty, pale pink flowers on stems that rise above neat leaves. (1973) (2n = 30)

'Distinction' (p. 199)
Many catalogues list this as new, and its colour does come as a surprise to many, but it is hardly a recent introduction! Every garden should have 'Distinction' because of its rich, beetroot colour

Pink and red hyacinths
Columns descending,
from top left.
First column: 'Pink Pearl' 4,
'Appleblossom' 3.
Second column:
'Lady Derby' 3, 'Fondant' 4.
Third column:
'Pink Surprise' 4,
'China Pink' 3.
Fourth column:
'Tubergen's Scarlet' 3,
'Vuurbaak' 4.
Fifth column: 'Jan Bos' 4,
'La Victoire' 3.

tepals are paler at the edge, smooth, and recurve a little. It is not such a harsh shade as 'Pink Pearl', and ages more attractively. (G th Weijers 1983)

'Hollyhock' (p. 198)
This bright red double is probably the most commonly available double, and one of the best. It is a sport of 'Tubergen's Scarlet', and the flowers are intensely double, their centres packed with dozens of tiny petals and stamens. Like all doubles, the flowers last longer than single-flowered hyacinths, though there are usually fewer flowers on the spikes. It is a wonderful hyacinth to grow in pots for the home. (A C van der Schoot 1936)

'Jan Bos' (p. 197)
Any average selection of hyacinths in garden centres will include this bright hyacinth, which stands out from the pinks, blues and whites because of its bright red colour. The florets are neat, and the spikes tend to be narrow, though densely set with small flowers with crinkled tepals. While an excellent plant, more adventurous gardeners could try 'Tubergen's Scarlet' or 'Vuurbaak' for a change. (J Bos 1910) (2n = 24)

'La Victoire' (p. 197)
A showy hyacinth with bright red flowers, their narrow tepals being paler at the edge. The flowers face outwards and do not hang, and the foliage is flat against the ground. (D Bakker 1875) (2n = 16)

'Lady Derby' (p. 197)
Once a common pink hyacinth, this is seen less often now. The flowers are pale pink, with deeper stripes down the centre of the tepals, and often with hooks. The flowers recurve, and the stems are flushed with red. (V H Veen 1875) (2n = 24)

'Lord Balfour' (p. 199)
This distinctive hyacinth has large flowers, with long tepals that recurve when mature. Each tepal is wine violet with a deep central stripe and paler edges. It is a great cultivar for the garden because of the bicolour effect. (J W van der Veldt 1883) (2n = 24)

'Mulberry Rose'
This pretty hyacinth has small flowers with rounded tepals of lilac-pink. Fairly commercial and a good novelty hyacinth, though it is not as

Hyacinths
Photographed with double primroses.
Top row:
'Gypsy Queen',
'Woodstock', 'Splendid Cornelia'.
Centre row:
'Hollyhock', 'Blue Jacket'.
Bottom row:
'L'innocence', 'Fondant',
'Gypsy Princess'.

and neat habit – even the dark stems are beautiful. It is at its best when interplanted with white hyacinths or white grape hyacinths, to show off its colour to advantage. Its foliage is darker than 'Woodstock', which is the only other hyacinth of similar colouring. (C W F Hoogeveen 1880) (2n = 16)

'Eddison' (p. 200)
This rare double has beautiful flowers of mid-pink. The triangular tepals are arranged in several rows, each laying on the other to give a starry shape. The colour fades as the flowers age, and the centre of each flower is deeper than the outer edge to create a fascinating effect.

'Fondant' (p. 197, 198)
This is possibly the best of the pink hyacinths. The flowers are carried on reddish stems and are of moderate size, starry and bright pink. The

common now as in the mid-1990s. (G van der Mey 1946)

'Nereus' (p. 195)
A bright hyacinth, this has small, bell-shaped blooms of deep pink, the tepals often hooked. (IVT 1980) (2n = 26)

'Nimrod'
Re-introduced from Lithuania, this hyacinth has large, fleshy flowers that are pale, blush pink. (P Ritter 1860) (2n = 19)

'Paul Hermann' (p. 199)
The intense, lilac-pink flowers of this modern hyacinth are enhanced by their large size. The tepals are glossy, narrow, and recurve, and often have twisted or hooked tips. (Walter Blom & Sons 1984)

'Perseus' (p. 195)
A modern, bright pink (phlox pink) with dense spikes of blooms. These fade considerably as they age. (IVT 1982) (2n = 24)

'Pink Pearl' (p. 197)
If you buy a pot of deep-pink hyacinths in spring, the chances are that they will be 'Pink Pearl'. The flowers have narrow tepals, but they are densely packed on the spikes and are an intense, deep pink. The flowers become deeper as they age and the petals wither. (N Dames 1922, AGM-RHS) (2n = 16)

'Pink Surprise' (p. 197)
A superb new introduction, this has starry flowers with broad, triangular tepals of bright pink, producing 'full' spikes. The centre of each tepal is a deeper shade, and the leaves are neat. It is distinct enough to make it a good choice for pots and indoor decoration, and makes a fine, showy garden plant. (C J Zonneveld 1984)

'Princess Victoria'
Another good bedding hyacinth, the rose pink flowers are augmented by the red-flushed stems. The flowers fade noticeably as they age. (1865)

'Purple Sensation' (p. 199)
This is a fine cultivar with stocky stems of starry, purple flowers that have smooth, long, slightly recurved tepals. Most flowers have a few extra tepals to give full spikes of colour. (new)

'Rosalie'
This pale-pink Roman or fairy hyacinth has delicate stems of small flowers. (van der Waveren-Kruyff 1948) (2n = 17)

'Rosette' (p. 200)
This double hyacinth is a sport of 'Delight' and has large flowers of mid-pink. The flowers consist of six outer tepals of normal size packed with a centre of smaller, curved tepals. (G Vreeburg & Sons 1971)

'Splendid Cornelia' (p. 198, 199)
A modern hyacinth, this has neat flowers of a rounded shape. They are lilac pink, much paler at the edge of the tepals, with a lavender tinge on the reverse when opening. It has reddish stems and neat leaves. (G Th Weijers 1984)

Hyacinths: pinks, blends and purples
Columns descending, from top left.
First column: 'Top Hit' 4, 'Distinction' 3.
Second column: 'Violet' 3, 'Splendid Cornelia' 4.
Third column: 'Woodstock' 4, 'Purple Sensation' 3.
Fourth column: 'Paul Hermann' 3, 'Amethyst' 4.
Fifth column: 'Blue Peter' 4, 'Lord Balfour' 3.

'Top Hit' (p. 199)
Pastel lilacs are not common, and this is a welcome addition to the range. It has large, fleshy flowers with broad tepals. The inner three are often hooked and the edges of the tepals are paler than the centre. (new)

'Tubergen's Scarlet' (p. 197)
This bright hyacinth is similar to 'Jan Bos', but is a sport of the beetroot 'Distinction'. Its bright, deep colour makes it useful in bold bedding schemes. (van Tubergen 1920) (2n = 16)

'Violet' (p. 199)
This attractive hyacinth has fine spikes of overlapping florets on sturdy, dark stems above very low foliage that opens flat. (unknown)

'Violet Pearl'
This sport of 'Pink Pearl' has broad spikes of

flowers with narrow, recurved tepals in a bright colour that, though hardly violet, is a bold, rich, purple. (G H van Went & Sons 1954)

'Vuurbaak' (p. 197)
Red stems add to the intensity of the colour of the flowers of 'Vuurbaak'. These have narrow tepals, and the red flowers develop pale edges as they age. It also has dark green, neat foliage, and is an excellent choice for bedding. (C J Zonneveld 1948)

'Woodstock' (p. 198, 199)
This fine hyacinth is valuable for its deep, burgundy/beetroot flowers on dark stems. These are larger but slightly paler than 'Distinction', and typically have obviously hooked tepals. The foliage is also less dark than 'Distinction'. (new)

Yellow and Orange

Forget your prejudices and give yellow and orange hyacinths a try. I find that the orange colours are the most pleasing – though they are orange mousse rather than freshly squeezed. Apart from being a pleasant shade, it is unusual and allows for some interesting colour combinations in the spring garden. If you are stumped for ideas, just plant them in a blue-glazed pot. The yellows can be rather disappointing, especially if you thought you were going to get something like the picture on the packet. They are lovely, but only a pale, creamy yellow. My favourites are 'Gypsy Princess' and 'Yellow Hammer'.

'City of Haarlem' (p. 201)
Every garden centre offers this yellow hyacinth in autumn, and prepared bulbs are often available. It is usually something of a disappointment because coloured labels give the promise of bright yellow flowers, whereas they turn out primrose yellow at best and, in full sun, quickly fade to cream. The tepals often have green tips, especially if the plants are ever deprived of water as they grow, and the flowers are rather small, with smooth tepals. (J H Kersten 1893, AGM-RHS) (2n = 23)

'Gypsy Princess' (p. 198, 201)
This sport of 'Gypsy Queen' has flowers with narrow tepals that are grooved and slightly twisted and hooked. The colour is pale yellow

Double hyacinths
Columns descending, from top left. First column: 'Eddison' 4, 'Dreadnought' 3. Second column: 'Ben Nevis' 4, 'Rosette' 3. Third column: 'Crystal Palace' 3, 'Madame Sophie' 4. Fourth column: 'Crystal Snow' 4, 'General Kohler' 3. Fifth column: 'Sunflower' 3, 'Chestnut Flower' 4.

and similar to 'City of Haarlem', slightly deeper in the centre of the tepals. (new)

'Gypsy Queen' (p. 198, 201)
Few hyacinths cause such strong emotions as 'Gypsy Queen'; as many people hate it as find it irresistible. Yet the colour is unusual and useful in spring. The salmon orange flowers have twisted and grooved tepals that are hooked. (G van der Meij 1927, AGM-RHS)

'Helena' (p. 195)
Yellow hyacinths can look rather similar to each other, and this newer cultivar seems unexceptional, with small flowers of pale yellow that have narrow inner tepals. (IVT 1988) (2n = 16)

'Helios' (p. 195)
This is a delicate hyacinth with spikes of small flowers of pale yellow, fading to cream. (IVT 1983) (2n = 16)

'Hermes' (p. 195, 201)
This hyacinth has flowers that are similar to 'Gypsy Princess', with narrow tepals but perhaps a little richer in colour. (IVT 1985)

'Odysseus' (p. 195)
A salmon-pink hyacinth with hooked, inner tepals and deeper stripes down the centre of each tepal. It is paler than 'Gypsy Queen', and the flowers are smaller but less wrinkled. (IVT 1983) (2n = 16)

'Oranje Boven' (p. 201)
The colour of this orange hyacinth is similar to 'Gypsy Queen', but the flowers have narrower tepals. (A Vanshie 1870) (2n = 16)

'Prins Hendrik' (p. 201)
A rich yellow hyacinth that is no longer grown commercially. (M van der Vlugt 1910)

'Prinses Maria Christina'
This variety's flowers are of a soft apricot colour. (P Hopman 1948)

'Sunflower' (p. 200)
Of all the ancient hyacinths that should be reintroduced to general cultivation, perhaps this has the greatest claim because its buff yellow, double flowers are so beautiful and unlike

anything else. The flowers are intensely double and a wonderful, pastel shade. However, Alan Shipp says it is very slow to increase, and it may never become a commercial cultivar again. (J H Veen pre-1897)

'Yellow Hammer' (p. 201)
This yellow hyacinth has flowers with narrow tepals that open quite a rich shade but fade as they mature, to primrose yellow. (J H Veen 1883) (2n = 16)

'Yellow Queen' (p. 201)
This sport of 'Gypsy Queen' has the same flower shape as the original, with rather crinkled tepals, the inner three being narrower than the outer. Most yellow hyacinths are rather disappointing, never quite fulfilling the promise of the pictures in catalogues, but this is among the most yellow of all, and is quite deep in bud. Probably the best bet if you really want a yellow hyacinth. (J S Pennings 1988)

Yellow, orange and white
Columns descending, from top left.
First column:
'Yellow Hammer' 4,
'City of Haarlem' 3.
Second column:
'Prins Hendrik' 3,
'Yellow Queen' 4.
Third column: 'Hermes' 4,
'Snow White' 3.
Fourth column:
'Gypsy Princess' 3,
'Gypsy Queen' 4.
Fifth column:
'Orange Boven' 3,
'White Pearl' 4.

Glossary

Acid – of soil, with a pH of less than 7 (which is neutral). It is the opposite of alkaline. The pH can be lowered (made more acidic) a little by the addition of sulphur.

Acute – pointed.

Alkaline – of soil, with a pH of more than 7 (which is neutral). It is the opposite of acid. Alkaline soils are found on limestone and chalk.

Alpine House – a greenhouse that is occasionally heated to prevent severe frosts reaching plants. Usually well ventilated and not heated.

Anther – the male part of the flower that sheds pollen.

Axil – the junction of a leaf and stem. In most bulbs the leaf axil is hidden within the bulbs itself, but the shoots in the axil develop into new bulbs.

Base plate – the bottom of the bulb – the compressed stem from which the leaves, often present as scales, grow.

Breaking – the process by which virus infection causes the colour to be removed from parts of the flower, usually in streaks. 'Broken' tulips were once highly prized but now only a few enthusiasts continue to cultivate them.

Breeder – a tulip that has been bred specifically, within rigid parameters, to be infected with virus to produce a 'broken' (rectified) flower.

Bulb – the storage organ, comprising a series of fleshy leaves or scales attached to the base plate.

Bulblet – a small bulb that forms in the axil at first and is then seen at the side of the parent bulb.

Corona – in daffodils, the petal-like structure in the centre of the flower.

Cultivar – a horticultural variety that is usually deliberately produced but is occasionally found in the wild. Cultivars are propagated by vegetative means, and not by seed.

Double – more than one set of tepals.

Eye – the centre of the bloom.

Filament – the part of the stamen that supports the anther.

Forcing – using a combination of chilling and then artificial heat to promote unseasonably early flowers.

Glaucous – grey or bluish in colour.

Hybrid – a cross of two different plants. These may be two species, two varieties, or two cultivars or a mixture.

Increase – the natural multiplication of the bulbs.

John Innes Compost – a loam-based (soil) compost with added peat and grit/sand and nutrients. There are three potting grades; No. 3 has the most nutrients.

Mucro – white curved tip of narcissus tepals that holds the bud closed.

Naturalize – planting bulbs in grass or some other area where they are grown with minimal maintenance and may increase naturally.

Offset – a small bulb that develops within the parent bulb at first but is later released as the outer scales dry.

Ovary – the female part of the flower that contains ovules, which, when fertilized, will develop into seeds.

Pedicel – the stem of a single flower. In *Narcissus*, the part of the stem that is above the spathe.

Peduncle – the strict term for the flower stem of a *Narcissus*. The lower part that might support more than one flower, according to species or cultivar.

Perianth – the six floral segments of the flower, comprising six tepals.

Pollen – (usually) yellow powder, produced by anthers, that contains the male gametes (sex cells).

Pollination – the transfer of pollen to the stigma of the same plant (selfing) or another (cross-pollination).

Raiser – the person that produced, by hybridisation or by noticing a sport, a new cultivar or hybrid.

Rectify – the 'breaking' of tulip flower colours by virus infection.

Scale – the fleshy leaves that comprise the bulb.

Scape – a term for the flower stem in daffodils and hyacinths.

Scooping – removal of the base plate of hyacinths to promote the production of bulbils, used by commercial growers for propagation.

Self, selfing – pollination of a plant by its own pollen.

Sepal – the outer part of the flower, which usually protects it when in bud. In most bulb flowers it is similar to the petals, and collectively they are known as tepals.

Spathe – the papery structure that surrounds the *Narcissus* flower in bud.

Spike – a flower stem with stalkless flowers (generally, any upright, unbranched flower stem).

Sport – a spontaneous mutation that usually affects one characteristic such as flower colour. Many plants produce colour sports but tulips seem especially prone to sporting, producing new flower shapes and variegated leaves.

Stamen – the male part of the flower, comprising anther and filament.

Stigma – the receptive part of the female part of the flower, at the end of the style, which leads to the ovary.

Stolon – a creeping underground stem.

Style – the tube that connects the ovary to the stigma.

Tepal – for many bulb flowers (including the three discussed in this book) the collective term for the sepals and petals, since these are similar in size and colour.

Variety – a unit of classification, that may divide a species in to smaller units.

Contacts

UNITED KINGDOM

Bloms Bulbs Limited
Primrose Nurseries
Melchbourne
Beds MK44 1ZZ
Tel: 01234 709099
www.blomsbulbs.com

Broadleigh Gardens
Bishops Hull
Taunton
Somerset TA4 1AE
Tel: 01823 286231
www.broadleighbulbs.co.uk

Carncairn Daffodils Ltd
Broughshane
Ballymena
Co. Antrim BT43 7HF
Tel: 01266 861216

Daffodil Society (UK)
Tel: 01257 425541
www.daffsoc.freeserve.co.uk

De Jager
Staplehurst Road,
Marden
Kent TN12 9BP
Tel: 01622 831235
www.dejagerflowerbulbs.co.uk

Hofflands Daffodils
Little Totham Road
Goldhanger
Maldon
Essex CM9 8AP
Tel: 01621 788678

National Plant Collection
Stable Courtyard
Wisley Garden
Woking GU23 6QP
Tel: 01483 211465
www.nccpg.com

Quality Daffodils
14 Roscarrack Close
Falmouth
Cornwall TR11 4PJ
Tel: 01326 317959
www.qualitydaffodils.co.uk

Steve Holden Daffodils
Sunny Corner
Copse Lane
Walberton
Arundel
West Sussex BN18 0QH
Tel: 01243 542070

Tyrone Daffodils
90 Ballynahatty Road
Omagh
Co. Tyrone BT78 1TD
Tel: 01662 242192

Van Tubergen UK
Bressingham Gardens
Thetford Road
Bressingham
Diss
Norfolk IP22 2AB
Tel: 01379 686900
www.vantubergen.co.uk

J Walkers Bulbs
Washway House Farm
Washway Road
Holbeach
Spalding
Lincolnshire PE12 7PP
Tel: 01406 426216
www.taylors-bulbs.com

UNITED STATES

American Daffodil Society
4126 Winfield Road
Columbus, OH 43220-4606
www.daffodilusa.org

Bill Welch
PO Box 1736
Carmel Valley, CA 93924
Tel: 531 659 3830
www.billthebulbbaron.com

Bloms Bulbs, Inc.
491–233 Glen Eagle Square
Glen Mills, PA 19342
Tel: 1 866 7 885477
www.blomsbulbs.com

Cherry Creek Daffodils
21700 S W Chapman Road
Sherwood, OR 97140-8608
Tel: 703 783 6237
www.cherrydaf.net

David Burdick Daffodils & More
PO Box 495
Dalton, MA 01227
Tel: 413 443 1581
www.daffodilsandmore.com

Dutch Flowers
PO Box 843
Babylon, NY 11702
Tel: 703 783 6237
www.dutchflowers.com

Dutch Gardens
4 Intervale Road
Burlington, VT 05401
Tel: 1 888 821 0448
www.dutchgardens.com

McClure & Zimmerman
PO Box 368
Friesland, WI 53935
Tel: 1 800 883 6998
www.mzbulb.com

Mitsch Novelty Daffodils
PO Box 218
Hubbard, OR 97032

Tel: 503 651 2742
www.web-ster.com/havensr/
mitsch/

Nancy Wilson Miniature Daffodils
6525 Briceland-Thorn Road
Garberville, CA 95542
Tel: 707 923 2407
www.asis.com/~nwilson

New York Botanical Gardens
200th St and Kazimiroff Blvd
Bronx, NY 10458
Tel: 717 817 8700
www.nybg.org

Old House Gardens
536 Third St
Ann Arbor, MI 48103-4957
Tel: 734 995 1486
www.oldhousegardens.com

Veldheer
12755 Quincy St & US 31 N
Holland, MI 49424
Tel: 616 399 1900
www.veldheertulip.com

Wooden Shoe Tulip Farm
33814 S Meridian Road
Woodburn, OR 97071
Tel: 503 634 2243
www.woodenshoe.com

AUSTRALIA

J N Hancock Daffodils
2 Jacksons Hill Road
Menzies Creek
Victoria 3159
Tel: 03 9754 3328
www.daffodilbulbs.com.au

Jackson Daffodils
PO Box 77, Geeveston
Tasmania 7116
Tel: 03 6297 6203
www.jacksonsdaffodils.com.au

NEW ZEALAND

Koanga Daffodils
PO Box 4129
Hamilton East
Tel: 07 829 5551
www.geocities.com/koanganz

G and F Miller Daffodils
564 Frontier Road
RD6
Te Awamutu

THE NETHERLANDS

Hortus Bulborum
Zuidkerkenlaan 23A
Limmen
Tel: 0251 231286
www.hortus-bulborum.nl/
index2.htm

Jan Pennings – Breezand
Schorweg I4 1764 MC
Breezand
www.pennings-de-bilt.nl

**KAVB (Royal General
Bulbgrowers' Association)**
PO Box 175
NL 2180 AD Hillegom
Tel: 0252 536951
www.kavb.nl

Keukenhof
Stationsweg 166a
2161 AM Lisse
Tel: 0252 465555
www.keukenhof.nl

Walter Blom & Zoon BV
Hyacinthenlaan 2
2182 DE Hillegom
Tel: 0252 519444
www.blomsbulbs.com

Bibliography

Blanchard, John, *Narcissus: A Guide to Wild Daffodils*, 1990
Bowles, E A, *My Garden in Spring*, 1914
Bowles, E A, *The Narcissus*, 1934
Royal Bulbgrowers' Association, *Classified List and International Register of Tulip Names*, 1996
Dash, Mike, *Tulipomania*, 1999
Hall, Sir Daniel, *The Tulip*, 1929
International Daffodil Register and Classified List (Sixth Supplement)
International Daffodil Register and Classified List, 1998
Jacob, Joseph, *Tulips*, 1912
Jefferson-Brown, Michael, *Narcissus*, 1991
Killingbeck, Stanley, *Tulips*, 1990
Mathew, Brian, *Flowering Bulbs for the Garden*, 1987
Pavord, Anna, *The Tulip*, 1999
Wells, James S, *Modern Miniature Daffodils*, 1989

Index

Page references for illustrations are in **bold**.

Daffodils (Narcissus)
'Abalone' 40, **59**
'Abba' 60
Aberfoyle' 40
'Accent' 40
'Achduart' 54
'Acropolis' 60, **65**
'Actaea' 83
'Admiration' 79, **79**
'Aircastle' 54
'Akepa' 68
'Alliance' 71
'Altruist' 54

'Ambergate' 40, **40**
'Amberglow'
'American Shores' 33
'American Heritage' 33
'Amor' **40**, 55
'Amstel' 61, **64**
'Angel Eyes' 83
'Apotheose' 61
'Apricot Lace' 85
'April Tears' 68
'Arcady' 40, **59**
'Arctic Gold' 33
'Arish Mell' 68

'Arkle' 33
'Armada' 40
'Articol' 86
'Ashmore' 41
'Askelon' 14
'Astropink' 86, **89**
'Audubon' 55
'Avalanche' 76, 79, **79**
'Avalon' 41
'Baby Moon' 74
'Badbury Rings' 55
'Baldock' 61, **61**
'Ballygarvey' 33, **35**

'Bandleader' **40**, 41
'Barleythorpe' 41
'Bantam' 41
'Barnum' 33
'Barri Conspiucuus' 16, **42**, 56
'Bartley' 71
'Bath's Flame' 16, 55, **58**
'Bawnboy' 33
'Beacon' 16
'Beauvallon' 61, **65**
'Bedruthan' 41, **58**
'Beersheba' 14

'Beige Beauty' 55, **59**
'Belcanto' 86
'Bell Rock' 33, **33**
'Bell Song' **52**, **70**, 74
'Ben Hee' 41
'Benbane Head' 83
'Berlin' **13**, 41
'Beryl' 71
'Binkie' 15, 41, **41**, **70**, 88
'Birma' 55
'Biscayne' 33
'Blarney' **44**, 55
'Blushing Maiden' 61, **64**

'Bobbysoxer' 74
'Border Beauty' 42
'Boscastle' 75
'Boscoppa' 86, **86**
'Boslowick' 86, **86**
'Bossa Nova' 55, 56
'Bossiney' 86, **89**
'Bosvale' 86, **89**
'Boulder Bay' 42
'Brabazon' 34
'Brackenhurst' 42
'Bram Warnaar' 34
'Bravoure' 34, **33**

'Brer Fox' 15
'Bridal Crown' **38**, 61
'Bright Spot' 79, 79
'Broadway Star' 86
'Broomhill' 42
'Bryanston' 42
'Budock Bells' 68
'Buffawn' **40**, 75
'Bullseye' 55
'Bunting' 75
'Butter and Eggs' 16, 61, **62**
'By Jove' 34
'Calgary' 62
'Camelot' 35, 42
'Candida' 62
'Cantabile' 83
'Cape Cornwall' 42, **42**
'Capisco' 55, **57**
'Carbineer' 16
'Carib' 71
'Carib Gipsy' 42
'Carlton' 42
'Caro Nome' 43
'Carrara' 55
'Cassata' 87
'Castle Rings' **61**, 62
'Cazique' 71
'Centrefold' 55, **57**
'Ceylon' 16, 43
'Changing Colours' 87
'Chanterelle' 87
'Charity May' 71, **73**
'Charter' 43
'Cheerfulness' 62
'Cheer Leader' 55, **56**
'Chesterton' 84
'Chickerell' 55, **57**
'Chinese Coral' 15, 34
'Chinita' 80, **81**
'Chit Chat' 75
'Chivalry' 34
'Chromacolour' 43
'C J Backhouse' 43, **58**
'Clockface' 55
'Codlins and Cream' 62, **62**
'Colorama' **86**, 87
'Coombe Creek' **42**, 71
'Congress' 87
'Conspicuus' 16, **42**, 56
'Content' 15
'Coquille' 43
'Corbiere' 15, **33**, 34
'Corbridge' 43
'Cornish Chuckles' **42**, 90
'Cotinga' 71, **73**
'Countdown' **51**, 56
'Courage' 14

'Crackington' **46**, 62
'Cragford' 80
'Craigywarren' 43
'Cristobal' 34
'Crock of Gold' 34
'Crocus' 15
'Curlew' 70, 75, **88**
'Dan du Plessis' **79**, 80
'Dawn Mist' 43
'Daydream' 43
'Delibes' **41**, 43
'Delnashaugh' 62
'Desdemona' 43
'Dickcissel' 75
'Dimity' 56, **56**
'Dimple' 84
'Dispatch Box' 34
'Doctor Hugh' 56
'Dolly Mollinger' 87
'Donore' 34
'Double Event' 63
'Double Fashion' 63
'Dove Wings' 71
'Dream Castle' 56, **59**
'Drumlin' 34
'Duet' 63
'Duke of Windsor' 43
'Dulcimer' 84
'Dutch Master' 34
'Early Splendour' **79**, 80
'Eastern Dawn' 44, **44**
'Eaton Song' 90
'Edna Earl' 56
'Eland' 75
'Elysian Fields' 44
'Elixir' 63, **65**
'Elvira' **39**, 80
'Emerald' 84
'Eminent' 56
'Empress' 14
'Empress of Ireland' 14, 35
'Ensemble' **46**, 63
'Entrancement' 35
'Envoy' 35, **59**
'Erlicheer' **51**, 63
'Evendine' 44
'Exception' 35
'Exemplar' 35
'Exotic Beauty' 63
'Falaise' 16
'Falconet' 80
'Fashion' **62**, 87
'Favourite' 44
'February Gold' 71
'February Silver' 71
'Feeling Lucky' 44
'Felindre' 84

'Ferndown' 56, **56**
'Festivity' 44
'Filly' 44
'Firebrand' 56, **62**
'Flower Record' 44
'Flying Saucer' 45
'Fort Knox' 35
'Fortune 15, 44
'Foundling' 71
'Fragrant Breeze' 45
'Fragrant Rose' 45
'Freedom Rings' 45, **49**
'Frostkist' **51**, 72
'Gay Kybo' 63
'Gaylord' 45
'Gay Time' 63
'Georgie Girl' 72
'Geranium' **41**, 80
'Gigantic Star' 45
'Gin and Lime' **33**, 35
'Glowing Phoenix' **62**, 63
'Glenfarclas' 35
'Gold Convention' 45
'Golden Aura' **35**, 45
'Golden Bells' **41**, 84
'Golden Bear' **61**, 63
'Golden Dawn' 80
'Golden Ducat' 16, 63, **76**
'Golden Jewel' 45
'Golden Rapture' 36
'Golden Riot' 36
'Golden Vale' 36
'Goldfinch' see 'Pet Finch'
'Goldfinger' 36
'Gold Medal' 36
'Good Measure' 45
'Gossamer' 57
'Gouache' **40**, 45
'Grand Monarque' 80
'Grasmere' 36
'Greenpark' 84
'Green Pearl' 84
'Hambledon' 45
'Hammoon' 57
'Hawera' 68, **70**
'Helford Dawn' 46, **46**
'Helford Sunset' 46, **49**
'Helios' 15, 46
'Hero' 15, 36
'Highfield Beauty' 81, **81**
'High Note' **35**, 75
'High Society' 46
'Hillstar' 75
'Holiday Fashion' 46
'Honeybird' 15, 36
'Honolulu' 63
'Hoopoe' 79, 81

'Horn of Plenty' 69, **69**
'Hospodar' 46, **58**
'Hugh Town' 81
'Ice Follies' 21, 46, **66**
'Ice King' 63
'Ice Wings' 69, **69**
'Icicle' 69
'Inca' 72
'Indian Maid' **75**, 76
'Indora' 64, **64**
'Intrigue' **75**, 76
'Irish Minstrel' 46
'Itzim' 38, 72, **76**
'Jack Snipe' 72
'Jack Wood' 87
'Jamage' 81, **81**
'Jamaica Inn' 64
'Jantje' **86**, 87
'Jenny' 72, **73**
'Jetfire' **38**, 72
'John Daniel' **61**, 64
'Jubilation' 46
'Jumblie' 90
'Kanchenjunga' 14
'Kaydee' 72
'Kazuko' 57
'Kenellis' **51**, 85
'Kildrum' 57
'Kilworth' **44**, 47
'Kimmeridge' **44**, 57
'King Alfred' 14, 36
'Kinglet' **75**, 76
'King of the North' 15
'Kingscourt' 36
'King's Grove' 36
'King's Ransom' 37
'Kissproof' **40**, 47
'Kiwi Magic' 64, **64**
'Kiwi Sunset' **61**, 64
'Klamath' 47
'Krakatoa' 47
'La Argentina' **41**, 47
'La Belle' 76
'Lady Ann' 47
'Lapwing' **35**, 69
'Larkwhistle' 72
'Last Word' 57
'Lavender Lass' 72
Leedsii 14
'Lemon Beauty' 87
'Lemon Cloud' 37
'Lemon Drops' 69
'Lemon Glow' 37, **76**
'Liberty Bells' 69
'Lichfield' 57, **59**
'Lilac Charm' see
'Lavender Lass'

'Limbo' 47
'Lingerie' 64
'L'Innocence' **38**, 81
'Little Beauty' 37
'Little Gem' 37
'Little Jewel' 57, **57**
'Little Witch' 73
'Liverpool Festival' **46**, 47
'Lizard Light' 47
'Loch Hope' 47
'Loch Owskeich' 47
'Logan Rock' **75**, 76
'Lorikeet' **33**, 37
'Lucifer' 47, **62**
'Lundy Light' **46**, 47
'Lyric' 84
'Madame de Graaff' 14
'Madam Speaker' **42**, 64
'Madison' 64, **65**
'Magnificence' 15
'Manly' 64
'Manon Lescaut' 47
'Marie-Jose' 70, 87, 88
'Marlborough' 48, **53**
'Martha Washington' 81, **81**
'Martinette' **18**, **38**, 76
'Matador' 81
'Mary Copeland' 16, 64
Mediicoronati 14
'Menehay' **86**, 88
'Merlin' 57
'Merry Bells' 69, **69**
'Merrymeet' **61**, 65
'Mike Pollock' **81**, 82
'Millennium Sunset' 42, 48
'Millgreen' 37
'Milan' 84
'Minnow' **76**, 82
'Mission Bells' 69
'Misty Glen' 48
'Mitylene' 48, **62**
'Mite' 73
'Modern Art' 48
'Mona Lisa' 48
'Mondragon' **86**, 88
'Mongleath' 48
'Moonlight Sonata' 15
'Mount Hood' 37
'Mountjoy' 76
'Mrs Ernst H Krelage' 14
'Mrs Langtry' 57, **58**
'Mrs R O Backhouse' 48
'Mulatto' 37
'My My' 48
'Nansidwell' 48, **49**
naturalisiing 23

'New-Baby' 76
'Newcastle' 15, **33**, 37
'New World' 48
'Night Music' 64, 65
'Niveth' 69, **69**
'Nonchalent' **56**, 58
'Nosie Posie' 37
'Notre Dame' 48
'Nuage' 49
'Obdam' **38**, 65, 66
'Odorus Rugulosus' 76, **76**
'Orange Ice Follies' 48, **66**
'Orange Phoenix' 16
'Orangery' 88
origin of name 12
'Ormeau' 49
'Oryx' 77
'Osmington' 49
'Palmares' 88
'Pampaluna' **86**, 88
'Panache' 37
Paper White
Grandiflorus' **23**, 82
'Papillon Blanc' 88
'Papua' 65
'Paricutin' 49
'Parisienne' 88
'Park Springs' **57**, 58
'Passionale' **44**, 49
'Pastorale' 49
'Patois' 84
'Pay Day' **30**, 37
'Peach Prince' **64**, 65
'Peeping Tom' 73
'Pengarth' 49
'Penkivel' 49, **49**
'Penril' 73, **73**
'Penstraze' **75**, 77
'Pentire' **86**, 88
'Peppercorn' 73, **73**
'Perdredda' 58
'Perimeter' **46**, 58
'Pet Finch' 77
'Petit Four' 65
'Petrel' 70, **70**
'Pheasant's Eye' see *N.
poeticus var. recurvus*
'Phoenix' 16
'Pimpernel' 49
'Pinafore' 49
'Pink Angel' 77
'Pink Charm' 50
'Pink Dew' 37, **38**
'Pink Formal' 89, **89**
'Pink Glacier' 89, **89**
'Pink Holly' 89
'Pink Pageant' 65

'Pink Paradise' 66
'Pink Smiles' **41**, 50
'Pink Tango' 89, **89**
'Pink Tea' 50
'Pinza' 50
'Pipe Major' 49
'Pipit' 70, 75, 77, **88**
'Pixie' 77
'Pixie's Sister' 77
'Polly's Pearl' **79**, 82
'Poppy's Choice' **61**, 66
'Potential' 37
'Praecox' 84
'Precedent' **44**, 50
'Precocious' **49**, 50
'Princeps' 38, **39**
'Printal' 89
'Professor Einstein' 50
'Prophet' 38
'Pueblo' 77
'Purbeck' 58
'Queensland' 50
'Quail' **24**, **41**, 77
'Quetzal' 84
'Quickstep' 77
'Quince' 90
'Radjel' **61**, 66
'Rainbow' 50, **53**
'Rapture' 73, **73**
'Ravenhill' **57**, 58
'Red Devon' 50
'Redhill' **41**, 50
'Redstart' **44**, 58
'Regal Bliss' 50, **51**
'Reggae' 73
'Replete' **38**, 66
'Riding Mill' 58
'Rijnvelds Early Sensation'
    38
'Ringleader' 51
'Ring of Fire' **41**, 50
'Rippling Waters' 70
'Rip Van Winkle' 66, **76**
'Rival' 73
'Romance' 51
'Rosado' 89
'Roscarrick' 73
'Rosemoor Gold' **75**, 77
'Rustom Pasha' **39**, 51
'Sabine Hay' 58
'Saint Keverne' **41**, 51
'Saint Keyne' **81**, 82
'Saint Patrick's Day' 51
'Salome' 51
'Sarah' 51
'Satellite' 74
'Satin Pink' 51

'Scarlet Gem' 82
'Seagull' 58, **58**
'Sealing Wax' 51
'Segovia' **52**, 59
'Serena Lodge' 66
'Sherborne' **61**, 66
'Shot Silk' 70
Showing 18
'Sidley' 59
'Silent Valley' 38
'Silver Bells' **69**, 70
'Silver Chimes' 82
'Silvermere' 51, **59**
'Sir Watkin' **39**, 52
'Sir Winston Churchill' 66
'Skerry' **51**, 52
'Snoopie' 74
'Snow Frills' 52
'Soldier Brave' **40**, 52
'Soleil d'Or' 83
'Sorbet' 89
'Spaniards Inn' 67, **89**
'Sparnon' **51**, 89
'Special Envoy' 52
'Spellbinder' **14**, 15, 38
'Sportsman' 52, **56**
'Spring Dawn' 52
'Standard Value' 38, **41**
'Stainless' **52**, 53, **70**
'Stratosphere' 78
'Strines' 53
'Stromboli' 53
'Sugarbush' 78
'Sugar Loaf' **64**, 67
'Sulphur Phoenix' 16, **62**,
    67
'Sun Disc' 78
'Sunnyside Up' 89
'Sunrise' **58**, 59
'Surfside' **73**, 74
'Suzy' 78
'Swaledale' 53
'Sweet Blanche' **75**, 78
'Sweetness' 78
'Swift Arrow' 74
'Tahiti' **61**, **65**, 67
'Tamar Fire' **46**, 67
'Tamar Lad' **56**, 59
'Tamar Snow' 53, **53**
'Taslass' **64**, 67
'Tater-du' 70
'Tedstone' 38
'Telamonius Plenus' 16, 67
'Testament' 53
'Tête-a-Tête' 16, **17**, **38**, 90
'Texas' 67
'Thalia' 70, **76**

'The Alliance' 71
'Thoughtful' **69**, 70
'Tibet' 53
'Tiffany' 85
'Tiffany Jade' **56**, 59
'Tiritomba' **86**, 90
'Tittle-Tattle' 78
'Topolino' 38, **38**
'Torrianne' 53, **53**
'Toto' 91
'Tracey' **73**, 74
'Tranquil Morn' 59, **59**
'Trappist' 14
'Trebah' **42**, 53
'Trena' 74
'Tresamble' **69**, 70
'Trevithian' 78
'Trewarvas' 53, **53**
'Tricollet' 90
'Trilune' 90
'Tripartite' 90, **131**
'Triple Crown' 59
'Trousseau' 39
'Tudor Minstrel' 53
'Tuesday's Child' 70
'Tullybeg' 59
'Tyrone Gold' 39
'Ulster Prince' 39
'Uncle Duncan' 39, **46**
'Unique' **65**, 67
'Unsurpassable' 39
'Valdrome' 90
'Valley Forge' 39
'Van Sion' 16, 67
'Variant' **38**, 54
'Vernal Prince' 60
'Verona' 60
'Vigil' 39
'Viking' 39
'Virginia Waters' 60
'Vulcan' 54
'Walton' **75**, 78
'Waterperry' 78
'Westward' 68
'Whang Hi' **73**, 74
'Wheal Coates' **75**, 78
'Whitbourne' 60
'White Lady' **58**, 60
'White Lion' 68
'White Marvel' 68, **70**, **88**
'Widgeon' 54
'Willy Dunlop' 54
'Windjammer' 39
'Winfrith' 54
'Woodgreen' 54
'Worcester' 54
'W P Milner' 39, **39**

'Yellow Cheerfulness' **65**, 68
'Yes Please'

Hyacinths
'Aeilos' **195**, 196
'Amethyst' 197, **199**
'Apple Blossom' 197, 197
'Ben Nevis' 196, **196**, **200**
'Bismark' **192**, 193
'Blue Blazer' **192**, 193
'Blue Haze' 193
'Blue Jacket' 193, **198**
'Blue Magic' **192**, 193
'Blue Peter' 193, **199**
'Blue Star' **190**, **192**, 193
'Borah' 193, **194**
'Carnegie' 196, **196**
'Chestnut Flower' 197, **200**
'China Pink' 197, **197**
'City of Bradford' 193, **194**
'City of Haarlem' **200**, **201**
'Colosseum' **196**, 200
'Concorde' 193
'Cote d'Azur' 193
'Crystal Palace' 193, **200**
'Crystal Snow' **196**, 200
'Debutante' **192**, 193
'Delft Blue' 193
'Diana' **187**, 193, **194**
'Distinction' 197, **199**
'Doctor Stresemann' 194
'Dreadnought' 194, **200**
'Duchess of Westminster'
    194, **194**
'Eddison' 198, **200**
'Fondant' **197**, 198, **198**
'Gainsborough' 194, **194**
'General Kohler' 194, **200**
'Goluboj Elektron' 194, **194**
'Grand Blanche Imperiale'
    196
'Grand Monarque' 194
'Gypsy Princess' **198**, 200,
    201
'Gypsy Queen' **198**, 201,
    201
'Helena' **195**, 201
'Helios' **195**, 201
'Hermes' **195**, 201, **201**
'Hollyhock' 198, **198**
'Indigo King' 194
'Jan Bos' **197**, 198
'Koh-i-nor' 194, **194**
'Kronos' **192**, 194, 195
'La Victoire' **197**, 198
'Lady Derby' **197**, 198
'L'innocence' **196**, 196, **198**

'Lord Balfour' 198, **199**
'Madame Kruger' 196, **196**
'Madame Sophie' 196, **200**
'Marie' **192**, 194
'Maryon' 195
'Minos' 195, **195**
'Miss Molly Gilroy' 195
'Mont Blanc' 196, **196**
'Mulberry Rose' 198
'Myosotis' **194**, 195
'Nestor' 195
'Nereus' **195**, 199
'Nimrod' 199
'Odysseus' **195**, 201
'Oranje Boven' 201, **201**
'Ostara' 195
'Pallas' 195, **195**
'Paul Hermann' 199, **199**
'Perle Brilliante' **194**, 195
'Perseus' **195**, 199
'Peter Stuyvesant' **192**, 195
'Pink Pearl' **197**, 199
'Pink Surprise' **197**, 199
'Polar Giant' **196**, 197
'Princess Victoria' 199
'Prins Hendrik' 201, **201**
'Prinses Maria Christina' 201
'Professor de Hertogh'
    192, 195
'Purple Sensation' 199, **199**
'Queen of the Blues' 195
'Rosalie' 199
'Rosette' 199, **200**
'Satana' **194**, 195
'Sky Jacket' **192**, 195
'Snow Blush' **181**, 197
'Snow Queen' 197
'Snow White' **196**, 197
'Splendid Cornelia' **198**,
    199, **199**
'Sunflower' **200**, 201
'Top Hit' **199**, 200
'Tubergen's Scarlet' **197**, 200
'Violet Pearl' 200
'Vuurbaak' **197**, 200
'White Pearl' **196**, 197
'Woodstock' **198**, **199**, 200
'Yellow Hammer' 201, **201**
'Yellow Queen' 201, **201**
Hyacinthus orientalis 193

Narcissus
N. asturiensis 91
N. bicolour 14
N. bulbocodium 91
N canaliculatus **28**, **76**, 92
N. cantabricus **27**, 92

N. cyclamineus 92
N. hispanicus 14
N. jonquilla 93
N. obvallaris 14, **39**, 93
N. moschatus 14, **39**, 93
N. poeticus 14, 16, 93, **131**
N. poeticus 'Plenus' 65
N. pseudonarcissus 14, 94
N. romieuxii 92
N. rupicola 94
N. serotinus 94
N. viridiflorus 93, 94

Tulipa
T. acuminata 96, 176, **176**
T. aucheriana 176
T. bakeri 176, **176**
T. batalinii 176
T. biflora 177
T. clusiana **88**, 95, **95**,
    169, **176**, 177
T. dasystemon see *T. tarda*
    179
T. eichleri 177
T. fosteriana 177
T. greigii 177
T. hageri 177
T. humilis 178
T. kaufmanniana 178
T. kolpakowskiana 178
T. linifolia 178
T. orphanidea **176**, 178
T. ostrowskiana **176**, 178
T. praestans **76**, 178
T. primulina **176**, 178
T. saxatilis 179
T. sprengeri 179
T. subpraestans 179
T. sylvestris 179
T. tarda 179
T. tetraphylla **176**, 180
T. turkestanica 180
T. undulatifolia 180
T. urumiensis 180
T. vvedenskyi **169**, 180

Tulips
'Abba' 116, **143**
'Abra' 119
'Abu Hassan' **119**, 124
'Addis' 171
'Adonis' 144, **146**
'Ad Rem' 130
'Adrian T Dominique' 153
'Agrass White' 119
'Air' 157
'Akela' 136, **136**

'Alabaster' 136
'Aladdin' 88, **143**, 144, **169**
'Aladdin's Record' 144
'Aleppo' 149
'Alfi' 119, **140**
'Alfred Cortot' 166
'Ali Baba' 172
'Allegretto' 162
'Allegria' 119
'Amazone' 119
'American Dream' 130
'Amethyst' 157
'Amsterdam Arena' 149, **150**
'Ancilla' 166
'Angelique' 162
'Anna Jose' 119
'Annie Schilder' 119
'Antonio Moro' 119
'Apeldoorn' 130, **132**
'Apeldoorn's Elite' 131
'Apricot Beauty' 113, **113**, **147**
'Apricot Impression' 131
'Apricot Parrot' **113**, 157
'Arabian Mystery' **117**, 119
'Arie Hoek' 119
'Aristocrat' 136
'Arlo' 119
'Arma' 149, **150**
'Artist' 153, **154**
'Astarte' 119
'Astor' 144, **146**
'Atilla' **119**, 120
'Atlantis' 136
'Avignon' 136
'Baby Doll' 116
'Bacchus' 137, **137**
'Ballade' 144
'Ballerina' **110**, **113**, **132**, 145
'Banja Luka' 131
'Barbados' 149
'Barcelona' 120
'Baronnesse' 137
'Bartigon' 137
'Bastogne' 120
'Beau Monde' 120
'Beauty of Apeldoorn' 131
'Beauty Queen' 113
'Belcanto' 137
'Bell Air' 162
'Bella Vista' 172
'Bellflower' 150
'Bellona' 113
'Ben van Zanten' 120
'Berlioz' 166
'Bestseller' 113

'Big Chief' 131
'Big Smile' 137
'Bill Clinton' 120
'Bing Crosby' 120
'Bingham' 137, **140**
'Bird of Paradise' 157, **158**
'Black Beauty' 137, **137**
'Black Diamond' 137, **137**
'Black Hero' 162
'Black Parrot' 157, **158**
'Black Pearl' 137, **137**
'Black Swan' 137
'Blenda' 120
'Bleu Aimable' 138, **147**, **155**
'Bleu Céleste' 162
'Blue Bell' 120
'Blueberry Ripple' 120
'Blue Champion' 120
'Blue Diamond' 162
'Blue Heron' 150, **152**
'Blue Parrot' **155**, 157, **158**
'Blue Ribbon' 120
'Blumex' **150**, 157
'Blushing Apeldoorn' 131, **131**
'Blushing Beauty' 138
'Blushing Bride' 138
'Blushing Lady' 138
'Bonanza' 162
'Boule d'Or' 162
'Brigitta' 120
'Brilliant Star' 113, **147**, **169**
'Bronze Queen' 138, **140**
'Burgundy' 145
'Burgundy Lace' 150
'Burning Heart' 131
'Burning Love' 114
'Buttercup' 172
'Cabaret' 145, **146**
'Caland' 157, **158**
'Calgary' 120
'Calibra' 150
'Calypso' 172
'Canasta' 150
'Candela' 96, 169
'Canova' 150
'Cantata' 169
'Cape Cod' 172
'Capri' 121
'Caravelle' 138
'Cardinal Mindszenty' 116
'Carlton' 116
'Carmine Parrot' 157
'Carnaval de Nice' 162, **162**

'Carnival de Rio' 121
'Carola' 121
'Casablanca' 162
'Cassini' 121, **132**
'César Franck' 166
'Charmeur' **102**, 121
'Charmeuse' 172
'Chato' 163
'Cherbourg' 138, **140**
'China Lady' 172
'China Pink' 145, **146**
'China Town' 153, **154**
'Chopin' 166
'Christmas Dream' 114
'Christmas Marvel' 114
'Clara Butt' 138
'Clara Carder' **162**, 163
'Cloud Nine' 138
'Coby's Spirit' 121
'Colour Spectacle' 138
'Companion' 138
'Compostella' 172
'Concerto' 167
'Coquette' 114
'Cordell Hull' 138
'Corona' 167
'Corsage' **101**, **169**, 172, **172**
'Couleur Cardinal' 101, 121, **150**
'Cramoise Brilliant' 157, **158**
'Crème Upstar' 163
'Crown Imperial' 114
'Cruquius' 121
'Crystal Beauty' 150, **169**
'Cum Laude' 139
'Cummins' 150
'Czar Peter' 172
'Daladier' 163
'Dance' 169
'Dancing Show' 153, **154**
'Davenport' 150
'Daydream' 131
'Daylight' 167
'Debutante' 121
'Deirdre' 153
'Demeter' 121
'Diana' 114
'Diana Ross' 157
'Dillenburg' 139
'Doll's Minuet' **147**, 153, 155
'Donna Bella' 173
'Don Quichotte' 121, **132**
'Doorman's Elite' see 'Karel Doorman' 159
'Doris' 121, **140**

'Double Fantasy' 158, **158**
'Double Focus' 163
'Double Sensation' 163
'Douglas Bader' 139
'Dover' 131
'Dow Jones' 121
'Dow Jones' 122
'Dreamboat' 173
'Dreamland' 139
'Dubbel Geel' 163
'Dubbele Roodkapje' 163
'Duplosa' 167
'Dutch Fair' 132
'Dynamite' 122
'Dynito' 145
'Eagle Wings' 158
'Early Glory' 122
'Early Harvest' 167
'Early Star' 173
'Easter Moon' 169
'Easter Parade' 169
'Easter Surprise' 173
'Electra' 116, **116**
'Elegant Lady' 145
'Elizabeth Arden' 132
'Empire State' 132
'Engadin' 173
'Erfurt' 163
'Erna Lindgreen' 158
'Eros' **162**, 163
'Esperanto' 154, **154**
'Estella Rijnveld' 158, **158**
'Esther' 139
'Eternal Flame' 163
'Etude' 122
'Exotica' 150
'Exotic Bird' 158
'Eye Catcher' 154, **154**
'Fancy Frills' 150
'Fancy Parrot' 158
'Fantasy' 158, **158**
'Farness' 151
'Fashion' 167
'Fats Domino' 122
'Flair' 114
'Flashback' 145
'Fly Away' **113**, 145
'Fidelio' 122, **122**
'Finola' 163
'Fire Queen' 122
'First Lady' 122
'Flaming Parrot' 159
'Flaming Purissima' **136**, 169
'Flaming Youth' 169
'Florosa' 154, **154**
Florist's 101, 103
'Flowerdale' 173

'Fokker Fan-Fan' 145
'Fontainebleau' 122
'Formosa' 154, **154**
'Fra Angelico' **137**, 139
'Frances Bremer' 122
'Franz Léhar' 167
'Fringed Beauty' 151
'Fringed Elegance' 151
'Fringed Rhapsody' 151
'Friso' 122
'Fritz Kreisler' 167
'Frohnleiten' 123
'Frosty Dawn' 151
'Fur Elise' 173
'Gander' 123
'Garant' 132
'Garanza' 116
'Garden Party' 123
'Gavota' **88**, 123, **124**, **169**
'Generaal de Wet' 114
'General Eisenhower' 132
'Gerbrand Kieft' **136**, 163
'Georgette' **132**, 139, **147**
'Ghandi' 116, **116**
'Giant Parrot' 159
'Gisella' 145
'Giuseppe Verdi' 167
'Glasnost' see 'Karel Doorman' 159
'Glück' 167
'Golden Apeldoorn' 132, **132**
'Golden Artist' 154, **154**
'Golden Melody' **122**, 123
'Golden Nizza' 163, **172**
'Golden Oxford' **122**, 132
'Golden Parade' 132
'Golden Show' 123
'Gold Medal' **162**, 163
'Goltu' 145
'Gordon Cooper' 132
'Goudstuk' 167
'Grand Prestige' 173
'Grand Style' 139
'Green Eyes' 154
'Green River' 154
'Green Spot' 154
'Green Valley' 154
'Green Wave' **100**, 159
'Groenland' 154, **155**
'Grower's Pride' 173
'Gudoshnik' 133
'Halcro' 139
'Hamilton' 151
'Hans Mayer' **132**, 133
'Happy Generation' 123, **155**
'Harlequin' 116, **116**
'Havran' 123

'Heart's Delight' 168
'Heart's Desire' 139
'Helga' 139, **140**
'Hellas' 151
'Helmar' 123, **124**
'Henley' 151, **152**
'Herman Broeckart' 116, **116**
'Herman Emmink' 163
'Hermitage' 123, **150**
'Hibernia' 123
'High Noon' 123
'High Society' 123
'Hit Parade' 169
'Hocus Pocus' 139
'Hofstra University' 139
'Holberg' 123
'Holland Candy' 164
'Holland Cherry' 145
'Holland Chic'
'Holland Happening' 159
'Hollandia' 124
'Holland Jewel' 145
'Hollands Glorie' 133
'Hollywood' **154**, 155
'Hollywood Star' 155
'Huis ten Bosch' 151
'Hummingbird' **154**, 155
'Ibis' 114
'Ice Follies' 124, **124**
'Ile de France' 124, **143**
'Inzell' 124
'Ivory Floridale' 133
'Jacqueline' 146
'Jane Packer' 146
'Jan Reus' 124
'Jaap Groot' 133
'Jeantine' 168
'Jerry Davids' 124
'Jet Set' 164
'Jewel of Spring' 133
'Jimmy' 124
'Joffre' 114
'Johann Strauss' 168
'Johan (van) Vlaanderen' 116, 116
'Juan' 170
'Judith Leyster' 124
'Juliette' 133
'Julius Caesar' 173
'Karel Doorman' **143**, 159
'Kees Nellis' 124
'Keizerskroon' 114
'Kingsblood' 140
'Koningin Juliana' 140, **141**
'Koningin Wilhelmina' 133
'La Courtine' 140
'Lac van Rijn' 114

'Lambada' 151
'Landseadel's Supreme' 140
'La Tulipe Noir' **137**, 140
'Lavendel Dream' 151, **152**
'Leen van der Mark' 124
'Lefeber's Favourite' 132
'Leo Visser' 125
'Libera' 146
'Libretto Parrot' **136**, 159
'Lighting Sun' 134
'Lilac Perfection' **117**, **162**, 164
'Lilac Time' 146, **146**
'Lilyfire' 146
'Lilyrosa' 146
'Lily Schreyer' 125
'Lilystar' 125
'Linda de Mol' 125
'Linette' 146
'London' 134
'Longfellow' 173
'Love Song' 168
'Lucky Strike' 125
'Lustige Witwe' 125
'Lydia' 125
'Maartje Kuiper' **162**, 164
'Macarena' 146
'Madame Lefeber' 170
'Madame Spoor's Favourite' 125, **140**
'Madison Garden' 151, **152**
'Madonna' 159
'Magazine Prima' 140
'Magier' 140
'Makassar' 125
'Maja' 151, **152**
'Mamasa' 125, **140**
'Margaret Herbst' 173
'Margot Fonteyn' 125
'Mariette' 146
'Marit' 134
'Marilyn' 146
'Marina' 173
'Marjolein' 146
'Markgraaf' **158**, 159
'Martha' 146, **146**
'Mary Ann' 173
'Matchpoint' **109**, 151
'Maureen' 140
'Maytime' **117**, **146**, 147
'Maywonder' 164
'Mazurka' **162**, 164
'Meissner Porzellan' 125
'Menton' 140
'Merry Christmas' 114

'Mickey Mouse' 115
'Miranda' 164
'Mirella' 125
'Miskodeed' 174
'Miss Fanny Kemble' 101
'Mistress' 125
'Mon Amour' 151
'Monsella' 116, **124**
'Monte Carlo' 116, **122**
'Monte Rosa' 126
'Montreux' 117
'Moonshine' 147
'Most Miles' 126
'Mount Tacoma' **162**, 164
'Mrs John T Scheepers' 140
'Mr Van der Hoef' **116**, 117
'Muriel' 160
'Murillo' 115, **116**, 117
'Musical' 126
'My Lady' 134
'Nairobi' 126
'Nashville' 126
'Negrita' 126
'New Design' 126
'Ninja' 126
'Niphetos' 140, **141**
'Nizza' 164
'Noranda' 151, **152**
'Odia' 174
'Olaf' 126
'Ollioules' 134
'Olympic Flame' **122**, **124**, 134
'Orange Bouquet' 126, **172**
'Orange Brilliant' 170
'Orange Cassini' 126
'Orange Elite' 174
'Orange Emperor' 170
'Orange Favourite' **158**, 160
'Orange Flight' 126
'Orange Goblet' 134
'Orange Monarch' 126
'Orange Princess' **113**, 164
'Orange Sun' see Oranjezon 134
'Orange Surprise' 126
'Oranje Nassau' 117
'Oranjezon' 134
'Oratorio' 131, 174
'Oriental Beauty' 174
'Oriental Splendour' 174
'Orléans' 127
'Oscar' 127, **172**
'Oxford' 134
'Oxford's Elite' **113**, 134

'Page Polka' 127
'Palestrina' 141
'Palmares' 152
'Pandour' 174
'Parabole' 152
'Parade' 134
'Parrot City' 160
'Parrot King' 160
'Pasadena' 152, **152**
'Passionale' 127, **155**
'Patriot' 127
'Paul Crampel' 117
'Paul Richter' 127
'Paul Scherer' **117**, 127
'Pax' 127
'Peach Blossom' 117
'Peach Blush' **52**, 127
'Peer Gynt' 127
'Peerless Pink' 127
'Perestroyka' 141, **169**
'Phillipe de Comines' **137**, 141
'Picotee' 147
'Picture' 141
'Pierot' 147
'Pieter de Leur' 147, **147**
'Pimpernel' 155
'Pink Diamond' 141
'Pinkeen' 170
'Pink Impression' 135
'Pink Jewel' 141, **155**
'Pink Panther' 160
'Pink Sensation' 174
'Pink Supreme' 141
'Pink Star' 164
'Pinocchio' 174
'Plaisir' 174
'President Kennedy' 135
'Pretty Woman' 147
'Primavera' 127
'Princeps' 170
'Princesse Charmante' 174
'Princess Margaret Rose' 141
'Princess Victoria' 127
'Prins Carnaval' 115
'Prinses Irene' 127, **150**, **172**
'Prinses Margriet' 128, 150
'Professor Röntgen' 160
'Prominence' 128
'Purissima' **52**, 170
'Purple Prince' 115
'Quasimodo' 160
'Quebec' **97**, **131**, **147**, 174
'Queen Ingrid' 131, 147, 174

'Queen of Marvel' **117**, 118
'Queen of Night' **132**, **137**, 142
'Queen of Sheba' 147
'Queen Wilhelmina' see 'Koningin Wilhelmina' 133
'Rai' 160
'Recreado' 142
'Red Champion' 160
'Red Emperor' see 'Madame Lefeber' 170
'Red Georgette' 142
'Red Impression' see 'Pink Impression' 135
'Red Nova' 165
'Red Paradise' 115
'Red Riding Hood' **52**, **169**, 175
'Red Sensation' 160
'Red Shine' 147
'Red Surprise' 175
'Red Wing' 152
'Regulus' 152, **152**
'Rembrandt' 165
'Renown' 142
'Renown Unique' 165
'Rex Rubrorum Bontleaf' **103**, 118
'Rheingold' **116**, 118
'Robassa' 170
'Rob Verlinden' 175
'Rockery Master' 175
'Rocket' **162**, 165
'Rocky Mountains' 128
'Rococo' 150, 160
'Rondo' 170
'Rosalie' 128
'Rosanna' 175
'Rosario Double' 165
'Rosy Dream' 170
'Rosy Wings' 142
'Royal Design' 147
'Royal Sphinx' 152
'Sagitta' 152, **152**
'Saint Tropez' 165
'Salmon Impression' see 'Pink Impression' 135
'Salmon Parrot' 160
'Salmon Pearl' 128
'Sapporo' 148
'Scarlet Baby' **52**, 168
'Scarlet Cardinal' 118
'Schoonoord' **116**, 118
'Seadov' 128
'Semper Augustus' 100
'Sevilla' 128
'Shakespeare' 168

'Shirley' 128, **136**
'Show Parrot' 160
'Showwinner' 168
'Silver Dollar' 128
'Singapore' 128
'Sjakamaro' 128
'Slim Whitman' 128
'Snow Parrot' **136**, 161
'Snowstar' 128
'Solva' 171
'Sombrero' 175
'Soroptimist' see 'Candela' 169
'Spring Green' 155
'Spring Pearl' 171
'Spring Song' 135
'Springtime' 135
'Starfighter' 152
'Stockholm' 118
'Strawberry Ice' 128
'Strawberry Swirl' 128
'Stresa' 168
'Striped Apeldoorn' 135
'Striped Bellona' 115
'Striped Oxford' 135
'Strong Gold' 129
'Sundew' 152
'Sunset Tropical' 165
'Super Parrot' 161
'Swan Wings' 152
'Swarovski' 142
'Sweet Harmony' 142
'Sweetheart' 171
'Sweet Lady' 175
'Swinging World' 129
'Sylvia van Lennep' 171
'Synaeda Amor' 129
'Synaeda Blue' 129
'Synaeda King' **146**, 148
'Talbion' **146**, 148
'Ted Turner' 129
'Telecom' 129
'Temple of Beauty' 142
'Temple's Favourite' 142
'Tender Beauty' 135, **172**
'Texas Flame' 161
'Texas Gold' 161
'The Cure' 129
'Theeroos' **116**, 118
'The First' 168
'The Sultan' **137**, 143
'Thule' 129
'Topparrot' 161
'Toronto' 175
'Toulon' see 'Juan' 170
'Toyota' 143

'Trés Chic' 148
'Tricolored Beauty' 155
'Trinket' 175
Triumph tulips 118
'True and Fair' 165
'Typhoon' 129
'Uncle Tom' **162**, 165
'Union Jack' 143
'Upstar' 165
'Valentine' 129
'Vermillion Parrot' 161
'Verona' 118
'Veronique Sanson' 129
'Viking' 118
'Violet Beauty' 143
'Violet Bird' 155
'Viridiflora' 155
'Virily Pink' 148
'Vivex' 135
'Warbler' 152, **152**
'Washington' 129
'Weber's Parrot' 161
'Wendy Love' **122**, 129
'West Frisia' 165
'West Point' 148
'White Dream' 129
'White Elegance' 148
'White Emperor' see 'Purissima' 170
'White Parrot' 161
'White Pearl' 165
'White Triumphator' 148
'White Wings' 148
'Wienerwald' **137**, 143
'Wildhof' 129
'Willemsoord' 118
'Willem van Oranje' 118
'Winter Gold' 115
'Wirosa' **155**, 165
'Wisley' 143, **143**
'Witty Picture' see 'Picture' 141
'World Expression' 143
'World's Favourite' 135
'Yellow Dawn' 175
'Yellow Dover' see 'Dover' 131
'Yellow Flight' 129
'Yellow Marvel' **146**, 148
'Yellow Present' 130
'Yellow Purissima' 171
'Youri Dolgoruckiy' 148
'Zampa' 175
'Zaza' **52**, 152
'Zombie' 171
'Zomerschoon' 143
'Zurel' 130